The Manhattan Directory of Private Nursery Schools

The Manhattan Directory of Private Nursery Schools

Victoria Goldman

SIXTH EDITION

SOHO

Published in the United States of America by
Soho Press, Inc.
853 Broadway
New York, NY 10003

SIXTH EDITION

www.victoriagoldman.net

I would like to acknowledge the previous authors of this directory, especially Linda Faulhaber, its originator, for they laid the groundwork on which this book rests. I also gratefully acknowledge and thank the many directors, administrators, and parents who have shared their insights and experiences, and provided the most accurate and up to date information about their schools. And, of course, my editor, Laura Hruska, for her guidance and expertise, as well as for giving me the opportunity to work on this book, and Melissa Gillis, for her invaluable and tireless efforts.

Also by Victoria Goldman

The Manhattan Family Guide to Private Schools and Selective Public Schools

The Los Angeles Guide to Private Schools

Contents

Individual school entries in this book appear alphabetically by geographic neighborhood

Please note: tuitions listed usually increase three to six percent annually.

PARENTS' PRESCHOOL PRIMER

This is Manhattan, and the gun goes off at 7:30 AM the day after Labor Day. Frenzied parents jam the phone lines of schools they deem most desirable to request nursery school applications. There are schools that run out of applications by noon. Some parents send their babies and toddlers to parenting programs and play groups that are supposed to be "feeders to the feeders" of the schools that will, they hope, secure a place for their offspring in an Ivy League college. Such pre-preschools, like Madison Playgroup, Free to Be Under Three at All Souls, Barnard Toddler Program or the Parenting Center at Central Synagogue help one- and two-year olds learn to socialize, share and play nicely so they can ace their nursery school interviews.

But since this is Manhattan, you need not take part in the madness unless you choose to. There are hundreds of nursery or early childhood programs available. The so-called top tier nursery schools or "Baby" Ivies have directors with over twenty years of experience, fabulous facilities, students with famous (or rich) parents, teachers with masters degrees, expertly thought out programs and strong track records of sending their graduates to all the best public and private schools in town. Yet there are many other schools that do as well by their students and frequently are a better match for a particular family. If you want to secure a place for your child at a supposed "feeder" nursery school, one that is thought to guarantee a place at a "top" ongoing school—most of which would honestly disclaim this ability—you have to prepare a balanced list of schools to apply to of no fewer than six and no more than twelve possibilities. Some of your choices should be schools that are less competitive, so-called "safeties." And before you can draw up any list, you must decide what sort of school would be best for your child.

What kinds of schools are there?

You have half a dozen and more from which to choose:

- **Montessori**
- **Developmental** (developmental-interaction)
- **Progressive** (included in developmental)
- **Traditional**
- **Eclectic** (a term used to cover the programs that combine several approaches or are not concerned with defining themselves in terms of methodology)
- **All-day or Day Care Center**

There are also such institutions as the Rudolf Steiner School, (a Waldorf school) which have developed their own individual teaching approaches. Other schools are distinguished from their counterparts by strong affiliations with religious groups. So there is a lot to think about and a lot of answers to find. The first concerns are mercifully practical—like birthday cutoffs, tuitions, proximity and school hours, for instance.

School hours for young children going into the 2s are either from about 8:30 AM to noon or from 1 PM to 4 PM. Older children attend from 8:30 AM until about 3 PM. Bringing children to school earlier than 8:30 AM is possible at most schools (called **early drop-off**), and many offer **extended hours** for the youngest preschool grades whereby the normal three-hour school day may be expanded to perhaps five hours, but rarely more.

There are alternatives to the traditional nursery school hours. For working parents requiring child care during normal workday hours there are **All-day** or **Day Care centers**. These centers consider themselves preschools and some are included here. They typically take children from 8:30 AM to 5:30 or 6 PM.

For parents who do not want to be separated from very young children by sending them to school there are **parent-toddler programs**. These not only permit, but actually require the presence of a parent. Some programs allow caregivers or sitters as substitutes, but the idea is to provide a preschool-like setting for parents and children not yet ready for the separation inherent in any school experience.

By law, mandatory enrollment in school only begins at 6 years of age. But not here in Manhattan where the sociocultural norms have families on a faster, earlier track.

The Law and Preschools

All schools listed in this directory are licensed by the New York City Department of Health, Bureau of Day Care. Each school must be relicensed every two years. Preschools caring for children under 2 are relicensed every year. Each facility is inspected at least twice a year.

Space. The legal requirement is 30 square feet per child. Every room in an all-day care center has an assigned maximum occupancy figure that specifies how many children may be in that room. The one variance is that all-day centers and nursery schools are allowed to enroll two children above the maximum allowance because daily attendance varies so greatly among preschoolers. Each classroom with children two years of age or older must have a minimum of one state-certified teacher.

Every classroom must have one teacher and one assistant for:

6 to 10 two-year olds
11 to 15 three-year-olds
13 to 20 four-year-olds
16 to 25 five-year-olds

Four other regulations you should know about:

All people working in schools or centers must be fingerprinted.
School staff members are forbidden to administer any medications.
All children under the age of 3 years are required to have a yearly physical examination within 30 days prior to attendance.
Children age 4 years and older must have a medical exam within 90 days of starting school.

Each program must also receive approval from the city's Buildings and Fire departments and from the Public Health and Sanitation Department.

Many schools also voluntarily elect to be chartered by the Board of Regents of the State University of New York. Its standards are stringent for classroom size, location, and construction, eating, rest and sanitary facilities, equipment and outdoor play space, and fire and safety requirements. Classrooms must include activities centers for block-building, housekeeping play, water play, creative arts, painting, clay and collage, science and nature study, cooking, and music, as well as adequate books, pictures, puzzles, games, and small play objects. Outdoor equipment must include well-anchored climbing and dramatic play structures, plus wheel toys, tricycles, wagons, trucks, building equipment, ladders, sawhorses, and a storage shed.

The maximum number of infants in any one room is 6, the maximum number of toddlers is 10; 4s, 20; 5s, 22

Schools must show evidence of a consistent curriculum and education program adapted to the ages, interests, and needs of the children. The child must be afforded the opportunity to choose and become involved in the manipulation of various materials and objects, large motor play, discussions and games, literature, music, science, and field trips.

Schools must also show positive parent collaboration in the education of their children, including conferences, parent workshops, classes or lectures, and newsletters.

These are the standards.

The Basics

What are the different pre-school grades?

• Infants	6 month to 1 year
• Toddlers: 2s, 3s, and preschoolers	$1\frac{1}{2}$ to 3 years
• 4s or preschoolers	4 years
• Kindergartners, 5s and prefirsts	5 years

What is an "ongoing" school?

A nursery school or preschool traditionally goes from age 2 or 3 years to age 5 or 6 years when the child is about to enter kindergarten—the first rung of most ongoing schools. An **elementary (or primary) school** goes through the 8th grade; **comprehensive schools** go all the way through high school to the 12th grade. An ongoing school refers to either one.

You will also hear teachers and administrators use such terms as "old 2s" or "young 5s" in describing children, depending on the relationship of their birth month to the school year. These terms simply mean that a child who is, say 2.1 (two years, one month) to 2.5 (meaning two years and five months) at the start of the school year is said to be a "young 2." A child who is from 2.6 (two years and six months) to 2.11 (two years and eleven months) in age would be considered an "old two." This same method of designating ages is used throughout the directory.

What is the first thing to look for in a nursery school?

The first consideration is practical: How far from home is it? Other basic questions come in quick succession:

- Are the days and hours right for our needs?
- What are the age qualifications?
- When should we apply?
- Is this school in our price range?
- Must children be toilet trained by the time school starts?

The answers to many of these questions are given in the individual entries. Do keep in mind, however, that programs change and that tuition usually goes up by about 6 to 8 percent a year depending on the school. (The tuitions listed in this book were being charged when the book was written.)

And then, of course, there is the biggest item of all: What **type** of school is best for my child? To answer this question, you need to know what the various educational approaches are about.

Just what is a Montessori school?

It is a school based on precepts formulated by Maria Montessori, who in the early 1900s created a strict method for training young children. She held that intelligence is the ability to classify and impose order on the apparent chaos of life. That was, for her, the paramount quality to be developed. At its most faithful, a Montessori school is one in which the Montessori-designed didactic materials (e.g., frames with buttons to be buttoned, color tablets to be matched) are to be used only in ways that demonstrate their unique pedagogic characteristics. Creative extensions by the child may arise out of the original presentation but are to be faithful to the original intention regarding the material.

Montessori, a medical doctor working primarily with orphans, observed that young children have an innate desire to learn, and in particular, a desire to master real-life tasks and skills. To nurture that desire, she developed the "prepared environment," an orderly, secure setting in which children feel free to explore sequential materials designed to stimulate and challenge. Learning skills embedded in real-life experiences, she was convinced, inculcates a sense of genuine achievement that is crucial to children's ongoing development. Thus, in addition to traditional academic and cultural subjects, the Montessori nursery emphasizes the mastery of such skills as putting on a coat, wiping the table and preparing a snack, sweeping the floor, watering plants, putting away materials, etc.

The mood of the classroom tends to be purposeful and task-oriented. While the classroom materials are often beautifully arrayed, children's original artwork is rarely displayed on the walls or in the hallways of a strict Montessori school.

Mme. Montessori did not believe that children were able to socialize at very young ages. Consequently, her program, where strictly followed, does not encourage social interaction in the classroom except perhaps for lessons in getting along with others. Children must always put away what they are working on—returning their materials to the proper place before embarking on another project—and file the results when they are finished. They must put away their mats. They must not disturb the projects of other children without permission, nor should they interrupt them. When finished with a project, the children raise their hands and wait for the teacher to come and review it.

Socializing takes place during outdoor play, on field trips, and during lunch, but this is not part of the curriculum. Children gather in large groups for demonstrations of proper usage of work materials or to be shown nature experiments: seeds growing, colored inks being absorbed by a plant, and so forth.

There is no room for "make believe" in the curriculum. There is no art work. Nor is there dramatic play, although children are read stories and, obviously, can engage in play fantasies during their outdoor periods. Children work individually for the most part, occasionally in pairs or small groups, and their interaction must further the work. Each activity is graded according to difficulty and the children must use the materials in the prescribed sequence until they have mastered the particular skill involved and are able to move on to more difficult projects. The idea of each undertaking is to have the child gain a particular bit of knowledge or skill from, for example, a pie-shaped puzzle that demonstrates the relationship of fractions to the whole, or from a series of boxes that resonate with different tones.

Three major skill areas are defined and practiced. *Practical life tasks:* tieing shoelaces, wiping surfaces properly, pouring liquids, operating a zipper or button. *Sensory:* handling three-dimensional geometric shapes, arranging color cards by tone, fitting cylindrical blocks of varying sizes into their proper holes, judging wooden tablets of different weights. *Language and math:* handling rough-textured alphabet letters and learning their sounds, tracing shapes to perfect small muscle control for writing and the development of penmanship, and counting beads strung on long chains.

Beyond these, there are geography materials (interesting puzzle maps of the world, three dimensional dioramas), and science materials (natural objects, small animals, perhaps a garden patch).

Age groups are mixed in the classroom and older children teach younger ones the correct use of materials and also serve as role models. The mix can vary from school to school: at one Montessori school it is from age 2.6 to 6 years, for instance. Although other kinds of nursery schools also mix ages, the differential is usually two years at most.

"The respect for the child is absolute," said child psychiatrist Dr. Yehuda Nir when describing his daughter's Montessori school experience. It is a statement with which every Montessori teacher would agree. Children are seen as immensely responsible and capable, and fully able to learn at a rate of their own choosing from a wide variety of materials and projects designed to intrigue and challenge. The primary relationship is between child and environment, not between the child and his peers or the child and his teachers. Teachers remain in the background.

Separation from parents is expeditious. Children are brought to the school door and from there they are escorted to their classroom by staff members or by older classmates.

The degree of adherence to the Montessori method varies from school to school. One clue to the strictness is a school's affiliation with one or the other of two Montessori federations. The first is the Association Montessori Internationale, which was organized by Maria Montessori herself, succeeded by her son. This is the purist or orthodox group. A good example of a school adhering faithfully to the original principles is Resurrection Episcopal Day School.

The Montessori schools that are members of the American Montessori Society have modified the basic method. They will provide the child with the prescribed project materials and also **open-ended** play things with undefined applications: sand, water, clay, art materials, blocks. They also allow for the child's dramatic or fantasy play, and are more flexible about the separation process when a child first enters school. An excellent example of a modified use of Maria Montessori's tenets is the West Side Montessori School.

What is a "child centered" developmental-interaction approach?

Schools with a **developmental** approach follow a curriculum that adheres to what teaching professionals would refer to as the **developmental-interaction** method. (You may hear the term "The Child Development Method" or the expression "The Total Child Approach.") **Progressive** schools basically use the same methodology.

Developmental-interaction is a concept which revolutionized early childhood education when first introduced more than eighty-five years ago at about the same time Maria Montessori was developing her theories.* The basic tenet is that the child has a need to explore, and then to

*Reggio Emilia, like Montessori, is Italian in origin. With roots dating back to the twelfth century, the Reggio Emilia is a progressive philosophy holding that community, democracy and citizenship are the most important components of a healthy society and should be taught to young children.

TriBeCa Community School, p. 337, *infra,* is an example of a Reggio Emilia nursery in New York City, and many schools have incorporated various elements into their programs. (*The Hundred Languages of Children—The Reggio Emilia Approach—Advanced Reflections,* 2nd Edition, Bolen, 1998.)

express his or her discoveries through a variety of channels: imaginative play, discussion, art, and the deceptively simple but central activity of blockbuilding.

Play is seen as the child's work. It is the means by which the child re-creates and re-examines, again and again, everything they have experienced and observed. Play is considered purposeful, exceedingly important, and serious. Hence activities chosen by the child are treated as important explorations. The developmental approach emphasizes the inseparability of the child's emotional life from his or her intellectual and physical development.

The child's emotional and fantasy life is indeed, thought paramount—the key. Social interactions are of major importance in these schools. To learn to be aware of emotions, to identify and talk about them, to express needs and negotiate their resolution with classmates and fac-ulty is considered vital. The idea is to encourage and facilitate interactions between the children. The teacher facilitates the forming of friendships.

Separation is seen as a part of the curriculum to which the teachers and parents devote a great deal of time, as all concerned learn and adjust to this new concept of going to school. Separation is approached as a major psychological and developmental milestone, a profound step in a child's life and not at all a minor, quick adjustment.

Developmental-interaction classrooms and progressive classrooms abound with what are called **open-ended** materials—water, sand, puzzles, fabrics, paint, clay, funnels, and lots of different size blocks. Children use the same materials at different ages in ever more elaborate ways. Free play time is generous, and even planned activities may sudden give way to the children's spontaneous interests. Rooms may be messy or noisy, teachers are addressed by their first names. Artwork tends to be varied, often beautiful, and sometimes rather more expressive than at other schools.

The aim of this approach is to allow the child to learn at his own pace through active play, and to facilitate constant interaction between emotional and cognitive development. There are no workbooks. There are no tests prepared for or given, and there are no prescribed points at which a child must master any skill, such as reading or arithmetic. There is no pressure to achieve prescribed levels at predetermined junctures. The teacher mediates, prepares materials, and observes. Specific learning and direct instruction are frowned upon, and hastening development through training or rote instruction is considered inappropriate, even possibly damaging.

Community is stressed, especially in the form of joint undertakings that require the continual interaction of the children. That is why so much emphasis is placed upon building with varieties of blocks. By the time children become proficient in blockbuilding, usually as 5s, they will build as teams, constantly discussing, deciding, and planning. The ambitiousness of their projects and their evident success can be truly impressive.

The Bank Street College of Education is the promulgator of this method. Established in 1914, its mission was to collect information on new teaching concepts then being developed in progressive schools such as City and Country. It resulted, four years later, in the founding of a new nursery school today known as the Bank Street School for Children. Over the intervening years it and the College trained many of the teachers and directors of developmental and progressive preschools in Manhattan, and fostered the growth of these approaches nationwide. It was and remains the hub of the innovative methods developed in City and Country School and the Little Red School House, all of which were avidly putting into practice the theories of psychologists Piaget, Anna Freud, John Dewey, and others. The philosophy and methodology that evolved profoundly influence educational approaches to this day.

As with the Montessori method, adherence varies from school to school and, in fact, many preschools in Manhattan call themselves adherents of developmental-interaction but are modified versions at best. So you cannot automatically accept labels or descriptions that schools apply to themselves. Developmental, child-centered, Bank Street, progressive—these terms may have been misappropriated or may be ill-fitting at best. The model developmental-interaction/progressive schools are quite open to inquiries and visits, Bank Street School for Children and City and Country School chief among them. They will give you an excellent idea of what a "Bank Street oriented" preschool is about.

The traditional schools are there too.

They are middle of the road, familiar, and often associated with a religious institution. They have definite curriculum goals that usually will include mastery of specific skills such as numbers or phonics and the like. The programs vary quite a bit school to school but most share basic elements. They have activities centers and a consistent class format that is usually teacher directed. There is a detailed curriculum with regular units of study and specific goals for the children. These are generally based on their skills or **readiness levels**, as they are called. Reading, writing, and math are stressed, often using workbooks and worksheets.

The term **academic** is often used in connection with traditional schools because of their emphasis on performance. Their goal is to develop skills, such as speaking, listening, time measurement, problem solving, and record keeping. Each day's activities are planned and the schedule closely followed in order to ground the children in an agenda of daily events and undertakings that are consistent and predictable.

Traditional programs also employ open-ended materials which can be explored and manipulated in innumerable ways: sand, water, blocks, paint, and clay. The classrooms resemble those of developmental preschools, with their housekeeping areas and, sand tables, water trays, blocks, story corner, carpentry tools, art supplies, science area, and so forth. But the approach is distinctly different. The teacher instructs, explains and organizes projects. Workbooks and worksheets may be used, and there may be formal lessons, particularly for older children. Classroom etiquette, and readiness to pay attention and to learn from a teacher are skills being taught.

The alphabet and numbers are systematically introduced, usually in the 3s, and games and books will further encourage their use. Printed artwork or teacher-made art objects will be displayed to illustrate lessons. The teacher directs the child's focus to the learning tasks at hand, urging the preschooler to color in a particular letter of the alphabet or, perhaps, to tell the class how many dots appear in an illustration. At more traditional schools that are dedicated to this approach, there is less "free-play" time and more academic activities like formal reading and arithmetic lessons. The children gather in groups and sit in their seats while the teacher covers specific curriculum areas. Workbooks and worksheets are used to practice reading, writing, mathematics, and to master certain concepts. Colors, shapes, letters and numbers were formerly introduced to the 2s at some schools. This is no longer the case.

Some traditional schools, such as Convent of the Sacred Heart or Temple Emanu-El Nursery School and Kindergarten, eschew the use of workbooks and similar "academic" materials and may resist such a label, but they are similar in that they, too, are performance oriented. And that, really, is the hallmark of the preschools described as traditional.

Some preschool programs are loosely described here as **eclectic**—a term coined purely for convenience—simply because they seem to have adapted a variety of methods in constructing their curriculum, or they do not promulgate any one approach. In such nursery schools you might find play and academic work, blocks and workbooks, all being utilized, and perhaps even some Montessori techniques or materials. Pieces and aspects of several theories may have been combined to create an effective hybrid.

All-day centers or **Day Care centers,** for instance, are generally more loosely structured and eclectic about the methods they employ.

These schools may use a variety of teaching techniques, often combining several approaches over the course of a day. They differ from their preschool counterparts only in that they offer daylong programs from early morning until early evening, and will, therefore, allow the children more free-time activities. As the director of Basic Trust pointed out, "We don't have to squeeze learning into two and a half or three hours. We have the whole day, and the children are learning all the time."

Unlike other nursery programs, they run year-round without a summer hiatus. Many also enroll children at much younger ages, beginning as early as six months, when the question of a particular approach is moot.

All-day centers consider themselves preschools in every way and somewhat resent the conventional preconception of their being simple caretakers. The Educational Alliance's Nursery School program is a prototypical example of the early child-care center concept.

Putting a particular school into one of these categories can be an art in itself. Even if you visit several schools before applying, you may be whisked through so quickly that you are unable to perceive the very real differences among them. Unfortunately, there is a tendency on the part of schools to be very general in briefing parents. Although the staff may be professional about teaching and extremely attentive to children, handling parents is not always their forte; sometimes vagueness is even deliberate.

Administrators worry. They may want their school to be seen as elite or desirable, but they do not want this exclusivity to be interpreted negatively. Or they may be trying to maintain and protect their image as a "child-oriented" school that emphasizes the child's development and disdains pressuring youngsters to perform especially when it comes to the touchy area of preparation for the test known as the ERB*, that most preschoolers will take and the scores of which will be used by ongoing schools to determine admission to their kindergarten/upper-school programs.

Directors and teachers will insist, devoted as they are to the education and welfare of "the total child," that they do not coach or train youngsters for these tests, even as they try to assure you that they do, in fact, produce students who succeed on these tests and get into the best ongoing schools.

Administrators and teachers are terribly sensitive about the alleged coaching of children for the ERB, used by ongoing schools to evaluate candidates. Often preschool staff will criticize such practices even while

*See ERB, pp. 377, *infra.*

showing prospective parents the tasks and other materials that, coincidentally, replicate the tasks and materials used by ERB tests. As a further convenience, and to make youngsters more comfortable and ostensibly help their scores, the tests may be administered in the school instead of at a testing facility. Such an advantageous arrangement may be emphasized, however subtly (and despite the testing organization's insistence that there is no statistical difference between the results of tests administered in the school and those given at its centers). Directors may even take children individually from their classrooms to familiarize them with the materials and testing procedure, insisting all the while that such is not the purpose.

An administrator may also eschew the use of workbooks and worksheets and cite their absence as evidence of a school's nonacademic orientation yet the program can be highly structured and academic in every other way. For instance, when introducing alphabet letters—let's say **W**—everything done that week from painting to cooking will involve **W** words. So even though workbooks are not being employed, the class activities may be highly structured to fulfill weekly and monthly learning units.

Other complications you may encounter: It is in the school's interest sometimes to maintain the impression that the demand for places in their class groups is far greater than the supply. You may get a lot of dire intimations about how few openings there are and how fast a decision needs to be made about accepting the school's possible offer of a place in their program. So another obvious obstacle to any probing discussion is the parents' anxiety about placing their child and the school representative's wish to depict the institution as desirable.

Finally, as often as not, tours are conducted by the parents of enrolled students who know the school as volunteers and not as teaching professionals, and report to the admissions director.

What are the admissions procedures like?

There are hundreds of nursery or early childhood programs to choose from. In all-day or day care centers for infants through five year olds, you will be invited to come informally, with or without your child, and spend time observing the program. This can be at any point in the calendar year. You will probably find on your visit that the all-day center is loosely structured and that the staff is used to parents visiting and being around. Most of these centers accept children on a first-come basis and receive applications all year.

Most preschools, for two through five year olds, are more formal. You will be asked the birth date of your child; you may be asked how you heard of the school, and some of the more exclusive preschools may even ask for references. In a few instances you will be able to arrange for a visit when you phone. The school visit may be a one-time individual family session for the parents and the child, or a collective meeting with another family or with both sets of parents. Or it may be a large gathering for twenty families and kids, depending on the school. Mostly, you will be expected to call for an application first and then schedule a visit; occasionally you will be asked to wait for the school to call you.

The majority of ongoing schools with nursery enrollments or lower schools start with either a tour or a personal interview with the parents. However, that word—**interview**—is used less now by school functionaries, so when arranging a "visit," make sure of what it is you are going for:

- A tour of the facilities
- An interview for you and your spouse
- An interview by the staff or director for your child.

Some schools collect all the applications before evaluating the applicants pool and making decisions. Other schools process applications in the order they are received *as* they are received and, once the vacancies are filled the admissions are simply cut off. After that they may only accept applications provisionally for unanticipated openings.

Ask each school what their policy is.

What should you look for on your tour of the school?

- Do the children look happy and involved?
- Are they too noisy/quiet for your taste?
- Are there "boys" activities and "girls" activities?
- How formal, or casual, is the atmosphere?
- Are the teachers working on the floor with the children, or do they keep their distance?
- How clean is everything?
- Do the windows have guards on them?
- What are the toilet facilities like and are they separate for adults?
- Does the temperature and air circulation of the school feel comfortable for the children?
- How do you feel about the level of order/disorder?
- Do the indoor and outdoor areas seem spacious enough for children to move with ease?
- Do the teachers seem warm?
- How are the interactions among children handled?
- How on top of things are the teachers?

- If you have a chance to see classroom conflict, how is it handled?
- How comfortable are you with the staff?

What's the most revealing question you can ask?

The one question that might reveal the most about a school is how they view and handle separation. There is a real difference among schools and it can be a significant indicator as to the nature of the school's program and philosophy. The more liberal (progressive, developmental-interaction, "Bank Street-oriented," "child-centered," modified Montessori) devote a great deal of time to it. The more conservative (traditional, academic, strict Montessori) tend to de-emphasize it.

Questions about separation you might ask if not already answered in the school's literature are:

- Do teachers make home visits before the school year begins?
- Does the school allow parents in the classroom?
- Do parents wait nearby?
- How many days or weeks does the school have parents in the classroom or standing by in the school?
- At what point do teachers usually begin suggesting the parent leave?

Another question that may suggest the totality of the program and the school's style involves the children's **free time**: How much of it do they have?

The developmental and progressive programs allow for a great deal of free time; the more traditional and conservative schools limit it.

Here is a checklist of significant questions you might pose during the tour, but be sure that the answers are not already available in brochures or elsewhere, such as the school's website.

- At what age does the school introduce phonics, the alphabet, numbers, formal lessons?
- Do they use learning games?
- Are children required to join activities?
- Does the school provide lunch?
- What kinds of snacks are served?
- Are naps mandatory or can the children just rest quietly?
- How are sick children cared for?
- Are there workshops for parents?

- How often during the year are parent-teacher conferences scheduled?
- How long do parent-teacher conferences last? (They can vary from between fifteen minutes to one hour.)

Typically, after the parent tour, an interview ("visit") with the child is scheduled at the school. This is usually a group-play session with two to six children of the same age (most often all applicants), who will be observed by the director and staff, sometimes without, but most often with, parents present.

A child may be seen singly for a play session with a teacher or the director, or the standard procedure may be to invite the child into a functioning classroom to participate (or not, as he wishes).

What is the school looking for?

The staff will be looking at your child's developmental level to decide if he or she is ready for school. They are interested in seeing:

- How the child responds to suggestions or directions.
- How well he or she can be understood.
- What are the interactions between your child and the others (if in a group).
- How are the parents responding? What are *your* personalities like?

To a great extent the admissions process is, as one nursery school director described it, "a numbers game." Once the school has allotted spaces for returning children, siblings, and legacies*, it must balance the ages, personalities, and sexes as best it can among its remaining applicants. If 15 three-year-old boys apply and four girls, the odds are astronomically in favor of the girls being accepted.

There is no point in taking acceptance, or rejection, as a judgment of you or your child. It may be a relatively random decision based on factors having nothing to do with you or your child.

Making a decision.

- When you get home think about what you observed.
- Compare what you observed at each school.

*alumni

- Reassess your feelings about each school.
- Call the school's director again if you have any further questions, but don't badger.
- Be sure that the schools that you like meet your needs for location, hours and cost.
- The most important thing you can ask yourself is "Do I feel comfortable leaving my child at this school?"

Certain schools will be looking at you, the parents.

A cooperative will want to know how well a prospective member may "fit in" because of the amount of time they will be spending with you in the collective work required to operate a cooperative nursery school.

Some preschools have chosen to cultivate specific populations. One institution's preeminence as a "society nursery school" was reported to be the result of a deliberate policy set years ago.

The level of privilege in a school may be a serious concern to parents. Many Upper East Side preschools, for instance, enroll extremely privileged children from this neighborhood. One nursery school director gave evidence of the wealth and sophistication of her charges by noting that even the youngest had been to Europe. Working middle-class parents, and even upwardly mobile two-career couples, have reported feeling uncomfortable with the ambience, and inconvenienced by required attendance at daytime functions, and the private SUV-with-driver-lock at pick up and drop off times.

The director of a school with a more mixed population commented that children are sensitive to social differences. "By the time children are five, they know who has a townhouse, chauffeur and cook, and who hasn't."

The attitude at some schools is actually condescending toward the less-privileged children enrolled. At one preschool, which offered several scholarships yearly to low-income children, the director commented that, "Yes. We have them, but you would hardly notice that they are in the classroom. I interview them as I interview everyone else." Other schools, like All Souls, encourage scholarship children by allowing them to bypass the school's application lottery system.

Yet another school, in its literature, congratulates its students' parents on their generosity in supporting the scholarship fund and entreats them to welcome scholarship children on an equal footing in their children's classrooms.

If your child's education is going to present a serious strain financially, you should know this: **Independent schools or centers which accept public funding offer up to half of their places to children funded by the Agency for Child Development.***

Some independent schools that accept public funding are:

- The Educational Alliance Nursery School
- Educare
- West Side Montessori

These programs generally have a better racial and economic balance than exclusively private programs.

The director of a nursery school observed that low-income and middle-class children learned a great deal from each other: "Middle-class children frequently cannot concentrate on a task alone. They are so used to being spoiled and pressured and attended to by parents who can't say 'no' to them. On the other hand, low-income children hear almost nothing but 'no.' They are often more independent and better able to take care of themselves." Some directors share this opinion and praise the mutual enrichment a variety of backgrounds provides. Others disagree. They feel that their more homogeneous classes allow them to spend more time on teaching and less time on negotiation and intervening.

If you are looking for a school with diversity at the primary and elementary levels, contact **Early Steps****, an organization that acts as the liaison for independent schools seeking students with a variety of backgrounds. It is the clearinghouse for information about programs, admissions procedures, and financial aid; and it will assist families to negotiate the admissions process.

Where can you get information to help make your decision about the right preschool for your child?

Neighbors are a terrific source of candid information, so call everyone you know with children in preschool. Finding a nursery school is a memorable experience for parents and most are happy to talk about it, while others' egos are deflated and they feel as if they have just been denied membership to the "club" of their dreams.

Also, look into **Child Care, Inc.*****. This is the leading private

*See ACD, p. 373, *infra*.
**See p. 377, *infra*.
***See p. 373, *infra*.

child-care advisory and advocacy organization. It is nonprofit and provides a great array of services. Telephone counselors give advice and information on over 2,000 licensed infant-toddler programs in the city, on nursery schools, all-day centers, after-school programs, kindergartens, and camps.

For a small fee, you can get a listing of all the licensed programs, and a counseling session will be arranged for you once you have several candidates in mind.

A professional advisor can also be retained.* Fees range from roughly $200 to $3,000, but still there are no guarantees.

Understanding the Program

Since the last publication of this book, most schools have discontinued woodworking as an activity. One of the main reasons for this is the necessity for young children to use their emerging dexterity for mouse control and keyboarding. Technology has clearly become of greater importance than the learning of handicraft activities or skills. However, a school like the Rudolf Steiner School continues to value the organic and natural, and handicraft activities; there is little if any plastic in the entire school.

What is "dramatic play"?

Dramatic play is simply make believe, or pretending. In most schools this consists of imaginative role-playing in the housekeeping corner, often including dress-up.

What are creative movement, music and movement, rhythms?

Anything from dancing around to a guitar or piano accompaniment, to extremely imaginative choreographic inventions that evolve in a rhythms program, answers to these descriptions.

What is large motor activity?

Active physical play on slides, see-saws, climbing equipment, swings and tricycles, and construction with large building blocks.

*See Advisory Services, p. 383, *infra*.

What are "manipulatives"?

Small play objects: beads, Legos, and the like.

The best way to get to know a school is to sit in the classroom and observe. Unfortunately, many schools do not allow this. It is not practical for them, and also many parents cannot commit the time this would entail. If an open house is coming up, go. Most schools arrange such visits. Be prepared with specific questions.

Be prepared to persist in asking until you are satisfied that you have answers but be respectful, don't be too pushy. In most instances, the director strongly sets the tone of the school, so the director's willingness to respond to your concerns is a significant clue as to what the school is or isn't. If you feel comfortable at a school, chances are so will your child. So, follow your instincts and your child will more than likely have a healthy and productive nursery school experience, and you will, too.

GLOSSARY OF ACRONYMS

ACD Agency for Child Development
ACEI Association for Childhood Education International
AMS American Montessori Society
AMI Association Montessori Internationale
ATIS Association of Teachers in Independent Schools
BJE Board of Jewish Education
ERB Education Records Bureau (also may refer to the test administered by the organization to pre-kindergarteners)
ISAAGNY Independent Schools Administration Association of Greater New York
NAES National Association of Episcopal Schools
NAEYC National Association for the Education of Young Children
NAIS National Association of Independent Schools
NYSAIS New York State Association of Independent Schools
NEST New Explorations for Science, Technology and Math
NYSAIS New York State Association of Independent Schools
SEIT A selective public school located on the Lower East Side

EAST SIDE

All Souls School

Ages: 2.6–6 yrs

Nonsectarian Nursery School

1157 Lexington Avenue (between 79th and 80th Streets)
Zip: 10021
Tel: 861-5232
Fax: 737-5271

Established 1965
Dr. Jean Mandelbaum, Director
Wendy Donoghue, Director of Admissions
Enrollment: 165

School year. September through early June.

Age	*Hours*	*Days*	*Tuition*
2s*	9:00–11:30	Tues and Thurs	$7,400
2s	9:00–11:45	Mon Wed Fri	$9,000
old 2s/young 3s	1:00–3:45	Mon–Thurs	$10,600
3s	9:00–11:45 or	Mon–Fri	$12,600
3s	1:00–3:45	Mon–Fri	
4s	9:00–12:00 or	Mon–Fri	$12,600
4s	1:00–4:00	Mon–Fri	
5s	9:00–3:00	Mon–Fri (until 12:00)	$16,800

*Must be 2.6 by September. Extended hours for 4s: The cost is $1,200 for one afternoon and $2,400 for two afternoons per year. Scholarships are available.

Program. Traditional/Developmental. The educational approach of the school is based on two principles: Children learn best when they are developmentally ready for new experiences and when these new experiences build upon earlier ones. Learning depends on the child's interaction with the social and physical environment. Long-range group projects and opportunities for individual work flow from children's interests and their readiness.

Activities include language arts (dictating stories, storytime, reading-readiness, and writing), blockbuilding (to discover math and aesthetic concepts), art, cooking, woodworking, sand and water play, math-readiness (measuring, quantifying, categorizing), science experiences, dramatic play, music and movement, social studies, and active play. Children do not use workbooks or worksheets.

Class projects develop from the interests of the children. Teachers and children collaborate on ideas that grow into trips, talks by guest experts and other special events.

All Souls is unusual in the amount of time it devotes to studying each child. Children are observed closely by all members of the staff in an attempt to see the world through each child's eyes, to learn who the child is, as opposed to evaluating that individual according to achievement norms (although this is done too, to meet ongoing school requirements). The staff's observations are discussed in staff meetings devoted to the children, and then a curriculum is developed.

ERB tests are given on the premises.

Scholarships are available.

Admissions. The application fee is $50. Inquire the first week after Labor Day. An open house is usually held in October. A lottery is being used to limit the number of applications.

Completed applications are processed in the order received.

Once the application is filed, the admissions director schedules a visit for the parents and, for another time, an afternoon play session for the applicant, at which four or five children of about the same age are brought together for about forty-five minutes with parents and faculty present.

Notifications are sent by early March. Preference is given to siblings. The school is nonsectarian.

Class size and staff. Twos have three teachers for each class of ten. Threes and older have fifteen or sixteen in each class, with three faculty. Most of the faculty, senior and junior, hold advanced degrees in early childhood education. Teachers are assisted by student teachers and a creative movement teacher. The school has a teacher's enrichment fund to support courses taken by teachers to increase their professional expertise. Teachers can obtain interest free loans. The school has a faculty that is unusual in its seniority and professional qualifications. The school sponsors staff attendance at important conferences, seminars, professional workshops and conventions, as well as further courses.

Facilities. The entry is through a garden. The classrooms are on the third, fourth, and fifth floors; the school's reception office, director's office, and a 2,500-book lending library are on the fifth floor. Since the elevator is tiny, many parents prefer to take the stairs (which function as a gallery for the children's art). There are six well-equipped, modern classrooms, two on each floor, a large multi-purpose basement room with a piano for movement and music. A roof playground houses a play structure, climbing and riding equipment, and large building blocks.

Summer program. An optional three-week summer program in June, from 9:00–12:30. Activities are similar to the regular curriculum with an expanded outdoor program.

Separation. Children are brought into the program in small groups for short class sessions. Separation may take a month for younger children. A home visit is made to each new child beforehand.

Parent involvement. Class-parent meetings and parent-teacher conferences are held periodically. Class-parent newsletters provide additional information. The school's Board of Trustees includes parents of children in the school. An active Parents Association sponsors many events, such as a children's carnival, a pancake breakfast, a cocktail party, and educational speakers. Parents also serve as classroom substitutes, librarians, and trip escorts. The auction, held in the community hall of the Unitarian Church of All Souls, is the school's major fundraising event, along with the book/bake fair. Funds raised go to the school's Scholarship Fund, Teacher's Enrichment Fund and the Director's Fund for Children's Special Needs. Parents meet regularly with the director to discuss issues of early childhood education, child development, and parenting.

Financial. The amount of financial aid was not available. However, there is a large endowment that helps keep tuition somewhat lower than at comparable schools.

Transportation. Parents bring their children to the classroom.

Graduates. Have gone to Allen-Stevenson, Bank Street, Brearley, Browning, Buckley, Chapin, Collegiate, Columbia Grammar, Convent of the Sacred Heart, Dalton, Ethical Culture, Friends Seminary, Hewitt, Horace Mann, Hunter, Marymount, Nightingale-Bamford, Riverdale Country, St. Bernard's, St. David's, Lab School, Spence, Town, Trevor Day, Trinity, PS 6, PS 158, PS 290, and UNIS.

Chartered. By the Board of Regents of the State University of New York.

Member. ERB, ISAAGNY.

Bright Horizons Children's Center

Ages: 6 weeks–5 yrs

All-Day Worksite Care

Main office:
New York Hospital
435 East 70th Street
(between First and York Avenues)
Zip: 10021
Tel: 746-6543
Fax: 746-5795
E-Mail: NYH@brighthorizons.com

Rachel Silver,
Director
Enrollment: 70–100

School year: Year round.

Age	*Hours*	*Days*	*Tuition*
6 Weeks–1 year	3–10 hours	2–5 days	$530–$2,247
1–3 years	3–10 hours	2–5 days	$442–$1,876
3s/4s	3–10 hours	2–5 days	$415–$1,760
4s/5s	3–10 hours	2–5 days	$389–$1,648

Program. Bright Horizons is a nationwide company providing high-quality early childhood education. Its philosophy is that children learn best through hands-on, concrete experiences under the observant eye of trained educators who can facilitate growth and development. Parents are considered partners in the children's educational experience and are welcome at all times. All of the company's centers are either accredited by the National Association for the Education of Young Children or currently in the accreditation process.

Admissions. Admissions are on a rolling basis.

Class size. There are eight infants per class, thirty toddlers, ages 1 to 2.5 years, and thirty-five preschoolers. In addition to regular class teachers, there are three floating assistants. A music and dance program is offered.

Facilities. The center is designed to offer developmentally appropriate learning areas and materials that encourage children to be self-directed. Located on the second floor of a high rise apartment building, the classrooms are all large and have big window that provide lots of natural light. There are two playgrounds, one for the infants and toddlers, the other for the older children.

Separation. The process entails careful planning and coordination between the classroom teachers and parents on an individual basis. Most children attend on an abbreviated schedule for the first two weeks.

Parent involvement. There's an open-door policy and parent advisory meetings are available. Parent-teacher conferences are held twice a year; parenting seminars, and family social events are scheduled.

Financial. Tuitions are collected on a monthly basis according to the individual child's schedule. There is a non-refundable registration fee of $100.

Transportation. Bright Horizons does not provide transportation to its center; most families live in the neighborhood or near-by community. Parents or caregivers drop off and/or pick up.

Graduates. Have attended a variety of public and private schools including Brearley, Chapin, Buckley, Collegiate, Churchill, Hunter, St. Davids, PS 6, PS 183, and PS 158.

Accreditation. NAEYC.

The Brick Church School

Ages: 3–6 yrs

Nonsectarian

62 East 92nd Street (between Madison and Park Avenues)
Zip: 10128
Tel: 289-5683
Website: www.brickchurch.org
E-Mail: lspinelli@brickchurch.org

Established 1940
Lydia Spinelli, Ed.D., Director
Enrollment: 145

School year. September through May. The optional summer program runs the first three weeks in June.

Ages	*Hours*	*Days*	*Tuition*
3s	9:00–12:00	Mon–Fri	$12,750
3s	1:00–4:00 1:00–3:30	Mon–Thurs, Fri	$12,350
4s–5s	9:00–12:00	Mon-Fri	$12,750
4s–5s	9:00–2:30	Mon–Thurs, Fri to 12:00	$16,350
K	9:00–2:30	Mon–Thurs, Fri to 12:00	$16,350

Children bring their lunches for the extended-day program, which is nonacademic. Morning drop-off and extended day available for a fee.

Program. Traditional. The director, Lydia Spinelli, has been at Brick Church School for close to twenty-five years. She runs the school with a combination of expertise in early childhood, humor, grace and good manners. Classrooms are well organized. Children choose from a variety of age appropriate early childhood materials, and take part in art, music and cooking, as well as pre-academic programs, which include science, math, social studies, language arts and literacy. There is a posted daily schedule of activities. The children have rooftime, activity time, etc. There is some scheduling flexibility except for the use of communal spaces. Although orderly and traditional, students can move freely from one activity area to the next. All children attend a weekly chapel service.

ERBs are administered on the premises.

Admissions. The application fee is $50. Inquiries begin right after Labor Day. The applications deadline is November 1st. Ask about tour schedules. Group interviews are scheduled by the admissions director. The applicants are observed in a classroom. Parents sit along the side and are asked to fill out a questionnaire, mainly (according to the school) so that the youngsters will see they are somewhat on their own and feel free to focus on their play. Parents may also complete the questionnaire at home and return it by mail. Once accepted, the director schedules a new parent conference and hosts a party for new families in the spring. Before school begins in the fall, teachers arrange to visit the child at home. Every October, Brick Church School holds an open house for parents already enrolled. It is a Back-to-School-Night, and is not for applicant parents.

Approximately fifty-three positions are open in the 3s. There are very few openings for older children. Preference is given to children of Brick Church members who have joined the church at least two years prior to the applications deadline, also to siblings, and to scholarship applicants. Children of church members account for about sixty percent of the enrollment. Notifications are sent according to ISAAGNY guidelines. The school maintains a waiting list.

Class size. There are four classes of 3-year-olds; three in the morning and one of fifteen children in the afternoon. Each has ten to fifteen children with two teachers per class. The 4s and 5s classes have eighteen to twenty children. In addition to the regular classroom teachers, there are three floating assistants and a music and movement teacher.

Facilities. This Carnegie Hill gem of a preschool recently renovated its building and church. The back wall of the large lobby is glass and faces the church's pleasant, walled garden which is where the children play on climbing structures, with wagons, and with other outdoor play items. Corridors and anterooms have cubby and storage space.

The classrooms are bright, clean, well organized, and well-equipped. There is a large, rubber-padded rooftop play area, as well as a carpeted music room and a chapel where the entire school gathers weekly for a brief chapel service. The downstairs area serves as a rainy-day play space. The children also use the church kitchen and gym.

Separation. After teachers visit the homes of new students, school begins with a four-day orientation period during which each half of each class meets for a short time. Parents stay with their children or wait in the garden room, depending on the child's ability to separate.

Parent involvement. Parents visit by appointment. Conferences are held with teachers semi-annually. Seminars are conducted on various aspects of parenting. There is a mix of working and nonworking parents who volunteer to various degrees, from occasional service to running the school library, Fall Fair, and other major fundraising events. Parents serve on the Day School Committee and the director meets with class representatives approximately once a month.

Financial. A deposit is required on signing the contract. The remainder of the tuition is payable in three installments due the 1st of

August, October, and December. An alternative payment schedule may be arranged upon request. About 13 percent of the students receive financial assistance, and the school encourages scholarship applicants.

Transportation. Most of the youngsters come from the immediate neighborhood and are brought by parents or caregivers.

Graduates. Have gone to Allen-Stevenson, Brearley, Browning, Buckley, Collegiate, Convent of the Sacred Heart, Chapin, Hewitt, Marymount, Nightingale-Bamford, Spence, St. Bernard's, and St. David's as well as to such co-ed schools as Birch Wathen-Lenox, Cathedral, Dalton, Manhattan Country, Riverdale, Town, Trevor Day and Trinity and to public schools.

Affiliations. Brick Presbyterian Church.

Member. ERB, ISAAGNY, NAIS, NYSAIS.

The Caedmon School

Ages: 2.9–10 yrs

Modified Montessori Nursery and Elementary School

416 East 80th Street (between First and York Avenues)	Established 1962
Zip: 10021	Carol Gose DeVine, Head of School
Tel: 879-2296	Erica Lowenfels
Fax: 879-0627	Admissions Director
Web site: www.caedmonschool.org	Nursery enrollment: 85
E-Mail: admissions@caedmonschool.org	Total enrollment: 215

School year. Mid-September through mid-June. No summer program.

Ages	*Hours*	*Days*	*Tuition*
2.9/3s	8:30–11:30	Mon–Fri	$11,258
4s–5s	8:30–3:30	Mon–Fri	$18,209

Children must be 2.9 by September 1st to begin and must be 5 years old by September 1st for kindergarten.

Extended hours. There is an extended/after school or "child-minding" program offered for children four years old through fifth grades. Activities include dance, ballet, cooking, computer, drama, sports, origami and art. An instrumental music program offers private lessons in piano, voice, guitar and violin and includes performance opportunities at recitals, and in workshops.

Program. Modified Montessori. The Caedmon School is a small, ongoing school with a strong sense of community and an actively involved group of families. Students have the unique opportunity to learn in a nurturing and academically challenging environment among a richly diverse group of peers. They graduate after completing the fifth grade, before entering adolescence, allowing the school to dedicate all of its attention and resources solely to these years of development.

The Beginners' Program, for children 2.9 to 3.0 years old, is specifically designed with developmentally appropriate tasks aimed to foster a sense of competence and confidence and social and emotional development. There is a predictable daily routine, a clear, accessible arrangement of materials, and special activities, all geared to make the experience a successful one. Social interaction within the deliberately small class of twelve students and two teachers is emphasized.

The Early Program for 3 and 4 year olds, combines Montessori philosophy and materials with art, open-ended activities, outdoor play, music and movement classes. In the Early Program, the curriculum emphasizes social and emotional development, as well as cognitive and sensory development, all geared to a child's individual pace. Caedmon utilizes and provides materials for fantasy play and there is a strong emphasis on group work and relaxed socialization among children. The program includes math, language arts and geography along with art, science and library classes for the four year olds once a week. Academics are taught in the afternoon and prepare children for the school's rigorous Elementary Program.

The Elementary Program, kindergarten through fifth grade, follows the spirit of the Montessori philosophy and offers a challenging academic program that is enriched by specialists in science, computers, library, art, art history, music, Spanish, writing workshop, physical education and yoga. Field trips around the city are incorporated into the program.

The Elementary Program builds a strong academic foundation based upon problem solving, work-study skills, and independent thinking. The fifth grade graduates are well prepared for a variety of middle schools and enroll in a range of independent schools and gifted public school programs. An extensive advisory service is provided to assist graduates in finding the most appropriate middle school.

Twenty-five percent of the students are from international families, representing twenty-two countries. Religious holidays are celebrated from a historical perspective and Catholic parents may request that their children receive religious instruction.

Admissions. The application fee is $50

The application deadline is November 30th. Parents may attend either a morning tour or an evening open house. Reservations are required as space is limited. The school strongly recommends that parents tour other ongoing schools as a basis for comparison. Parents are interviewed at a separate time from their child's visit; small groups of children visit with several teachers in a classroom for about a half an hour. In accordance with ISAAGNY policy, notification letters are mailed in early March for Beginners and the Early Program; and in mid-February for Kindergarten and higher grades. Caedmon maintains a strong commitment to diversity.

Tests. Applicants for the elementary program must take the WPPSI or WISC-III given by the ERB.

Class size. There is one toddler class of twelve children (2.9-3 years old) with two teachers. The 3s/4s meet in classes of eighteen children with two teachers. The elementary classes average sixteen to eighteen children and also have two teachers as well as specialists.

Staff. Caedmon has a highly trained staff of teachers. Early Program head teachers are experienced Montessori trained educators supervised by an Early Program Coordinator. Teachers meet weekly, as a group and individually, with the Early Program Coordinator to discuss each child's progress, the curriculum, and to share ideas. The Educational Director oversees the entire program. A school psychologist is available as a resource to parents and teachers.

Facilities. Caedmon occupies a bright and spacious building with four floors housing classrooms, an art studio, science lab, gym, library, computer lab, and music room. The science lab was recently renovated and has all brand new, state of the art equipment. The gymnasium was also renovated to include new gymnastics equipment and a rock-climbing wall (for Elementary Program students only). Classrooms are beautiful, bright and well equipped with Montessori and traditional equipment. The 3s and 4s use the large, cheerful lunchroom for movement classes, conducted by a professional dancer. They also visit the school's art room library and science lab each week and use the fully equipped music room. Elementary children use the school's gym three days a week, as well as the art, library, computer room, science, and music rooms. There is also an attractive private courtyard with modern playground equipment which the children use daily, weather permitting.

Separation. Separation is explained at a parents' orientation meeting before school begins. In September, new children begin school in small groups of four to six, and work up to the full program within two weeks. Most children settle in easily within that time period. Those with additional questions or concerns may consult the school psychologist. Parents may remain in the classroom until the child has made a comfortable adjustment.

The Parents Auxiliary hosts a coffee hour in the lunchroom for the parents of children who are able to separate. This provides an opportunity for new parents to meet each other at the beginning of the year, and volunteer to plan upcoming school events.

Parent involvement. The Parents Auxiliary acts as a formal liaison between the parents and staff. It organizes fund-raising events and sponsors social functions. The president of the PA is a member of the school's board of trustees. Parents are welcome to observe class sessions in the morning. Formal conferences are held three times each school year. The school also gives several workshops throughout the school year to demonstrate the use of educational materials and discuss various aspects of the curriculum. There are also several opportunities throughout the year for parents to do special projects or be guest readers in their child's class. Parents may be invited to read a favorite book, share a holiday treat or tell a story about their family.

Financial. A non-refundable deposit of $2,000 is required with the enrollment contract.

Transportation. Private bus service can be arranged for children 4 and older with a company recommended by the school.

Graduates. Have gone to Allen-Stevenson, Birch Wathen-Lenox, Brearley, Brooklyn Heights Montessori, Calhoun, Chapin, Collegiate, Columbia Grammar, Convent of the Sacred Heart, Dalton, Dwight, Ethical Culture, Friends Seminary Hewitt, Horace Mann, Hunter Elementary, Manhattan Country School, Marymount, Nightingale-Bamford, Poly Prep, Riverdale Country, Rudolph Steiner, Spence, Trevor Day, Trinity, York and gifted and talented public school programs.

Chartered. By the Board of Regents of the State University of New York.

Member. AMS, ERB, the Guild of Independent Schools, NYSAIS, NAIS, ISAAGNY, Early Steps.

Central Synagogue May Family Nursery School

Ages: 2.6–5 yrs

The Parenting Center

Ages: 4–36 months

SNAP (Special Nurturing Achievement Program)

Ages: 3–5 yrs

Jewish, Reform

123 East 55th Street (between Park and Lexington Avenues)
Zip: 10022
Tel: 838-5122 ext. 233
Website: www.centralsynagogue.org

Established 1965
Susan Alpert, Director
Ann Obsatz, Associate Director
Enrollment: 175

School year. September through first week in June. Separate June program.

Ages	*Hours*	*Days*	*Tuition*
2.6	9:30–12:00	3 days	$9,100
3s	9:15–12:15	Mon–Fri	$12,785
4s	9:15–2:15	Mon–Fri (Fri till 12:15)	$15,790
SNAP	9:00–12:00	Mon–Fri	$22,000

Families enrolled in the nursery are eligible for special membership rates at the synagogue. Tuition does not include a $2,500 required Temple membership fee.

Program. Developmental. Children's intellectual and emotional growth, competence, and work habits are addressed in a warm and healthy learning environment. The program welcomes children from diverse backgrounds and its objective is to encourage each to reach optimal development as an individual as well as a participant in group life. The staff give the children hands-on, open-ended, explorative materials and activities such as art, water and sand play, music, literature, expressive writing, science, cooking, dramatic play, and discussion. Children have music and movement once a week as well as a library class. For older children there are class trips to Donnell Library, The Jewish Museum, an apple orchard to pick apples, a picnic in Central Park's Conservatory Garden, etc.

Shabbat is celebrated every Friday.

ERBs are given on the premises, and the school works closely to counsel parents in selecting an ongoing school. Early in the fall a meeting for parents of 4s/5s is held to discuss admissions procedures to public and private ongoing schools.

Admissions. The application fee is $40. Inquiries are from September on. Call for an application and to sign up for the parent tours, held throughout the fall. Children are seen in January for a half hour of play and snack. Notifications are sent in accordance with ISAAGNY guidelines.

Class size. Each class has a head, associate, and an assistant teacher.

Staff. The staff is notable for its experience and its low rate of turnover.

Facilities. The school occupies the seventh, eighth and ninth floors of the Synagogue's imposing Community House, built in 1966. There are cheerful, light, and well-equipped rooms on each floor, also offices, a well-stocked library of children's and professional literature, and kitchenettes. Cubbies line the corridors. The rooftop playdeck is equipped with an extremely large climbing and exploration structure and slide. The floor is safety-surfaced. It has a large toy-filled sandbox, and is well equipped with tricycles, wagons, building blocks, planks, and other riding toys housed in a charming barn structure. Children bring their lunches and the school provides snacks.

Separation. Teachers pay home visits to the children shortly before school begins. Separation is gradual. The youngest children are introduced to one another and to the school in groups of as few as three youngsters. Size and length of stay increase until, after a month, all the children come together for the full session. Parents remain in the classroom or nearby as long as needed.

Parent involvement. Parents are welcome in the classroom for various activities, including art or music projects, storytelling, and cooking. They also join the classes on field trips, run the major benefit/fundraiser, and join holiday observances, including weekly Shabbat, outdoor Sukkah, and Hannukah and Purim services. Parents are occasionally asked to attend school events during the daytime. One day a week a consultant from the Jewish Board of Family and Children's Services is available. There are also two additional consultants, an occupational therapist and a speech and language specialist. Parent-teacher conferences are held twice yearly.

Financial. Some financial aid is available.

Transportation. Private bus transportation can be arranged for children age 3 years and older.

Graduates. Go on to both public and private schools.

Affiliations. Jewish Board of Family and Children's Services, JECA.

Member. ERB, ISAAGNY, Parents League of New York, NAEYC.

Special Programs:

The Parenting Center. The Parenting Centers offers support and guidance to enrich parents' relationships with their very young children during the critical early years. Once a week, professional facilitators meet with mothers of same-age children (0–12 months, 12–18 months, 19–30 months) to discuss child development, parenting skills, women's issues, etc. The children play in a cheerful adjacent space under teachers' supervision. (Children unwilling to separate may stay with their mothers.) The session ends with a snack, music, and a story. Father's Sunday is offered four times during the year. Jewish holidays are celebrated. A similar weekly program is offered for caregivers.

SNAP (Special Nurturing Achievement Program). Established in 1998, SNAP offers a full early-childhood experience that meets the needs of children ages 3.6–5 years old having difficulty in an average to large nursery school class. For three hours a day, from Monday through Friday, eight children meet in a small program tailored to the needs of the individual child. The class is led by three special education teachers and offers enrichment (music, movement, library) as well as consultant services (speech/language and occupational therapy). Parent discussion groups are conducted once a month as a key component of the total education of the children.

Children's All Day School and Children's All Day Pre-Nursery

Ages: 6 mos–5 yrs

Nonsectarian

109 East 60th Street (between
Park and Lexington Avenues)
Zip: 10022
Tel: 752-4566
Fax: 752-4567
Website: www.childrensallday.org
E-Mail: cadskids@aol.com

Established 1975
Roni Hewitt, Director
Anne Walsh, Administrative Assistant
Karen Vernoski, Educational Consultant
Enrollment: 90

School year. Year round.

Ages	*Hours*	*Days*	*Tuition*
Infants	8:00–6:00	Mon–Fri	$22,500
Toddlers (1–2)	8:00–6:00	Mon–Fri	$22,000
2s	8:00–6:00	Mon–Fri	$21,000
3s–5s	8:00–6:00	Mon–Fri	$20,500
Half-day*	8:30–12:30	Mon–Fri	$14,500

*Half-day programs are only available for children over two.

Program. Developmental Eclectic. The school was founded in 1975 as an alternative to nannies or baby-sitters for children of working parents. Young children are provided safe, nurturing and developmentally appropriate environments where learning takes place through play, hands-on and academic experiences.

The developmental interaction philosophy is the main focus of the school's approach. In the 3s and 4s, more emphasis is placed on reading and math readiness activities so that children will be able to handle an academic kindergarten. Social skills and emotional well-being are important aspects of the program. Morning programs from 8:30–12:30 as well as 3 and 4 day schedules are available for children over two years of age.

Admissions. The application fee is $40. The school has a fall admissions process, but will enroll children throughout the year if there is a place available. A completed application form and fee must be sent before the school will schedule a tour. Parents are met in small groups and children are observed in play groups of four to six. Admissions preference is given to siblings and legacies. The ERB test is given on the premises.

Class size. There is one Infant Group of 9 children (ages six to fourteen months) with four full time caregivers, and two Toddler groups of 8 children, each with two full time teachers and one part-time floater. There are two 2s classes of 12 children with three full-time teachers; two 3s classes of 15 children, each with two full time and one part time teacher; and one 4s or Pre-K class of 18, with two full-time and a part-time teacher.

Staff. Six teachers currently have masters degrees in early childhood education. There is a music teacher on staff and an outside movement specialist for all classes, from toddlers on. The educational consultant works with all teachers on curriculum and child development concerns.

Facilities. The school occupies most of two contiguous townhouses. The school is open from 8:00–6:00, and children arrive between 8:00 and 9:30 and leave between 4:30 and 6:00. Parents and children climb stairs to the various rooms, which are colorful and bright. All eight classrooms have either lofts or climbing platforms. Rooms and hallways are decorated with children's art. On the first floor is the director's office and a large, handsome, and formally furnished parlor. The school has one infant class, two toddler classes, two 2s, two 3s, and one 4s–5s class.

A tree-shaded backyard contains a treehouse, climbing and sliding structure, outdoor building blocks, tricycles, wagons, and other toys. The school uses a closed-circuit television camera for security purposes.

Children bring lunch from home. Snacks of juice, crackers, cereal, and fruit are provided by the school.

Summer sessions (July and August) are part of the yearly contract and offer sprinklers, water play, bi-weekly shows and weekly picnics.

Separation. Parents of children under age 3 are required to participate in a seven day orientation process to assist with separation. Young children are gradually introduced into the program, in small groups, for progressively increased time periods. For the first three days parents remain in the classroom. Generally, by the end of seven school days, children are ready to be on their own but if necessary, parents are asked to stay longer. For older children the process is modified.

Parent involvement. Parents may visit without an appointment. Most parents participate in fund-raising events and field trips. Conferences are arranged twice a year or at the parents' or teachers' request.

The student body is diverse and international, coming from NYC and surrounding areas.

Financial. Upon signing a contract (which runs from September through August), a deposit of ten percent of the total annual tuition is required. The year's tuition is paid in ten instalments. About ten percent of the students receive some financial aid, and sibling discounts are offered.

Transportation: All students are brought and picked up by parents or caregivers.

Graduates. Have gone on to such schools as Birch Wathen-Lenox, Brearley, Browning, Buckley, Chapin, Columbia Grammar, Dalton, Ethical Culture, Hunter Elementary, Lycée Français, Manhattan Country, Trinity and UNIS.

Chartered. By the Board of Regents of the State University of New York.

Member. ERB, ISAAGNY, NAIS, National Association for the Education of Young Children.

Christ Church Day School

Ages: 2.3–6 yrs

Nonsectarian Nursery School

520 Park Avenue
(at 60th Street)
Zip: 10021
Tel: 838-3039
Fax: 593-3744
Website: www.christchurchnyc.org
E-Mail: pmarble@christchurchnyc.org

Established 1949
M. Margaret Marble, Director
Luanne Vrattos, Administrative Assistant
Enrollment: Approximately 100

School year: September to end of May. June camp available to currently enrolled students.

Ages	*Hours*	*Days*	*Tuition*
2s	9:00–11:30	Tues Thurs or	$7,780
		Mon Wed Fri	$9,405
3s	9:00–11:45	Mon–Fri	$13,170
4s	9:00–11:50	Mon–Fri	$13,170
5s	9:00–2:30	Tues–Thurs, Mon and Fri until 12:00	$17,680

Extended day option available Tues and Thurs for 3s and Tues, Wed, and Thurs for 4s until 2:30 at an additional cost of $3,700 and $4,510, respectively.

Program. Developmental. Founded in 1949 by the Board of Trustees of Christ Church United Methodist as a day nursery for parishioners as well as neighborhood families, but without religious instruction.

M. Margaret Marble, known as "Peggy," has been with the school as director for over twenty years. Ms. Marble's expertise in early childhood development, as well as her strong leadership, is the reason why the Day School has become one of the prominent nursery schools in the city.

The Day School emphasizes a child centered program. The school sees learning as a process in which children gather information and concepts through direct discovery and exploration and then externalize them through creative activities. The children are expected to have a good time, with a wide range of materials and activities, including blockbuilding, art, music and movement, woodworking, and dramatic play.

ERBs are given on the premises. The school has set aside a quiet room for ERB testing. At the beginning of the year, teachers introduce the tester. The children visit and play in the testing room with the teacher before any of them are tested. A number of meetings are arranged for parents to discuss the ongoing schools' application process.

Admissions. The application fee is $45. Inquiries are received from the first Monday in October on. Apply promptly. The school automatically accepts siblings, who take most of the openings. Few additional places are available, and applications may be cut off early. Reserve a place in a group tour, given during November and December, when you call for an application form. The school notifies parents by mail that it has received their application and requests that they call to make an appointment in January or early February for the child's interview. Children are seen individually with their parents for half an hour to forty-five minutes. Parents who apply after the application cutoff pay no application fee unless the school is able to schedule an interview.

Notifications are sent by early March.

Class size. There are two classes of 2s, with ten to twelve children and one of twelve to fourteen children. The two 3s classes have sixteen children each, and there is one class each of eighteen to twenty 4s or 4s/5s.

Staff. The larger classes have three staff members: two co-teachers with an assistant, including at least one teacher with a masters in early childhood education. The faculty are reputed to be among the highest paid in any New York City nursery school. The school has a Teachers Fund, the interest from which is used for yearly bonuses for Senior teachers. In addition, ongoing workshops within the school provide continuing professional development, and further training is paid for by the school. A professional artist works with the four-and five-year-olds in the extended day program. There is also a music and movement specialist for the children. The school encourages grandparents to assist on a weekly basis as intergenerational docents.

Facilities. Visitors enter through the church's small courtyard on Park Avenue, or through the main entrance to the church. Once inside, there is a manned elevator to the sixth floor, where they must be buzzed into the school through a glass door. The stairs are locked above the second floor, although parents can use the stairwells. The school has five spacious classrooms and a large, well-equipped state of the art playroof with a colorful modular play system. An indoor playspace is used for movement and music classes.

Separation. A separation workshop is given by the director before the term begins to explain how parents can help their child. Parents of 3s are encouraged to step out of the room on the second day, if the child is comfortable with this. The 2s have a longer separation period. However, because each child's needs are different, separation is handled individually.

Parent involvement. The parent body is homogeneous and cohesive, and very involved in the school. In addition to arranging social and fund-raising events, parents can volunteer to work in the school's library. There are frequent workshops on parenting issues such as children's fears, sibling rivalry, discipline, and ongoing school selection given by outside experts. Conferences are arranged twice yearly and as needed.

Financial. Financial aid is available.

Transportation. Private bus service can be arranged.

Graduates. Tend to prefer single-sex schools and a fair number go on to schools such as Allen-Stevenson, Brearley, Chapin, Collegiate, Nightingale and Spence as well as to Columbia Grammar, Dalton, and Trinity.

Affiliations. Christ United Methodist Church, but school is nonsectarian.

Member. ERB, ISAAGNY, NAEYC.

Convent of the Sacred Heart

Ages: 3–18 yrs

Girls Catholic Nursery and Comprehensive School

1 East 91st Street (at 5th Avenue)
Zip: 10128
Tel: 722-4745
Fax: 996-1784
Website: www.cshnyc.org
E-Mail: broot@cshnyc.org
Total enrollment: 650

Established 1881
Patricia Hult, Head of Lower School
Barbara Root, Director of Admissions

Nursery enrollment: 31
Kindergarten enrollment: 54

School year. September through June. No summer program.

Ages	*Hours*	*Days*	*Tuition*
3s	8:15–12:15	Mon–Fri	$15,210
4s	8:15–2:00		$20,025
5s	8:15–3:00	Mon–Fri	$28,000
Fees for lunch for grades 1–4			$1,000

Program. Traditional. At 8:15, the young children pass through the school's enclosed, cobblestoned courtyard into a cavernous hall fragrant with flowers. Each joins the line for Morning Greeting and takes her turn, curtsying to and taking the hand of the Lower School Head before going on to class.

The children begin to wear uniforms (gray jumpers) in Pre-K. In kindergarten, work becomes distinctly academic, although there is time for free play. There is an emphasis on social skills; instilling confidence and a strong sense of self esteem is the focus of the lower school's program. Each student is encouraged to recognize the spiritual dimensions of personality.

The oldest girls' school in the city, Sacred Heart has deep ties with an international network of 118 schools (21 in the United States) under the direction of the Society of the Sacred Heart, founded in France in 1800 and now headquartered in Rome. The schools are centrally evaluated every five years for their intellectual rigor, sense of community, social awareness, and ethical sense. The academic program is designed to foster competency and creativity. Children develop effective problem-solving skills; logical ways of thinking are taught aned encouraged. There are exchange programs with European sister schools.

There is a daily community prayer, and children from second grade on attend weekly mass.

Admissions. The application fee is $65. Inquire from April on. After the school has received the completed application and fee, parents are contacted to arrange an interview and tour. Plan to spend about one to one and a half hours for this visit; your daughter's interview will be in a group setting and last about half an hour and will consist of free play, teacher-directed activities and a story. The school's multiracial, multicultural student body consists of girls from the New York area as well as many foreign countries. While religion plays little part in the preschool, it enters the curriculum in later grades.

The preschool admits older 3s for a two-year program. The school maintains a waiting list, but will not admit a child who has already accepted a place at another ISAAGNY school.

The preschool was founded to accommodate families already involved with Sacred Heart. Preference is given to siblings and children of alumnae.

Notifications are sent by early March. ERB tests are required for 4s and 5s applicants. Children who enter the school through the nursery program go automatically into kindergarten and therefore need not prepare for the ERB.

Class size. There are two preschool groups, one for 3s and one for 4s, of between fifteen and seventeen children, with two teachers each. There are fifty-four children in the kindergarten in three sections with two teachers each.

Facilities. These are easily among the most elegant school buildings in the city—two interconnecting mansions, the James Burden House (circa 1900) and the magnificent Otto Kahn mansion (completed in 1918 in the Italian Renaissance style), both landmark buildings. The Burden House was built for a granddaughter of Cornelius Vanderbilt and was designed by Warren & Wetmore, the architects who designed Grand Central Terminal and the old Biltmore Hotel. Its marble staircase swirls up several flights to a cupola executed by the French artist Hector d'Espouy. On the third floor is a ballroom with mirrored panels and doors, rose and white marble walls, and an ornately decorated ceiling. There is a large music room. Older children lunch in a banquet hall with immense, deeply inset, arched windows and green marble walls accented with gold.

The school completed an extensive construction and renovation project in 2004. It has thirty-six classrooms, a large chapel, two libraries with automated card catalogues and over 25,000 volumes, five science laboratories, five computer centers, an independent computer network, a theater, five art and music studios, two gymnasiums, a ballroom, and a banquet hall, as well as a dining hall. There are two handsome, cheerful prekindergarten classrooms. These are arranged into distinct activity areas and filled with well-ordered materials, both task-centered and open-ended. There are two rooftop play areas; one extends the length of the building fronting 5th Avenue and has a spectacular view of Central Park and the reservoir. Preschoolers use the lower school library, the ballroom for dancing lessons, the rooftop play spaces, and the gyms.

Separation. Children are brought into the school in small groups for three days to acclimate them. Parents remain on the premises until the child is comfortable. A parents' office is computerized and also has telephones. It is staffed five days a week.

Parent involvement. There is an active parents association. Conferences are scheduled twice a year and can be called for by parents or teachers whenever a need arises.

Financial. Limited financial aid is available for students of special ability. The endowment is approximately $25 million.

Transportation. Children come from all over the metropolitan New York City area. Private bus transportation can be arranged.

Graduates. Approximately half those enrolled eventually graduate from the upper school. Those who leave usually do so because their families leave the New York area.

Affiliations. The school is informally affiliated with the Archdiocese of New York. It is chartered by the Board of Regents of the State University of New York.

Member. The Network of Sacred Heart Schools, National Coalition of Girls' Schools, ERB, ISAAGNY, NAIS, NYSAIS, the European Council of International Schools and the International Schools Association.

The Creative Playschool

Ages: 2.0–3.10 yrs

A Jewish Preschool

Fifth Avenue Synagogue
5 East 62nd Street
Zip: 10021
Tel: 750-8793
Website: www.5as.org/sections/playschool.asp

Paulette Stein Meyer, Director
Rochelle Hirsch, Chairperson
Enrollment: 39

School year. Third week in Sept.–June.

Age	*Hours*	*Days*	*Tuition*
2.0–2.6	9:15–12:15	Tues, Thurs	$6,950
2.5–2.11	9:15–12:15	Mon, Wed, Fri	$8,200
2.10–3.8	9:00–1:00	Mon–Friday	$11,500

*Children need not be toilet-trained.

Program. Eclectic, centered on experiential learning. Classroom atmosphere is warm, respectful and unpressured. If they show an interest, 3/4s are encouraged to write their names, but this is not required. If a child does not want to join an activity, that choice is respected. Curriculum centers around the seasons, Jewish holidays and secular holidays, the development of self and the recognition that each child is unique. As part of scientific study, children go on nature walks, picking a tree in autumn and making notes throughout the year.

Admission. Inquiries should be made in autumn of the year preceding attendance. Applications are generally made by December with notification by March. After the application form is submitted with a $100 fee, the director will contact parents to arrange a meeting.

Class size. Two classes of 2s with 12–13 children and 3 adults. One class of 3s/4s with 12 children and two adults.

Facilities. Very clean and new. An elevator to the fifth floor opens into the entryway of the very large, high ceilinged 2s/3s class. Windows fill the top third of one long wall. The 3s/4s room is smaller but equally bright with the same high windows. A large windowed room serves as a gym where children play daily.

Separation. "Slow and easy," says the director. The first day is divided into two sessions with half the class attending each. Parents or caregivers are required to stay for the first day and thereafter, based on cues from their children, take their leave usually within a few weeks.

Parent involvement. An orientation meeting for parents is held one evening before the start of school. Parents are always welcome to visit, but must call first; they often come in for cooking and baking, to celebrate Shabbat or accompany groups on trips. A parent committee has been formed; it coordinates fundraising activities like raffles, breakfasts, book fairs and lectures. Close home/school communications are encouraged. Parents may call to arrange conferences.

Financial. Upon a child's acceptance into the program, a nonrefundable deposit of $1,000 must be paid, credited towards tuition. Fifty percent of tuition is due by September 1, the remaining half by December 1.

Graduates. Go to Ramaz School, Park East Day School, Horace Mann, the Abraham Joseph Heschel School and Park Avenue Synagogue.

Affiliation. Fifth Avenue Synagogue.

The Elizabeth Seton Pre-School

Ages: 2 mos–6 yrs

An All Day Montessori Developmental Educational Program

1675 Third Avenue (at East 93rd Street)
Zip: 10128
Tel: 369-9626
Fax: 369-1337
Day Care Enrollment: 40 (2 mos.–36 mos.)
Preschool Enrollment: 35 (2.9–6 yrs.)

Established 1972, 1980
Mrs. Maria Gravel, Infant Program Preschool Director
Susan Pomilla, Assistant to Director

School year. All Year.

Age	*Hours*	*Days*	*Tuition*
2 r	8:00–6:00	Mon–Fri	$385–410 weekly

Program. Montessori based. Seton serves as a model of Montessori day care programming. Observers from all over the country visit frequently. Children are introduced with remarkable gentleness to its modified Montessori curriculum, which includes many activities and materials found in more traditional programs: dramatic play, open-ended materials such as blocks, sand, and water, as well as many ordinary toys. There is a strong emphasis on the nurturing and personalized care of children as well as on their social and emotional growth.

In the preschool, children are given free choice in the various curriculum areas and are encouraged to work individually or in small groups. A teacher in each activities center pays close attention to the children's progress in a curriculum area, and encourages development through small group and one-on-one work. Skills and materials are introduced in small groups or as one-on-one.

Admissions. The application fee is $40. Inquiries can be made at any time; filing an application form places your child on a waiting list. You may then make an appointment to visit the preschool or the infant/toddler program, with or without your child. Applicants are accepted on a first-come basis. In the infant/toddler program, a number of families are eligible for sliding scale fees through a limited purchase of service plan with the Agency for Child Development.

Class size. The four small groups in the infant/toddler center meet in separate rooms. There are seven infants, 2 to 10 months; nine toddlers 10 to 18 months, and two classes of twelve children, each 18 to 36 months. Each group has a staff of three adults. Foster grandmothers and student interns assist staff.

Children in the preschool (which is really an extension of the infant/toddler program) function in flexible, constantly changing small mixed-age groups. Students on field placement assist the five regular staff members. There is also a music teacher.

Facilities. The school is located near two parks. The environment is described as safe and homelike.

Separation. A phasing-in plan is worked out for each family based on its needs and the child's.

Parent involvement. On a daily basis parent involvement is informal. The staff works in partnership with parents. Throughout the year, small group and large group meetings are held.

Financial. Tuition for the preschool and the day care center is payable monthly.

Affiliations. Sponsorship by The New York Foundling Hospital/Center for Parent and Child Development.

Member. Affiliated with AMS, ERB, ISAAGNY, Association of Children's Services (ACS); ACD, Child Care, Inc.

Epiphany Community Nursery School

Ages: 2–5 yrs

Nonsectarian

510 East 74th Street
(off York Avenue)
Zip: 10021
Tel: 737-2977
Fax: 737-2993
Website: www.74magic.com
E-Mail: w.levey@ecns.org

Established 1975
Wendy Levey, Director
Enrollment: 150

School year. Mid-September through the end of May.

Age	*Hours*	*Days*	*Tuition*
young 2s	9:00–12:00	Tues and Thurs	$9,100
older 2s	9:00–12:00	Mon Wed Fri	$11,000
3s	9:00–12:00 Tuesday to 2:30	Mon–Fri	$15,000
4s/5s	9:00–2:30	Mon Wed Thurs and Tues Thurs until 12:00	$17,200

Extended hours. Children 3 through 6 may be dropped off at 8:30 for an additional daily charge of $5.

Program. Traditional. The school has a strong program using a core curriculum for social, emotional, cognitive, language, and motor development. Weekly study units explore themes through experiment, cooking, painting, music, and other pursuits. The school celebrates holidays through food and music. For example, in celebration of the Chinese New Year there's a parade, the children make lanterns and prepare a typical Chinese dish. Current events and history are discussed with older children.

The ERB tests used to evaluate kindergarten candidates are given on the school's premises. Students tend to choose independent schools, but also attend parochial and public schools.

Admissions. The application fee is $75. Inquire from the day after Labor Day on. There are openings for 24 to 25 young 2s, 24 to 28 older 2s and openings vary for 3s, 4s, and 5s.

Group tours are scheduled during October and November. The application and fee may be submitted after the tour. Call right after your tour to arrange a forty-five minute interview with the director, during part of which the child will be observed at play with parents present. Interviews for 2s, 3s and 4s applicants are conducted after Thanksgiving until the end of February with both parents and the child.

Acceptance notifications are sent in March.

Class size: There are four classes of 12 to 14 2s with 3 teachers; 16 3s with 3 teachers; and 20–22 4/5s with 3 teachers.

Staff. All head teachers have masters degrees in early childhood education. Parent–teacher conferences are held twice a year. The school pays for teachers to attend workshops, lectures and weekend classes.

Facilities. The school is located in a large air-conditioned, newly painted four-story facility. There is a playground on the roof. The facility has ten classrooms. There is a full kitchen, conference room, and library. Children bring their own lunch; parents provide the school's snacks. No nuts are allowed.

Summer program. From June through August there is a summer day camp for 2–5.5s on the premises. Schedules are flexible; an additional fee is required.

Separation. All new children are visited at home by their teachers before school begins. They are eased in slowly, especially the 2s, who are introduced to the school environment in fifteen-minute sessions with half of their eventual classmates. The length of each introductory visit is increased and the class members are brought together, so that by the first week in November they are on the full morning schedule.

Parents stay in the classroom the first day, and stand by out of sight thereafter, unless a child seriously objects. They are encouraged to stay in the school in a room other than the classroom, until their child is comfortable with complete separation. For 3s and 4s the process is speedier.

Parent involvement. Parents are encouraged to take part in classroom activities and field trips, to share their expertise with students and faculty, and to help in fund-raising and development drives, community service projects, with admissions tours, and with the school's newsletter.

Several meetings are held each year on curriculum, ongoing schools, and other topics of interest. These are usually held during the day, often at breakfast.

Parents' visits are by appointment. They confer with their child's teacher twice a year for formal developmental progress reports.

Financial. A $2,500 deposit is due upon signing the contract. Half the balance remaining is due May 1st, the last installment by August 1st. There are no refunds. Some scholarship aid is available.

Transportation. No private bus service.

Graduates. Have gone on to schools such as Allen-Stevenson, Birch Wathen-Lenox, Brearley, Browning, Buckley, Chapin, Collegiate, Convent of the Sacred Heart, Dalton, Ethical Culture, Hewitt, Horace Mann, Marymount, Riverdale, St. Bernard's, St. Davids, Spence, Town, Trevor Day, Trinity, UNIS and PS 158, among others.

Chartered. By the Board of Regents of the State University of New York.

Member. ERB, ISAAGNY, Parents League, ATIS, NAEYC.

The Episcopal School

Ages: 2.6–5+ yrs

Non-sectarian Early Childhood School

35 East 69th Street (between Park and Madison Avenues)
Zip: 10021
Tel: 879-9764
Fax: 288-7505
E-Mail: office@episcopalschool.org

Established 1961
Judith Blanton, Director
Jane Arnold, Director of Admissions
Enrollment: 220 boys and girls; 110 AM; 110 PM

School year. September through mid-June

Ages	*Hours*	*Days*	*Tuition*
2s	9:15–11:15 or 1:15–3:15	Mon–Fri	$12,190
3s, 4s,5s	8:30–11:30 or 12:30–3:30	Mon–Fri	$13,600

Program. Traditional. Instruction is individualized to meet each child's needs. The program provides experiences in reading- and math-readiness, science, cooking, music, art, and literature. Creative movement and story-telling are also offered. The atmosphere of the school is formal. Weekly chapel services are held.

ERBs are given on the premises, and the admissions directors of some of the ongoing schools visit to observe the children they are considering for admission.

Admissions. The application fee is $50. Inquiries from Labor Day on. Apply promptly. Openings are limited. Call for an application form and return it promptly. Upon receipt, the school contacts the parent and arranges a parent tour and interview, given in October and November. The child will visit later in the winter for a play session at which parents are present. Notifications are sent by early March.

Facilities. The school occupies a well-appointed, seven-story townhouse with a rooftop playdeck. In addition to spacious, sunny classrooms, there are an indoor all-purpose room, a library, and a small backyard play area.

Summer program. For three weeks in June, 9:00 to 1:00.

Separation. New children are visited at home by their teachers before school begins. Twos and 3s are introduced to the program in small groups and shortened sessions.

Parent involvement. The parent body is cohesive. Parents are heavily involved in school activities.

Financial. A non-refundable deposit of $1500 is due by mid-March with the signing of the contract. Financial aid is readily available. A form should be requested when applying.

Transportation. Greetings and leave-takings are with a formal handshake for each child. Children are accompanied to the classroom by a parent or caregiver.

Chartered. By the Board of Regents of the State University of New York.

Graduates. Tend to choose single-sex ongoing schools.

Member. ERB, ISAAGNY, NAES, NAEYC, NYSAIS, NAIS.

The Family Schools

Ages: 1.6–12 yrs

Nursery and Elementary School

Established 1975
Lesley Nan Habermann, Founder and Headmistress

Dag Hammarskjold Plaza
323 East 47th Street
(between 1st and 2nd Avenues)
Zip: 10017
Tel: 688-5950
Fax: 980-2475
E-Mail: famschool@aol.com
Total enrollment: approximately 160
Preschool enrollment: approximately 130

See also The Family School West under West Side listings.

School year. September through June.

Age	*Hours*	*Days*	*Tuition*
1.6–3s	8:15–3:00	Mon–Fri	$13,500
1.6–3s	8:15–11:15	Mon–Fri, 2 or 3 days	$7,300–$12,500
	12:30–3:30	Mon–Fri	
3s*–6s	8:15–3:00	Mon–Fri, 2, 3 days half or full	$7,600–$13,900

*Should be toilet trained.

Extended day programs are available until 6:00 PM for an additional fee.

Program. Montessori. Toddlers spend time in both cognitive and gross motor rooms each day. The cognitive room offers children a variety of areas to choose from including language, math, sensory play, practical life, science and geography. Toddlers start the day with circle time, where they learn to focus and use language for increasing periods of time. Music, art and foreign languages as well as social interaction are central to the toddler program. Toddlers visit the library and have their own enclosed outdoor play area.

The pre-primary program for three, four and five-year olds, also includes language, math, activities of practical life and cultural areas. Children begin their day with a group meeting in a circle, then break up into smaller groups for independent and collaborative work and are exposed to academic materials. They play on the playground before lunch. Specials include music, art, foreign languages, physical education, dance and yoga.

ERBs are given on the premises; applicants 5-years-old and older must take the ERB. Assistance is given parents who want to take advantage of ongoing school placement.

Admissions. The application fee is $40. Inquiries are always welcome. Applications are followed up with a call to schedule an appointment for parents to visit and observe a classroom, and to meet with faculty. Families are encouraged to visit the school as many times as they desire. Children may join their parents during the first visit; the headmistress is available to meet with and will spend time with applicants and their families.

Class size. Including both part- and full-time students, there are approximately sixty children in the toddler program, with no more than twelve to a class, each with three to four teachers; 3s through 6s, have three groups of twenty children. with three to four teachers.

Facilities. There are seven classrooms, a gym, an art room, a library, and an outdoor play area. The botanical area in Dag Hammarskjold Plaza, of which the headmistress is a vice president, is a commonly used play area.

Summer program. Mid-June through August; $4,000 for the full 10-week program, or $400 a week for part time programs.

After-school program. All children may take part in creative and recreational activities on a full-time basis or at a per diem cost.

Separation. The school's summer program is a good time to introduce toddlers to the school. In September children have several days of transition with their parents.

Parent involvement. Parents are encouraged to share their cultural backgrounds and traditions in the classrooms. Each week, parents, extended family, and friends are welcome to join the school for lunch. Two parent workshops are offered each year; parents receive two detailed evaluations each year, attend two parent/teacher conferences, and three mandatory observations. Class parents are well-informed and available.

Financial. A $1500 non-refundable deposit is required on contract signing. The remainder of the year's tuition is payable July 1st and December 1st. Payment plans are available.

Transportation. About a quarter of the children come from the immediate neighborhood: 1st to 5th Avenues, between 37th and 57th Streets. The remainder come from other parts of Manhattan or other boroughs.

Graduates. Have attended Brearley, Browning, Buckley, Cathedral, Chapin, Columbia Grammar, Convent of the Sacred Heart, Dalton, Ethical Culture, Friends Seminary, Horace Mann, Lycée Française, Marymount, Nightingale-Bamford, Riverdale, Spence, St. David's, Town, Trinity, Trevor Day, and UNIS, as well as Hunter, and Gifted and Talented programs in the public schools.

Chartered. By the Board of Regents of the State University of New York.

Member. AMS, ERB, ISAAGNY, Parents League.

Garden House School of New York

Ages: 2.6–6 yrs

Nonsectarian Preschool

593 Park Avenue (at 64th Street) — Natalie Williams, Co-Director
Zip: 10021

40 Sutton Place (at 59th Street) — Mary Cantwell, Co-Director
Zip: 10022
Tel: 421-3282 — Enrollment: 220
Website: www.gardenhouseschool.org
E-Mail: info@gardenhouseschool.org

Ages	*Hours*	*Days*	*Tuition*
2s	8:45–11:15 or 12:30–3:00	Mon–Fri	$12,900–18,500
3s–6s	8:45–11:45 or 12:30–3:25 or 8:45–12:00	Mon–Fri	

Program. Traditional/academic. Programs are designed to meet the social, physical, emotional, and intellectual growth of each child. The day is structured with an enriched curriculum that includes art, singing, gym, cooking, early science, and math-readiness. There are daily class discussions as well as storytime, dramatic play, and use of small motor manipulatives. The juniors (3s/4s) and seniors (4s/5s) are introduced to French, ballet/movement, computer, as well as an early reading and writing program. The 4s and 5s take field trips throughout the year.

Typical units of study are introduced through projects, readings, trips and discussions. One unit on the Olympics was the focus of interest; others include farm animals, friendship and personal stories.

The core of the program is traditional values combined with academic learning. The school maintains a highly structured and formal nursery environment which is beautiful, comfortable, and orderly. There are always fresh flowers in the school's entryway, and the children wear uniforms designed uniquely for Garden House School.

ERBs are given on the premises. The examiner is introduced to the children before testing begins in October. Directors from ongoing schools visit to observe children they are considering for admission.

Admissions. The application fee is $100. Requests for applications begin the Tuesday after Labor Day. Upon application, visits and interviews for the parents and child are scheduled from October through mid-December. Parents are given a group tour and an informal interview. The child is invited to a brief playdate. Families are notified in March.

Staff. Each class has a head teacher with a masters degree and an assistant teacher. A ballet/movement teacher and a French teacher work with the children throughout the school.

Facilities. The Park Avenue facility occupies two floors of the Central Presbyterian Church. Classrooms have pleasant open space and good natural light. There is a large, vaulted-ceiling, well-equipped gym space where children play happily and freely. A rooftop garden, with architecturally stimulating vistas of cupolas and cityscapes, is equipped with climbing structures and riding toys.

The Sutton Place facility is the flagship for Garden House School of New York. It occupies the entire ground floor of a condominium building.

Summer program. A three-week program is available in June. Daily activities include arts and crafts, gardening, dramatic play, music, and outdoor water play.

Separation. Toddlers are gently introduced to school for shortened sessions and in smaller groups over a two- to three-week period. A parent or caregiver stays in the classroom for the first few days and then remains nearby until the child is comfortable.

Parent involvement. Parents participate in field trips. All parents are members of the Parent/Teacher Association. A class representative(s) from each class organizes social events. Parent-teacher conferences are arranged in November and May.

Financial A non-refundable deposit is required to secure a place. The remaining tuition is paid in three additional installments due in May, September, and December.

Graduates. Have gone to all "the leading ongoing independent and public schools."

Affiliations. Garden House School of London.

Chartered. By the Board of Regents of the State University of New York.

Member. ERB, ISAAGNY.

Horace Mann School Nursery Division

Ages: 3–5 yrs

Nonsectarian Nursery School

55 East 90th Street (between Madison and Park Avenues)
Zip: 10128
Tel: 369-4600
Website: www.horacemann.org
E-Mail: admissions@horacemann.org

Established 1954
Dr. Thomas M. Kelly, Head of School
Mrs. Patricia Yuan Zuroski, Head of the Nursery Division
Ms. Dana Haddad, Associate Director of Nursery and Kindergarten Admissions
Enrollment: 150

School year. September to June.

Ages	*Hours*	*Days*	*Tuition*
3s	9:00–3:00 and 1 half day	2 full days and 1 half day	$20,860
4s	9:00–3:00 (Fri until 2:00)	Mon–Fri	$26,880
5s	9:00–3:00 (Fri until 2:00)	Mon–Fri	$29,110

Program. Developmental/Traditional. Active learning is the operative principle here with a strong focus on social and emotional, as well as intellectual, development in an academically appropriate environment. Activities include blockbuilding, cooking, free or structured dramatic play, including puppetry and putting on plays; art, woodworking, music, including singing, improvisation, instruments, and movement to music; daily storytime, reading- and math-readiness, and science, computer readiness, physical education, and chess. Phonics, sight words, and writing are introduced.

The school was founded in 1954 as the New York School for Nursery Years by the staff of the former Harriet Johnson Nursery School; in 1968, as a service to alumni, it merged with the Horace Mann School in Riverdale and then the Horace Mann-Barnard Elementary School, providing an academically appropriate preschool program of the ongoing school. There are approximately 1750 children in the entire school, ages 3 through 18. Many children admitted to the nursery division go all the way through twelfth grade at Horace Mann.

Admissions. The application fee is $50. Inquire from June 1st on; apply promptly. The school requires two interview appointments: one for the parents, and one for the child. The children are observed in play groups of five or six with parents sitting on the side for about forty-five minutes, ending with juice and cookies. Notifications are sent by early March. Preference is given to siblings and legacies.

Test. Kindergarten applicants must take the ERB.

Class size. There are eleven classes for the various age groups, including kindergarten. Each class has a head teacher and an assistant teacher. Often there is a third adult present. Threes classes have up to fifteen children, 4s have eighteen, and kindergartners have up to nineteen.

Staff. A psychology consultant is available to parents and teachers on a regular basis.

Facilities. The school is located in a completely renovated coach house between Park and Madison Avenues. Each group has a colorful, comfortable, and well-ordered classroom. Two rooftop playgrounds are equipped with a sandbox, large blocks, and climbing apparatus, and there is a large yard. Fours and 5s go to Central Park or to a neighborhood gym. A hot lunch is provided for full-day groups. The 5s take a school bus to Riverdale to use the gym facilities and become acquainted with the lower division.

Parent involvement. There is an active parent association. Conferences are scheduled twice yearly, and other conferences are encouraged as needed. Parent volunteers run the school library.

Separation. The teacher visits the child at home at the start of the school year, and each child is helped to make a comfortable transition from home to school.

Financial. A nonrefundable deposit of $3,000 is payable upon contract signing.

Financial aid is available. A form may be requested from the Nursery Division and filed with the admissions office of the Horace Mann School at 231 West 246th Street, Riverdale, NY 10471.

Transportation. Children from all parts of Manhattan attend. Private bus transportation can be arranged.

Member. ERB, ISAAGNY.

House of Little People

Ages: 6 mos–5 yrs

Nonsectarian

122 East 91st Street
Zip: 10128
Tel: 369-2740
Fax: 369-3298
E-Mail: hlp90@verizon.net
Website: the houseoflittlepeople.com

Established 1976
Barbara Robinson,
Founder, Executive Director
Enrollment: approximately 35

Second location:
House of Little People, Too
Ages: 3 mos–2.9 years
129 East 90th Street
Zip: 10128
Tel: 860-8118

Established: 1999
Debra Tuohy, M.S.Ed.,
Managing Director
Enrollment: 45

Third location:
Your Kids "R" Our Kids (see entry page 345)

Age	*Hours*	*Days*	*Tuition (monthly)*
All	7:30–6:00	5 days, M–F	$1,500

The school offers a year round program.

Program. The program is designed to provide a warm, nurturing and family-like atmosphere. The environment demonstrates sensitivity to the different needs of infant, toddler and preschool children, affording comprehensive learning experiences, socialization skills and growth enhancement. The comprehensive program is recognized by the New York City Department of Health as an innovator within the field of infant/toddler and preschool care.

Admission. Open enrollment: children are enrolled as space becomes available. Interested parents may call to arrange enrollment and/or tour. Tuition is payable monthly. There is no financial aid.

Class Size. Class size is age appropriate as indicated below:

Infants = 1 adult to 3 infants
Toddlers = 1 adult to 5 toddlers
Preschool, 4–5 years = 1 adult to 6 preschoolers

Facilities. The school is located in the first two floors of a brownstone with a garden play yard area. Two neighborhood parks are within safe walking distance offering substantial physical activity opportunities.

Parent Involvement. Parent meetings are held throughout the year. Children's progress conferences are conducted twice a year. Special issues and/or concerns are managed on a daily basis with parent input. Parents participate in all field trips and special in-house activities.

Graduates. House of Little People graduates have been accepted at many private schools including Chapin, Dalton, Nightingale-Bamford, St. Ignatius, Spence, PS 6, 87, 151, Hunter Elementary, and Gifted and Talented public school programs.

House of Little People, Too

Ages: 3 mos–2 yrs, 6 mos

Established 1999
Debra Tuohy, M.S.Ed,
Managing Director

Program. Infant Toddler Learning Program, specializing in quality care for very young children. The environment is nurturing and stimulating. Activities are sensory related, giving each child the opportunity to develop at his/her own pace.

Admission. Registration is open all year. It is recommended that parents apply as early as possible, as spaces fill up rapidly. Call to arrange an onsite tour. A one time registration fee and one month advance payment are required at the time of enrollment. Tuition is paid monthly.

Class Size. There are three age groups: infants, young toddlers and older toddlers, staffed at a ratio of 1 adult : 4 infants; 1 adult : 5 toddlers.

Staff. Staff members all have early childhood education backgrounds. The music teacher plans creative music and movement activities weekly. Directors hold masters degrees in education. The managing director has a masters degree in Infant/Toddler Development from Bank Street College.

Facilities. A safe, clean, cozy and stimulating environment on Manhattan's Eastside. Located on the ground floor of a brownstone, the center has central air-conditioning and heat. Children's bathrooms have age appropriate fixtures, which encourage toilet training. A private backyard contains climbing equipment designed for infants and toddlers. During the summer months, outdoor water play and sanitized creative sand related activities are available.

Parent Involvement. Parents may request individualized conferences regarding progress and development at any time. Parents are encouraged to participate in holiday celebrations and special occasions. New mothers are encouraged to breast-feed during the day.

Graduates. Have gone on to the sister school on East 91st Street which accepts children until they are 5 years old. Children have also gone on to attend some of Manhattan's most selective schools.

The International Preschools

Ages: 1.6 yrs–6 yrs

Nonsectarian

330 East 45th Street (between 1st and 2nd Avenues)
Zip: 10017
Tel: 371-8604
Web site: www.ipsnyc.org
E-Mail: 45street@ipsnyc.org
E-Mail for admissions: admissions@ipsnyc.org

Established 1963
Valerie Kennedy, Director
Kevin Abernathy, Admissions Director
Total enrollment approx. 600 (for all locations); 200 (for 300 East 45th Street)

1010 Park Avenue (between 84th and 85th Streets) — Enrollment: 55
28 East 35th Street (between Park and Madison Avenues) — Enrollment: 101
120 West 76th Street (between 1st and 2nd Avenues) — Enrollment: 55
57 West 75th Street (between Amsterdam and Columbus) — Enrollment: 175

School year. Mid-September through early June.

Age	*Hours*	*Days*	*Tuition*
1.6–2 years (Crêche program)	8:30–10:30 or 11:00–1:00	2 days	$4,800
2.4–3.3 (Toddler program)	9:00–11:30 or 1:15–3:45	2, 3 days	$5,800–$7,700
3s	9:00–12:00 or 1:00–4:00	3 days	$7,700
3s/4s	9:00–12:00 or 1:00–4:00	Mon–Fri	$10,800
4s/5s; Kindergarten	9:00–3:00	Mon–Fri	$12,000–$15,700

Different schedules are available at each location; the most common are listed above. A young toddler program, "The Crêche," for children under 2, is only available at the 45th Street location. There are additional charges of from $85 to $110 per year; $150 for Kindergarten, for books and computer fees.

Program. Developmental/Interactive. Valerie Kennedy, the school's director has been with IPS for about 30 years, first as a parent, later as a teacher, and has shaped the program. The teaching backgrounds and approaches of staff members are as varied as the backgrounds of the students, and they meet frequently to evaluate goals and develop curriculums. Children in the crêche and toddler groups are offered an age appropriate program that includes socialization skills, language development, social studies, reading, quantitative reasoning, creative expression, scientific exploration creative movement, and physical development, music, and library. All classrooms are divided into learning centers. Children select activities and materials in the early years; active exploration forms the core of the program.

The nursery and pre-kindergarten programs stress basic number concepts and reading readiness while the kindergarten children participate in a variety of structured learning tasks and group activities. Both nursery and kindergarten programs are developmentally appropriate but offer strong pre-academic preparation through a variety of structured activities.

The celebration of varied national customs, cultures, languages and cuisine, and dress are part of the curriculum, as well as stories, songs, and games from around the world.

Admissions. There is a $50 application fee. The school's admissions process begins the fall prior to the year in which the child will be enrolled. Applications are available either by phone, mail, or Internet. After a completed application is received, parents are invited to an admissions information meeting. An admissions representative will call parents to schedule a visit to the location of their choice with their child. Notifications are sent out by early March but IPS accepts applications from families being transferred to New York throughout the year.

Class size. Young toddlers (crêche and young 2s), are limited to ten children per group. Older twos and young 3s have ten to twelve children with three teachers. Older 3s have up to fifteen per class; 4s and 5s classes each have between fifteen and twenty children with two or three teachers.

Staff. One teacher in each class is "international." Each class has a licensed early childhood teacher and one or two qualified assistant teachers. There's a librarian, and there are specialists in science, music, and creative movement, and an education director who works closely with teachers for all children including those who have special needs.

Facilities. Parents have called the school warm and boisterous. Those with children in the most "international" of the preschools feel the varied cultural exposure is invaluable. In 1983 the school's major center moved to a building on East 45th Street with a modern preschool facility specially designed for it and erected with the help of the United Nations Development Corporation's Board of Directors.

Each location has its own character and personality. Outdoor and indoor active play areas provide plenty of space for exercise.

Summer program. There is a creative and recreational program from early June through the end of July. The program is open to children 2 to 5 years old. Preference is given to children currently enrolled.

Separation. Special care is taken with children of all ages, since many of them face major adjustments in coming to a new country. The crêche and toddler programs offer a gradual separation process that includes parents and caregivers who stay until the child is comfortable. According to the director, "We don't hurry parents out of the classroom."

Parent involvement. The Parents Association is active, it organizes social and fundraising events. Educational meetings are held on a variety of subjects and there are social activities and events. Parent/teacher conferences are held each semester. Parents join on field trips and classroom celebrations.

Financial. Tuition is due in two instalments each year, July 1st and November 1st. Financial aid is available, especially for families attached to the United Nations, embassies, consulates, etc.

Transportation. Parent or caregiver brings the child directly to the classroom.

Graduates. Have attended almost every private school in Manhattan including, Allen-Stevenson, Brearley, Buckley, Chapin, Collegiate, Convent of the Sacred Heart, Dalton, Ethical Culture, Friends Seminary, Grace Church, Hunter Elementary, Lycée Francais, Nightingale-Bamford, St. Bernard's, St. David's, Spence, Town, Trinity, UNIS, other independent schools, and various public and parochial schools.

Member. ERB, ISAAGNY, NAEYC, Parents League, chartered by the Board of Regents of the State University of New York.

The Stanley H. Kaplan Nursery School of Sutton Place Synagogue

Ages: 2–5 yrs

Jewish Nursery School

225 East 51st Street
(Between 2nd & 3rd Avenues)
Zip: 10022
Tel: 826-6204
Fax: 893-8116
E-Mail: akmorgano@aol.com

Established 2001
Amy K. Morgano,
Director

School year: Mid-September through early June.

Ages	*Hours*	*Days*	*Tuition*
2s*	9–11:30	Tues/Thurs or	$8,300
		Mon/Wed/Fri	$9,650
3s**	9–12	Mon-Fri	$12,800
	Extended day option (until 1:30)**	Tues/Thurs	$900
4s	9–1:30	Mon–Thurs	$15,950
5's	9:00–2:15	(Fri until 12)	

*Children entering the 2s class must be 2 by September 1st.
**Children entering the 3s class must be 3 by September 1st. Extended day option is available at an additional cost.

Program. Developmental. The Kaplan Nursery School just completed its sixth year of operation. Amy Morgano, the school's director, was a teacher at Christ Church Day School, and former director of Purple Circle. This preschool aims to "foster a deep sense of community, where a young child's social and emotional growth and intellectual development can flourish." The program offers both structured and open-ended play. Children are encouraged to ask questions and interact with a variety of stimulating materials. The Jewish holidays are integrated into the school's curriculum and on Fridays the children take part in a Shabbat snack.

Admissions. The application fee is $50. Inquiries are from September on. Preference is given to long-term synagogue members and siblings. Group tours are given. Families come for individual visits in December through February. Notifications are sent in early March. *

Class size. There are ten to twelve children in the 2s classes, eleven to fourteen children in each of the two 3s classes and, and ten to fifteen children in the 4s classes and ten to fifteen children in the 5s class.

Staff. The school provides each teacher with $1,200 towards tuition or workshops, such as the NAEYC conference. The development of staff is a primary focus, and the staff is supported by occupational therapy, speech, language and child psychology consultants.

Facilities. Classrooms are housed in the newly constructed Sachs Family Educational Center, a six-story building that includes a large outdoor play area and a children's garden.

Parent Involvement. Parents are welcomed in the classrooms to read books or cook. The Parents Association is an integral part of the school's community; parents can volunteer to work on a variety of fundraising and community building events.

Transportation. None

Graduates. Children from the first three graduating classes attend Brearley, Columbia Grammar, Chapin, Browning, Calhoun, Horace Mann, Nightingale-Bamford, Trevor Day, Lower Lab, Hunter and other private and public schools.

Affiliations. Sutton Place Synagogue.

Member. Application pending ISAAGNY; member of ERB.

*The school is in the process of joining ISAAGNY. In the meantime, it voluntarily adheres to ISAAGNY guidelines and admissions dates. The school offers on-site ERB testing.

La Scuola d'Italia "G. Marconi"

Ages: 3yrs–12th grade

Bilingual Italian Nursery and Comprehensive School

12 East 96th Street — Established 1977
Zip: 10128 — Pia Pedicini,
Tel: 369-3290 — Deputy Headmistress-
Fax: 369-1164 — Director of Admissions
Preschool and nursery enrollment: 32
Website: www.lascuoladitalia.org — Total enrollment 210
E-Mail: admin@lascuoladitalia.org

Ages	*Hours*	*Days*	*Tuition*
3–5*	8:30–2:50	Mon–Fri	$15,000–17,000 plus $1,100 in fees, (3s–12th grade).

*The birthday cut-off for kindergarten is 5 years of age by December 31st.

Program. The school was founded by the Italian Ministry of Foreign Affairs to meet the academic needs of Italians living in the New York City area. The curriculum seeks to foster self-esteem, trust, and autonomy by building physical and linguistic abilities and introducing children to the first elements of literacy. Preschoolers are introduced to Italian through a variety of activities in language, drama, art, music, science, and psychomotor projects. There is total immersion in foreign languages from preschool on, and an in-depth study and appreciation of American, European and Italian civilizations and cultures.

Admissions. The application fee is $100. There is no deadline for submitting applications but parents should be prepared to apply as early as September for the following school year. After the application is completed, the family is invited for an interview. The child stays in the classroom, where the head teacher evaluates social skills and capacity to relate to peers. Notifications are sent in accordance with ISAAGNY guidelines.

Class size. There are two preschool classes, one with nine children and one with fifteen children. There is also a kindergarten class of twenty.

Staff. Two head teachers, one who instructs in Italian, one in English, alternate during the school day. Larger classes have bilingual assistants who remain in class at all times.

Facilities. Entering the school's limestone, five-story mansion through a bright-red door, one crosses the hall and takes a central staircase down to the high-ceilinged rooms of the preschool area. The main room, walls hung with murals painted by the children, has two windows onto the yard. Another long, bright room with easels, kitchen facilities and long tables on which children were shaping playdough and painting, has windows and a door opening onto a ground-level wooden deck with riding toys, seesaws and a balance beam. A child-size bathroom adjoins.

Separation. For the first week, children attend a half class, on an abbreviated schedule, and parents stay as needed.

Parent involvement. A curriculum meeting opens the school year, and three parent/teacher conferences are held during the year. An annual open house offers prospective parents the opportunity to become acquainted with the bilingual curricula and educational activities. The Parents Association is very active in organizing annual fundraising events.

Financial. A $1,000 deposit is required upon acceptance. Tuition is paid in three installments. No financial aid is available at the preschool level.

Graduates. Most children stay on at La Scuola through 12th grade. At the end of their senior year, the students are required to take the Italian Ministry of Education State Exam, the *Maturita,* equivalent to the International Baccalaureate degree honored by all universities in Europe and the United States.

Affiliations. Chartered by the Board of Regents of the State University of New York and the Ministry of Education of Italy.

Imagine Early Learning Center at Mount Sinai Medical Center

Ages: 3 mos–5 yrs

60–62 E. 97th Street
Zip: 10029
Tel: 410-2077
Fax: 410-6992
E-Mail: maryann@imagineelc.com

Maryann Gaggi,
Director
Enrollment: 85

School year. Year round.

Ages	*Hours**	*Days*	*Tuition (monthly)*
3 mos–2 yrs	6:45–6:00	Mon–Fri	$1,350
3s–5s	6:45–6:00	Mon–Fri	$1,225

*Part-time hours and fees can be arranged.
**Fees are for hospital employees. Fees for community families are about 10 percent higher.

Program. Developmental/Progressive. Imagine Early Learning Center is a full-day, full-year early childhood program affiliated with Mount Sinai Medical Center. This multi-cultural program offers a hands-on child-centered curriculum and encourages learning through play. Since the Center is so close to Central Park, children enjoy outdoor experiences like garden walks, playing at different playgrounds, picnics in the meadows, and viewing the lake.

The school has a "Learning Healthy Early" program, encouraging healthy eating habits, and daily exercise and fitness. The program extends to the home and is encouraged throughout the day with the daily routines and snack options.

The Center has a special relationship with Mount Sinai which provides a volunteer and intern program, guest speakers and community service visits to the hospital.

In the full-year program children learn Spanish, sign language, movement and music. The summer program offers a more outdoor-based curriculum, a nature and animal program, swimming at the Y, a visiting musician and a soccer program.

Admissions Parents are required to tour the center. Admission is on a rolling basis depending on availability. If a place is not available, there is a waiting list.

Class size. There are three groups: fifteen infants in two classrooms with six teachers; thirty-seven toddlers in three classrooms with six teachers; and thirty-three preschoolers in two classes with five teachers.

Facilities. The school is housed in two stories of a brownstone on the Upper East Side. The Center has a backyard space and children play in Central Park.

Separation. A transition period is encouraged for new children. The school suggests that children and a parent visit the school before starting, and parents are welcomed to stay for the transition period and beyond. The process is welcoming and individualized for each family.

Parent involvement. The school seeks to promote a family atmosphere, with close home/school communication often on a daily basis. There is an open door policy. Parents may drop in at any time without an appointment. All parents have the directors' and teachers' home phone numbers. Teachers give a daily report to parents regarding their child's moods, toileting, favorite activities and who they play with. The Parent Advisory Board meets once a month. Parent workshops have included how to enhance creative arts with children.

Financial. Some children are funded through ACD. Because about 90 percent of parents work for Mount Sinai, children come from different cultures around the world. (Mount Sinai dependents have priority.) About 10 percent of children are not affiliated with Mount Sinai.

Chartered. By the Board of Regents of the State University of New York.

Member. Mt. Sinai Medical Center, Imagine Early Centers Inc., NAEYC.

A late addition is **Little Dreamers of NYC,** 336 East 53rd Street, New York, NY 10022, Tel: 486-0597; Fax: 917-591-4565, website: www.littledreamers of nyc.com, E-mail: info @littledreamersofnyc.com. Half and whole days for children two to five years of age.

Lycée Français de New York

Ages: 3–18 yrs

Bi-lingual French Nursery and Comprehensive School

505 East 75th Street (York Avenue)
Zip: 10021
Tel: 369-1400
Website: www.lfny.org
E-Mail: mail@lfny.org
Total enrollment: 1260

Mr. Yves Theze, Head
Joel Guignolet, Primary School Director
Ms. Martine LaLa-Katz, Director of Admissions
Nursery enrollment: 300

School year. Mid-September through mid-June. There is also a summer program, from mid-June to mid-July.

Ages	*Hours*	*Days*	*Tuition*
3s	8:30–11:30 or	Mon–Fri	$12,300
	12:30–3:30 or 8:30–2:45		$12,300
4s	8:45–2:45	Mon–Fri	$14,500
	Fri until 12:30		
5s	8:45–2:45	Mon–Fri	$14,500
	Fri until 12:15		

*Children must be toilet-trained upon entrance, but extra clothes are kept on hand in case of accidents.

Extended hours. There are two options: 2:45–3:45 p.m. or 2:45–4:45 p.m.

Program. Traditional. The early childhood program offers a complementary bilingual English and French educational curriculum for 3s, 4s, and 5s. Children starting kindergarten must be proficient in French. An American certified teacher and a French-educated and certified teacher share the classroom at all times, encouraging the students to develop their personality, talents, and skills while acquiring a new language. This is accomplished by means of interrelated individual and small-group activities planned by the coteachers around a class project, with common pedagogical objectives covering all facets of the curriculum, including art, music, and movement. There are clear academic expectations for each age. At the same time, a calm, nurturing, and accepting atmosphere prevails.

The children participate in a music and movement class, conducted in a newly built glass dome, two to three times a week. Gymnastics classes are held in the gym. Computer studies are introduced in kindergarten. As early as the 3s, children keep song and poetry books. The 4s and 5s are prepared for cursive writing. School trips are planned regularly and include an apple orchard, farm, zoo, nature center, museums, and other local attractions. The student body represents over 40 countries.

The Lycée confers a New York State high school diploma and prepares its students to pass the baccalaureate at the end of "Terminale." The dual French and English curriculum allows students to attend leading American as well as foreign colleges and universities. The Lycée is neither owned nor operated by the French government. It is accredited by the French Ministry of National Education and chartered by the Board of Regents of the State of New York.

Admissions. The application fee is $150. Inquiries are from mid-September on. Preschool applicants are given individual evaluations in a small-group setting conducted by a faculty member. A tour follows the evaluation. Admissions are rolling. Notifications are sent in February, and are ongoing for international transfers, depending on availability.

Class size. From 15 to 25. Each classroom is shared by two co-teachers.

Staff. All American teachers are certified by New York State and hold a masters degree. All native French teachers are certified by the French Ministry of Education.

Facilities. The new building is situated on 75th street at York Avenue, offers a spectacular space with large gymnasiums, gross motor climbing structures, a roof play area cushioned with a rubber surface for the youngest, computer and science labs, art and music studios and a spectacular 350-seat auditorium which opened in May 2005. With this opening, the Lycée has a cultural center which provides a unique venue in which students can express their artistic creativity or to listen to leading speakers addressing a variety of international topics.

Dress code. Beginning at age 3, boys wear a navy-blue blazer, classic-cut gray pants, a white shirt and tie, or a white turtleneck and blue pullover. Girls wear a navy-blue blazer; a gray skirt, jumper, or slacks; a white blouse or turtleneck and navy-blue cardigan. A chambray smock is worn over the "uniform."

Parent involvement. Parents are encouraged to participate in their child's education and in all major social, cultural, educational, and fundraising events. These activities include pedagogical meetings and conferences, regularly scheduled school trips, concerts, United Nations week, the spring fair, and other special projects. Progress reports are issued twice a year. Parent-teacher conferences are scheduled in the spring.

Financial. 27 percent of the student body receives some form of aid.

Transportation. Arrangements for private transportation are made by parents. Children 5 and older may use Department of Education buses.

Graduates. Most students continue at the Lycée through 12th grade.

Chartered. Chartered by the Board of Regents of the State University of New York and the French Ministry of Education.

Member. Association of French Schools in America, NYSAIS, Parents League.

Lyceum Kennedy French International School

Ages: 2.5–18 yrs

French Bilingual Nursery and Comprehensive School

225 East 43rd Street
Zip: 10017
Tel: 681-1877
Fax: 681-1922
Website: www.lyceumkennedy.org
E-Mail: info1@lyceumkennedy.org

Established 1964
Yves Rivaud, Head of School

Nursery and Kindergarten enrollment: 60
Total enrollment: approximately 190

School year. September through mid-June.

Ages	*Hours**	*Days*	*Tuition*
2.5/3s/4s	8:45–3:00	Mon–Fri	$15,550
5s	8:45–3:00	Mon–Fri	$15,550

*Extended hours of daycare as well as extracurricular activities, from 3:00 to 5:30, are available at a reasonable fee.

Program. The children are immersed in the French language beginning in the nursery year, and become comfortable with the language through songs, games, and creative play. Teaching is geared toward the psychological, emotional, and physical development of the individual. By pre K and kindergarten, language of instruction is 60% French and 40% English with a greater emphasis placed on reading readiness and the beginning of mathematical concepts. Art, creative movement, and music are integral to the program.

Admissions. The application fee is $200. The application form must include a copy of the child's birth certificate, two photographs of the applicant, and the child's most recent school report. An interview will be scheduled after the application has been completed. Children are invited to attend the preschool during two days, "Discovery Days," in February or March before they are admitted.

Class size. Ten to twenty children.

Financial. A deposit of $1,000 is required upon admission. Tuition is payable on August 1st and December 1st. Children of French citizens may receive a scholarship from the French government.

Transportation. Children receive free public bus or subway passes starting in first grade.

Affiliations. The school is managed by a French head of school and is accredited by the French Ministry of Education as well as by the Board of Regents of the State University of New York.

The Madison Avenue Presbyterian Day School

Ages: 2.9–5.11 yrs.

Nonsectarian Nursery School

921 Madison Avenue
(between 73rd and 74th Streets)
Zip: 10021
Tel: 288-9638
Fax: 717-4152
Website: www.mapc.com

Patricia Pell, Director
Michael Zimmerman, Admissions Coordinator
Enrollment: 90

School year. Mid-September through May. June program.

Ages	*Hours*	*Days*	*Tuition*
All*	8:30–12:45	Mon–Thurs (Fri until 12:00)	$14,000
	8:30–2:45**	Mon–Thurs	$4,400***

*Must be 3 by December 31.
**optional extended day.
***in addition to tuition listed above.

Program. Developmental-interactive. The school's goal is to provide, and encourage children to engage in, activities that will allow them to acquire skills, learn new concepts and discover by themselves the information that they need. Recognizing that play is the work of children, tactile materials such as sand, water, clay, paint, and blocks are emphasized. Explorations with pre-academic materials encourage children to think, plan, re-create, and thereby to make sense of the world. The programs are rich in language-usage experiences as well as reading and math readiness so as to encourage in each child a love of learning, curiosity, creativity, self-confidence, and independence.

Each class visits the school library weekly. Chapels and assemblies are held for Christmas, Hanukkah, Passover, and Easter as well as other significant cultural holidays celebrated by families in the school.

The school is an integral part of the church and serves not only the member families but also the community beyond.

Admissions. The application fee is $50. Inquiries begin in September, and parents may tour the school prior to applying for admission. Children are seen later in groups of six.

Church members and siblings may request an early decision on admissions.

Class size. There are six classrooms; group size depends on the ages of the children as well as the size of the classroom. There are twelve to fourteen 2s and 3s, fifteen to sixteen each of 3s and 4s, and eighteen to twenty-one 4s and 5s.

Staff. There is a head teacher and associate or assistant in each class. Specialists teach music, movement and art.

Facilities. The eighth and ninth floors of the church house contain the school's six classrooms with self-contained bathrooms, as well as staff offices, along a cubby-filled corridor. All of the rooms enjoy plenty of natural light. The two largest rooms overlook Madison Avenue and are windowed on three sides.

Classroom materials include a wide variety of manipulative items, including blocks, games, and puzzles. Children's artwork is displayed on classroom walls and the school hallways. Portable ovens and hot plates are available for cooking in the classrooms.

On the eighth floor there are two classrooms, a full kitchen used by all classes, a children's lending library, and a multipurpose room used for music and movement, as well as for assemblies. The eleventh floor play roof is extremely large, enclosed, and well equipped for play.

Parent involvement. The school's parent committee plans social and fund-raising events. There is a library committee and parent volunteers are responsible for the lending library and weekly story-time.

Financial. An initial payment of 25 percent of the annual tuition is due with the contract. Tuition aid is supported through fund-raising and an endowment fund.

Transportation. Most parents bring their children to school. Private bus service is not available.

Affiliations. The Madison Avenue Presbyterian Church.

Member. ERB, ISAAGNY, NAIS, NYSAIS, Early Steps, ACEI, ATIS.

Marymount School of New York

Ages: 3–18 yrs

Catholic Nursery and Comprehensive School for Girls 3–18
Nursery Program includes sibling and legacy Boys 3–4

1026 5th Avenue (between East 83rd and 84th Streets)
Zip: 10028
Tel: 744-4486
Fax: 744-0163
Website: www.marymount.k12.ny.us
Nursery enrollment: 16
Uniforms are required of all students.

Established 1926
Concepcion Alvar, Headmistress
Eleanore Bednarsh, Head of Lower School
Lillian Issa, Admissions Director

School year. First week in September through second week in June.

Ages	*Hours*	*Days*	*Tuition*
3s–4s	8:20–12:00 or	Mon–Fri	$17,040
5s	8:20–3:00	Mon–Thurs	$27,790
	8:20–1:45	Fri	

*The birthday cut-off is August 31st.

Program. Traditional. It is one of an international network of Marymount schools founded by the religious order of the Sacred Heart of Mary. Chapel services, lessons and carols, vespers, and other Catholic rituals, are part of the curriculum. Nursery children follow a balanced program of work, rest, and play, which prepares them for later learning. Nursery students are the youngest users of the lower school science lab. They are exposed to language arts, mathematics, science, social studies, and religion. Music, art, and physical education are also part of the curriculum.

Reading instruction for kindergartners is approached with structured phonics lessons, whole language and literature-based instruction. Mathematics instruction employs materials such as unifix cubes, cuisenaire rods, weights, and graphs. Language arts and math are taught in small groups of 3 to 5 children.

Admissions. The application fee is $60. Inquiries are accepted throughout the year. Sixty percent of the students are Catholic, but the school welcomes students of other faiths.

Parents should call in September for an admissions packet. After a completed application is received, parents are called to schedule a parent interview, a child interview and a tour. Notifications follow ISAAGNY guidelines.

Facilities. The school is housed in three adjoining landmark Beaux Arts mansions, constructed near the turn of the century—the Vanderbilt Burden Mansion, the Herbert Pratt, and the Dunlevy Milbank. These form part of the Metropolitan Museum historic district known as "Museum Mile." A new middle school building is located on East 82nd Street just off Fifth Avenue. The buildings contain classrooms, a chapel, an auditorium, a gymnasium, five science laboratories, three computer centers and a language lab, two library complexes, four art studios, a commons and a courtyard play area.

After-School Program. Starting in kindergarten, a variety of optional activities are available, Monday–Thursday until 6:00; Friday until 2:00.

Summer program. Three 5-week co-ed sessions; varied programs are open to children from ages 4 to 13. Cost: $2,900–3,150.

Financial. A nonrefundable deposit of $5,000 is required upon enrollment. It is credited toward the second term tuition. Two-thirds of the annual tuition is due by May 15th, and one-third by November 1st.

Graduates. Girls attending the nursery school usually continue at Marymount; boys attend a variety of independent schools including Allen-Stevenson, Browning, Buckley, Collegiate, Dalton, St. Bernard's, Saint David's, and Trinity.

Chartered. By the Board of Regents of the State University of New York and accredited by NYSAIS and the Middle States Association ges and Schools.

Member. ERB, Guild of Independent Schools, IES, ISAAGNY, NAIS, the National Catholic Educational Association, NCGS (National Coalition of Girls' Schools), RSHM Schools (Religious of the Sacred Heart of Mary).

Memorial Sloan-Kettering Cancer Center Children's Center

Ages: 6 wks–5 yrs

Nonsectarian

(Employer-sponsored and open to employees' children only.)

475 Main Street
Roosevelt Island, NY
Zip: 10044
Tel: 224-0129
Fax: 224-0136
Website: www.brighthorizons.com
E-Mail: mskccbrighthorizons.com

Established 2003
Jennifer Polatnick, Director
Cindy O'Neill, Regional Manager
Enrollment: 45

School year. Year round.

Ages	*Hours*	*Days*	*Tuition* (monthly)
6 wks–12 mos	7:00–6:00	Mon–Fri	$1400
13 mos–36 mos	7:00–6:00	Mon–Fri	$1400
3–5 yrs	7:00–6:00	Mon–Fri	$1300

*The birthday cut-off is August 31st.

The program is NAEYC accredited.

Merricat's Castle School

Ages: 2–5 yrs

Nonsectarian Nursery School

316 East 88th Street (between 1st and 2nd Avenues)
Zip: 10128
Tel: 534-3656
Fax: 534-4141
Enrollment: 110

Established 1974
Linda Wosczyk, Education Director
Gretchen Buchenholz, and Mimi Broner Co-Directors

Ages	*Hours*	*Days*	*Tuition*
2s/3s	9:10-11:40 or	Tues/Thurs	$4,300
	12:40-3:10	Mon/Wed/Fri	$6,400
		4 days	$8,500
		Mon-Fri	$11,000
3s/4s*	9:15-11:45 or	Tues/Thurs	$4,000
	12:45-3:15	Mon/Wed/Fri	$6,000
		4 days	$8,000
		Mon-Fri	$10,000
4s/5s*	9:05-3:05	Mon/Wed/Fri	$12,000
		4 days	$16,000
		Mon-Fri	$19,000

*Combined full and half day weeks available, tuition is adjusted to reflect the program selected.

Program. Developmental. Merricat's Castle offers a preschool program where children both with and without special needs come together in a supportive and nurturing environment. Children are encouraged to participate in both structured pre-academic work and open-ended activity such as dramatic play, cooking, music, reading, arts and crafts, social studies, science, blockbuilding, physical activities, and outdoor play. The school serves as a model for preschool integration, having a richly diverse group of children from many New York City neighborhoods. The directors see Merricat's as a family that other families join.

Admissions. The application fee is $35. Applications are available after Labor Day. There are about forty openings per year. After receiving the application, the school will call to schedule a tour for parents without the child. The child will be invited at a later date to participate in a short play group.

Class size. The school accommodates fifty-five children at a time, in three groups with four staff members each plus volunteers. There are twelve 2/3s, seventeen 3/4s, and twenty-two 4/5s.

Staff. In addition to the full-time teaching staff, teaching interns from Hunter, BMCC, CUNY, La Guardia, Bank Street, Marymount, NYU, and Columbia Teachers College are present in the classrooms.

Facilities. On the second floor of St. Christopher's House, a four-story building constructed in 1887 and part of the complex belonging to the Church of the Holy Trinity (inspired by England's Litchfield Cathedral). The school has three large classrooms, divided into activity centers. In addition, there is an office, kitchen, conference room, and parents' lounge. There are two outdoor play areas with climbing structures.

Separation. Parents are asked to remain nearby during the first two weeks of school. Coffee and treats are served in the parents' lounge, where new parents have the opportunity to meet each other and returning parents.

Parent involvement. The active parents' association comprises a number of committees, with opportunities for involvement for all parents. Parent-teacher conferences are scheduled annually at mid-year and as needed.

Financial. A 20 percent deposit is required upon signing of contract. A monthly payment plan is available for families upon request. The school, committed to racial and economic diversity, makes every effort to provide financial assistance.

Graduates. Have gone on to Allen-Stevenson, Birth Wathen-Lenox, Brearley, Browning, Cathedral, Caedmon, Chapin, Collegiate, Columbia Grammar, Convent of the Sacred Heart, Dalton, Ethical Culture, Manhattan Country, Marymount, Riverdale Country, St. Bernard's, St. David's, St. Ignatius, Spence, Town, Trevor Day, and many other private schools as well as Hunter Elementary and a variety of public school programs.

Member. ERB, ISAAGNY.

Special programs. Merricat's is one of the programs of the Association to Benefit Children, a service-based advocacy organization with headquarters at Cassidy's Place on East 86th Street. ABC serves hundreds of children each year from families struggling with poverty, homelessness, serious illness and disability, through programs at several sites on Manhattan's East Side.

The Montessori School of New York International

Ages 2–14 yrs

Nonsectarian Montessori Nursery and Elementary School

347 East 55th Street (between 1st and and 2nd Avenues)*	Established 1969
Zip: 10022	Anil K. Sinha, Executive Director
Tel: 223-4630 or 718-857-3341	Lina Lee, Educational Director
Fax: 644-7057	Hannah Sinha, Coordinating Director
Website: www.montessorischoolny.com	
Total Enrollment: 150	Nursery Enrollment: 50

*Other locations include: 105 Eighth Avenue (Park Slope), Brooklyn 11215, 55 Junction Boulevard, (Elmhurst), Queens 11373

School year. September through June. A summer camp program is available.

Age	*Hours*	*Days*	*Tuition*
2–6	9:00–11:30	Mon–Fri	$8025
2–6	12:30–3:00	Mon–Fri	$7800
2–14	9:00–3:00	Mon–Fri	$7500
2–14	8:15–5:45	Mon–Fri	$10,000

Twos must be toilet trained before enrollment.

Program. Montessori. The school's early childhood curriculum includes classes in practical life, language and speech, writing, reading, phonics, grammar, math, French, music and movement, science, art, social studies, and free play. Children choose activities in which they are interested and for which they are ready. Older children use workbooks. Conversational French and Spanish are begun in the early years.

Admissions. The application fee is $25. The admissions deadline is March 1st, though it may be earlier if applications are numerous. Admission is based on group orientations followed by an interview with the child, at which time parents may observe a class. If they wish, parents may visit the school first, without their children, after they have applied.

Class size. The primary class contains children age 2 to 5 years. The children meet together in one large room with four teachers. The room is divided into two areas, one for older and one for younger children, with mixed age groups.

Staff. Staff have postgraduate Montessori diplomas from the Association Montessori Internationale.

Facilities. The school occupies a specially designed townhouse. The school has branches in Brooklyn and Queens.

Separation. Children are phased in during the first two weeks of school according to their comfort and ability to separate.

Financial. A nonrefundable deposit of $2,000 is required on acceptance. Approximately half the tuition is due August 1st, another third on October 1st, and the remainder in December and January.

Transportation. Private bus service can be arranged.

Chartered. By the Board of Regents of the State University of New York.

Member. Staff members belong to a variety of educational societies including AMI and AMS.

92nd Street YM-YWHA Nursery School

Ages: 2.6–5 yrs

Jewish Nursery School

1395 Lexington Avenue
(at 92nd Street)
Zip: 10128

Tel: 415-5532
Web site: www.92y.org

Established 1938
Mrs. Nancy Schulman, Director
Mrs. Ellen Birnbaum, Associate Director
Ms. Marcia Thaler, Director of Admissions
Mrs. Gail Raybin, Administrator
Enrollment: 175

School year. Third week in September through the first week of June.

Age	*Hours*	*Days*	*Tuition*
2.6–2.8	9:00–11:30	Tues Thurs.	$9,500
2.8–2.10	9:00–11:45	Mon Wed Fri	$11,000
3s	9:00–12:00	Mon–Fri	$15,400
4/5s	9:00–2:00 (Fri until 1:00)*	Mon–Fri*	$18,900

Extended hours. Parents may drop children off early (at 8:30).

Program. Developmental/Traditional. The 'Y' was founded in 1938 with three classes and has grown to ten classes. Since 1990, Nancy Schulman, a former teacher and director of admissions at Horace Mann School, has been the school's director. The school's warm, creative atmosphere seeks to preserve and foster young children's imagination, curiosity, and intellect. The children's social, emotional, physical, and intellectual growth is facilitated through a curriculum attuned to the individual child's unique pattern of development. The school feels children learn best in a clearly structured program which emphasizes creative expression through hands-on experiences, provides opportunities for play, and encourages respect for others. Favorite projects include an archeology "dig" and a sculpture unit and gallery opening. Tzedakah (community service) is performed through Passover Food Drives for the elderly and toy collections for needy children. The school's goal is to help children establish a secure sense of self-esteem in order to fulfill their potential. Shabbat and the Jewish holidays are celebrated. "I have the best job in New York City," says Ms. Schulman. "Every day is different, challenging, and fun."

Admissions. The application fee is $50. Inquiries are from the day after Labor Day. Most children enter as 2s or 3s but the school accepts older children as well. Application forms are not mailed. Call early to arrange a parents-only visit between mid-October and the end of November. Children are observed in playgroups of six to eight, with one parent present, for thirty minutes.

The school welcomes children of all faiths.

Class size. The 2s classes have about ten children, with three teachers. The older classes have fifteen to twenty-one children, with three teachers each.

Staff. There are specialists for movement, science, music, gym, dance, speech and language, and a psychologist visits once a week. The director meets with all members of the staff once a week. There is a teacher enrichment fund of $1.5 million that is used for enhancing teacher salaries, funding teacher education and for special projects.

Facilities. Parents enter the large marble lobby of the Y's "old building" and take the elevator to the sixth floor. There are extremely large, inviting, and well-furnished classrooms, offices, a music/assembly room with a skylight, a quiet-time room (where ERBs are given), and three rooftop play areas (one with a retractable roof), with innovative climbing structures that run nearly the full length of the building. Children use the Y's large library, which they visit once a week, and the kitchen. Children who enroll in the Y's enrichment programs use these also.

Summer programs. Summer day camp is housed in the nursery school.

Separation. Teachers visit their new students before school starts. Twos begin with brief, small-group classes; the full session begins after about six weeks. A parent or caregiver needs to be available during phase-in. The schedule is staggered for the beginning weeks of school.

Parent involvement. The parents association takes an active role in fund-raising. The Nursery School Benefit usually held in March is legendary; about 400 people attend including the entire parent body and over $100,000 is raised. Parents participate in classes frequently. Conferences are arranged twice yearly. About half the mothers work.

Financial. Approximately 5 percent of children receive financial aid.

Graduates. Graduates attend approximately 25 different private and public schools including Allen-Stevenson, Brearley, Chapin, Collegiate, Columbia Grammar, Dalton, Ethical Culture, Heschel, Horace Mann, Nightingale-Bamford, Riverdale, Spence, Town, Trinity, PS 6 and PS 290.

Affiliations. YMHA, UJA/Federation.

Member. ATIS, ERB, ISAAGNY, NAEYC, BJE.

Park Avenue Christian Church Day School

Ages: 2.7–5 yrs

Nonsectarian

1010 Park Avenue (between 84th and 85th Streets)
Zip: 10028
Tel: 288-3246, ext. 2
Enrollment: 180

Established 1963
Betsy Newell, Director

School year. September through May.

Age	*Hours*	*Days*	*Tuition**
2s	9:15–11:30	2 or 3	$7,100–$8,500
3s	9:00–11:45	Mon–Fri	$11,750
4/K	9:00–12:00	Mon–Fri	$12,100
4s	plus three afternoons until 2:30		$3,200
5s	plus four afternoons until 2:30		$15,600

Program. Developmental. Emphasizes blocks, dramatic play, learning from hands-on experience rather than traditional academic skills. Children's social skills and interaction are of the foremost importance. There are no worksheets. In art, teachers do not show a model for replication. Representational drawing and abstract work are equally valued. While some of the children's paintings are quite representational, they vary in subject and style.

Threes study the family, talk about themselves as babies and make family books to take home. Walls display each child's artwork. Fours begin to explore the neighborhood with trips, e.g., to the shoe store. There is no formal math for 4s, but measurement is introduced. 5s use a modified version of the Writing Process. 5s also have scheduled work time for math, writing (inventive spelling is used), and reading, but reading is not expected of the children.

Children in all groups were observed to listen attentively while teachers read aloud, and readily joined in discussion. Teachers take dictation of the children's own stories.

ERBS are given on the premises and directors from ongoing schools visit the classrooms.

Admissions. The application fee is $50. Inquiries begin after Labor Day. The school accepts twenty toddlers and forty 3s. A few places are open for older children. It is best to call on the day after Labor Day for an application. When parents have submitted an application, they will be contacted by the school to schedule a parent tour and a child interview. Small group visits begin in October and continue through January. Children visit with the director for half-an-hour in groups of four. One parent per child stays through the interview.

Applicants for the 4s and K are seen beginning in November and visit one at a time in a classroom setting. Applicants for 3s are seen mainly in November and December. Toddler interviews are January through February. The school follows ISAAGNY notification dates.

Admissions priority is given to siblings of current and past students and to children of church members.

Class size. The toddler classes have ten children each. The five 3s classes have ten or fifteen children. The three 4s classes have twenty. The 5s class has up to 20 children.

Each class has a head teacher with a masters degree and an

assistant teacher. In addition there is a music teacher and four roving assistants.

Facilities. Children and mothers climb a short flight of stairs once they enter the building. Children escorted by a parent use the elevator to reach the four floors of spacious, bright classrooms with white brick walls and large windows. There is a separate kitchen on each floor. Each class spends 30 minutes daily in free play in the big cheerful rooftop playground with extensive equipment, and an equally large basement used for cold or rainy-weather play. The International Preschool uses the three fifth-floor classrooms when the school is not in session. During the mornings that the Park Avenue school occupies these rooms, the International Preschool's wall displays are covered with drapes.

Separation. Varies with the child's age. Teachers make home visits to all toddlers and 3s before school begins in September. The school requires parents to stay in the room for six days with toddlers; three days in the room with 3s and on site for the fourth day; on site for one day with the 4s.

Parent involvement. The home-school connection is highly valued and nurtured. An active parents' association organizes the fund raising for scholarship, teacher tuition reimbursement and other program enrichments around the building. Scheduled parent visits—to share a special skill, introduce a new baby or tell a story—form a crucial part of the curriculum in the 3s and 4s. Parents may also visit to observe by appointment. Conferences are held twice a year.

Financial. A deposit is due with the signed contract. Diversity in racial and economic backgrounds is encouraged. A generous scholarship program exists, ranging from almost full scholarships to 50 percent aid.

Transportation. Bus transportation cannot be arranged.

Graduates. Go to the full range of ongoing independent schools, including Allen-Stevenson, Brearley, Buckley, Chapin, Collegiate, Dalton, Hewitt, Nightingale, Sacred Heart, Spence, St. David's, Town and Trinity. Some parents choose parochial or public schools, including PS 6, 158, 290, and Hunter.

Affiliations. The church founded the school in 1963. Nonsectarian. Children do not attend chapel.

Member. ERB, ISAAGNY.

Park Avenue Methodist Church Day School

Ages: 3–6 yrs

Nonsectarian

106 East 86th Street
(between Park and
Lexington Avenues)
Zip: 10028
Tel: 289-6997
Fax: 534-0410

Established 1953
Ms. Judith Keisman,
Director

Enrollment: 74

School year. Mid-September through May.

Age	*Hours*	*Days*	*Tuition*
3–6	9:00–12:00 or 1:00–4:00	Mon–Fri	$13,200

Program. The school eschews an identification as "eclectic." However, according to the director, "We value the children as they are, not for what we will make them. We want to provide them with a good experience appropriate for their age. We emphasize play. There are no workbooks. We talk a lot with the children and encourage them to talk to one another. They do see words, letters, and numbers. They come to school to socialize and have a good time. We provide them with a well-thought-out program." Limits are clear; the goal is to help children become happy integral members of the community.

Activities include sand, and water play, housekeeping, dress up, play-dough, painting and other art materials, blockbuilding, play with small objects, musical instruments, toys, and books. Group activities include music and storytime.

Admissions. The application fee is $75.

Inquiries are from Labor Day on. Parents are encouraged to apply after touring the school. After filing an application, parents make an appointment to come in with their child for a visit in a play group setting with four to five other families. Notifications are sent in March.

Class size. There are two groups of younger children, one in the morning and one in the afternoon, each with sixteen children and three teachers. There are two groups of older children, one in the morning and one in the afternoon, each with twenty-one children and three teachers.

Facilities. The school uses the fourth floor of Park Avenue Methodist Church. Parents or caregivers bring the children up in the elevator. Everything is well maintained. The school is an extremely large room divided in half by shelves (on one side) and cubbies (on the other). One side accommodates the younger children, the other, slightly larger area is occupied by the older ones. There is plenty of room for both, but they are not in the room at the same time. At the far end is a large alcove—almost another room—which houses the blocks, musical instruments, records, and a sand table. Shelves and cupboards line the walls, and there are lots of small tables and chairs. There are also housekeeping areas, a science area and art materials, small play objects, puzzles, games, and toys. There are large windows all around. The room is organized, yet messy, and the children's art and projects are everywhere. Down the corridor are staff offices, a small kitchen, and a small, pleasant room used as the library. Up two short flights of stairs is the rooftop playground, quite large, with lots of climbing equipment, two slides, wagons, blocks, crates, and chairs. For rainy-day play, the children use the basement play area.

Summer program. The eight-week summer program, June through July, is open to children currently enrolled in the school.

Separation. According to the director, "We find most children are ready to say good-bye in a week. School begins with small groups coming for short sessions. It takes one to three weeks to get the whole group together for the whole session."

Parent involvement. There is no formal parents association, though parents do involve themselves in various school activities including administration of the school library. They host the holiday party, and have access to administration and teachers. Parents also participate by cooking and offering music and language instruction among other activities.

Graduates. Go to the full range of public and private schools. ERBs are given on the premises.

Member. ERB, ISAAGNY.

Park Avenue Synagogue Early Childhood Center

Ages: 2.6–5 yrs

Jewish Nursery School

50 East 87th Street (corner Madison Avenue and 87th Street)
Zip: 10128
Tel: 369-2600
Fax: 410-7879
Website: www.pasyn.org;
E-Mail: mmorse@pasyn.org

Established 1965
Carol Hendin, Director

Enrollment: 125

School year. Late September through first week in June.

Ages	*Hours*	*Days*	*Tuition*
2.6	9:00–11:30	Tues Thurs	$9,125
2.8	9:00–11:30	Mon Wed Fri	$10,600
3s	9:00-12:00	Mon-Fri	$14,850
	1:00-3:30	Mon-Thur (Fri till 12:00)	$11,450
	9:00-1:00	Mon-Thur (Fri till 12:00)	$16,450
4s/5s	9:00-2:00	Mon-Thur (Fri till 12:00)	18,025

Children should be toilet-trained for the 3s program.

Program. Developmental. The school strives for a balance between flexibility and structure and between self-initiated and guided work and play. There is blockbuilding, dramatic play, music, art, language arts, math, science, and trips. There is no specific reading program, but teachers respond to their children's readiness in an individual way.

The children celebrate major Jewish holidays and close each week with a Shabbat celebration. Blessings are said in Hebrew and English.

ERB testing is done on the premises. The director sees each parent individually to talk about which ongoing school options. An early Fall meeting is held to discuss the admissions process.

Admissions. The application fee is $40. Inquiries begin in early September. Most children enter as 2s or 3s. Once an application has been submitted, parents call to schedule a date for a group tour. Children are seen in groups of about seven beginning in December. There is no separate interview for parents. Special consideration is given to siblings and long-term synagogue members. Notifications are sent in March.

Class size. There are two 2s classes of eleven to thirteen children each, three 3s classes, and three 4s classes of sixteen to eighteen children each.

Staff. Three staff members for each class. There is also a part-time music and movement teacher and several consultants available one day a week.

Facilities. On the fifth and sixth floors, there is a small, cheerful lobby surrounded by benches. Hallways on either side lead to the classrooms and an interior space used for indoor play on rainy days. The classrooms are large and beautifully equipped. A full kitchen opens off the interior playroom and is used for cooking by all but the toddlers. There is also a large rooftop play space.

Children bring their own dairy or vegetarian lunches.

Separation. All children who are new to the school are visited at home before school begins. Returning students make classroom visits prior to the beginning of school. Parents and caregivers are encouraged to be available for the first two weeks of school, sometimes longer. Parents will spend some time in the classroom. The children begin classes in small groups for gradually increasing hours. The whole process takes less than a month. An effort is made to allow the children to come to trust the adults involved.

Parent involvement. Family orientation meetings are held in the fall and spring. There is an active Parents Association and parents are closely involved through holiday celebrations. Parent-Teacher conferences are held twice yearly. Additional conferences may be requested.

Financial. Once children are enrolled in the school, families are required to become members of the synagogue. Financial aid is available.

Graduates. Go on to public and private schools.

Affiliations. Park Avenue Synagogue, a Conservative congregation.

Member. ERB, ISAAGNY.

Philosophy Day School

Ages: 2.11–9

12 East 79th Street (between Madison and 5th Avenue)
Zip: 10021

Tel: 744-7300
Fax: 744-5876
Web site: www.philosophyday.org
E-Mail: secretary@philosophyday.org

Nursery program (Formerly The Ark Nursery School) Established 1975, the Day School (formerly Abraham Lincoln School) Established 1994

William Fox, Headmaster
Kathy Kigel, Director Preschool Program
Enrollment: 86

School year. Early September—early June.

Ages	*Hours*	*Days*	*Tuition*
2.11–4.11	8:30–12:45	Mon–Fri	$12,550
5–9	8:10–3:20	Mon–Fri	$14,860 +$1,000 fees

Program. The mission of the Philosophy Day School is to provide a rigorous classical education incorporating knowledge and approaches to life from Eastern and Western civilizations.

The school's focus is on educating the "whole child": intellect, body and spirit. The school values academics, arts and athletics and is integrated with teachers who encourage students to make connections not only between subject areas but also between subjects and themselves and their fellow students.

In a structured, unpressured environment, the physical surroundings are intended to enhance the sense of intimacy, beauty and light. There is a dress code, and a formal system of address between students and teachers.

Teachers model personal values, good manners and social skills to develop a sense of self, a respect for others, a commitment to community and a belief in a Divine Spirit. Students take responsbility for areas of the classroom and parts of the daily schedule in an atmosphere that values each individual's thinking and efforts so that students do not shy away from taking risks or doing their best.

Admissions. The application fee is $50. Parents should call or e-mail inquiries on or after Labor Day. Parents are encouraged to attend an open house (held every Wednesday, September through December) before applying. After applying, parents are given a 45-minute personal tour with the preschool director, or with the headmaster if applying for K–4th grade. Playgroups of one hour with 3–4 children are held during the winter. Parents or babysitters stay in the room.

Class size. There are 15 3s and 18 4s.

Staff. Head teachers have their masters and certification, or are in graduate school. Assistant teachers have BA degrees, or are in college presently.

Facilities. The school is located in a beautiful townhouse with large rooms near both Central Park and the Metropolitan Museum of Art.

After School Program. Pre-K (4-year-olds) 12:45–1:30, 4 days a week optional, $30 per class; K-4th 3:30–4:30, 4 days a week optional, $30 per class

Separation. Gradual separation for 3 year olds: At first they stay for 1½ hours for two days, parents welcome to remain; 2 hours for the next week; 3 hours for the third week; and have a full program by the 4th week. Parents can remain as long as necessary.

Parent involvement. The school has an active Parents Association. Parents help in the classrooms, escort the 3s and 4s to the park, and help serve lunch.

Financial. Tuition assistance is available from K–4th grade.

Member. NAIS, NYSAIS, ISAAGNY.

Rabbi Arthur Schneier Park East Day School

Ages: 2–13 yrs

Jewish Nursery and Elementary School

164 East 68th Street
(between Lexington and
Third Avenues)
Zip: 10021
Tel: 737-6900
Fax: 570-6348
Website: www.rasped.org
E-Mail: harriet@parkeastdayschool.org

Established 1976
Mrs. Barbara T. Etra,
Principal
Mrs. Harriet Ingber,
Director of Early Childhood
Mrs. Debbie Rochlin
Director of Admissions
Total Enrollment: 350
Nursery/K Enrollment: 185

School year. Early September through mid-June. Summer program available for registered students only.

Ages	*Hours*	*Days*	*Tuition*
2s	9:00–12:00	2, 3 days	$8,450, 9,700
3s	9:00–12:00	5 days	$12,475
3s	9:00–2:00	Mon–Fri	$15,150
4s	9:00–2:00	Mon–Fri	$15,150
4s	9:00–3:30	Mon–Fri	$17,500

Extended hours are available for 4s and 5s, for an additional fee. A tuition reduction is available for families with more than one child enrolled. Members of Park East Synagogue receive a tuition reduction of $500 for one child.

Program. Developmental. The Park East Day School was founded by Rabbi Arthur Schneier as a nursery school and merged with East Side Hebrew Institute in 1979, when an elementary division was added. The school is sponsored by a traditional orthodox Jewish synagogue; all the Jewish holidays and Shabbat are observed. Classes for children in the toddler and nursery programs are experiential, they learn through play and hands-on activities. Formal reading instruction begins in the 4s class, computers are used beginning with the 4s and 5-year-olds have chess instruction. In kindergarten, children also begin to learn about The Writing Process.* For those who choose to continue at Park East, the elementary school offers an award-winning program in math, and also has strong programs in science, art and computers.

Admissions. The application fee is $50. Inquiries are from mid-September on. The school has a three-to-one applications to acceptances ratio. Call no earlier than mid-September. After an application form has been submitted, the school will arrange a conference with the parents. A play session will be arranged for the child in late January or the beginning of February. Notifications are sent in March.

Class size. "A Taste of School" for sixteen-month to twenty-four month-olds meets twice each week in two groups for ninety minutes, with a parent or caregiver. For 2s there are two classes, there are three classes of 3s, three classes for 4s and two classes for 5s.

Staff. Each class has two staff members. There are specialists for music and movement, computers and other activities.

Facilities. The school is located in ten large, modern classrooms on the third, fourth, and fifth floors of the Minskoff Cultural Center. There is a large outdoor play terrace and a large gym, as well as other facilities of the on-going school. A Kosher lunch is served.

Separation. The children are introduced with short schedules and in small groups over two weeks. Parents usually stay in the hall.

*Sometimes called Writers' Workshop, this is a four-step program in which students learn to clarify their thoughts by drafting ("brain drain"), revising ("sloppy copy"), editing ("neat sheet") and, finally, publishing ("final fame"). Formal grammar and spelling are taught in this context.

Parent involvement. The parents council is extremely active and arranges many programs for parents and children. The school psychologist is available for consultations. A social worker is also available and holds parent workshops.

Financial. A deposit of $1000 is required on signing the contract. Parents must pay by four quarterly checks postdated June 30 to March 30 enclosed with the contract. There is additional $300/$400 registration and materials fee.

Transportation. Private bus service can be arranged.

Graduates. Many continue on to the upper school.

Affiliations. Park East Synagogue. Chartered by the Board of Regents of the State University of New York; BJE.

Member. ERB, ISAAGNY.

Ramaz School

Ages: 3–18 yrs

Orthodox Yeshiva (bilingual Hebrew School)

Early Childhood and Lower school:
125 East 85th Street

Established 1937
Rabbi Haskel Lookstein, Principal
Rabbi Alan Berkowitz, Headmaster, Lower school
Ms. Judith Fagin, Dean, Ramaz School
Ms. Deena Bloom, Director, Early Childhood Center
Ms. Shira Baruch and Ms. Kim Ganz Wexler Early Childhood Center Coordinators
Mrs. Daniele Gorlin Lassner, Dean of Admissions

Zip: 10028
Tel: 774-5610
Fax: 774-8039
Website: www.ramaz.org
E-Mail: earlychildhoodadmissions@ramaz.org

Total enrollment: 1078
Early Childhood Center: 135

Ages	*Hours*	*Days*	*Tuition*
3s	9:00–2:00	Mon–Fri	$13,950
4s	9:00–3:00	Mon–Fri	$14,250
5s	8:20–3:15	Mon–Fri	$14,550

Program. Academic. Ramaz offers a rigorous curriculum of general and Judaic studies as well as a program in the Torah and mitzvot, Zionism, the State of Israel, and the religious and cultural traditions of Judaism. It gives equal emphasis to American democracy and Western culture.

The Early Childhood Center's curriculum includes cooking, math, verbal and social skills, science, music, art, dance, social studies, field trips, and physical activity. Jewish and national holidays are celebrated and Jewish history, laws, customs, prayers, and blessings are explored. The program also stresses social and emotional growth.

Children who may require extra support in developing readiness skills may participate in the school's Early Intervention program.

Admissions. The application and testing fee is $150. Parents should call early for an appointment with Mrs. Lassner; September 1 may be too late.

Class size. There are two classes of eighteen 3 year-olds, two classes of eighteen 4s, and three kindergarten or 5s classes of 22 children each.

Facilities The Early Childhood Center is located in the lower school, and has two outdoor play areas, one with a custom-designed play sculpture the other with a full-sized playground. There is also access to a fully equipped gym, library, a media center, science lab, and music and art centers.

Financial. A variety of additional fees for 3s through 5s ranges between $5,000 to $7,500 and includes registration, parents council, activities, lunches, security, educational materials and a mandatory foundation pledge.

Transportation. Private bus service can be arranged.

Affiliations. Congregation Kehilath Jeshurun.

Member. NYSAIS, Middle States Accredited.

Renanim Preschool and Nursery

18 mos–5 yrs

Jewish

336 East 61st Street (between First and Second Avenues)
Zip: 10021
Tel: 750-2266

Established: 1977
Rachel Goren, Director

School year. September through June, plus summer camp.

Ages	*Hours*	*Days*	*Tuition*
All	8:30–12:00	Mon–Fri	$9,900
	8:30–3:30	Mon–Fri	$14,500
	8:30–6:00	Mon–Fri	$15,000

Flexible schedules are available and tuition is prorated.

Extended stay. $10.00 per hour, by prior arrangement.

Program. Developmental. "Renanim" means happiness in Hebrew. The school, founded in Israel, offers an English-Hebrew education, although no prior knowledge of Hebrew is required or necessary. The program seeks to develop the whole child—i.e., the social, emotional, physical, and cognitive aspects—through meaningful, concrete experiences. There is a strong focus on the arts, including drama, arts and crafts, music and dance. In addition, the school offers an emergent literacy curriculum, computer, math and science, cooking, and fun-filled educational trips. The goals are to build self-esteem, to develop a positive attitude toward school, to learn respect for oneself and others, to develop math and reading readiness skills among the older children, and to encourage curiosity and foster independence.

Admissions. The application fee is $85. Inquiries are welcomed from Labor Day on. The school offers two open houses, one in November, one in December. Parents are encouraged to call to schedule a tour with their child throughout the year.

Class Size. All classes have two head teachers, one who speaks Hebrew, one who speaks English, as well as an assistant teacher or aide. There are twelve children in the 20 mos–2.6 yrs group, fourteen in the 2.6–3.6 group, and sixteen in the 3.6–5 group.

Staff. All head teachers have a masters degree in early childhood education. A music, a yoga, and a ballet teacher work with the children on a weekly basis.

Facilities. Open, spacious classrooms with custom-made and brightly painted furniture provide a unique and cheerful environment for indoor play and learning. Every classroom has its own bathroom, which allows the teacher to help children become successfully toilet-trained. A special diaper-changing area is also available. A large, safe outdoor playground is connected to the school and is used exclusively by Renanim children. In addition to balls, hoops, and sand play, it is fully equipped with a carousel, climbing apparatus, two slides and bicycles.

Separation. For the first week, the parent is asked to be available, either in the classroom or outside in the lounge, as needed. The school wants both the parent and the child to be comfortable.

Parent involvement. Parents are encouraged to visit the classroom. There are three parent-teacher conferences each year and two Sunday afternoon arts-and-crafts workshops for parents and children. Parents are invited to accompany the class on field trips and also to celebrate holidays and their children's birthdays with special programs. A monthly calendar and weekly letters inform parents of activities the children will be involved in during the coming week.

Summer program. A separate summer program is available during July and August. The children play outdoors, garden, swim, and exercise; indoor activities include cooking, arts and crafts, music, musical instruments, movement and dance, movies, and visits to museums.

Financial. A non-refundable registration fee of $85 and a non-refundable deposit (applied toward tuition) of $500 is due upon registration. The remainder of tuition is due in equal installments upon arrangement with the school administration.

Graduates. Have gone on to private schools such as Abraham Joseph Heschel, Rabbi Arthur Schneier Park East Day School, and Solomon Schecter, as well as a variety of public schools, including Hunter.

Affiliations. BJE.

Member. ERB.

Resurrection Episcopal Day School (REDS)

Ages: 2.9–5 yrs

Episcopal Nursery School

119 East 74th Street
(between Park and
Lexington Avenues)
Zip: 10021
Tel: 535-9666, Admissions, ext 11
Fax: 535-3191
Website: www.redsny.org
E-Mail: info@redsny.org

Established 1990
Laurie Boone Hogan,
Director
Rhea Shome,
Assistant to Director and
Director of Admissions
Enrollment: 80

School year: Second week in September until early June. Two week summer program.

Ages	*Hours*	*Days*	*Tuition*
2.9–6	8:45–11:45	Mon–Fri	$14,400
3.6–5	8:45–2:45 (Fri until 11:45)	Mon–Fri	$17,606

Full-day children bring their own lunches. A snack is laid out for half-day children who help themselves to it.

Extended hours. For children 3.6–4.6, the Afternoon Enrichment Program operates from 12:00 to 2:45. On any particular day there may be three or four activities for children to choose from.

Program. Classic Montessori curriculum, member of the Association Montessori Internationale. Children are given the freedom to learn at an individual pace and are allowed to gain in self-confidence, initiative, and independence as they master each level of material. There is a three-year age span in the classroom, which allows the individual to socialize with both older and younger children, and an opportunity to experience help joyfully given and received.

Admissions. The application fee is $60. Inquiries start in the fall prior to the application year. Parents attend an open house with a school tour, complete an application, observe a classroom, and have an interview. A child visit follows. Parents are notified in early March.

Class size. The ratio is 8 to 1.

Staff. Two staff members per class: one AMI*-trained teacher and one credentialed assistant. There are two full time assistant teachers (floaters) and four specialists, one to four days a week.

Facilities. The school's four sunny, spotless, and well-organized rooms are on the garden level, second and third floors of the parish house of the Church of the Resurrection. On street level, a large indoor playroom opens onto an attractive, fully equipped playground. The rooms are filled with colorful and beautifully displayed Montessori materials. There are child-sized bathrooms. The whole environment is designed for children.

Separation. Before school starts, a parent accompanies the child on a "transition visit," an opportunity to meet the teachers, become familiar with the classroom, and establish a connection between school and home. Once school starts, new children are "phased in" a few at a time. Some new children are more comfortable with shortened sessions that gradually extend to a full session. For the first week of school, parents are invited to remain as long as they wish in the school lobby, where the school hosts a coffee morning for the first two weeks.

Parent involvement. The school believes that communication and partnership between home and school are critical for children's positive development. REDS publishes a weekly newsletter and sponsors periodic workshops and lectures on educational and parenting issues. There is an active parent association which meets once a month. Parents serve as Room Parents, are invited to a variety of social events throughout the year (Welcome Back Pot-Luck Dinner, Book Fair, etc.), and help organize the REDS Dinner and Auction fundraiser.

Financial. A $1000 deposit is required on signing the contract. The balance of tuition is paid in two equal installments. Limited financial aid is available.

*Association Montessori Internationale

Transportation. Most children come from the immediate neighborhood and are brought by parents or caregivers.

Graduates. Have attended leading ongoing independent and public schools.

Member. AMI, ISAAGNY, North American Montessori Association, NAEC.

The Rhinelander Nursery School

Ages: 2.6–4

350 East 88th Street
(between First and Second Avenues)
Zip: 10128
Tel: 876-0500
Fax: 876-9718
Website: www.rhinelandercenter.org
E-Mail: Stephanie@rhinelandercenter.org

Established in 1993
Felicia Gordon,
Nursery Director
Stephanie Katzman,
Assistant Director
Enrollment: 75

School year. Second week in September through the last week in May.

Summer program. Optional summer program June through August.

Ages	*Hours*	*Days*	*Tuition*
2's	12:45-3:15	Tues, Thurs, Fri	$6,500
3's	9:30–11:30	Mon, Thurs, Fri	$8,925
3's	12:30–3:00	Mon, Tues, Thurs, Fri	$7,675
4's	8:45–11:45	Mon-Fri	$9,725
4's	12:15–3:15	Mon,Tues,Thurs,Fri	$8,350

Program. Developmental. The program focuses mostly on the development of social skills, self-esteem and individuality, through relationships with the other children and with teachers. Children learn through hands-on play that is tailored to meet their individual abilities and interests. The core of the program consists of support and enhancement of each child's ideas, feelings and thoughts. Age appropriate activities are incorporated into group and individual instruction times in the school's learning centers. On site outdoor playgrounds provide a place for the children to exercise and play.

Admissions. The application fee is $45. Applications are accepted the day after Labor Day for the following year. After applying, parents are invited to join a small group tour of the school. Children are invited to return for a playgroup along with their parents later in the year. Parents are notified in early March.

Class size. There are fifteen children in each 3's class and sixteen children in each 4's class. The 2's classroom has thirteen children. All classes have three teachers, one head teacher and two assistants.

Staff. Head teachers have masters degrees in education. Most teachers have acquired their state certification.

Facilities. The school is located in a brownstone. There are two sunny classrooms with areas for block building, art, science, reading, imaginative play, puzzles and manipulatives. The children play outdoors on two rooftop decks.

Separation. Separation is a two-step process: For the first three weeks the school day is shorter and classes are smaller. Parents bring their children into the classroom and either stay in the classroom or in an adjacent family room that has a one-way mirror. Parents are expected to stay at school for the first couple of weeks until their child is comfortable. If the process takes longer than three weeks, the school is flexible and gently guides parents through the separation process individually.

Parent involvement. Parents play an important role and choose to be involved in many ways. There are parent committees, conferences, newsletters and trips. Parents are welcome in the school at any time.

Financial. A nonrefundable deposit of $1,500 is required upon signing the contract. The balance of tuition is to be paid in one or two payments. There are flexible payment plans and financial aid is available.

Transportation. Most students come from the Upper East Side and walk to school.

Graduates. Have attended leading on-going private and public schools.

Affiliations. Children's Aid Society.

Member. ISAAGNY, Parents League, ERB.

The Rockefeller University Child and Family Center

Ages: 3 mos–5 yrs

Nonsectarian Nursery School

1230 York Avenue
(at 66th Street)
Zip: 10021
Tel: 327-7072

Established 1966
Dr. Marjorie Goldsmith,
Director
Enrollment: 93

Ages	*Hours*	*Days*	*Tuition**
3 mos–3 yrs	8:30–5:45	Mon–Fri	
3s–5s	8:30–2:30 or 8:30–5:45	Mon–Fri	

*The Child and Family Center accepts only children whose parents are affiliated with Rockefeller University. These affiliated families pay tuition on a sliding scale depending on the amount of hours their children attend.

Program and Admissions. There is no application fee. Applications are accepted throughout the year. Parents may visit the school during January and February. The director does not meet the children until after they are admitted.

The school has an international flavor and takes pride in the multiplicity of its children's traditions.

Class size. There are two infant groups, four toddler groups, two 2/3s groups, and two 4s groups, ranging in size from eight to eighteen children, depending on the age.

Staff. The director, thirty-four full-time teachers, and several part-time teachers.

Facilities. The school occupies the ground floor of the Graduate Students Residence and Sophie Fricke Hall on the Rockefeller University campus. Its classrooms look out on the beautifully landscaped fifteen-acre campus.

Summer program. The summer program is for students already enrolled and runs five days a week from July through August.

Separation. Children attend for short periods in small groups during the first week. Parents are expected to stay until their child is comfortable.

Parent involvement. Parent involvement in the school's activities is encouraged.

Financial. There is a nonrefundable registration fee of $400 applicable to tuition.

Transportation. No private bus service is available.

Graduates. Have gone on to such schools as Brearley, Collegiate, Dalton, Ethical Culture, Nightingale-Bamford, Spence, and Trinity, as well as neighborhood public schools.

Affiliations. Rockefeller University.

Member. ERB, ISAAGNY.

Roosevelt Island Day Nursery

Ages: 2.6–5 yrs

Nonsectarian

4 River Road
Zip: Roosevelt Island 10044
Tel: 593-0750
Fax: 593-1342
Website: www.ridn.org
E-Mail: ridndlc@netscape.net

Established 1977
Diana Carr, Director
Enrollment: 40

School year. Early September through mid-June. Working parents may drop off children at 8:00.

Age	*Hours*	*Days*	*Tuition*
2.6/3s	9:00–12:00	Mon–Fri	$8,880
3s	9:00–3:00	Mon–Fri	$10,800
4s	9:00–3:00	Mon–Fri	$9,740*

*Universal Pre-K funds provided by the NYC Board of Education subsidize the full day 4s program.

Program. Eclectic. The school describes itself as an open-classroom, child-centered school. The curriculum stresses the development of concepts and skills that are needed for the formal learning of reading, writing; math, science and social studies. Block building, dramatic play, art, music, and physical development are an integral part of the curriculum.

Admissions. The application fee is $25. Registration begins in March. Most children enter as 3s, although there are usually some openings for 4s as well. Children are admitted on a first-come basis. Parents visit the school with their children.

Class size. Classes for 2.6s/3s, have 15 children, and for 4s, up to 18 children. The youngest groups have 3 teachers, while older groups have 2.

Facilities. The rooms are spacious, bright and well equipped, with views of the river. All classrooms are divided into activities areas for block-building, art, science, cooking, dramatic play, puzzles, and games.

Summer program. There is an eight-week summer program similar to the school-year program with emphasis on water and other outdoor activities.

Parent involvement. Parents may visit any time and are involved on the board of directors, with fund-raising, and with classroom activities such as cooking, art projects, field trips, and parties.

Financial. A tuition deposit is required on registration. Payments of the balance are made quarterly or monthly. There is a $10 bookkeeping charge for monthly payments. Financial aid is available from the Agency for Child Development or school's scholarship fund.

Graduates. Have gone on to local public schools and private schools such as Brearley, Browning, Collegiate, Dalton, Ethical Culture, Town, Trevor Day, and UNIS.

Member. ERB, ISAAGNY

Accreditation. NAEYC.

The Rudolf Steiner School

Ages: 2–18 yrs

Nonsectarian Nursery and Ongoing School

Elementary School:	Established 1928
15 East 79th Street (between Fifth	Josh Eisen,
and Madison Avenues)	School Administrator
Zip: 10021	Irene Mantel,
Tel: 327-1457	Director of Admissions
Fax: 861-1378	Nursery enrollment: 70
Lower School	Total Enrollment: 350
Fax: 744-4497	
Upper School: 15 East 78th Street	
Tel: 879-1101	
Website: www.steiner.edu	

School year. September to early June.

Ages	*Hours*	*Days*	*Tuition*
2s	90 minutes	T or Th	$825
3s	8:30–12:00	Mon–Fri	$17,400
4s/5s	8:30–12:00	Mon–Fri	$17,900
4s/5s	8:30–2:45	Mixed Week	$21,500
4s/5s	8:30–2:45	Mon–Fri	$24,400

The 2s attend ten parent-child sessions. For all other programs, children must be age-appropriate by September 1st.

Program. Developmental. The Waldorf method, established by Rudolf Steiner, is based on the belief that children pass through three basic stages of development, and the curriculum is designed to engage the abilities of the growing child at each of these stages. In preschool this is accomplished through creative guided play and activities that foster imagination such as nursery rhymes, stories and songs that prepare for language arts; eurythmy, a form of music and movement, and counting games, which build a foundation for later math work. The preschool uses only natural materials including chestnuts, sand and water, shells and stones, pinecones, and other objects found and gathered from nature. The children model in beeswax (a favorite Waldorf material), paint with watercolors, bake bread and make soup every week. You will never find a LEGO here.

Admissions. The application fee is $55 Inquiries begin after Labor Day. The application deadline is October 31st. Tours and open houses are offered in the fall and require a reservation. Applicants' parents meet with the admissions director, while children are interviewed in small groups.

For the 2s Plus Program, children must be 2 by June 30th. There are 23 spaces available for 3 year olds. Places for 4 and 5 year olds are limited and depend on attrition. The 2s program offers 28 places but does not provide automatic acceptance into the 3-year-old nursery program. Five years of age is a typical entry point. Preference is given to siblings and legacy applicants.

Notifications are sent in February and March. Children may be put on a wait list pending openings that can sometimes occur in late spring or summer.

Class size. There are two classes of 3 year olds, one group of fifteen older 3s, and a second group with eight young 3s, each with two teachers, and two mixed-age (4s/5s) kindergartens, one with twenty-four students and the other with twenty-one students, each of which has a head teacher with two assistants. The 2s program has two groups of twelve children with three teachers.

Staff. The head teachers have masters degrees in Early Childhood Education as well as training in Waldorf education. An elected committee composed of faculty and staff governs the school. This committee must approve all decisions affecting the school and the students.

Facilities. The lower school building houses the nursery, kindergarten and first through sixth grades and is located in a limestone mansion by McKim, Mead & White fronting East 79th Street. Its entrance hall is white marble. On the first floor are two nursery rooms, and one mixed-age kindergarten; a second kindergarten is on the second floor. The rooms are filled with materials chosen to stimulate the children's imagination such as building blocks, soft dolls and puppets, and colorful cloths. Each classroom is equipped with a kitchen area for baking, cooking, and preparation of a daily snack. An organic lunch is served to full day students. Central Park is the school's play yard. Everyday the children walk the half block from the school and cross Fifth Avenue holding on to a long rope with loops. They carry buckets for gathering acorns or leaves, jump ropes, balls, and in the spring their snack and a large blanket for picnics.

Separation. Separation is gradual and varies with the needs of each child. Threes come together in small groups for abbreviated periods of time. After a few weeks they are in their regular group for a full morning. Most children learn to separate within two to three weeks.

Parent involvement. Ongoing parent education is offered. Formal parent/teacher conferences are held twice a year, and informal exchanges are frequent. Either the parent or the teacher may request a meeting at any time. There is also an active parents association, which has a role in activities such as the annual Fall Fair, where beautiful crafts are sold, a major showcase for Waldorf education.

Financial. Tuition includes all fees. A non-refundable tuition deposit [illegible]rcent is required on signing the contract. Half the tuition is due August 1st, the remainder on January 1st. Parents can subscribe to a commercial tuition payment plan. Financial aid is rarely available at the nursery or kindergarten level.

Transportation. About half the school's students come from the immediate neighborhood, the remainder from the Upper West Side, downtown, Brooklyn, Queens, the Bronx and New Jersey. Most children are brought to school by their parents or caregivers, but some come by private bus.

Graduates. Many children continue through high school.

History. Rudolf Steiner (1861-1925), an Austrian scientist, artist, educator, and founder of anthroposophy, began the first Waldorf school in Stuttgart in 1919. Integrating intellectual and artistic development, Steiner sought to sustain and deepen the child's capacity for life and creative thought. Driven underground during the Hitler years, Steiner's ideas survived and now inspire some 900 schools in more than 40 countries. There are approximately 200 Waldorf schools in North America.

Member. ERB, ISAAGNY, NAIS, NYSAIS, Early Steps, Waldorf Schools Association.

St. Bartholomew Community Preschool

Ages: 2.4–5 yrs

Episcopal

109 East 50th Street
(between Park and
Lexington Avenues)
Zip: 10022
Tel: 378-0223/0238
Fax: 378-0281
Website: www.stbarts.org
E-Mail: ponce@stbarts.org

Established 1973
Susan Kotite,
Director
Mary Ponce,
Admissions Director
Enrollment: 60

School year. September through May.

Ages	*Hours*	*Days*	*Tuition*
2s/young 3s	9:00–11:45	2 or 3 days	$7,600–9,200
3s/4s	9:00–11:45	Mon–Fri	$13,000
	9:00–3:00	Mon–Fri	$16,500
4s/5s	9:00–3:00	Mon–Fri	$16,500

Children in the 3s program must be toilet-trained. Early morning drop-off is available from 8:30–9:00 AM at a minimal fee.

Program. Eclectic. The preschool cultivates an environment in which children are encouraged to learn about themselves, and the community around them. Teaching is individualized according to the child's need, development, and readiness. The program is structured but not rigid and includes music and movement, library, chapel, cooking, and swimming. One of the main goals of the school is to foster a sense of enjoyment and help children feel confident about going to school.

Unique to St. Bart's is its swimming program. Children learn water safety and basic swim strokes in the school's indoor pool which has a special tot dock to accommodate the younger ones.

Foreign languages and tennis are offered as afterschool programs.

A first step playgroup, sponsored by the preschool, meets once or twice a week from 9:30–11:30. Children must be 12 months or older.

Admissions. The application fee is $35. Inquiries are from September on. There are openings for approximately twenty 2s, limited spaces for 3s, 4s, and 5s.

Once the application is submitted, the Admissions Director schedules a visit for the family. Children are seen with their parents and have an opportunity to play with toys in the director's office, participate in a classroom, and tour the school. Preference is given to children of parishioners of St. Bartholomew's. However, the student body and the faculty are highly diversified; ten different religious affiliations are currently represented. Notifications are sent in March.

Class size. There are two 2s groups of ten to twelve, one group of fifteen to seventeen 3s, and one group of eighteen or nineteen 4/5s. Each class has two staff members. Specialists teach dance and movement, swimming and science.

Facilities. Children arriving in the morning take the elevator with their parents to large, sunny, cheerful classrooms on the fourth and fifth floors of the church's community house. The children make use of a large multi-purpose room for music, dancing, and other activities; a children's 2,500-volume circulating library; a swimming pool (with a special tot "dock") and full-size gymnasium; and a new 1900-square-foot fully equipped rooftop playground with a garden and climbing equipment. Many of the school's resources (the library, video equipment, gym equipment, the charming cubby mural) were donated by generous parents of past and present students.

Summer program. The June program—three weeks of "Adventurous Summer" camp—is open to the community.

Separation. Handled gradually and individually. The 2s begin with small groups and short sessions. Parents remain in the classroom until children are comfortable with their leaving.

Parent involvement. The school strongly encourages parent participation in their children's lives at school. There are monthly parent-child luncheons that parents gladly attend, a newsletter staffed by parents, library activities, and numerous committee, fund-raising, and social events (Family Play Days, Thanksgiving/Passover exchange program with Central Synagogue, Parents Night, farewell picnic) that bring the community of families together. As one parent said, "Finding a school that allows parents to be this involved makes us feel like we are a part of, and not just an observer of, our children's school experience."

Financial. A deposit of $1500–$2000 is required on signing the contract. Limited scholarship aid is available.

Graduates. Go on to such schools as Allen-Stevenson, Birch Wathen-Lenox, Brearley, Browning, Buckley, Cathedral, Chapin, Columbia Grammar, Convent of the Sacred Heart, Dalton, Ethical Culture, Friends, Gateway, Grace, Hewitt, Nightingale-Bamford, St. Bernard's, St. David's, St. Hilda and St. Hugh's, Spence, Trinity, Trevor Day, and UNIS.

Affiliations. St. Bartholomew's Episcopal Church.

Member. Day Care Council of New York, Child Care Inc., Ecumenical Child Care Network, ERB, ISAAGNY, National Association of Episcopal Schools.

St. Ignatius Loyola Day Nursery

Ages: 2–5 years

Catholic

240 East 84th Street
Zip: 10028
Tel: 734-6427 (Office);
734-0043 (Admissions)
Fax: 734-6972
Website: www.saintignatiusloyola.org

Established 1915
Theodora L. Crist, Director
Luz M. Mezza Robledo,
Assistant Director
Rosario Murray
Admissions Director
Enrollment: 130

School year. September through June.

Ages	*Hours*	*Days*	*Tuition*
2–5	8:00–5:30	Mon–Fri	$15,500
2s and 3s	9:00–12:00	3, or 5 days	$11,500–12,500
3s and 4s	1:30–4:30	3, or 5 days	$11,500–12,500

Program. The Day Nursery offers a challenging child-centered preschool program that stresses social, emotional, and cognitive growth. Creative play with manipulatives (blocks), as well as a variety of other materials is stressed. Teachers support learning and act as nurturing guides in a variety of ways. Themes are central to the program: units include transportation, recycling, life at the North Pole, insects, New York City, *Aesop's Fables,* the solar system, dinosaurs, and other topics of interest to the children. Snacks are nutritious and prepared in the nursery's remodeled kitchen. The lunch menu reads like those of many Madison Avenue restaurants offering raisin bread, frittatas, pasta primavera, puddings, and parfaits. Afternoons include a "tea time" with freshly baked goods and yogurt prepared on the premises. ERBs are given on-site.

Admissions. The application fee is $50. Inquiries and requests for applications from September on. Completed applications must be received before a tour is scheduled.

Parents are called to schedule appointments; children visit the school with parents for interviews. The nursery maintains a wait list. Preference is given to children of members of the parish of the Church of St. Ignatius Loyola and siblings.

Class size. There are two classes of 2s, four classes of 3s, two classes of 4s, and one junior kindergarten of 4s and 5s. Each class has a head teacher and an assistant teacher.

Staff. There's a strong feeling of connection between home and school. Faculty members teach at the school on average of twelve years. There are extensive professional development opportunities including tuition assistance for coursework. A staff development coordinator adds to these opportunities through conferences and evaluations. A consulting psychologist is available to meet with parents and teachers on a weekly basis. A Spanish teacher meets with children twice a week integrating art, music and movement into the foreign language program. A yoga instructor introduces the fundamentals of yoga weekly.

Facilities. The Day Nursery occupies an historic five-story building on the Upper East Side. Each floor contains two generously proportioned, sunny classrooms, divided into separate areas for instruction, play and reading, eating and napping. The enclosed rooftop playground includes 2,000 square feet of open play space, equipped with tricycles, slides, climbing equipment and plenty of room for running and playing.

Parent involvement. A breakfast orientation meeting is held for new parents. Each class conducts a meeting for its parents during the gradual separation period. Two informational meetings are held for parents during the year; parent-teacher conferences are held twice a year, more frequently if requested. Each class has at least two parent representatives who fundraise, recruit volunteers and arrange special classroom activities.

Separation. A gradual process that begins with abbreviated sessions and small groups. The staff lounge is available for parents during the separation process.

Financial. There is an enrollment fee of between $1,800 and $2,000 due upon signing the contract. Tuition payments are made in three installments, June, September and February. A building maintenance fee of from $700 to $900 is due in June. Financial aid is available for the full day program.

Transportation. The school does not provide bus service. The closest public transportation includes the numbers 4, 5 and 6 Lexington Avenue trains and the 86th Street and Second and Third Avenue bus routes.

Graduates. Have been accepted to Allen-Stevenson, Bank Street, Birch Wathen/Lenox, Brearley, Browning, Buckley, Caedmon, Chapin, Collegiate, Convent of the Sacred Heart, Dalton, Ethical Culture, Horace Mann, La Scuola, Lycée, Marymount, Spence, St. Bernard's St. David's, St. Ignatius Loyola, St. Joseph's Yorkville, St. Stephen's of Hungary, P.S. 6, 158, 290, The Anderson Program, Hunter and Lower Lab.

Affiliations. The Church of St. Ignatius Loyola, Yorkville Civic Council, Parents League, ACEI, ASCD.

St. Thomas More Play Group

Ages: 2–5 yrs

Nonsectarian Nursery School

65 East 89th Street
(between Madison
and Park Avenues)
Zip: 10128
Tel: 534-3977
Fax: 427-9015

Established 1972
Nancy Godreau,
Director

Enrollment: 110

School year. September through May.

Ages	*Hours*	*Days*	*Tuition*
2s	1:15–3:15	T/W/Th	$9,550
3s	12:45–3:00	M/T/Th	$10,050
	8:45–12:00	Mon–Fri	$13,950–$14,250
4s/5s	8:45–1:00	Mon–Fri	

Program. Traditional/Developmental. The Play Group provides a nurturing and supervised environment where separation is sensitively handled. Daily schedules and movement of the groups between rooms and interest areas is structured yet flexible enough to allow for spontaneity. Developmentally age-appropriate activities include arts and crafts, movement and music. Children make weekly visits to the schools library where even the youngest children are encouraged to explore and borrow books of their choosing.

Admissions. The application fee is $50. Inquiries are in September. Parents call after Labor Day to arrange for a visit to the school between October and December. Applications are given after the school tour. No interview is required of the child. Parents are notified of decisions in mid-February and must respond by early March.

Class size. There are two 2s classes with ten to twelve children and two 3s classes with fifteen children. The 4s class and the two 4s/5s classes each have fifteen to eighteen children. Each class has three teachers.

Facilities. When children enter the school they are met by their teachers and escorted downstairs where they each have a cubby. The classrooms and special activity areas are well lit, and well equipped, and there are two padded outdoor play area. The children have music or creative movement each day in a large music room with a piano.

Summer program. Two weeks in June, for enrolled students only.

Separation. Students receive at home visits from their teachers prior to the beginning of the school year. The 2s and 3s begin school in small groups, which meet for shortened sessions during a three-week orientation period.

Parent involvement. There is an active parents association, which meets monthly and serves as liaison between parents and school. The parent body is homogenous; families are likely to reside in the immediate Upper East Side neighborhood.

Transportation. No private bus service is available. Most children walk to school with a parent or caregiver.

Temple Emanu-El Nursery School and Kindergarten

Ages: 2.7–6 yrs

Jewish Nursery School

One East 65th Street (between 5th and Madison Avenues)
Zip: 10021
Tel: 744-1400
Enrollment: 135
Website: www.emanuelnyc.org
E-Mail: info@emanuelnyc.org

Established 1950
Mrs. Ellen Davis, Director
Mrs. Emily Bau, Registrar

School year. September through beginning of June. Summer program available to children in and outside of the school community.

Ages	*Hours*	*Days*	*Tuition*
2.7–2.9	9:00–12:00	2 days per week	$7,740
2.10–3.1	9:00–12:00	3 days per week	$9,070
3.0–3.5	9:00–12:00	Mon–Fri	$12,850
3.5–6 yrs	9:00–2:00	5 mornings + 3 afternoons	$15,150
3.5–6 yrs	9:00–2:00	5 mornings + 4 afternoons	$15,150

Children of temple members and siblings may be 2.5 on entering. Toilet training is not necessary for 2s or 3s.

Program. Traditional. The curriculum includes a full readiness program. In a typical day, children have an hour of free-choice time, which includes group time, music, gym, nature, science, a cooking or art project, or library time. The older children dictate and illustrate stories, which are collected and saved for their parents. The last part of the morning is spent on one of the school's two outdoor playgrounds. The children also take many field trips. The classes contain a balanced number of boys and girls.

The director stresses that the children are not schooled for the ERB other than by being helped to learn to sit, focus, and complete a task. She strongly disapproves of tutoring and considers it self-defeating for children to be placed in schools that are inappropriate for them. The ERB test is given on the premises.

Major Jewish holidays are celebrated and others are discussed when appropriate. The children's snack on Fridays is challah.

Admissions. The application fee is $50. Inquiries are from Labor Day on. Parents begin calling after Labor Day to reserve a place in a group tour. These commence at the end of October. Parents are notified by letter of their tour date. Applications must be received before a tour is scheduled. The school invites children for play sessions with members of the staff in January and early February. Five or six children come at a time, and the session lasts thirty minutes. Only one parent accompanies the child. Preference is given to siblings and children of longstanding congregation members.

Class size. There are three 2s classes of fourteen students each. The two 3s classes have eighteen children, the 4s and 4/5s each have twenty. Each class has at least three staff members, allowing teachers to split up the group for concentration in various areas, such as woodworking or cooking. Movement, music, and nature specialists work with each group once a week. The nature specialist brings in a variety of plants and animals—from parrots to snakes—to enrich nature presentations. Each Friday a reading program takes place in the library. This program is run by parent volunteers.

Facilities. In addition to six spacious, beautifully equipped and maintained classrooms on the third floor of the temple's Community House, there are two large outdoor playgrounds (equipped with playhouses, large construction blocks, slides, tricycles, wagons, and intricate climbing structures), a large carpeted playroom, a library, a conference room, offices, and a room for cooking and woodworking. The classrooms have adjoining toddler-sized toilets, sinks for water play, and mirrored-window observation booths for parents. Many of the rooms have pianos. Classrooms are divided into well-equipped activities centers, including a block corner. Creative artwork as well as project art adorn walls and bulletin boards. Sand tables are filled with kosher salt or cornmeal. The children gather together for a school sing-along once a month.

Summer program. A six week summer program is available Monday through Thursday at 9 AM to 1 PM, at an additional cost of $1500. It is held in the school's facility and is open to the community.

Separation. Handled gradually and individually. Two teachers visit each new child before school begins. In addition, there is a tea in the classroom for parents to meet and talk with the director about separation. Extra staff is available to the 2s during separation. Twos come daily for the first week in small groups for short sessions. By the end of the month they stay for the full session. When school begins, the 2s are encouraged to get used to the room and the other children. They are not expected to share yet, so there are duplicates and triplicates of things. The 3s are introduced in small groups for shortened sessions over two weeks. Some parents may be able to leave their children at the door and wait in the conference room; others may be needed in the classroom.

Parent involvement. There are two formal conferences each year and others as needed. Teachers are always available by phone. Parents are encouraged to use the observation booths, and to join the classroom for lunch, or to read a story or arrange an art project (if their children can handle having them leave afterward). They are also involved in the book fair, library, newsletter, occasionally substitute in the classroom, and help arrange events such as the Seder.

Financial. Some scholarship aid is available.

Transportation. Parents bring their children to the school floor where they are greeted by three teachers. No bus service is provided by the school. The children come from the East and West Sides down to Tribeca.

Graduates. Have gone to Abraham Joshua Heschel, Allen-Stevenson, Birch Wathen-Lenox, Brearley, Browning, Buckley, Chapin, Collegiate, Columbia Grammar, Dalton, Ethical Culture, Friends Seminary, Hewitt, Horace Mann, Nightingale-Bamford, Riverdale, St. Bernard's, Spence, Town, and Trinity.

Affiliations. Temple Emanu-El.

Member. ERB, ISAAGNY.

Temple Israel Early Childhood Learning Center

Ages: 2.4–5 yrs

Jewish Nursery School, Reformed

112 East 75th Street
(between Lexington and
Park Avenues)
Zip: 10021
Tel: 249-5000 ext 101 (between 9:00 and 5:00)
Website: www.templeisraelnyc.org

Established 1966
Nancy-Ellen Micco,
Director
Enrollment: 90

School year. September through early June. June school available for three weeks.

Ages	*Hours*	*Days*	*Tuition*
2s	9:00–11:30	2, 3 days a week	$8,200 or $9,800
3s	9:00–11:45	Mon–Fri	$13,600
3s	12:30–2:45	Mon–Thurs	$10,250
4s	9:00–2:15	Mon–Fri (Fri to 12)	$16,600
5s	9:00–2:45	Mon–Fri (Fri until 12)	$17,250

Extended days available for 3s (11:45–2:00) for an additional fee of approximately $2,500, Tuesday and Thursday afternoons.

Program. Developmental. The Early Childhood Learning Center provides a warm, nurturing, structured and stimulating environment emphasizing individual and small group activities. Teachers understand the individual needs of young children. Experiences are provided in the arts, math, reading readiness, handwriting without tears, music, literature, science, block building literature and science. Each child is encouraged to develop his or her own strengths. The goal is to have all the children leave school feeling confident, independent, and secure in themselves and their abilities.

Learning through play on an age-appropriate level is stressed. Projects related to the individual curiosity and interests of the child are incorporated into the curriculum. There are always specific projects available, as well as a range of other activities. Each group is offered a cooking curriculum which incorporates aspects of math and science.

There is a strong Jewish component to the curriculum. Children are introduced to Jewish traditions and holiday celebrations, through art, music, and food. Shabbat is celebrated on Fridays in every classroom; families participate.

ERBs are given on the premises, in both spring and fall.

Admissions. The application fee is $50. Requests for applications begin on the first Monday in October, unless this conflicts with the High Holy Days. Dates to call may be found on the summer voice mail message. Parents should call for an application form and return it with the fee. The school will call to arrange a parent group tour. Individual family interviews begin in early December. Preference is given to siblings and children of long-term temple members.

Class size. There are two 2s classes, two morning classes for 3s, one afternoon 3s class, one class for 4s, and a class of older 4/5s. There are three teachers for each group.

Facilities. Located on the fourth floor of Temple Israel, the school's walls are fire brick, painted white and accented with primary-color-painted doorways. Each of the five classrooms has a wall of windows, its own bathroom and direct access to the play terraces. The rooms are well equipped and divided into activity areas for art, blockbuilding, storytime, dramatic play, science, puzzles, manipulatives and special projects. The school has a new library and a music and movement room. In warmer weather children can take classroom activities out onto the terrace; in rainy weather they use the temple's auditorium for active play.

Separation. All children visit their classrooms before school begins. There is a separation workshop, prior to the first day of school, for all incoming parents. Separation for the 2s is gentle and gradual.

Parent involvement. The parents association sponsors social events, parenting seminars, and special programs for children and is solely responsible for all fund raising events. Parents are welcome to visit any time to observe. The staff makes a point of being accessible. Formal conferences are held twice yearly, in November and April.

Transportation. This is primarily a neighborhood school. Parents or caregivers bring their children to the classrooms.

Graduates. The majority of students go on to independent schools such as Abraham Joshua Heschel, Allen-Stevenson, Bank Street, Beit Rabban, Birch Wathen/Lenox, Brearley, Browning, Collegiate, Calhoun, Cathedral, Chapin, Columbia Grammar, Dalton, Dwight, Ethical Culture/Fieldston, Friends Seminary, Hewitt, Horace Mann, Manhattan Country, Nightingale/Bamford, Rabbi Arthur Schneier Park East, Ramaz, Riverdale, Rudolf Steiner, Rodelph Sholom, Solomon Schecter, Spence, St. Bernard's, St. David's, St. Ignatius Loyola, Town, Trevor Day, Trinity, UNIS, The Anderson Program at PS 9, Hunter, Lower Lab and PS 166.

Affiliations. Temple of Israel. Chartered by the Board of Regents of the State University of New York.

Member. ERB, ISAAGNY, BJE.

Temple Shaaray Tefila Nursery

Ages: 2.5–5 yrs

Jewish nursery school, Reform

250 E. 79th Street	Established 1993
Zip: 10021	Sari Schneider,
Tel: 535-2146	Director
Fax: 288-3576	Bonnie Blanco,
Website: www.shaaraytefilanyc.org	Associate Director
E-Mail: administration@tstnyc.org	Enrollment: 135

School year. September through June.

Ages	*Hours*	*Days*	*Tuition*
2.6	9:00–11:30	Tues Thurs	$8,500
		Mon Wed Fri	$10,200
2.9–3.9	9:00–11:30	Mon–Fri	$12,000
3	8:45–11:45	Mon–Fri	$13,000
3	12:45–3:15	Mon–Thur	$10,250
3.6–4.6	8:45–1:00	Mon–Fri (Fri till 12:45)	$14,000
4	9:00–2:30	Mon–Fri (Fri till 12:45)	$15,500

There is a $1,750 discount for temple members.

Program. The school incorporates the traditions and values of Judaism in a nurturing close-knit environment. The curriculum is designed to promote self-esteem and offers a program that includes block building, art projects, dramatic play, and the exploration of many different kinds of open-ended materials.

Children are introduced to Jewish traditions through weekly Shabbat and holiday celebrations, songs and games.

Admissions. The application fee is $25. Parents fill out an application and call ahead for a tour appointment. During the tour, they meet the director. The school gives priority to temple members and siblings. Remaining spaces are filled via lottery. Notifications are sent out in March.

Class Size. Class size varies from 10 to 20, depending on age and class. There are three teachers per class.

Staff. The head teachers are certified with masters degrees in early childhood education.

Facilities. The school is located in the temple building on the third and fourth floors. There is a rooftop playground, and a playroom in the basement. The seven classrooms all have windows. There are rugs in the reading area. Children display their art on the walls. There is a library. The bathrooms have been adapted for children. Children bring their own lunches.

Separation. Gradual phasing-in process. Parents and caregivers are asked to remain in the classroom until the school feels that the child is comfortable. Separation is considered an individualized process.

Parent involvement. There is a strong Parents Association. Parents are very involved in fundraising activities, organizing parent programs, working in the library and publishing a biannual school newspaper. There are also monthly discussions on child development with the director.

Financial. Partial financial aid is available. Payments are made four times a year. Parents sign a contract for the year. There is a nonrefundable deposit of $2,500.

Transportation. Transportation must be provided by parents.

Graduates. Have gone on to independent and public schools, with about one-half of the children choosing private schools including Jewish and single-sex schools.

Affiliation. Temple Shaaray Tefila.

Member. BJE, ERB, ISAAGNY.

Town House International School

Ages: 2–6 yrs

Nonsectarian Nursery School and Kindergarten

1209 Park Avenue (at 94th Street)
Zip: 10128
Tel: 427-6930
Fax: 427-6931
Website: www.townhouseinternationalschool.org
E-Mail: info@thisny.org

Established 1976
William M. Nagy, Director
Mary E. Cousins, Director of Admissions
Enrollment: 35

School year. September through June.

Ages	*Hours*	*Days*	*Tuition* (monthly)
2–6	8:30–12:30	Mon–Fri	$939
2–6	8:30–4:00	Mon–Fri	$1,298
2–6	8:15–5:45	Mon–Fri	$1,598

Two or three half or full-day sessions can be arranged. Children on these schedules can occasionally be accommodated for additional half or full days for which an additional payment is required.

Program. Developmental. The school was started by former Head of School and present chairman of the board, Joseph Villamaria III, 25 years ago as an early childhood center. For the past fifteen years William Nagy has been the school's director. Emphasis is placed on nurturing individual talents in an intimate, yet challenging way to foster confident learning.

Admissions. The application fee is $50. Students are accepted throughout the year, there is a fall open house.

Facilities. The school is located in the headquarters of the Filipinas-Americas Science and Art Foundation (which founded and partially funds it) in a renovated Carnegie Hill townhouse with a large outdoor area in the back of the first floor. Children bring their own lunches; the school provides snacks.

Summer program. July and August.

Parent involvement. Conferences are scheduled quarterly and as parents request them. Parent-teacher workshops are held periodically. A parent advisory committee works on two fundraisers each year. The funds help purchase more educational materials. There is a parent head in each of the four classes who assists teachers, go on field trips and fundraisers.

Financial. An initial payment of one month's tuition is due before school begins. There is a monthly payment plan, financial aid is available.

Graduates. Have attended Manhattan Country School, Convent of the Sacred Heart, Ramaz, Trevor Day, and PS 6.

Affiliations. Filipinas-Americas Science and Art Foundation, City University of New York. Chartered and accredited by the Board of Regents of the University of the State of New York, ISAAGNY, Parents League, East Side Tenants Association and CIVITAS.

The Town School

Ages: 3–14 yrs

Nonsectarian Nursery and Elementary School

540 East 76th Street
(at the East River)
Zip: 10021
Tel: 288-4383
Fax: 988-5846
Website: www.thetownschool.org

Established 1913
Christopher Marblo,
Head of School
Natasha Sahadi,
Admissions Director
Odette Muskin,
Head of Nursery-Kindergarten Division
Nursery enrollment: 80
Total enrollment: 395

School year. Second week in September through second week in June.

Ages	*Hours*	*Days*	*Tuition*
3s	8:15–12:00	Mon–Fri	$13,500
Pre–K	8:15–2:30	Mon–Fri	$22,900
K	8:15–2:30	Mon–Fri	$26,700

Program. Traditional. Each division of the school, nursery-kindergarten, lower, and upper, has its own director and an organization that reflects the developmental needs of its particular group.

In the nursery and kindergarten classrooms, which are alive with plants and animals, children are encouraged to make choices, ask questions, try new experiences and find new friends. Learning is organized around simple themes, such as family, or the school itself, and is reinforced through books, songs, discussions, artwork and trips. In the preschool, children are introduced to English, math, history and science. In kindergarten, the children begin to learn a basic Spanish vocabulary.

Kindergarten applicants must take the ERB.

Admissions. The application fee is $60. Inquiries are from Labor Day on. Parents should reserve a place on a tour when they call for an application form. Tours are given between mid-September and mid-December. After submitting the application, parents call to make appointments for interviews for themselves and their children. Threes candidates are seen singly (with parents) in January; older applicants in October through December in groups of eight.

For applications completed by December 1, notifications are sent by February for kindergarten, March for nursery and PreK.

Class size. There is one class each of sixteen 3s and of eighteen prekindergartners. Each of these has two staff members. The two kindergartens each have twenty-two children with three staff members each.

Facilities. The school overlooks the East River and John Jay Park. It was modernized in 1986 with funds obtained from the sale of the school's air rights. The four spacious and well-equipped classrooms in the nursery-kindergarten wing were recently refurbished in August 2001.

In addition to classrooms, the building complex includes a luxurious auditorium, a full-size gymnasium, a technology center, a two tier library, studios for dance, music, and arts and crafts, a darkroom, two science laboratories, a dining room, and three play roofs, one of them enormous and facing the river. Many classrooms have windows looking out onto the water. Children also use John Jay Park and Randall's Island sports complex.

Children below first grade do not wear uniforms.

After-school program. Postscript is offered Monday through Friday. Pre-Ks and Ks may take Junior Postscript from 2:45 to 3:45 Monday through Thursday. Activities include sports, art, jujitsu, woodworking, photography, cooking and drama.

The course fees vary and are available for children 2.6–7 years of age.

Summer program. SummerSault, is a day camp for three through nine year olds, staffed both by Town School teachers and teachers from other independent schools.

Staff. A full-time nurse is on staff as well as fourteen teachers. There are four reading specialists in the nursery and kindergarten divisions.

Separation. The children are introduced in small groups with shortened sessions. The process is handled in a very individualized manner.

Parent involvement. The parents association meets monthly, and its representatives liaise between parents and school. Annual dues are $100. The association runs the Town School Store, the book fair, the uniform exchange, and special fund-raising events. Parent volunteers work in the library, on street patrol, share special talents or interests in the classroom, go on class trips, and join in other activities.

Conferences for the nursery-kindergarten division are arranged twice yearly, and written reports are sent at the end of the school year.

History. Founded as the Hyde School in 1913, the school was purchased by four teachers in 1935 and renamed The Town School. It was the first in New York City to use a consultant psychologist and to require that teachers be trained in child development. Accorded nonprofit status in 1952 and extended through eighth grade in 1956, it moved to its present location in 1962. In 1977 the school purchased and renovated an adjoining warehouse. The sale of its air rights in 1985 provided an endowment fund, and was used to raise teachers' salaries and improve facilities.

Financial. A $3,500 reservation deposit is required on signing the contract. The tuition balance is payable on July 1st and January 1st. The school reserves the right to charge 1.5 percent per month on past-due invoices. A tuition refund plan is available. Parents are asked to support an annual fund-raiser.

The school has a budget of approximately $1 million for financial aid. Guidelines of the Princeton School Scholarship Service are followed in determining need; 12 percent of students receive assistance.

Transportation. Private bus transportation is available.

Graduates. Most graduates go to independent day schools, a few to boarding schools, and a few to selective public high schools. Among the schools graduates have attended in the last five years are (in order of popularity) Trinity, Dalton, Horace Mann, Riverdale, Fieldston, Columbia Prep, Spence, Brearley, Nightingale.

Member. ERB, Guild of Independent Schools, ISAAGNY, NAIS, NYSAIS.

Trevor Day School

Ages: 3–18 yrs

Nonsectarian Comprehensive School

Early Childhood Division
11 East 89th Street
Zip: 10128

Tel: 426-3355
Website: www.trevor.org

Established 1930
Pamela Clarke,
Head of School
Deborah Ashe,
Admissions Director (Nursery through Gr. 5)
Total Lower School enrollment: 370
Preschool enrollment: 120
Elementary enrollment: 250

School year. September 7th through June 8th.

Ages	*Hours*	*Days*	*Tuition*
3s* mornings	8:30–11:30	Mon–Fri	$18,500
3s afternoons	12:30–3:30	Mon–Fri	$18,500
4s (Sept–Feb	8:25–2:00	Mon–Thur	$22,250
(Feb–June)	8:25–2:55	(Fri until 12)	
5s	8:25 – 3:00	Mon–Fri	$24,750

*Must be 3 by September 1st.
**Extended day available from 2–2:55 Mon–Thurs, Sept–Feb, at an additional charge.

Extended hours. Afterschool programs are available Monday through Friday, for Kindergarten–Grade 5 from 3:00–6:30 PM at an additional cost.

Program. Developmental. Emphasis is placed on providing a nurturing, appropriate environment, with careful attention to developmental and cognitive milestones. Activities include blockbuilding, cooking, art (painting, clay, rubbings, collage, sculpting, weaving, puppetry), dramatic play, sand and water play, games, puzzles and stories. The pre-kindergarten and kindergarten curriculum includes formal reading and math instruction as well as social studies, science, and field trips. Specialists teach art, music, physical education and foreign languages.

Admissions. The application fee is $50; There is no cost if you apply online. Inquiries may be made from April on.

A parent visit and interview are arranged following receipt of an application. Nursery and Pre-K applicants are observed with parents, the admissions director, and a teacher. Kindergarten applicants are observed in groups without their parents. Notifications are sent according to ISAAGNY guidelines. Preference is given to children of alumni and to siblings; in the N–K division, roughly 40% of children represent minorities; eleven foreign languages are spoken.

Class size. There are two classes of fourteen nursery students, morning and afternoon, two groups of approximately fifteen 4s (prekindergarten), and four classes of approximately fifteen each for 5s (kindergarten).

Staff. Most teachers and many assistants have masters degrees in early childhood education. The school utilizes a variety of innovative techniques emplying traditional manipulatives (blocks, etc.) as well as technology.

Facilities. Trevor Day School occupies a former townhouse across from the Guggenheim Museum. Four floors house the nursery, prekindergarten, and kindergarten. There are two rooftop play areas. In between are the art room, music room, gymnasium, kitchen, and library. Bright, cheery, and stimulating, the school was built for children.

Children enrolled pre-K and kindergarten bring their lunches. Snacks include fresh fruits and and crackers, which are provided by the school. The school is a peanut controlled environment.

Summer program. The summer program, Summer Day, which is open to the community, is a five-week program for 3s–6s, in late June to late July. For more information, call Shelley Miller, Director, at 426-3351; two, three, four and five week options are available.

Separation. Nursery children and their parents visit individually with homeroom teachers, just before school starts. When the term begins, the new children come together in small groups for a week for periods that gradually lengthen over about a month, building up to a full day's program. Gradually parents leave the classroom. Separation is very individual, and the teachers work out plans to suit the needs of each family.

Parent involvement. All parents are members of the Parents Association. Parents also serve on the board of trustees, are involved in fundraising and school committees, give admissions tours, read to children in the library on a regular basis, and assist with field trips. Evening workshops for parents are given two or three times a year, and family conferences are held semiannually.

Financial. A non-refundable deposit of 15 percent of the tuition is due in February on signing the year's contract. Three payment plans are available. The school has a tuition refund plan for emergency withdrawals from school. About 20 percent of the full student body receives financial aid, which becomes available in kindergarten.

Transportation. Children come from the East Side and West Side, as well as downtown, Roosevelt Island, New Jersey, Brooklyn, Queens and the Bronx. Most are brought by parents or caregivers, but starting in kindergarten transportation is available by either private or Board of Education buses.

Graduates. Most children go directly into the Trevor Day School Elementary School.

Chartered. By the Board of Regents of the State University of New York.

Member. ERB, ISAAGNY, NAIS, NYSAIS, Early Steps.

Vanderbilt YMCA

Ages: 6 mos–5 yrs

Nonsectarian Nursery School

224 East 47th Street
Zip: 10017
Tel: 912-2507
Fax: 752-0210
Website: www.ymcanyc.org
E-Mail: sconroy@ymcanyc.org

Sally Conroy,
Early Childhood Director
Enrollment: 55

School year. Open year round, except the last week of August and the week between Christmas and New Years.

*Ages**	*Hours*	*Days*	*Tuition (monthly)*
6 mos–5 yrs	8:30–6:00	Mon–Fri	$1,400
		M, W, F	$944
		T, Th	$672
	8:30–12:30	Mon–Fri	$926
		M, W, F	$602
		T, Th	$428
	2:00–6:00	Mon–Fri	$885
		M, W, F	$525
		T, Th	$383

*Call for more information. Full-day children bring their own lunches. A snack is provided in the morning and afternoon. There is an annual membership fee of $82.

Program. Developmental. Children learn through hands-on play using the plentiful supply of blocks, weighing and measuring and utilizing other forms of direct experimentation. Exploration of materials is open-ended. Children's self-esteem and feelings of success are encouraged. Children have a choice of activities provided within the structure created by teachers.

The Infant/Toddler class follows the same curriculum as the other aged classes, which includes nurturing active learning in all areas of development.

A music specialist visits all groups once a week and full time children swim twice a week. Gym and play yard activities are scheduled daily. A science specialist and a movement specialist work with the 3s and 4s weekly; yoga is introduced.

Admissions. The application fee is $50. The school maintains an active and ongoing waiting list. Inquiries are year round and families should call to be placed on the school's extensive waiting list. A tour of the school is scheduled prior to enrollment. Parents do not sign a contract and there is no rigorous screening process for the children. The important requirement is that the school should be a good match for the child and family. A nonrefundable deposit of one month's tuition is required to hold a child's place. Tuition is payable monthly.

Class size. There are four classes. The Infant/Toddler and 2s classes have ten children and the 3s and 4s have fifteen children each.

Staff. There is one teacher in each class with three assistants in the toddler class, two assistants for the 2s and 3s, and one assistant in the 4s class.

Facilities. Large, clean classrooms have windows looking onto the inner court, water tables, art tables, tables for Legos and bristle blocks, adjoining bathrooms and cots for rest time. Large areas are devoted to block play. The 3s/4s room has a listening loft with headsets and story cassettes. A long, narrow, but sunny, outdoor yard, padded on three sides and screened on top, offers a climber, seesaw, wagons, tricycles and outdoor blocks. In warm weather, water tables and sprinklers are made available outdoors.

Separation. Varies according to the individual child and is definitely not rushed.

Parent involvement. Parents help with fundraising for scholarships. Monthly parent meetings and potlucks, to which parents bring food of their native countries, are held. Parents and teachers communicate on a daily basis.

Financial. Limited scholarships are available, based on need. Because of proximity to the U.N., children come from diverse ethnic backgrounds.

Graduates. Go on to Bank Street, Calhoun, City and Country, Dalton, Ethical Culture, Little Red School House, Rudolf Steiner, UNIS, Village Community, PS 6, PS 116, PS 178, PS 183, PS 59, Hunter Elementary and other public school Gifted and Talented programs.

Wee Care Preschool

Ages: 6 wks–6 yrs

Nonsectarian Nursery School

451 East 83rd Street #BA (between York and First Avenues)
Zip: 10028
Tel: 472-4481
Fax: 472-2442

Established 1994
Carol Carrozelli, Director
Enrollment: 56

School year. September through June. Summer program July and August. (School is open year round.)

Ages	*Hours*	*Days*	*Tuition* (monthly)
Infants	8:00–6:00	2 days–5days	$704–$1507*
Toddlers	8:00–6:00	2 days–5 days	$655–$1274**
Nursery	9:00–3:30	2 days–5 days	$626–$1059***
	8:00–6:00	2 days–5 days	$652–$1274****
Preschool	9:00–3:30	2 days–5 days	$570–$952*****
	8:00–6:00	2 days–5 days	$603–$1148******

*Drop-in rates $78/day.
**Drop-in rates $73/day.
***Drop-in rates $69/day.
****Drop-in rates $73/day.
*****Drop-rates $63/day.
******Drop-in rates $69/day.

Program. Developmental. Children's learning is encouraged through interaction with their environment through play. Teachers plan activities that support emerging skills and recognize individual differences. The focus is on the development of the whole child: physically, emotionally, socially, creatively and academically. The program aims to foster respect for others, the equipment and the materials. A wide variety of activities are provided within the daily routine and cooperative play is encouraged. Activities are drawn from the curriculum areas of art, math, science, cooking, music and movement, large muscle, social studies, practical life, dramatic play, language arts and manipulative activities. Each child is encouraged to develop an active curiosity and an enthusiasm for learning which stimulates exploraton and creativity.

Admissions. The application fee is $75. Prospective parents should call to schedule a tour. Siblings are given priority.

Class size. The 2's class has ten students and two teachers. The 3's class has twelve students and two teachers. The pre-kindergarten has fourteen students and two teachers.

Staff. Teachers are CPR certified.

Facilities. The school has a play yard and the park is two blocks away.

Summer program. The summer program features field trips, play in the sprinklers, picnics and other activities.

Separation. New children begin the program gradually, an hour or two a day to start with.

Parent involvement. Parents are welcome anytime.

Financial. Siblings are given a ten percent discount.

Graduates. Go on to PS 290, PS 158, Hunter, Lower Lab and a variety of private schools.

The William Woodward Jr. Nursery School

Ages: 2.6–5 yrs

Nonsectarian

1233A York Avenue
(67th Street)
Zip: 10021
Tel: 744-6611
Website: www.woodwardns.org
E-Mail: wwjns@aol.com

Established 1961
Serena Fine English, Director
Mary Fracchia, Admissions Director
Enrollment: 90

School year. Mid-September for 3s up, late September through May for 2s.

Ages	*Hours*	*Days*	*Tuition*
Younger 2s*	9:30–11:30	Tues Thurs	$6,405
Older 2s	9:30–11:30	Mon Wed Fri	$7,560
Young 3s	1:00–3:45	Mon–Fri	$10,500
3s	9:00–11:45 or 1:00–3:45	Mon–Fri	$10,500
4/5s	9:00–11:45 or 1:00–3:45	Mon–Fri	$10,500

*Toilet training is not essential for the 2s. Children must be 2 by March 31st.

Program. Developmental/Traditional. The program includes a variety of experiences in blockbuilding, art, dramatic play, sand and water play, cooking, music, language arts, science, math, movement, and other activities aimed at developing social, emotional, physical and cognitive skills.

Admissions. The application fee is $35. Inquiries are from early September on. Parents should call for information and to arrange for a tour of the school, followed by a child's play visit. Admissions preference is given to families connected with New York-Presbyterian Hospital, New York Weill Cornell Center, Memorial Sloan-Kettering Cancer Center and The Hospital for Special Surgery. This accounts for 65 to 70 percent of the available places. Community children are accepted as space is available.

Parents are notified in March. Families connected with affiliated hospitals are given the option of early notice.

Class size. The school has two 2s classes of ten to thirteen with three teachers each; three 3s classes of thirteen to fourteen each; and two 4/5s classes of fifteen. Each of the older classes has two teachers. The staff is experienced in helping English and non-English speaking children communicate with each other. A music specialist works with the children. A consultant is available for children, families and staff.

Facilities. The school occupies four well-equipped classrooms; there is a one-way observation window, on the ground level of 1233A York

Avenue. In addition, there is a library and a large multipurpose room for special events, movement and rainy-day play; offices; and a large, landscaped outdoor playground equipped with sandbox, slides, climber and wheeled toys. The entire playground is covered with a safety surface. There is a full kitchen for cooking projects. Families provide snacks twice weekly.

Summer program. There is a four-week morning June program for currently enrolled students ages 3 to 5 taught by Woodward staff.

Separation. Children are introduced to school during two-three weeks of shortened, small-group sessions. Parents are expected to stay until children are comfortable.

Parent involvement. The parent body is active and international. Daytime and evening meetings on parenting and educational matters are held during the year by the school's parent facilitator and consultant. Parents serve on the board of directors and help with fundraising and in the classroom. Conferences are held twice yearly.

Financial. A payment of $3,000 to $3,500 is required upon signing the contract. Tuition is payable in three annual installments. Children of families of affiliated hospitals pay tuition on a sliding scale.

Transportation. Most children come from the East 50s through 80s.

Graduates. Have gone on to leading independent and public schools such as Allen-Stevenson, Brearley, Browning, Buckley, Chapin, Collegiate, Dalton, Friends Seminary, Hewitt, Lycée Français, Marymount, Nightingdale-Bamford, Sacred Heart, Spence, St. David's, Town, Trevor Day, Trinity, PS 6, PS 9, PS 77, PS 158, PS 183, PS 290, and Hunter.

History. The school was founded and is partially funded by grants from the Woodward Foundation.

Affiliations. New York-Presbyterian Hospital, New York Weill Cornell Center, Memorial Sloan Kettering Cancer Center, Hospital for Special Surgery. Chartered by the Board of Regents of the State University of New York.

Member. ERB, ISAAGNY, ATIS, NAEYC.

York Avenue Preschool

Ages: 2.3–5 yrs

Nonsectarian

1520 York Avenue (80th Street)
Zip: 10028
Tel: 734-0922
Fax: 861-8901
E-Mail: admissions@yorkavenuepreschool.org
Website: www.yorkavenuepreschool.org

Established 1989
Dr. Michele Starr, Director
Preschool Enrollment: 120

School year. Mid-September through May.

Ages in September	*Hours*	*Days*	*Tuition*
2.3-2.6	8:50–11:45	Tues & Thurs	$9,150
2.7-3.0	8:50-11:45	Mon, Wed, Fri	$10,950
3.1	8:50-12:00	Mon-Fri	$14,850
4.1	8:50-2:30	Mon-Thurs	$17,150
	8:50-12:00	Fri	

*Children in 3s program must be toilet trained before school begins.
**Children in the 4s stay for lunch. After school program available for 3s and 4s.

Program. Traditional/Developmental. The program is developmental, but the foundation is laid for the academic skills needed later on. Language, motor skills, and social and emotional development are considered on an individual basis. The program also integrates art, music, physical education and French in to the curriculum for the 4s group.

Children may be tested by the ERB in the library.

Admissions. The application fee is $50. Applications are available the day after Labor Day. After filing an application, parents call to schedule a tour. Following the tour parents schedule a child evaluation.

Class size. The young toddler group, 2.3 years through 2.6 years, has ten children. The older toddlers group, 2.7 years through 2.11 years, has about twelve children. Pre-nursery 3s has 15 children and nursery 4s has 18 children. Each class has a head teacher and an assistant at all times.

Staff. Dr. Michele Starr, the school's current principal is a licensed New York State School Administrator and holds a doctorate in early childhood education. All head teachers hold a master of education degree. Assistant teachers hold bachelor degrees. There are specialists in music, physical education and art.

Facilities. The school has one spacious gym adapted for young children, a library, an art studio and several classrooms, each with its own kitchenette and toilets. There is a well-equipped playground.

Summer program. June through mid-August; an additional fee is required.

Separation. Before school starts there are pre-entry meetings with parents. The separation process for the children is handled gently and on an individual basis. Toddler 2s begin with a schedule that consists of small group sessions and parents either remain in the classrooms, wait nearby or join other parents for coffee.

Parent involvement. Parents are encouraged to participate in their child's education, social activities, workshops and scheduled conferences with teachers, as well as take part in class trips and parent-run activities such as library and book club. The Parents Association sponsors activities that foster friendship and a strong sense of community.

Financial. A non-refundable tuition deposit of $2,500 is required on signing the contract.

Graduates. Recent graduates have gone onto both private and public schools, including competitive public school programs.

Affiliations. ERB, ISAAGNY, Parents League. Chartered by the Board of Regents of the State University of New York.

WEST SIDE

Abraham Joshua Heschel School

Ages: 3–18

Jewish

Nursery–Grade 5
270 West 89th Street
(between Broadway
and West End Avenue)
Zip: 10024
Tel: 595-7087
Website: www.heschel.org

Established 1983
Roanna Shorofsky,
Director
Judy Wolf-Nevid,
Early Childhood Head
Nursery enrollment: 118
Total enrollment: 730

School Year. Early September through mid-June.

Ages	*Hours*	*Days*	*Tuition*
3s	9:00–12:00*	Mon–Fri	$17,100
4s	8:30–3:00**	Mon–Fri	$22,210
5s	8:30–3:15**	Mon–Fri	$22,210

*Optional afternoon hours available. **Friday until 1:15.

Program. Eclectic/Progressive. The school describes itself as "a pluralistic independent Jewish school." Curriculum themes emerge from the Jewish and American holidays, nature and Shabbat observance. The school believes that young children learn best by doing, and encourages experimentation and active involvement with their environment. The school aims to help children become independent, self-confident and inquisitive learners.

Admissions. The application and testing fee is $45 for nursery and pre-kindergarten, $75 for kindergarten and above. Inquiries from September on. The admissions deadline is mid December. A tour of the school is required before applying. Tours are given weekly from September through December. After the application is received, the school will arrange for play-visits in small groups and parent interviews. The school expects that children who enroll in the nursery division will continue on at the school for the upper grades. ERB testing is required for kindergarten and above.

Class Size. There are two classes per grade. Each class has two co-teachers (or three, depending on class size).

Facilities. The entire school occupies three facilities. The lower school is at 270 West 89th, the middle school at 314 West 91st Street and the high school at 20 West End Avenue. All are fully equipped with large classrooms, library, science lab, computers, chapel, art room, music studio, gym, and outdoor play areas.

Separation. The school requires parents to be available during separation. The children start with shortened sessions and work up to the full program over the course of a month. Parents stay in the classroom or in the hall just outside as long as the child—or parent—needs them.

Parent involvement. Parents share personal and professional experience with classes, raise funds, escort school trips, plan and join in holiday celebrations and social events, serve on the board of directors, attend lectures on matters of general interest, and participate in the school's support group, which meets to discuss developmental parenting and curriculum topics.

Conferences are held twice yearly.

Financial. A tuition deposit of $2,000 is required on signing the contract. Half of the balance is due July 1st; the remainder, December 1st. Each family makes the school an interest-free loan of $1,000 for the period of the child's enrollment. Financial aid is available.

Transportation. Private bus service can be arranged. Department of Education buses are available for children 5 and older.

Graduates. Some students go on to independent schools, select public schools and Jewish schools; the majority of students continue.

Chartered. By the Board of Regents of the State University of New York.

Member. ISAAGNY, NAIS, NYSAIS.

Basic Trust Infant/Toddler Center

Ages: 3 mos–5 yrs

Nonsectarian Day Care Center

225 West 99th Street
(between Broadway
and Amsterdam Avenues)
Zip: 10025
Tel: 222-6602
Fax: 665-6855
Website: www.basictrust.org
E-Mail: basictrust@verizon.net

Established 1976
Peggy J. Sradnick,
Director

Enrollment: 39 per day

School Year. September through mid-August.

Ages	*Hours*	*Days*	*Tuition**
3 mos–5 yrs	8:00–5:45	3 days	$16,050
		4 days	$20,150
		5 days	$23,590

*There are no make up classes for absences. A non-refundable deposit of $750 is required.

Program. Progressive. The environment is warm and homelike, with many couches and chairs for snuggling. The children's day, structured around eating and sleeping, is filled with a wide variety of activities. The babies play with water, sing songs, read books, and are taken for walks. The Toddlers explore the neighborhood and nearby playgrounds. The Big Kids do all this plus baking, painting, blockbuilding, and eventually take on more sustained "project work." Social skills are a priority and relationships are fostered in many ways.

Admissions. The application fee is $75.

Basic Trust has openings every September. Parents may make an appointment to look at the program after receiving a brochure. The school asks that both parents (of two-parent households) visit the program with their child. After visiting, parents are given an application. Applications must be completed by early February for children who turn 2 before September 1st, and by May 1st for children turning 2 after September 1st.

Class size. The infant group has between eight and nine children (3 months to 14 months) a day with three full-time caregivers. There are ten or eleven toddlers from 17 months to 2.6 years. The 3/4s group has eighteen children with four staff.

Staff. In addition to the director, twelve full-time teaching staff, a full-time chef, and seven part-time staff, Basic Trust often has interns from Bank Street, and City-as-School. The staff have diverse backgrounds; some have master's degrees from Bank Street, some have B.A.'s in early childhood education, yet others have no formal education but a wealth of experience and on-the-job training. When special needs children are enrolled, the school works closely with a variety of specialists.

Facilities. An exceptional, multi-level, well-lit, completely renovated space in the basement of St. Michael's Church thoughtfully designed for young children. Each age group has its own room but all areas are connected to all others around a central, fully equipped kitchen. The bathrooms have child-size toilets; the kitchen has a low counter so children can bake and work on other projects; the couches are low and accessible to toddlers. The Baby Room is warm and cozy, with mobiles for the babies to gaze at, bells to ring, and many hanging plants. The Toddler Room has a pass-through window to the kitchen so children can watch and smell food being cooked. The Big Kids' Room has an upstairs level for working, eating, and reading, as well as a downstairs level for dress-up, blocks, toys, etc. There is also a large, carpeted gym area. There is also a large, grassy back yard with a sandbox, swings, climbing equipment, and a big garden for flowers and vegetables.

Meals are cooked and served family-style, and snacks are provided. The school does not allow candy, gum or nuts.

Separation. The separation process lasts a week, during which parents stay in the classroom attending to the needs of the child. Gradually the caretaking shifts from parent to teacher. Even if children will be attending part-time, the first week should be on a full-time schedule. The staff see separation as a developmental stage for both parents and children and therefore help both with the process.

Parent involvement. The staff feel their relationship with parents is central and are committed to sharing information with parents about child care as well as early childhood learning and development. Parents serve on the board of directors and are primarily responsible for the two to three major fund-raising events of the year. Parents are welcome to visit at any time.

Financial. A nonrefundable $750 deposit is required on signing the full-year contract. Tuition is paid monthly on the first of the month from September to June. No financial aid is available.

Transportation. No private bus service is available.

Graduates. Go on to independent schools and select public schools such as Bank Street, Manhattan Country School, Manhattan New School, Trevor Day, UNIS, Hunter, Manhattan School for Children, PS 163, PS 87, PS 75.

Member. ISAAGNY, Parents League.

The Brownstone School and Daycare Center

Ages: 2–4.11 yrs

Nonsectarian

128 West 80th Street (between Amsterdam and Columbus Avenues)	Established 1963
Zip: 10024	Cristina T. Huang, Director
Tel: 874-1341	Lorraine Lilley, Director of Admissions
E-Mail: brownstoneschool@verizon.net	Enrollment: 70
Website: www.brownstoneschool.com	

School year. Early September through mid-June.

Ages	*Hours*	*Days*	*Tuition*
2–4.11	9:00–12:30	2, 3 or 5 days	$5,900–11,800
	9:00–3:30	2, 3 or 5 days	$7,600–15,300
	8:00–5:45	2, 3 or 5 days	$9,033–18,169

Flexible schedules are available for 2, 3 or 5 day attendance; fees vary according to schedule, not age. Children need not be toilet-trained; they must be 2 by September 1st of the year they enter.

Program. Progressive. The approach is developmentally appropriate and child-centered, focusing on the social, emotional, intellectual, and physical needs of each child. Daily schedules offer a broad range of structured and unstructured activities, and provide children with the security of a routine. Working independently and in small groups, the children learn through play and hands-on exploration of selected materials. Dramatic play, children's literature, foreign language, puppets, games, puzzles, blocks, various artistic mediums, music, creative movement, outdoor activities, water play, and manipulatives promote the development of pre-reading, pre-math, and scientific concepts. Social interactions with peers and teachers through such activities challenge children to learn appropriate ways to express their feelings and develop their interests.

Admissions.
Applications are available on the third Monday in September until an adequate pool of applications is received. It is advisable to return applications promptly. After completing and submitting the application, parents should call to arrange a parent tour. Tours are scheduled for October through December, child visits for January through late February. Notifications are sent in accordance with ISAAGNY guidelines.

Class size. Child-staff ratios are 4:1 for the 2s; 6:1 for old 2s and young 3s; 7:1 for old 3s and young 4s as well as for older 4s/5s. The 2s class consists of 12 children, the 2s/3s of sixteen to seventeen, the 3s/4s of eighteen to nineteen, and the 4s of nineteen to twenty children.

Staff. Each class is staffed with a qualified group teacher, assistant teacher, and teacher's aide. Student teachers and interns enhance the program throughout the year. Music and creative movement classes are provided once a week, and a social worker is available as a consultant. Staff backgrounds are diverse but all have expertise in working with young children; in addition, all have been cleared by appropriate agencies.

Facilities. The school occupies a roomy, five-story, renovated brownstone on a street that has become gentrified. The rooms are lofty, with handsome old fireplaces and floor-to-ceiling mirrors. Each classroom has a floor to itself. The large rooms are divided into activity areas. Standard early childhood equipment, such as water/sand tables, easels, and dramatic play and block areas are available. Toys and cubbies line the walls, and there are child-size bathrooms and sinks.

There is a newly renovated outdoor play area, with slides and climbing frames with a poured rubber surface on the ground. The children use Central and Riverside Parks daily for outdoor and gross motor activities.

ERB testing is available on-site.

Summer program. From mid-June through end of July for Brownstone families only. Families may choose days and weeks in which their children will attend. Activities include arts and crafts, water play, outdoor recreation, tennis and day trips throughout New York City.

Parent involvement. The school attracts families of diverse economic, cultural, and professional backgrounds. Although many live or work on the Upper West Side, some commute from the surrounding boroughs of the city. The strength of the school lies heavily on the participation of its parent body. Utilizing individual talents, skills, and professional affiliations, parents volunteer in and outside the classrooms. They become involved with the organization of social events, fund-raising, and are encouraged to become members of the board of trustees.

Financial. A nonrefundable reservation deposit of $1,500 is required. Parents sign a contract for the school year and tuition is payable in six monthly installments. Some places are funded by the NYC Agency for Child Development.

Transportation. No private bus service is available.

Graduates. Go on to a wide range of school settings, including independent schools such as Allen-Stevenson, Bank Street, Collegiate, Columbia Grammar and Prep, Dalton, Ethical Culture, Marymount, Rodeph Sholom, Saint David's, Spence, Town, as well as gifted and talented programs and other public school programs throughout the city.

Member. Child Care, Inc., ERB, ISAAGNY, Parents League.

The Calhoun School

Ages: 3–18 yrs

Nonsectarian Preschool and Comprehensive School

3s through 1st grade:
Robert L. Beir Building,
160 West 74th Street
Tel: 497-6550
497-6575, Admissions Office
Grades 2 through 12:
Main Building
433 West End Avenue
(at 81st Street)
Zip: 10024
Tel: 497-6500
497-6510, Admissions Office
Website: www.calhoun.org
E-Mail: robin.otton@calhoun.org

Established 1896
Kathleen Clinesmith,
Lower School Director
Robin Otton,
Admissions Director, 3s–1st grade
Nancy Sherman,
Admissions Director, 2nd–12th grade

Total enrollment: 700
3s–1st grade enrollment: 200

School year. September through early June.

Ages	*Hours*	*Days*	*Tuition*
3s	9:00–12:00	Mon–Fri	$16,700
3s	9:00–12:30	Mon–Fri	$18,300
4s	8:45–2:30	Mon–Fri	$24,700
K, 1st	8:30–2:45	Mon–Fri	$25,600

Extended hours. Afterschool program for 4s–1st graders until 4:30, and extended care until 5 PM, at an additional cost. early dropoff at 8 AM at no additional charge.

Program. Developmental. The program is based on the principle that all children want to learn and that all children learn best when actively involved and when learning is relevant to their lives.

The 3s and 4s programs emphasize developing socialization skills, strengthening a child's sense of self, and laying the groundwork for a successful academic path. A team of teachers creates an environment, both physical and social, in which children can absorb information and then use it in their play. There are opportunities for open-ended play as well as directed activities and thematic studies. Each room features areas for blockbuilding, dramatic play, cooking, water and sand play, art, science, quiet reading, and perceptual/manipulative materials.

The kindergarten and first-grade programs emphasize an integrated curriculum in language arts, math, social studies, and science. Notable is the comprehensive lanugage arts program and the extensive integration of music and Spanish into the curriculum.

There is a strong sense of community at the school, with visits between classrooms, school-wide assemblies, weekly sing-alongs, shared performances, visits from older Calhoun students, and, for first-grade students, trips to the ongoing building.

Admissions. The application fee is $50. Inquiries are from mid-August on. Call for an applications packet and apply promptly. (The school frequently wait-lists applications received after a critical number has been received.) Most children enter at age 3 or in kindergarten. Open houses are held in April, May, October and November. Interviews and school tours are arranged once the application is received. The child's interview consists of a small-group visit with a teacher. In a separate visit, parents attend an information session and tour followed by a meeting with the Lower School Director.

Notifications are sent in February for kindergarten and in March for the 3s and 4s. The school seeks students with academic potential who bring diversity in talent and background.

Tests. ERB testing is required for applicants beginning at the kindergarten level.

Class size. There are four classes at the 3s through 1st grade levels. Class size is ten to sixteen, with one teacher and one assistant in a class.

Staff. Calhoun teachers are experienced professionals, most with masters degrees in early childhood education. There are also specialists in music, theatre/movement, physical education, Spanish, and art. Calhoun maintains a strong professional developmental program. Many teachers are given grants for study leading to new curricula.

Facilities. A completely renovated five-story brownstone with spacious, light-filled classrooms, a library, gym, art room/wood shop, auditorium/theater, and outdoor play terrace.

Summer program. A full six-week program is offered to children in the community. Some part-time registration is available.

Separation. Phase-in is gradual, beginning with brief classroom sessions with small groups of children. Parents and teachers work closely together to ease the home-to-school transition.

Parent involvement. Parents are welcome in the classroom. They may, for example, share in holiday celebrations, cook with the children, offer their expertise in a curriculum area, or volunteer in the parent-run library. There is daily contact with teachers; formal conferences are scheduled twice a year and parents receive reports about their child's progress. The school offers workshops and monthly parent-education forums. There is a very active parents' association which sponsors social events and raises funds for special improvements.

Financial. There is a registration fee of $150 for new students. A deposit of $3,000 is required on signing the contract. Tuition is normally paid in two installments: June and January. A ten-month payment plan is also an option. Limited financial aid is available at the kindergarten level.

Transportation. Department of Education bus service information is available upon request.

Graduates. Students are automatically admitted to Calhoun's ongoing school, which goes through 12th grade.

Chartered. By the Board of Regents of the State University of New York.

Member. Early Steps, ERB, ISAAGNY, NAIS, NYSAIS, Prep for Prep, The Oliver Program.

Cathedral Parkway Towers Pre-School, Inc.

Ages: 2–6 yrs

Nonsectarian All-Day Care

125 West 109th Street, Suite Three (between Columbus and Amsterdam Avenues)
Zip: 10025
Tel: 749-0291

Established 1968
Sandra Hunt-Smith
Director

Enrollment: 35

School year. All year.

Ages	*Hours*	*Days*	*Tuition*
2–6	8:00–6:00	Mon–Fri	$230 weekly

*Children must be toilet-trained before enrollment.

Program. Eclectic. Cathedral Towers employs many Montessori teaching techniques and believes that its program is unique. Activities include arts and crafts; blockbuilding; sand and water play; prereading, prewriting, and premath activities; early science; play with puzzles, games and small play objects; music and dance; field trips; films; storytelling; and active outdoor play.

Admissions. There is a $10 application fee. Inquire any time. Interviews are scheduled only when positions are open, and children are accepted on a first-come basis. Parents may visit to see the school in operation and meet the director, with or without their children. They are notified of acceptance as soon as possible.

Class size. There is one class of 2s/3s and a mixed group of 4/5s.

Facilities. The preschool is located in rooms on the third floor of a residential high-rise. It also has use of a backyard play space.

Parent involvement. Three evening seminars are given each year. Parents are involved in fund-raising and help with field trips. Conferences are twice a year or as requested. Parents may visit any time.

Financial. Tuition is payable monthly or weekly. A $100 deposit is required; parents sign a contract for the full year. Parents more than a month in arrears must withdraw their child until payments are up-to-date. No financial aid is available.

Transportation. Parents bring their children directly to the classroom. No private bus service is available.

Graduates. Have attended Cathedral and Manhattan Country, as well as neighborhood public schools.

Chabad Early Learning Center

Ages: 18 mos–5 yrs

Jewish Nursery School

(Toddler Location)
101 West 92nd Street
(corner of Columbus)
(Location for 3–5 yrs)
160 W. 97th Street
Zip: 10025
Tel: 864-1207
Fax: 932-8987
E-Mail: celec@chabadwestside.org
Website: www.chabadwestside.org/celc

Rabbi Shlomo Kugel,
Executive Director
Pearl Stroh,
Educational Director

Enrollment: 160

School year. September through mid-June.

Ages	*Hours*	*Days*	*Tuition*
18 mo–2 yrs*	1:00–3:45	2–3 days	$6,600–8,610
2s	9:30–12:30 or 9:30–2:30	2 days	$6,600–10,650
3s	9:30–12:30 or 9:30–2:30	3 days	$8,310–10,650
4s	9:00–12:30 or 9:00–2:30	Mon–Thur	$9,870–12,090
5s	9:00–12:30 or 9:00–2:30	Mon–Fri (until 12: 30 on Fri)	$10,950–13,110

*Tuition includes daily hot lunch, except for afternoon toddler class, and field trips.

Program. Activity-based. The program carefully balances structured play and free play throughout the day. The children become acquainted with many mediums to encourage proper growth in cognitive, physical, and social-emotional areas. Structured play includes group activities such as stories, music, movement, discussion, and dramatic play. Free play involves manipulative toys, sand and water tables, clay, and an outdoor and indoor gym. Jewish holidays are taught through hands-on preparation and participation throughout the year. Readiness and self-help skills are naturally integrated throughout the curriculum to prepare the children for school. Each child's unique style of living and learning is valued and nurtured.

The school provides a daily lunch program. Mid-morning and afternoon snacks are also served, usually crackers or fruit.

Admissions. Inquiries begin at the end of October. Call for an application. Once an application is submitted the school will call to schedule an appointment to visit the school. Notification is usually within three weeks of school visit.

Class size. There are three toddler classes of ten, three 2s classes of twelve, two 3s classes of fifteen and two 4s classes of twenty. Each class has three teachers.

Staff. Each head teacher is certified in early childhood education and is usually a parent or comes from a large, close-knit family or both.

Facilities. Both locations of the Chabad Early Learning Center are newly renovated. Each have bright classrooms and a mobile library.

There is a covered play area and outdoor playgrounds with state of the art play equipment.

Separation. Teachers encourage parents to visit and stay in our classrooms as long as necessary for a smooth transition.

Parent involvement. The Parents Association is involved in fund-raising activities and coordinates parent support groups. Formal conferences are held twice yearly. Parents are welcome to visit the classroom for special activities and holidays.

Financial. Registration fee is $250
There is a $250 non-refundable registration fee payable upon enrollment and a one-time $1,000 Building Fund contribution payable per family. Parents are required to pay an additional $720 for Chabad's annual dinner, which is held in May or June.

Transportation. The school is happy to assist parents in forming carpools.

Graduates. Have gone on to Abraham Joshua Heschel, Manhattan Day School, Ramaz, Solomon Schechter, and other local public and private schools.

Children's Center of John Jay College of Criminal Justice Inc.

445 West 59th Street
Zip: 10019
Tel: 237-8310

William Altham,
Director

For John Jay students' children only.

All-day care. Serves 55 children. Ages: 6 mos–5 yrs, September through July. Tuition: $34 to $67 weekly. Parent education workshops are also offered.

Children of Today/Niños De Hoy

Ages: Infant–5 yrs

Nonsectarian Nursery School

Westside Locations:
131 West 72nd Street Studios
939 Eighth Avenue at 56th Street
520 Eighth Avenue at 36th Street
Administrative Offices:
117 West 70th Street, Suite 622
Tel: (212) 799-7810
Web site: www.hometown.aol.com/childtdy/myhomepage/index.html
E-Mail: childtdy@aol.com

Established 1998
Alena Gabriel,
Executive Director
Enrollment: 110

School year. Annual seasonally.

Ages	*Hours*	*Days*	*Tuition*
Birth–5	P/T AM or PM	Mon–Sun	$18 per hour*

Program. Developmental. The program integrates inquiry and directed learning with technology, language and creative arts. Children are encouraged to express themselves individually at age appropriate levels. Children learn in an exciting atmosphere of creative arts and materials with a multicultural flare.

Admissions. The application fee is $10. Parents need to call the admissions office at 70th Street to see the program. When families visit, children are encouraged to join in the group activities.

Staff. Each group has a head teacher/performing artist with a BA/BS or a masters degree, many in fine arts. An assistant teacher also works with the group if necessary. Groups are typically small and visiting teachers join classes depending on the interests and talents of the children. Teachers participate in on-going classes, seminars and workshops in early childhood education.

Facilities. The facilities vary from location to location, but they are "safe, sunny and healthy."

Summer Program. The program includes water play in a pool.

Separation. Separation is handled individually with care to meet the child's particular needs.

Parent Involvement. Parent involvement is welcomed, but not necessary.

Financial. Tuition is paid seasonally, and is not refundable.

Graduates. Have gone on to attend independent and public schools.

Claremont Children's School

Ages: 2–Pre-Kindergarten

Nonsectarian

747 Amsterdam Avenue
(between 96th & 97th Streets)
Zip: 10025
Tel: 865-4020
Fax: 865-3435
Website: www.claremontschool.org
E-Mail: info@claremontschool.org

Established 2001
Donna Cohen, Director
Laurie Uffner, Educational Director
Dianne Williams, Educational Director
Candida Gray, Admissions Coordinator
Enrollment: 180

School year. Mid-September through mid-June. Summer program from mid-June through July.

Ages	*Hours*	*Days*	*Tuition*
2s*	8:45-11:45	Tues Thurs	$7,000
	8:45-11:45	Mon Wed Fri	$8,750
3s	8:45-11:45	Mon-Fri	$14,000
	8:30-2:30	Mon-Fri	$18,000
4s	8:30-2:30**	Mon-Fri	$18,000

*Children must be two years of age by September 1st.
**Optional extended day.

Program. Traditional. This Upper West Side nursery school provides a comfortable setting, offers teacher directed activities with an enriched curriculum and is based on the philosophy that preschool aged children can learn and therefore should be taught. The main goal of the program is to provide an atmosphere that fosters a sense of community, encourages participation, and is structured so that children can function independently. Children learn both individually and in groups through activities that include block building, sand and water play, dramatic play, language arts, paint, clay, cooking, story time, outdoor play and trips into the community. In addition, the school has seven specialists on staff to teach music, art, science, gymnastics, yoga and library and computers.

Admissions. The application fee is $50
Inquiries begin in September. Parents must apply before taking a tour of the school. Children are seen later in playgroups of five. The school maintains a sibling priority policy.

Class size. There are six 2s classes with up to twelve children and three teachers and four 3s classes of up to sixteen children; the three 4s classes of up to twenty children have three teachers in each class.

Staff. The school's director has a clinical social work degree and the educational director has a masters in social work. All head teachers have masters degrees in early childhood education. Assistant teachers have some credits towards a bachelors degree or have a B.A. The school uses specialists, who are trained in their particular fields, to teach art, music, gymnastics, science, yoga, library, and computer. All teachers have previous experience working with children.

Facilities. Claremont Children's School is housed in a landmarked building that was formerly the East River Savings Bank. The renovated space has magnificent floor to ceiling windows, which provide natural light to the ten classrooms from both 96th Street and Amsterdam Avenue. In addition, there is a computer lab, a library, an art room, a gym/auditorium, a kitchen for children's cooking activities and a rooftop play area. The classrooms are set up as centers so that children can easily navigate their way around. Each classroom has an area for dramatic play, an art area, and a carpeted area for floor activities, circle and story time.

Summer program. Camp Claremont, which runs from mid-June through July.

Separation. For two-year-olds, teachers visit new students at home before school begins. Before the first day children visit the school. A parent or caregiver is expected to be available and on the premises during the first three weeks of school.

Parent involvement. The school encourages parental participation in the Parents Association. Each class has two class parents and parents are invited to celebrate holidays and cultural events in the school. Conferences are arranged twice yearly.

Financial. Claremont is a for profit school. Limited financial aid is available for the preschool program.

Transportation. The school is convenient to public transportation; the cross-town bus route at 96th Street, the Seventh and Eighth Avenue subway lines, and the uptown M7 and M11 buses stop right in front of the school. The school does not provide transportation.

Graduates. Attend approximately twenty-six different private and public schools including Brearley, Cathedral, Columbia Grammar, Dalton, Ethical Culture, Little Red School House, Trinity, Anderson, Hunter and the Region 10 Gifted and Talented Program.

Member. ATIS, ERB.

Columbus Park West Nursery School

Ages: 2.9–4.9 yrs

Nonsectarian Parent Cooperative

100 West 94th Street
(Corner of 94th Street
and Columbus Avenue)
Zip: 10025
Tel: 866-1567
Website: www.cpwn.org
E-Mail: admissions@cpwn.org

Established 1964
Emily Shapiro,
Director

Enrollment: 20

School year. Second week in September through the first week in June.

Ages	Hours	Days	Tuition
2.9–3.9	8:45–12:00	Mon–Fri*	$14,800
2.9–3.9	8:45–1:00		$11,500
3.9–4.9	8:45–2:30	Mon–Fri	$13,350

Toilet training is not necessary.
*All morning children leave at 12:00 on Fridays.

Program. Developmental. The school was started by neighborhood parents over forty years ago. The program provides a warm environment which supports children's emotional, social, cognitive, and motor development. Children are encouraged to express their thoughts and feelings and to exercise their newly developing competence with the support and guidance of caring adults. They are helped in learning to maintain their own individuality while functioning effectively as part of a group. The program is designed to provide a child-centered environment which enables the child to move comfortably out of the home environment and move on with confidence after nursery school.

Admissions. The application fee is $35. Inquiries are from September on. After receiving the application form, the school schedules tours for parents from late October through January.

Facilities. A large sunny community room on the second floor of a high-rise residential building. Tables offer a variety of art materials, puzzles, and other manipulatives, Play-doh and sand. There is also a generous block area, house and dress-up corner, painting easels, and a story corner. A large adjoining patio has outdoor play equipment. There is a full kitchen.

Summer program. Six weeks in June and July.

Separation. School starts in September on a staggered schedule. Separation proceeds gradually according to the needs of each child.

Parent involvement. As members of a co-op, parents serve on the school's board of directors, take responsibility for organizing fundraising activities or social events, and help with the daily setup of the outdoor play space. Parents run a preschool appropriate block fair and their occupations range from potters to journlists to bankers. Families also come together several times a year for events at the school to strengthen the sense of community.

Financial. A tuition deposit of ¼ of the year's tuition is due on signing the contract, and the remainder is payable in April, June, and October. The contract is for the full school year. Some scholarship aid is available.

Transportation. Most children come from within a ten-block radius, and are brought by parents or caregivers.

Graduates. Have gone on to Bank Street, Calhoun, Ethical Culture, Horace Mann, Manhattan Country, Trevor Day School, and others; half go on to public schools.

Columbus Pre-School and Gym

Ages: 2.5–4 yrs

Nonsectarian nursery school

606 Columbus Ave.
(89th Street)
Zip: 10024
Tel: 721-0090
Website: www.columbuspre-school.com

Established 1988
Marcia Lery,
Director
Enrollment: 110

School year. September through June.

Ages	*Hours*	*Days*	*Tuition*
2s	8:30–11:30	T, Th	$6,830
2s	8:30–11:30	M, W, F	$8,750
2–3s	1:00–4:00	Mon–Wed–Fri	$7,000
3s	8:30–12:00	Mon–Fri	$9,270
3/4s	8:30–1:00	Mon–Fri	$13,135
4s	8:30–2:30	Mon–Fri	$15,810

There is a nonrefundable application fee of $50.

Program. Focuses on the individual child as an active learner within a supportive learning environment that maintains developmentally appropriate standards. Children explore, manipulate, discover, question, make choices, problem-solve, and create as they participate in a variety of interactive play activities, music, science, and art experiences. In addition, the specialized gymnastic program offers every child the opportunity to develop physical strength and coordination as they learn a progression of basic gymnastic skills under the direction of qualified gymnastic instructors.

Facilities. Classrooms are bright and spacious. Children also have access to the outdoor rooftop play area, which is equipped to safely meet the needs of the growing, energetic young child.

Parent involvement. Parents are actively involved both in the classrooms and the school community. Parents volunteer to go on school trips and run the annual book fair and the toy and food drives, as well as the auction and school carnival.

Graduates. Go on to Bank Street, Calhoun, Cathedral, Claremont Prep, Collegiate, Columbia Grammar, Dwight, Ethical Culture, Riverdale Country, Trinity, Anderson, and other Gifted and Talented Programs.

The Family School West

Ages: 2.6–6

Nonsectarian Montessori Nursery School and Kindergarten

308 West 46th Street	Established 1989
(between Eighth and	Lesley Nan Haberman,
Ninth Avenues)	Founder and Headmistress
Zip: 10036	Enrollment: 40
Tel: 688-5950	
E-Mail: famschool@aol.com	

School year. September through June. Optional vacation programs are available.

Hours. 8:15–3:00, extended day program until 6:00.

Tuition. From two half days to five full days: $6,300–$12,500.

Program. This Montessori school is a satellite of The Family School located at 323 East 47th Street. The school cites its cultural and socio-economic diversity. The Montessori based program includes math, language, practical life, sensory play cultural arts and geography.

Admissions. See The Family Schools entry, page 53.

Class size. Including part and full-time students, there are approximately 40 students, with no more than 28 at a time, with 4 teachers and several part time specialists.

Facilities. Located in St. Luke's Lutheran Church, a landmark building in a former basketball gym, with high ceilings which proves a large open classroom, and a music room with a garden/play area.

Parent involvement. Parents are actively involved in all areas of the curriculum and in the life of the school. Class parents are knowledgeable and available throughout the year.

Graduates. Have gone on to many independent schools and selective public schools; see Family School.

Affiliation. American Montessori Society.

Member. ERB, ISAAGNY, The Parents League.

First Friends Preschool

Ages: 2–4.11 yrs

Nonsectarian

245 West 74th Street
(between Broadway and
West End Avenue)
Zip: 10023
Tel: 769-1088
E-Mail: ffpreschoolnyc@yahoo.com

Established 2001
Ruth Summer Keller,
Director

Enrollment: 90

School program. Mid-September through first week of June.

Summer program. June through early August.

Age	*Hours*	*Days*	*Tuition (Monthly)*
2–4	9:00–11:30, 11:30–3:30, 3:30–5:30	Tue, Thur, or Mon, Wed, Fri or Mon–Fri*	$925–2,100

*The school offers a variety of class sessions depending on the child's age and space availability.

Program. Developmental. Formerly, Ruthie's Toddler Time, this cozy and supportive nursery program offers children a variety of activities and materials that provide them with hands-on learning experiences in science, art, music, drama, movement, free play, cooking and literature. The school fosters a strong sense of community in a low-key atmosphere where individual differences are appreciated.

Admissions. The application fee is $25. Parents may call the school to schedule a visit, at which time they receive an application. An informal meeting for parents with the director is held along with a group tour of the school.

Class size. There are two classrooms, the size of the group varies depending on the ages of the children. One morning class consists of young two-year olds; older two and three year olds comprise the other morning group. The afternoon class consists of two and three year olds, four-year olds attend a pre-kindergarten program in the afternoon. The late session is for two and three year olds.

Staff. The school offers a high teacher to student ratio. Teachers are well trained and parents depend on their observations and judgements.

Facilities. The school has two classrooms, a kitchen and a resource room for small group activities. Children's artwork adorns the walls, there is age-appropriate furniture and play equipment. Children play at Riverside Park, two blocks away.

Separation. For most children this is their first school experience, the separation process is handled in a variety of ways to suit the needs of the child.

Financial. Limited scholarship aid is available.

Parent Involvement. After the separation period, parents are welcome as visitors and observers; they are also encouraged to volunteer in classrooms, either reading or telling stories. Some take dictation from the children, others who have special skills or hobbies are invited to perform demonstrations. Recently, a professional cellist performed and another parent taught orgami techniques.

Graduates. Have gone on to a variety of private and public schools including Abraham Joshua Heschel, Dalton, Calhoun, Columbia Grammar, Ethical Culture, West Side Montessori, St. David's, Marymount, Trinity, PS 87, PS 199 gifted and talented programs and The Anderson Program.

Affiliations: none.

43rd Street Kids Preschool, Inc.

Ages: 1–5 yrs

Nonsectarian Parent Cooperative

484 West 43rd Street
between 9th and
10th Avenues)
Zip: 10036
Tel: 564-7496
Website: www.43rdstreetkids.org
E-Mail: prekids43@aol.com

Established 1986
Nancy Lilienthal,
Director

Enrollment: 70

School year. September through early June.

Ages	*Hours*	*Days*	*Tuition***
1–2* (with parent)	9:00–10:30	Tues, Thurs	$1,425 yearly
2–3 (with parent)	9:10–11:00	M, W, F	$2,000 yearly
2.4–3	11:00–12:30	T, W, Th	$2,000 yearly
2.9–5	8:30–12:30	Mon–Fri	$5,575
	8:30–6:00	Mon–Fri	$10,825
	1:00–5:00	Mon–Fri	$5,250

*Children must be 1 by December 31st. Families are not required to join the co-op.

**The non-cooperative tuitions are 40 percent higher than those listed above.

Program: The school's director, Nancy Lilienthal, has given workshops on the Reggio Emilia schools in Italy*, and has been with the school from its inception. The Steps Classes, for one and two-year olds offer an environment where parents can meet and discuss their children's milestones while their children play with blocks, sand and water, age-appropriate art materials and listen to music. Two-year olds begin a separation process that takes about half the year for some and longer for others. The 2s classes are small and are supervised by a teacher and parent aide. The preschool group is larger with approximately 20 children per class, offering three and four year olds the opportunity to learn from pretend play, block building, games, art, manipulatives, puzzles and books.

The program is integrated and revolves around a social studies or science curriculum. Past projects have focused on fall harvest, families, celebrations and fish. Children discuss the program, sing, and read stories, as well as talk about social and emotional issues every day. They help with cleanup and choose daily jobs that include caring for the school's pets and plants. Children swim twice a week and play outside every day, weather permitting.

Admissions. The application fee is $30. Inquire from January 1st on. Parents should call to arrange a visit. There is no application deadline.

Class size. The parent/toddler groups each accommodate 13 children. The 2s program without parents accommodates 6. The preschool can accommodate twenty children, 2.9 to 5. The three staff

*See page 7, *supra*.

members in the preschool classes include a parent aide. Music and creative movement are taught. A mental health consultant visits monthly and is available to parents and staff and to speak on parenting issues.

Facilities. The school's large, bright, and modern space is donated by the Manhattan Plaza complex, where many families live. It consists of two rooms: one class and an extremely large rehearsal space, and indoor and outdoor play terraces, and a kitchen. Children swim twice weekly at the health club in the complex.

Summer program. Summer program from mid-June through July, for 3s through 8s.

Separation. Separation is handled individually. Parents are in the classroom as long as they are needed and withdraw gradually.

Parent involvement. Co-op parents assist in the classroom once a month, work two hours on a "work day" once a year and join one of many school committees. All families participate in fundraising.

Parents, some of whom have careers in entertainment, volunteer to perform in plays and concerts.

Financial. Families that are not residents of Manhattan Plaza pay a surcharge of $165. A deposit of 15 percent of tuition is required on signing the contract. The balance is paid in installments. Limited financial aid is available. Preschool families pay a $70 cleaning fee. Younger classes pay a $30 fee.

Transportation. None.

Graduates. Have attended Bank Street, Ethical Culture, and Hunter and UNIS, as well as public schools such as PS 9, Anderson, Midtown West and NEST. Many children enter public school Gifted and Talented programs.

The JCC in Manhattan
The Saul and Carole Zabar Nursery School

Ages: 2.9–5 years

Jewish Nursery School

334 Amsterdam Avenue
(at 76th Street); 2nd floor
Zip: 10023
Tel: 646 505-4400
Fax: 646 505-4388
Website: www.jccmanhattan.org/nurseryschool
E-Mail: tekelman@jccmanhattan.org

Established 2001
Ilana Ruskay-Kidd, Director
Felicia Gordon, Associate Director
Tara Ekelman, School Administrator
Enrollment: 184

School year. September through mid June. Summer program from the end of June through August.

*Ages**	*Hours*	*Days*	*Tuition*
2.7–2.11	8:45–11:30 or	M/W/F or	$9,870
		T/Th	$11,080
	12:30–3:00	M/W/F	$10,600
3**	8:45–12:00	Mon–Thurs	$14,070
	12:30–3:30	(Friday until 3)	
3.0–3.11	8:45-12:00	Mon–Fri	$12,257
4/s5s	8:45-2:45	Mon–Thurs	$18,340
		(Fri until 1:00)	

*Bridge Program for siblings only, 12:30–2 PM, Tu/Th, $5,500
**Extended 3s Program, $15,500.

Program. Connection is the philosophy of this nursery school housed in the newly built Jewish Community Center. Children are encouraged to learn ways to connect to one another, to their teachers, to Jewish life, and to their community.

JCC's parenting resource center offers parents and caregivers an opportunity to learn from one another, as well as from experts.

Admissions. The application fee is $75

Inquiries begin in September after Labor Day. The school offers tours during October and November. Applications are only given out on tours. Small group play sessions are scheduled on Sunday mornings in January and early February for prospective students. Acceptances are mailed at the beginning of March in accordance with ISAAGNY guidelines.

Class size. There are three classes of 2s with ten to twelve children, five classes of 3s with thirteen to seventeen children, and three classes of 4s/5s with sixteen children in each class. There are three teachers in each class.

Staff. Each class has one head teacher with, or studying for, a master's degree in the field of education, and two associate teachers.

Facilities. The JCC Nursery School is housed in a new eleven-story building with a separate and secure entrance and elevator dedicated to nursery school use only. The learning areas are flooded with natural light. The school has the exclusive use of the facilities of the Jewish Community Center, which include the gym and rooftop playground, during school hours.

Separation. The separation process at the beginning of the year is gradual and individual. During the first week of school parents stay in the classroom building. A parent or caregiver is expected to be available if needed for the first three weeks of school.

Afterschool programs. There is an extensive afterschool program, available to children ages four through thirteen, including homework help. Check website: www..jccmanhattan.org/afterschool.

Parent involvement. The nursery school welcomes parent involvement, both in the school and in the JCC. Parents serve on many committes, and attend birthday and other holiday celebrations at the JCC and in their child's classroom. There is an additional $375 in PA dues, payable with July's tuition.

Financial. Once enrolled in the JCC Nursery School, the parents automatically belong to the JCC. The school maintains a generous financial aid program.

Transportation. The school does not provide transportation. Most children are accompanied to school by a parent or caregiver.

Graduates. Former students have gone onto many private schools as well as selective public schools, Gifted and Talented programs and Jewish day schools.

Member. ERB, BJE.

La Escuelita

Ages: 2–5 yrs in the preschool program
12 mos to 3rd grade in the playgroups program
K–3rd grade in the afterschool program

302 West 91st Street
(at West End Avenue)
Zip: 10024

Tel: 877-1100
Fax: 917-591-3023
Website: www.laescuelitanyc.org
E-Mail: info@laescuelitanyc.org

Established 2003
Carolina Weissenbock,
Director
Jennifer Woodruff,
Co-Founder and Admissions Director
Jennifer Friedman,
Co-Founder and
Director of Development
Enrollment: 80
Playgroups: approximately 100
Afterschool program: approximately 20

School year. Early September to early June. Summer program for six weeks in June and July.

Ages	*Hours*	*Days*	*Tuition*
2s*	9–11:30 am	Mon–Fri	$11,200
2s	9–11:30 am	Mon Wed Fri	$6,700
2s	9–11:30 am	Tues Thurs	$4,500
2/3s	2–4:30 pm	Mon Wed Fri	$6,700
3s	9–12 pm	Mon–Fri	$11,200
3/4s	1:30–4:30 pm	Mon Wed Fri	$6,700
4s	9–2:30 pm	Mon–Fri	$14,400

*Children must be two years of age by September 1st.

Program. Developmental. The mission of La Escuelita is to support bilingualism in children from English and Spanish speaking families of one to eight years of age. The curriculum is based on an understanding of children's linguistic, social, physical, and cognitive development. Thematic units which emerge from children's interests provide organization for activities and concepts; for example, classes have studied transportation, restaurants, outer space, and babies. A music teacher instructs children once or twice a week. Academic skills, including early literacy and mathematical concepts, are introduced in a developmentally appropriate way at a child's individual level of understanding. There is a wide variety of linguistic backgrounds among the families of La Escuelita, including English-only, Spanish/English bilingual, and families who already speak other languages and are adding Spanish to their child's repertoire.

Admissions. Applications are available in September. Parents should plan to attend a small group information session in the fall, which combines a tour and an open house. A written application includes a page of contact information and short essays regarding what a parent is looking for in a preschool program. Upon receiving an application, a family meeting is scheduled with the director of admissions. Children are not observed or evaluated as part of the admissions process. Siblings are automatically accepted providing that the school meets their developmental needs. Legacies and children enrolled in La Escuelita's playgroups are given preference.

Class size. In the 2s and 2/3s classes there are eleven children with one head teacher and two assistant teachers. In the 3s class there are sixteen children, one head teacher and two assistant teachers. The 3/4s and 4s classrooms have 20 children each, with one head teacher and two assistant teachers in each classroom. There are also two floater teachers available to assist in the classrooms.

Staff. All head teachers have masters degrees in education or are completing masters degrees. Assistant teachers have a variety of backgrounds, including decades of working with young children and bachelors degrees in education or development. Several assistant teachers are working toward masters degrees. All teachers and assistant teachers are native Spanish speakers, and speak English as either a native or second language.

Facilities. La Escuelita is located on the Upper West Side in the newly renovated basement of the Greek Orthodox Church of the Annunciation. The classrooms are spacious with high ceilings and plenty of light, but with limited windows. Classrooms have centers for art, blocks, dramatic play, books, manipulatives, water, sand and music. The school is one block from the Hippo Playground in Riverside Park, which provides an area for outdoor activities. A large meeting room is used for parties and gross motor activities. An outside ramp and an elevator provide convenient access for strollers.

Summer program. A six-week summer session is held in June and July. It is similar to the regular preschool program with an expanded outdoor and sports component. Often, the entire school works on one theme such as "water" or "sports" and participates in activities together. Preschool children are given priority for enrollment, but children from other preschools are also welcome.

Afterschool programs. The afterschool program, which runs from 3:30 to 5 PM, is aimed toward children in kindergarten through third grade who are already bilingual. Many of the afterschool program students are La Escuelita graduates. Conversational Spanish is emphasized, with Spanish literacy skills introduced for children who are ready.

Separation. The separation process includes a teacher visit to the child's home in August, during which the teacher speaks to the child in his/her dominant language (Spanish or English). The first week of school has shortened days and smaller groups, and parents are expected to accompany children for the first few days at least. Thereafter, separation is discussed between a parent and the head teacher and proceeds at a pace appropriate for each child.

Parent involvement. Parents are welcome to participate in a variety of ways, including organizing social events, serving on the Parent Advisory Board, leading classroom activities, or organizing the school library. Parent participation is not expected, particularly for parents who are working full time.

Financial. Tuition assistance is available; families must fill out a financial statement which is reviewed by the school administration. Tuition reduction is offered at the time of acceptance and is first available to families continuing in the school who have a change in financial circumstances, and then to new families. The school [illegible] hat as a matter of preserving an atmosphere of equality for all families at La Escuelita, it does not engage in fundraising activities among its families. Some families contribute spontaneously, and all funds are directed toward tuition reduction for families who need it. Families who have connected at corporations or foundations are encouraged to present La Escuelita as a potential recipient.

Transportation. The 2/3 express and 1/9 local subway stop at 96th Street is three blocks from the school. The M104 Broadway bus and the 96th and 86th Street cross-town buses come within a few blocks of the school.

Graduates. La Escuelita has graduated only two classes. Students have gone to Dalton, Bank Street, Rodeph Sholom, St. Luke's, Manhattan Country School, The School at Columbia University, Special Music School, Hunter, Anderson, PS 199, PS 87 dual language program, PS 75 dual language program, PS 163 dual language program, Manhattan School for Children and Hamilton Heights Academy.

Member. ERB, NAEYC. La Escuelita is organizing the first consortium of dual language preschools.

Le Jardin a L'Ouest (The Garden of the West) French-American Preschool

Ages: 2.6–5 yrs

French-American Preschool

164 West 83rd Street (between Columbus and Amsterdam Avenues)
Zip: 10024
Tel: 362-2658
Fax: 362-3419
E-Mail: dbh@lejardinalouest.com
Website: www.lejardinalouest.com

Established 1972
John Arden Hiigli, Dominique Bordereaux-Hiigli, Co-Directors
Enrollment: 28

School year. September through June.

Ages	*Hours*	*Days*	*Tuition*
2s and 3s	9:30–11:45	Mon–Fri	$15,400
4s and 5s	1–4	Mon–Fri	$15,400

Program. Progressive. The teacher/directors, a husband and wife team, are Bank Street–trained and hold masters degrees in early childhood education. It is a French language immersion program. The children follow clear routines with plenty of of time for free play as well as organized activities they join at will. Above all, an early exposure to the French language and culture is offered to young children. Teachers are experienced and are native French speakers who also speak English fluently. Children discover that although they speak to teachers in English, teachers only respond in French; the environment is a bi-lingual one.

Admissions. The application fee is $50. Inquiries are from September until December. Parents must return the application form before arranging an interview. These are scheduled beginning November 1st. The application fee will be refunded if no interview is arranged.

All applicants who have been interviewed will be notified no later than March 15th. The school maintains a waiting list for openings that may occur in mid-year.

Class size. There are 12–14 children in each class.

Staff. There are two native French-speaking teachers to each class plus an assistant. The directors also participate in special projects throughout the year.

Facilities. The school is located on the bottom floor of a townhouse. (The directors live and have their offices directly above.) The two large rooms that are used by each class have a cathedral ceiling and walls lined with shelves holding materials. In addition, the children use a kitchen, and a well-equipped backyard playground. One of the rooms also functions as a children's art gallery, "La Jardin Galerie Inc."

Summer program. A four-week, 4 morning summer program is available for children 3 to 5 years old.

Separation. Parents or caregivers remain for the two-week period when school begins; then they must leave. Parents are encouraged to leave sooner if the child is ready.

Parent involvement. Parent/teacher conferences are scheduled once a year and whenever needed and also to discuss specific topics or issues. The school has an open door policy and parents are welcomed in the classrooms anytime to participate. Parents must attend the initial orientation before school begins in the fall and are expected to actively fundraise.

Financial. A nonrefundable deposit of $3,000 is due on signing the enrollment contract. The remaining balance is payable in two equal installments, May 1st and September 1st. An alternative payment plan is available. There are no scholarships, financial aid or sibling discounts.

Graduates. Have gone on to Brearley, Dalton, Dwight Calhoun, Collegiate, Columbia Grammar, Ethical Culture, Riverdale Country, Horace Mann, Hunter Elementary, Lyceé Français, Marymount, Spence, Trevor Day, Trinity.

Affiliations. The preschool is a Limited Liability Corporation (for profit); the art gallery is not-for-profit; ERB.

The Mandell School

Ages: 2–6 yrs

Nursery School and Kindergarten

128 West 95th Street,
Administrative Offices
127 West 94th Street; Pre-School
(between Amsterdam
and Columbus Avenues)
Zip: 10025
Tel: 222-1606
Fax: 665-0665
Website: www.mandellschool.org
E-Mail: admissions@mandellschool.org

Established 1939
Barbara Mandell Rowe,
Head of School
Gabriella Rowe,
Director
Myrna Stuart,
Asst. Director of Admissions
Enrollment: 60 Toddlers
120 Pre-Schoolers

School year. Second week in September through beginning of June. There is a Summer Program for all classes through the third week in July.

Ages	*Hours*	*Days*	*Tuition*
Younger 2s*	8:45–10:45; 12:30–2:30	Tues, Thurs	$8,500
Older 2s	8:45–11:15; 12:30–3:00	Mon, Wed, Fri	$13,800
Younger 3s**	8:30–11:45; 12:45–3:00	Mon–Fri	$15,650
Older 3s	8:30–11:45	Mon–Fri	$15,650
4s and 5s	8:30–2:45 (Fri until 12:45)	Mon–Fri	$17,450

*Children must be 2 by October 1.

**Children must be 3 by December 15 and must be toilet-trained.

Program. Traditional, Structured and Academic. The curriculum focuses on Good Citizenship, Academic Preparedness and Parental Involvement. It includes social studies, reading and math readiness, music, art, cooking, science and computers.

In the 2s program the children are provided with an educational environment designed to support their physical and developmental needs and enable a smooth transition from home to school. The primary focus in the 3s program is to promote independence, community and collaborative learning. The children are encouraged to move freely about the room choosing different activities while learning to share both their classroom and their ideas. The 3s classroom activities include block building, art projects, puzzles, manipulatives and skill work.

The 4s and 5s are divided into three sections based upon age. All sections are full-day. The first two sections of 4s and 5s are composed of children in their first year of Pre-K; the third section is especially for children with fall birthdays in their second year of Pre-K.

The curriculum for the 4s and 5s program is designed to further the development of each child with the goals of social, emotional and academic preparedness. This curriculum includes theme based social studies, large art projects, science experiments, math surveys, story writing and publishing.

The director of the school works closely with each family at every stage of the process of applying to ongoing schools. Children take the ERB at the school.

Admissions. The application fee is $60. Inquiries are accepted from the first working day after Labor Day. Applications should be returned promptly. The school interviews one-on-one with families, with either the director or admissions director; interviews are limited. Parents of already enrolled toddlers do not need to re-apply to the nursery school and may go on to the pre-nursery or toddler level.

The parents' probable compatibility with the rest of the parent body is a consideration. In January, an open house offers applicant parents an opportunity to speak to Mandell teachers and currently enrolled parents. Acceptance notifications are sent in accordance with ISAAGNY guidelines.

For Mandell Elementary, (kindergarten through fourth grade), the school will offer its families an early notification that is expected to include more than half of any class.

Facilities. A photo from 1939 of the school's founder, Barbara Mandell's father, greets you as you enter the reception area. The school occupies two brownstones. Classrooms are floor-through rooms with windows at front and back. The 3s classrooms are on the lower floor; the 4s and 5s classrooms are reached by a narrow staircase.

There is a 4,500 volume lending library as well as nine computers, a piano, and various musical instruments. There are two well-equipped play yards with a tree-house, jungle gym, bicycles and sandbox. The 4s and 5s bring their lunches, which are refrigerated. They have a half hour rest period with a video (education in nature is a favorite), and a half hour of quiet rest.

Separation. Parents stay with children as long as teachers feel it is necessary. This generally takes under two weeks for the threes and longer for the twos. Summer "bridge" programs are offered to ease separation.

Parent involvement. Parents serve on school committees and help with community-based activities, the library, scholarships and field trips. There are conferences twice a year or as requested.

Financial. Approximately $5,000 is due on signing the contract. The remainder is payable in mid-May and mid-October. Approximately 10 percent of the school receives some financial aid; all students are eligible.

Transportation. The children come from between 60th and 100th Streets on the East and West Sides. There is no private bus service.

Graduates. Have gone to Bank Street, Brearley, Browning, Chapin, Collegiate, Columbia Grammar, Convent of the Sacred Heart, Dalton, Ethical Culture, Hewitt, Hunter, Nightingale-Bamford, Riverdale, Spence St. Bernard's, St. David's.

Chartered. By the Board of Regents of the State University of New York.

Member. ERB, ISAAGNY. For profit.

Manhattan Day School

Ages: 2–5 yrs

Orthodox Yeshiva

310 West 75th Street
(between West End
Avenue and Riverside)
Zip: 10023

Tel: 376-6800
Fax: 376-6389

Established 1943
Rabbi Mordechai Besser,
Principal
Aviva Yablok,
Assistant Principal and
Director of Early Childhood
Enrollment: 120

School year. September through June. Day camp, end of June until August.

Ages	*Hours*	*Days*	*Tuition*
2s	8:45–12:45	2, 3, or 5 days	$4,800–10,400
3s	9:00–2:00 or 9:00–3:00	Mon–Fri	$9,900 $12,175
4s, 5s	9:00–3:00	Mon–Fri	$12,175

Children must be 3, 4, or 5 respectively by December 1st.

Program. Eclectic. The school is bilingual. Hebrew is introduced as part of the daily routine. The curriculum revolves around the Jewish holidays and the secular calendar and includes both free and teacher-directed activities such as painting, collage making, cooking, storytelling, singing, dancing and movement, and dramatic play. Activities are often coordinated with a classroom study unit. All children participate at their level in daily Tefila and Brachot. The development of social skills and the expression of feelings and ideas is also stressed. The children spend at least a half hour per day in the outdoor playground and forty-five minutes each day in the gym, and visit the library once a week. Fours have prereading, computers, math and science skills. The preschool program is committed to learning by doing, and to recognizing the unique learning styles and interests of each child. The 5s program develops a firm pre-academic foundation in both Judaic and general studies.

Admissions. The application fee is $250. Inquiries are from mid-September on. The school will mail application forms and a parent visit and private tour can be arranged. After visiting the school an appointment may then be made to meet the principal who may arrange a time to observe the applicant in a small group.

Class size. There are two classes for each age level, varying between fifteen to twenty-two children in each class.

Staff. All head teachers have masters in early childhood education. Assistants are present in each classroom and work individually with each child.

Facilities. Built in 1972, the school has a separate early childhood area, a gym with adjoining cafeteria, an art room, a fully-equipped science laboratory, a library and Bet Midrash, classrooms, and offices. Wide corridors serve as assembly spaces and extra learning areas. The outdoor playground is equipped with a large, multi-purpose climbing apparatus.

The school has a hot lunch program; preschoolers eat in their own lunchroom. Lunch is followed by Birkat Hamazon.

Separation. Children start school in small groups and in abbreviated sessions. Parents or other caregivers withdraw gradually.

Parent involvement. The Parents Association conducts social and fund-raising activities, coordinates the class-parents functions, and helps with extra-curricular activities. Conferences are twice yearly.

Financial. Tuition assistance is available, based on need. The school declines to break down the numerous fees charged along with tuition. Parents are expected to make a contribution of at least $1,500.

Transportation. The school services the area within a five-mile radius of the school. The youngest children come only from the midtown area. Private bus service can be arranged for the midtown area.

Graduates. To Yeshiva High Schools.

Affiliations. Torah U'Mesorah, BJE.

Metropolitan Montessori School

Ages: 2.9–12 yrs

Nonsectarian Montessori Nursery and Elementary School

325 West 85th Street (between West End and Riverside Drive)	Established 1964
Zip: 10024	Mary M. Gaines, Head of School
Tel: 579-5525	Jeanette Mall, Director of Admissions and Communications
Fax: 579-5526	Total enrollment: 200
Website: www.mnsny.org	Nursery enrollment: 90

School year. September through beginning of June. Seven-week summer program.

Ages	*Hours*	*Days*	*Tuition**
2.9–4.9 (Primary)	8:45–11:45	Mon–Fri	$17,600
4.9–6 (Extended Day)	8:45–2:45	Mon–Fri	$20,500
6–9 (Lower Elementary)	8:45–3:00	Mon–Fri	$21,100
9–12 (Upper Elementary)	8:45–3:15	Mon–Fri	$22,100

Children must be 2.9 in September. Toilet training is preferred but not necessary.

Program. Montessori. Metropolitan Montessori is a nursery school and an ongoing school as well. Specific concepts, properties, and skills are explored at the nursery level. However, children here are not required to follow strict sequences for using materials. Teachers are addressed formally and record the materials children are using in order to determine their skills levels. New materials are introduced in small groups or individually. Sometimes teachers will ask an older student to demonstrate a material's use to a younger one. As the children are ready, they will write, read, and learn basic math skills using materials that demonstrate these in tangible ways.

Head of School Ms. Mary Gaines has been at Metropolitan Montessori for a decade, and often greets students at the front door.

Nursery children exchange their shoes for slippers shortly after arrival. Usually the children work alone, either at tables or on little floor mats, which they roll up and put away when they are finished. Curriculum areas include practical life, sensory explorations, language (playing with sandpaper letters gives youngest children a swift introduction to phonics), and math skills, music (Orff instruments), science, geography, and art. Opportunities for social exchanges come with circle time, outdoor play, and at lunch. Field trips supplement classroom learning. Metropolitan Montessori holds a schoolwide Art Fair in the spring.

ERBs are given to students in grades one and above (but not to nursery or kindergarten age children) on the premises. About 10 percent of the children transfer to ongoing schools before graduation. The head of school is an active member of ISAAGNY and has close relationships with many ongoing school directors.

Admissions. The application fee is $40. Inquiries are accepted from mid-September on. The applications deadline is November 15th for children who will be age 2.9 to 10 years old, with preference given to younger children. After receiving an application, the admissions office calls parents to schedule two appointments, one for the parents' tour and another for the child's visit with a teacher. (One parent can be present in the classroom during the child's visit.) Parents tour the school with the admissions director in small groups followed by a question and answer session. Notifications of acceptance are given the second week of February for 5s applicants and the first week of March for younger children.

Class size. Nursery children are grouped into four mixed-age classes (2.9s through 5s) of about twenty-one to twenty-four children, each staffed with two teachers. Children remain in the same classroom for three years. Every head classroom teacher has Montessori training.

Facilities. The school's newly renovated carriage house is a state-of-the-art early childhood facility furnished with small tables, and chairs made of pastel painted wood or wickerwork. Baskets hold the children's rolled up mats. The white, immaculate floors reflect light flooding in through huge windows. There are plants and animals in each room.

The full-fledged kitchen provides an optional hot natural foods lunch for all-day students. There is also a gym, a ground-level playground with a climbing structure and a rooftop play area.

Afterschool program. Children can join after-school classes in movement, art, puppetry, chess, and sports-related activities. There is an additional charge for participation.

Separation. New children visit, one at a time, before the term begins to see the classroom and meet the teacher. During the first weeks of school, coffee is offered by the Parents Association. Parents may come to observe after six weeks. Two new children per week are introduced into each class of older children, allowing teachers to focus on them.

Parent involvement. Parents are very important to the school; they organize social events and serve as fund-raisers. There is a spring gala, a fall social and a parent run book fair.

Classroom observation and conferences are provided two times each year. A complete personal and academic profile for each child is prepared twice a year; parent/teacher conferences are held twice a year for nursery school children.

Transportation. Not available for nursery children, older children use public transportation.

Graduates. Have gone on to Brearley, Calhoun, Collegiate, Columbia Grammar, Convent of the Sacred Heart, Dalton, Delta Honors Program (a gifted and talented program), Ethical Culture, Fieldston, Friends Seminary, Horace Mann, Hunter College High School, Nightingale-Bamford, Riverdale Country School, Spence, Stuyvesant High School, Town School and Trinity.

Member. AMI, AMS, ERB, Early Steps, ISAAGNY, North American Montessori Teachers Association, NYSAIS.

Morningside Montessori School

Ages: 2–5.6 yrs

Nonsectarian Parent Cooperative

251 West 100th Street
(at West End Avenue)
Zip: 10025
Tel: 316-1555
Fax: 866-2128
Website: www.morningsidemontessori.org
E-Mail: info@morningsidemontessori.org

Established 1966
Susan Gemberling, Director
Deborah Gonzalez, Admissions Director
Enrollment: 90

School year. September through mid June. Summer Camp mid-June through August.

Ages	*Hours*	*Days*	*Tuition*
2.0–2.9	9:00–12:00	2 days	$7,325
2.9–5	9:00–12:00	3 days	$9,470
	9:00–12:30	Mon–Fri	$13,460
	1:30–4:30	Mon–Fri	$9,095
2.9–5	9:00–3:30	Mon–Fri	$16,080
2.9–5	8:00-6:00	Mon–Fri	$19,390

*Additional schedules are available.

Program. Modified Montessori. Morningside offers a secure nurturing environment where children can develop according to their own pace and interests in an organized and stimulating environment. Important features of the mixed-aged classrooms include Cuisenaire rods, blocks, Legos, computers, and fantasy-play materials, as well as Montessori materials. Activities are divided into sensory, practical life, and academic. Older children use workbooks. Skills demonstrations are given to the entire class. Descriptions of recent class projects are mounted on a bulletin board and later put into a loose-leaf binder. Visitors are invited to look through this detailed record, impressive for the volume and variety of activities.

Admissions. The application fee is $40. Inquiries are from mid-September on. The deadline for applications is mid-December. Call for an applications package and arrange a time to observe activities in a classroom. Parents may visit individually or in pairs. Once the application has been filed, parents call for an appointment for an interview. The child will be invited to participate in class activities with the parents present. Notifications are given by March. All children who apply are interviewed.

Class size. There is one toddler class of 12 children, one 3s class of fifteen children and four half-day mixed-age classes of twenty and sixteen children each, with a minimum of three teachers per class. Two classes share a Montessori teacher.

Facilities. Four old-fashioned classrooms on the sixth floor of Temple Ansche Chesed, reached by an automatic elevator. One is an extremely large room which has been divided into two separate classrooms. Two smaller rooms adjoin. Every classroom has building block areas. The toddler room has a high climbing loft. A teacher commented that a child's first task was to master climbing up and down the loft stairs. Two other preschools housed in the temple, Yaldaynu and the Purple Circle, share the large, well-equipped rooftop play area with Morningside.

Summer program. Camp Morningside offers an optional, full-time program as well as half-day programs, for children ages 2.6 through 6 years.

Separation. For the toddlers, this takes about four weeks. Parents stay in the classroom for the first week then stay outside classrooms by cubbies, then in the near-by kitchen. New children in the mixed-aged program are in school for the first two days by themselves before the old-timers join them. Parents may stay in the classroom for half an hour or so the first day or two, and can remain on the premises longer. New 3s can also join the summer program.

Parent involvement. The school is guided by a parent-elected and -run board of trustees. Parents are required to donate eighteen work hours (nine for a single parent) and sign a parent work agreement on joining. They may work in the classroom, although this is not encouraged. Committees include work coordination, fund-raising, social, maintenance, communications, scholarship, admissions, and personnel; or the work assignment may consist of office assistance or help on field trips.

Financial. A tuition deposit of $1,000, plus a $350 loan to the school, are required on signing the contract. The balance of the tuition is payable in two or eight installments. (There is a $100 charge for the latter.) Limited financial aid is available.

Transportation. No private bus service is available; parents bring their children to the classroom.

Graduates. Have gone on to Bank Street, Brearley, Cathedral, Calhoun, Collegiate, Columbia Grammar, Dalton, Ethical Culture, Friends, Fieldston, Horace Mann, Hunter, Manhattan Country, St. Hilda's and St. Hugh's, Town, and Trinity and local public schools.

Member. AMS, ERB, ISAAGNY.

The Nursery School at Habonim

Ages: 2.6–5 yrs

Jewish Nursery School

44 West 66th Street
(Between CPW and Columbus Avenue)
Zip: 10023
Tel: 787-5347
Fax: 595-3542
Website: www.habonim.net
E-Mail: rramsay@habonim.net

Established 1997
Barbara Kohn Katz, Director

Enrollment: 40

School year. Mid-September through mid-June. No summer program.

Ages	*Hours*	*Days*	*Tuition*
2s	9:00–11:30	Mon Wed Fri	$8200
3s*	8:45–12:00	Mon–Fri	$9600
4s	8:45–2:15	Mon–Thurs (Fri until 1:00)	$11,300

*There is an extended program 2 days a week, 12–2 PM.

Extended hours. Parents of 3s and 4s may drop children off early at 8:30. For 3s, extended days are available at an additional cost.

Program. The Nursery School is beginning its tenth year, and is dedicated to educating the youngest children of the community, in accordance with the desire of the synagogues founding members, all Holocaust survivors. The goal of the program is to foster self-esteem, social skills, and confidence as a learner. The atmosphere is nurturing with age appropriate activities that include manipulatives, block building, sand and water, arts and crafts, dramatic play, science, cooking and baking.

Children are introduced to Jewish traditions through weekly Shabbat and holiday celebrations, story time, music and food. The older children participate in short, age-appropriate Torah services in the Sanctuary.

Admissions. The application fee is $50. Inquiries begin in September. Parents may call to request an application. Upon receipt of application, the school will arrange for a tour of the school. Children are interviewed individually.

Class size. There are ten to twelve children in the 2s class and fifteen children in the 3s class with three teachers in each class. The 4s class has up to eighteen children in the class with two teachers.

Staff. Each class has one head teacher, and one or two assistants or co-teachers. There is a movement specialist and a music teacher who meet with all the children once a week. A school psychologist is on staff.

Facilities. Located in three bright classrooms on the ground floor of the synagogue. There is an outdoor play area with climbing apparatus, large wooden blocks, and a large multi purpose room that is used daily and for movement. The school also uses the sanctuary and the kitchen of the synagogue.

Separation. The separation procedure at the beginning of the school year is gradual and individual.

Parent involvement. Parents work in the library and are involved with fundraising events. Formal conferences are scheduled in the fall and spring, and as needed. The school psychologist is available for consultation when needed.

Financial. Tuition includes synagogue membership, and High Holy Day tickets for the immediate family.

Transportation. The school does not provide transportation. Most children are accompanied to school by a parent or caregiver.

Graduates. Have gone to Abraham Joshua Heschel, Brearley, Calhoun, Columbia Grammar, Dwight, Ethical Culture, Hewitt, Horace Mann, Hunter, Ramaz, Rodeph Sholom, Soloman Schechter, as well as a variety of public elementary schools.

Affiliations. Congregation Habonim

Member. ERB. Applying for ISAAGNY.

Twin Parks Park West Montessori School (part of Twin Parks Schools formerly Park West Montessori School)

Ages 3 mos–6 yrs

435 Central Park West
(between 103rd and
104 Streets)
Zip: 10025
Tel: 678-6072
Fax: 678-1998
Website: www.twinparks.org
Park West E-Mail: pwoffice@twinparks.org

Dr. Kathy Roemer,
Director
Shelly McBuire
Director of Admissions
Enrollment: 150

School year. September through June. Summer program, July and August.

Ages	*Hours*	*Days*	*Tuition*
3 mos–1.5 yrs	8:00–6:00	Mon–Fri	$16,760
2.9–5 yrs	8:00–6:00	Mon–Fri	$13,000
1.6–2.8	8:00–6:00	Mon Wed Fri	$14,380
1.6–2.8	8:00–6:00	Tues Thur	$10,880
1.6–2.8	9:00–3:00	Mon–Fri	$17,880

Birthday cut-off is September 1st. Additional scheduling options available.

Program. Developmentally based Montessori program. Park West Montessori, one of the Twin Parks Montessori schools, offers a flexible curriculum in a homelike setting that is tailored to meet the individual needs of each child. Activities are chosen to foster the joy of learning, as well as cooperation. Children work at their own pace, alone or with others.

In the infant program, babies learn by responding to gentle touch and move freely as they interact with their environment. Materials are displayed on low, open shelves and on floor mats, all within reach of even the youngest child.

The toddler class focuses on trust, separation, independence and self-control. Toddlers learn to use verbal and non-verbal skills to resolve social conflicts as well as to facilitate toilet training.

In the early childhood class the aim is to cultivate the child's natural desire to learn. Children use manipulatives and are encouraged to make choices, work independently and become capable and confident learners. Music and physical education are scheduled daily; for art, children use paint, clay, paste and colors. Although the school offers individualized instruction, cooperative learning is encouraged.

Admissions. The application fee is $25. After a completed application is received, the director of admissions will call to schedule an appointment to tour classes and discuss the program. There is a meeting/interview for three-and four-year-old applicants.

Class size. There is one infant class with twelve children; four toddler classes with ten children in each, and three early childhood classes with up to twenty children. The teacher to child ratio is 1:3 for infants; 1:5 for toddlers, and 1:8 for early childhood.

Facilities. The school is located on the ground floor of an apartment building. It has a rear play yard with a climbing structure, tricycles and seesaw. The children use Central Park, which is across the street, for outdoor playtime daily. The school has a separate playroom, library and an indoor gym.

Summer program. There is a summer program during July and August.

Separation. During the first week of school, parents/caregivers are expected to remain nearby until their child has adjusted comfortably.

Parent involvement. Parents are invited to read in the classrooms and share their skills and family traditions and attend field trips. The teachers send home a weekly notebook/portfolio to keep parents informed of the events of the week. There are two parent-teacher conferences each year. Social events include potluck dinners, coffee chats, parent education nights, grandparents day, an ice cream social, and pick-up-in-the-park days. Parents Voice, made up of parent representatives from each class, meets monthly with the director.

Financial. There is a $500 nonrefundable annual tuition deposit, which also serves as a materials fee. Quarterly or monthly payment schedules are available.

Transportation. No private bus service is available.

Graduates. Have gone on to public school gifted and talented programs and independent schools.

Affiliation. AMS, NAEYC, and the Middle States Commission on Elementary Schools.

The Poppyseed Pre-Nursery Inc.

Ages: 8 mos.–3.5 yrs

Nonsectarian Pre-Nursery School

424 West End Avenue (corner of 81st Street)
Zip: 10024
Tel: 877-7614

Established 1986
Gail Ionescu, Director
Enrollment: 120

School year. September through June; summer program June and July.

Ages	*Hours*	*Days*	*Tuition*
8 mos.–1 yr	1 hour	1 day	$390/semester
1–1.5 yrs	2 hours	2 days	$3,195/year
1.6–3.5 yrs	2 hours	2 days	$3,195/year
1.6–3.5 yrs	2 hours	3 days	$4,495/year

*Semesters are: October through February and February through May.

Program. The program offers a gradual bridge between home and school with its small, brief classes. Age appropriate activities include, music, art through brush and finger painting, collages, clay and Play-doh, waterplay and cooking. A mini gym that's fully equipped keeps kids fit rain or shine.

Class size. The center serves up to fourteen children at a time. There are two staff members per class (in addition to the parents and caregivers).

Admissions. Call for an application by January; inquiries are ongoing.

Facilities. A large carpeted play room with a variety of toys (train set, Duplo table, dolls, kitchen area, cars and trucks to ride in), a piano, and several musical instruments. There is also a well-equipped mini-gym (including a ball pit and slide), a snack area, and an arts-and-crafts area.

Separation. Parents or caregivers are required to remain with the children and participate in the program.

Financial. Payment is made in three installments. There is a $25 or $50 registration fee depending on which class is chosen.

Summer program. Tuesdays, Wednesdays and Thursdays for two hours for children ages 1 year through 3.5 years.

Purple Circle Day Care Center, Inc.

Ages: 2–6 yrs

Nonsectarian Parent Cooperative

251 West 100th Street
(at West End Avenue)
Zip: 10025
Tel: 866-9193
Website: www.purple-circle.org

Established 1971
Eleni Karas,
Director
Enrollment: 60

School year. Open fifty weeks a year.

Ages	*Hours*	*Days*	*Tuition*
2–5	8:30–1:50	Mon–Fri	$13,778
2–5	8:30–4:00	Mon–Fri	$16,806
2–5	8:30–6:00	Mon–Fri	$19,756
2–5	2:30–6:00	Mon–Fri	$10,914

Program. Eclectic. A community-based diverse program within a nurturing environment, blending cognitive, emotional, social and physical development. Teachers focus on individual interests and strengths using space, time and materials that are geared for problem solving and investigating. Children explore their ideas through story-telling, blocks, sand, water, clay, books, drawing, writing, music, movement, neighborhood trips, dramatic play, painting, and cooking.

Admissions. The application fee is $35. Inquire from September on. Tours are scheduled upon receipt of application. Children are not interviewed. Notifications are sent in early March, and parents are asked to reply within one week.

Class size. There are four groups of 2s, 3s and 4s. Each has three teachers.

Facilities. Two sunny and spacious classrooms on the fourth floor and two on the fifth floor of Temple Ansche Chesed and a large playroof. Children also use local parks and library. They bring their own lunches; morning and afternoon healthy snacks are provided.

Separation. Teachers make home visits with families before school starts, for a gradual and more positive separation process. New children are introduced over a two to three week period in gradually lengthening sessions. Parents remain in the classroom for several days, then move to the hall, and then may leave the floor briefly for refreshments with other parents downstairs. From then on, the process is handled at whatever pace each child and parent seems to need.

Parent involvement. The school sees itself as a close community. Parents contribute to the running of the school in a variety of ways. Opportunities include serving on the board of directors, participating in the physical upkeep of the school, fundraising, or donating time or services to the school.

Financial. A deposit of approximately 11 percent of tuition is required on signing the full-year contract. Half of this is refundable until May 30th. The balance is paid in ten monthly installments. There is limited financial aid. There is a tuition reimbursement of $200 each for teachers who are pursuing their undergraduate or graduate degrees. There is also about $2,000 available for general staff development.

Transportation. Children come from 70th to 145th Streets on the Upper West Side, and are brought by their parents or caregivers.

Graduates. Have gone on to Abraham Joseph Heschel, Bank Street, Calhoun, Cathedral, Chapin, Columbia Grammar, Dalton, Ethical Culture, Manhattan Country, Trevor Day, Solomon Schechter, Saint Ann's, as well as public schools including The Anderson Program in District 3 and Hunter Elementary.

River School

Ages: 2 months–5.6 yrs

Nonsectarian Nursery School

75 West End Avenue
(at 63rd Street)
Zip: 10023
Tel: 707-8300
Fax: 707-8600
Website: www.theriverschool.com
E-Mail: info@theriverschool.com

Established 1989
Jane Kresch,
Director
Enrollment: 100

School year. All year.

Ages	*Hours*	*Days*	*Tuition*
2 mos–18 mos	7:30–7:00	Mon–Fri	$850–$1,865*
18 mos –3.5 yrs	7:30–7:00	Mon–Fri	$800–$1,735*
3.5 yrs–5.5 yrs	7:30–7:00	Mon–Fri	$760–$1,600*

*Children may be enrolled for 2, 3 or 5 days per week.

Program. Developmental. The program is highly nurturing and emphasizes creative participation in the learning process. Children explore their environment via active play involving art, music, dance, literature, drama and sports. Outside instructors in swimming, music, art and frequent field trips enrich the regular curriculum. Age appropriate literacy experiences and the encouragement of a relaxed social milieu are regarded as the essential foundation of the learning process.

Admissions. There is no application fee. Applications are accepted on an ongoing basis and admission is offered as space becomes available. Parents are welcome to stop in or make an appointment. Siblings are given priority.

Class size. There are eight infants, eleven toddlers, and 12 to 16 preschoolers per individual class.

Facilities. The school occupies a dramatic 7,000-square-foot, light-filled ground floor space located on a cul-de-sac with a park and playground directly adjacent. Creative design integrates library, computer areas and an indoor amphitheatre with comfortable classrooms, each with its own bathroom. An active gym space and swimming pool in the building complement the convenient outdoor play space.

Summer program. The summer program for preschoolers includes field trips, swimming, sports, and special projects involving science, nature, art and dramatic play.

Separation. The separation process is individualized to suit the needs of the child. It can range from just a few days up to two weeks. Parents are encouraged to stay until the child feels at ease with the environment.

Parent involvement. Parents are encouraged to volunteer as chaperones on class trips. Families come in to read stories, talk about their culture or to participate in school activities. Parent workshops with guest speakers are offered throughout the year.

Financial. A deposit of the first month's tuition is required to reserve a space. Tuition is payable monthly. A ten percent discount is offered for siblings.

Transportation. The school is conventiently located near public transportation: the M104 bus and the 1/9 trains are located on Broadway. The school does not provide transportation.

Graduates. Have gone on to Ethical Culture, Columbia Grammar, Chapin, Nightingale, Spence, Bank Street, Cathedral, Calhoun and Dwight. Many children attend parochial school or public schools, including Anderson, Hunter, PS 199, PS 87 and various Gifted and Talented programs.

River-Park Nursery School and Kindergarten

Ages: 2.8–5 yrs

Family Cooperative

711 Amsterdam Avenue (at 94th Street) — Established 1967
Zip: 10025 — Desiré J. Ford, Director
Tel: 663-1205 — Maria Nunziata, Co-Director
Fax: 663-1205 — Enrollment: 40
Website: www.riverparknurseryschool.com
E-Mail: riverparksns@earthlink.net

School year. September through mid-June.

Ages	*Hours*	*Days*	*Tuition*
2.8–3s	8:45–11:30	Mon–Fri	$7,980
3s	8:45–1:00	Mon–Fri	$9,345
3s–4s	8:45–4:00	Mon–Fri	$14,175
4s	1:00–4:00	Mon–Fri	$7,980
4s	11:30–4:00	Mon–Fri	$9,345

There is a $350 equipment and emergency fund fee; and a furniture moving fee of $50.

Extended hours. Available at 8:00 AM until 6:00 PM.

Program. Eclectic. The school's philosophy stresses "meeting each child where he or she is and helping them grow and develop from there," encouraging exploration at their own pace without undue pressure. With a strongly diversified student body, the staff particularly emphasizes a non-sexist, non-racist approach, the keystones of which are "trust, dignity, and respect for yourself," and also for other people. Self-expression in the creative arts as well as reading and math readiness anchor the curriculum. Teachers use the term "sciencing," which means learning through investigation. The staff encourages children to learn from each other's diverse backgrounds as well as from the formal program.

Admissions. The application fee is $40. Inquiries are from September on. After applying, parents tour the school with their child, who is invited to participate in that day's activities. Testing runs counter to the school's philosophy and is thus not required. The school is interested in families that will benefit from participating in a cooperative and that will contribute to this "extended family" (now extended to two generations). Families are accepted on a first-come, first-served basis, so parents are encouraged to file applications as soon as possible.

Class size. The school day is divided into half-day sessions for 3s in the morning and 4s in the afternoon. Lunch can be added to the half-day program for a slightly longer day. Approximately one-half of the students are in the full-day program. There are 14 to 18 children in the morning and afternoon sessions, with two teachers and two teacher directors working in the classroom.

Staff. All teachers have a minimum of 20 years teaching experience, are certified early childhood educators and/or have a masters degree in early childhood education. The school also draws student teachers and teaching assistants from a number of New York City educational institutions.

Facilities. The spacious ground-floor area, (the size of three classrooms), is adjoined by a large, private outdoor play yard. The bright, airy classroom has high ceilings and two walls of floor-to-ceiling windows. It includes a full kitchen, which is used frequently for children's projects. Both the indoor and outdoor spaces permit even the most physically active child to use his/her energies constructively.

Separation. A teacher visits each child's home before school begins to develop a one-to-one relationship. The first two weeks of school are adjustment weeks. As with all issues, the staff works closely with parents to allow the child to adjust as his or her own pace.

Parent involvement. Each family contributes 35 hours of service during the school year. The River Park co-op has worked for over thirty-nine years, and many alums return to the annual International Dinner in May to meet and greet former teachers and friends. The school sponsors a bazaar in December, the proceeds of which benefit the school fund. There are at least two parent-teacher conferences annually, monthly parent-staff meetings, and special programs focusing on topics such as "how to apply to elementary schools."

Financial. A deposit of 25 percent of the annual tuition is due upon signing the contract. The remaining payments are due August 1 and

December 1. Limited scholarship assistance is available. The deadline for scholarship applications is December 15th. In addition, a non-refundable equipment fee of $225, and a $500 reservation which is deducted from the first tuition payment, is required.

Transportation. Children come from many Manhattan neighborhoods and other boroughs. No private bus service is available, but the school is located at the junction of many city bus and subway lines.

Graduates. Alumni are represented at a broad range of both public and private schools throughout Manhattan.

Chartered. By the Board of Regents of the State University of New York.

Riverside Montessori (Part of Twin Parks Schools)

Ages: 3 mos–5 yrs

Nonsectarian Montessori Nursery

202 Riverside Drive (South corner of West 93rd Street)
Zip: 10025
Tel: 665-1600
Fax: 665-1775
Website: www.twinparks.org
E-Mail: rmoffice@twinparks.org

Established 1997

Enrollment: 111

School year. September through June. Summer Session from mid July through August.

Ages	*Hours*	*Days*	*Tuition*
3mo–20 mos	8:00-3:30	Tues/Thurs	$9,160
		Mon/Wed/Fri	$12,660
		Mon-Fri	$16,900
1s/2s	8:00-3:30	Tues/Thurs	$8,080
(Toddler I)		Mon/Wed/Fri	$16,580
		Mon-Fri	$15,580
20 mos–3 years	8:00-3:30	Tues/Thurs	$7,900
& 3s/4s (Preschool)		Mon/Wed/Fri	$11,200
		Mon-Fri	$15,360

Aftercare is included in the tuition.

Program. Progressive. Children are free to work at their own pace, alone or with others. In the infant program, babies learn by responding to gentle touch and move freely as they interact with their environment. The school does not use high chairs, swings, or activity chairs. After six months, babies sleep in custom made infant beds, not cribs. The toddler class focuses on the tasks of trust, separation, independence and self-control. Children are guided towards appropriate behaviors in a non-judgmental atmosphere where they can learn the balance between freedom and limits. Toddlers learn to use verbal and non-verbal skills to resolve social conflicts as well as to facilitate toilet training.

In the preschool class children use manipulatives and are encouraged to make choices and work independently. Music and physical education is given daily; for art children use paint, clay, paste and colors. Although individualized instruction is emphasized, cooperative learning is encouraged.

Admissions. The application fee is $25

Inquiries are on-going. The school maintains an active waiting list. Upon receipt of the completed application, the school will call to make an appointment for a class tour, and a meeting with the director. Tours are held once a month. There are no tours in September. An opportunity to meet with a child two or older will be arranged at a later date. Notifications are mailed in late March for September enrollment, or within two weeks for more immediate enrollment.

Class size. There are eight to ten children in the infant and toddler classes and sixteen to twenty children in the preschool classes with two teachers in each class, plus one floater among a few preschool classes.

Staff. All teachers hold advanced degrees. The school pays for professional development courses and will sponsor any teacher or aide for Montessori certification at the College of New Rochelle.

Facilities. Located on two floors of a residential building on 93rd Street and Riverside Drive, the beautifully renovated, bright classrooms offer a comfortable, carefully prepared, homelike setting. Materials are displayed on low, open shelves and on floor mats, all within easy reach of even the youngest child. The school recently finished constructing a full size gymnasium as well as an infant playroom.

Separation. The separation process at the beginning of the school year is gradual and individual.

Parent involvement. Most of the parents are full time professionals and at least 40 per cent of the mothers hold part-time positions. Parents are present in the school on a daily basis and often socialize at day's end or on weekends. There is a Parents Voice that meets once during the school year. Parents participate in the school's snack program and are very supportive.

Financial. The reservation fee is $500, and is not applicable toward tuition which is due upon signing of the contract. In addition, a deposit of the first and last month's tuition is also required at this time.

Transportation. None

Graduates. Have gone on to Bank Street, Calhoun, Columbia Grammar, Dalton, Ethical Culture, Hunter, Horace Mann, Manhattan Day School, Riverdale, Rodeph Shalom, Saint Ann's, UNIS, The Anderson Program, and PS 9, PS 87, PS 166 and PS 163.

Affiliations. AMS.

Member. ERB.

Rocking Horse Nursery School

Ages: 2.6–5 yrs

Nonsectarian Nursery School

120 West 69th Street
(between Broadway and Columbus Avenue)
Zip: 10023
Tel: 874-9269
Fax: 877-5783
Website: rockinghorsenurseryschool.org
E-Mail: guyjoe@aol.com

Established 1981
Judy McGerald, Director
Andy Marcus, Co-Director
Enrollment: 30

School year. September through May. Summer program runs mid-June to mid-August.

Ages	*Hours*	*Days*	*Tuition*
2.6/3s	9:00–12:30	Tues Thurs	$3,291
3/4s	9:00–12:30	Mon Wed Fri	$4,782
4/5s	9:00–12:30	Mon–Fri	$7,074

Program. Eclectic. The school's objectives are to facilitate the development of good social relationships, to nurture self-esteem, and to stimulate cognitive growth and creativity in an intimate environment. Its multifaceted program offers such activities as art, dance, music, cooking, etc., integrated around particular topics. Topics studied include Native American culture, celebrations around the world, families, the school's city block, and the weather. One focus of the curriculum is an in-depth use of children's literature—poetry, tales, fables, Native American myths, as well as classic children's books—to instill a love of language and learning. Another important strand of curriculum is the arts, which get children to open up to their own creative and expressive potentials. The school's art program was developed by the director's husband, Andy Marcus, a professional visual artist.

Parents linger in the morning as their schedule permits. One mother said, "There's a wonderful free, easy-going atmosphere here combined with attention to the children as individuals and lots of things for them to do. I also like its varied population—there are mixed-race kids and kids who are adopted here."

Admissions. The application fee is $40. Inquiries are from mid-September on. Families may visit with their child. During the visit teachers are available to answer school-related questions and children may take part in all classroom activities. A Parent Handbook contains detailed information about the school. Notifications are sent between mid-February and mid-March.

Class size. There is one mixed-age class each morning, varying in size from sixteen to twenty depending on the age of the majority of the children in the class. There are three teachers at all times. Three specialist instructors teach dance, drama and yoga.

Staff. The director is board-certified by the New York State Department of Education. The co-director and assistant teacher both hold advanced degrees.

Facilities. Located in the undercroft of a landmark church with a lawn and garden. The spacious main classroom (40 by 60 feet) is divided into activity areas which are rearranged for large-group activities such as dancing. There is a fully equipped kitchen for cooking projects, an outdoor yard with climbing equipment, a playhouse, and two large trees.

Summer program. From mid-June through the first weeks of August, open to the community. A twelve-foot-wide wading pool is set up in the play yard and many other outdoor activities are offered. Children may attend on a weekly basis.

Separation. Each child is an individual and each adjusts at a different pace. School begins with shortened sessions that lengthen gradually over a two-week period. Parents or caregivers stay in the classroom until the children are comfortable with their leaving.

Parental involvement. Parent involvement is encouraged in a variety of ways. Parents make up the board of directors and actively organize social events as well as fundraising drives. Parents are welcome to visit at any time and also free to share their expertise with the children in the classroom. Social events (a wine and cheese party, potluck dinner, spring picnic) are held throughout the year. A monthly newsletter informs families about curriculum topics and projects.

Financial. A deposit of two months' tuition is required upon acceptance of a place; a third month's tuition is due on the first day of school. The remaining tuition is due December 1 and March 1.

Transportation. Most children come from the Upper West Side with a parent or caregiver.

Graduates. Have gone on to a variety of public and private schools, including Calhoun, Columbia Grammar, Ethical Culture, Hunter, Midtown West, and The Anderson Program and PS 87 and 199.

Member. Child Care Inc., Parents League.

The Rodeph Sholom School

Ages 2.5–14 yrs

Jewish Nursery and Elementary School

10 West 84th Street
(between Central Park West
and Columbus Avenue)
Zip: 10024
Tel: 362-8769
Fax: 874-0117
Website: www.rodephsholomschool.org
Total enrollment: 700

Established 1958
Mr. Paul Druzinsky,
Acting Headmaster
Ms. Susan Weiss Newman,
Director, Nursery Division
Ms. Alexandra Mustonen,
Admissions Director
Nursery enrollment: 130

School year. September through mid-June.

Ages	*Hours*	*Days*	*Tuition*
2s*	9:00–11:30	2, 3 days	$9,250 or $10,350
2s	12:30–3:00	M,Tu,W,Th	$11,450
3s	8:45–11:45	Mon–Fri	$12,600
3s	8:45–1:00	Mon–Fri	$15,900
4s (pre-K)	8:45–2:45	Mon–Fri	$23,550
5s (kindergarten)	8:15–3:15	Mon–Fri	$26,250

*Children need not be toilet trained. All families in the school are automatically members of Congregation Rodeph Sholom. Extended hours are available to 5:00 beginning with pre-kindergarten.

Program. Eclectic. The school offers a program that aims to foster both self-expression and cooperative behavior. In the nursery division, children explore a wide variety of materials and activities such as block building, dramatic play, sand and water, art, cooking, planting, manipulatives and music. In Pre-K, students are offered a curriculum which includes math, writing and reading readiness. Each Pre-K classroom has a computer with age-appropriate software programs. Children are introduced to Jewish traditions through weekly Shabbat and holiday celebrations, songs games and blessings. All classes, starting in nursery, are taught about *tzedakah** through city-wide programs, such as Common Cents, a penny harvest that collects coins for various charitable organizations.

Admissions. The application fee is $60. Inquiries are from Labor Day on. Call for an application package and to schedule a group tour. After the application is filed, call for a family interview and tour in November. Twos are interviewed with their parents; 3s participate in playgroup interviews. Once enrolled at Rodeph Sholom students may continue through eighth grade. The school welcomes children of all faiths.

Class size. There are six 2s classes of ten, six 3s classes of up to fifteen, six pre-K classes of up to eighteen, and four kindergarten classes of about eighteen. Each class has two teachers.

Facilities. The campus comprises three buildings: the Temple building at 7 West 83rd Street houses the 2s and 3s; 10 West 84th Street houses the pre-K, kindergarten, and 1st grade; 168 West 79th Street houses grades 2–8. In Nursery, there is a fully equipped roof playground and gym. Pre-K and Kindergarten students travel outside their classrooms for specials, including physical education.

Summer program. Summer camp, located in the 7 West 83rd Street building, runs from late June through mid-August.

Separation. Before school begins, teachers visit the family at home. If the need arises, parents or caregivers may be expected to be on the premises for two or three weeks. School begins with small, staggered classes and shortened sessions.

*Charity

Parent involvement. The school encourages strong communication among parents, teachers, and administration. An active PTA organizes fundraising events and parent outreach programs. All parents are automatically granted membership in Congregation Rodeph Sholom, including reserved High Holy Day seats.

Financial. A $3,500 nonrefundable deposit is due on acceptance. Parents with more than one child in the school receive a $500 tuition reduction per sibling for each child beyond the first. Financial aid is available.

Transportation. Private bus service can be arranged for all children. Elementary children can use Department of Education buses.

Graduates. Eighth-grade graduates go on to both private and public schools, including Brearley, Bronx High School of Science, Collegiate, Columbia Prep, Dalton, Fieldston, Heschel, Horace Mann, Hunter, LaGuardia High School of the Performing Arts, Riverdale, Stuyvesant High School, and Trevor Day.

Affiliations. Congregation Rodeph Sholom.

Member. ERB, ISAAGNY, NYSAIS.

Stephen Wise Free Synagogue Early Childhood Center

Ages: 1.6–5 yrs

Jewish

30 West 68th Street (between Central Park West and Columbus Avenue)	Established 1983
Zip: 10023	Lori Schneider, Director
Tel: 877-4050. ext 224	Enrollment: 125
Fax: 787-7108	
Website: www.swfs.org/ecc	

School year. Parents contract for the school year, September through June. The center also operates a summer camp through early August. Toddlers and 2s attend 2 or 3 days per week. Threes to 5s ive days a week.

Ages	*Hours*	*Days*	*Tuition*
18 mos–2 yrs	9:10–12:45	Tu/Thurs	$10,450
18 mos–2 yrs	9:00–12:45	M/W/F	$12,865
3s–4s	9:00–12:45	Mon–Fri	$15,490
Pre–K	9:00–2:45 (Fri 1:15)	Mon–Fri	$17,905

Tuition includes synagogue membership. Second child in family receives a tuition discount. An extended day program is available for an additional fee.

Program. Developmental. The overriding philosophy at Stephen Wise is that learning does not occur in narrowly designated subject areas but is a process where the curriculum is integrated into all areas. This is accomplished in an environment in which children can explore, experiment and interact with their peers and teachers in an age appropriate way. Play is an essential component of the developmentally appropriate curriculum. The program emphasizes Jewish values and traditions. The Early Childhood Center has been inspired by the Reggio Emilia approach to education. A significant number of teachers have attended Reggio Emilia study tours in Italy.

Admissions. The application fee is $45. Inquiries may be made after Labor Day. Request a tour date. Applications are due in December. Contracts are sent according to ISAAGNY guidelines.

Class size. There are single groups of eight young 2s, twelve older 2s, three groups of thirteen 3s, and two groups of fifteen 4s; all groups have three staff members.

Staff. All head teachers have or are working toward masters degrees. Teachers have attended conferences and workshops.

Facilities. Seven comfortable classrooms on the fifth floor of the synagogue building. There is an indoor play space with lofts and climbing equipment plus a newly renovated outdoor terrace for older children. The youngest children use a huge rubber-protected rooftop play area with its own toilet, storage, and shaded areas.

Separation. This is carefully scheduled and handled slowly. Small groups and abbreviated hours lead into the full program. Parents or a caregiver must be available for at least two weeks, sometimes longer.

Parent involvement. An educational consultant is available to work with parents. Conferences are held twice a year and as needed. Parents are involved in fundraising, social and educational activities, as well as celebrations.

Summer program. A four-week and six-week program are offered. Prices range from $780 to $2,160, based on full-day or half-day schedules. Spaces are for 3s to 5 year olds who have been through the separation process.

Transportation. None. Children come from about 54th Street through 120th Street on the East and West Sides.

Graduates. Have gone on to Abraham Joshua Heschel, Allen-Stevenson, Bank Street, Brearley, Chapin, Columbia Grammar, Dalton, Ethical Culture, Fieldston Lower, Horace Mann, Lycée Français, Manhattan Country, Ramaz, PS 87, 163, 199, Hunter, Trevor Day, Riverdale Country, Rodeph Shalom, Solomon Schecter, Spence, UNIS, Anderson and the Lab School.

Affiliations. BJE, Early Childhood Education Council, ERB, ISAAGNY, Federation of Jewish Philanthropies.

The Studio School

Ages: 2–14 yrs

Nonsectarian Nursery, Elementary and Middle School

115–117 West 95th Street	Established 1971
(between Columbus and Amsterdam Avenues)	Janet C. Rotter,
Zip: 10025	Head of School
Tel: 678-2416	Jennifer Tarpley,
Website: www.studioschool.org	Director of Admissions
E-Mail: info@studioschoolnyc.org	Nursery enrollment: 50
	Total enrollment: 115

School year. Early September to early June.

Ages	*Hours*	*Days*	*Tuition*
2s–nearly 2s	9:15–11:15	2, 3 days	$5,140–$7,710
3s–nearly 3s	9:00–12:00	Tue Wed Thur	$8,455
Early childhood/	8:30–12:30	Mon–Fri	$12,390
kindergarten	or 8:30–3:00	Mon–Fri	$18,400

Program. Developmental/Progressive. Children at Studio are given ample space and time for experimentation and investigation. Believing that play is a child's work the school offers children the opportunity to make sense of their internal and external worlds and prepares students for the larger world utilizing a varied curriculum. In work period, each student has the experience of taking a project from start to finish, with a teacher's guidance. Children learn to choose and plan projects, think about what materials they want to use in the process, and enjoy seeing the results of their own handiwork. Open-ended materials are available, as well as mural paper for large pictures or group work, to stimulate and inspire students' creativity and originality. Children work with both large outdoor blocks and wooden unit blocks daily. Trips are specially arranged for them to learn more about the world, and to bring their new experiences into their work.

Other aspects of the curriculum are music, movement, physical education, reading and telling stories, natural and social sciences, art, and problem-solving. Children also help prepare lunch for the whole school in "Kitchen Science" class together with older elementary and middle school students. Morning and afternoon snacks are provided. Studio's Early Childhood program reflects the school's philosophy that teaching cognitive and social skills in these early years is essential for a child's further academic success.

Admissions. The application fee is $50. Inquiries are from mid-June on. Children are accepted throughout the year if openings are available; however, tuition is pro-rated only to the trimester. Parents inquiring during the fall are encouraged to attend an open house or tour. Morning tours are held during the months of October and November. A group interview is arranged after an application is submitted. Preference is given to siblings of students currently enrolled in the school.

Class size. The 2s and nearly-2s class has ten children, and the 3s and nearly-3s has fourteen with a teacher and an assistant in each classroom. Early childhood and kindergarten classes have sixteen children with one teacher and an assistant.

Facilities. The Studio School moved into its new home at 115–117 West 95th Street in the fall of 2006. Some highlights of the new building are spacious classrooms, a multi-media library, gymnasium, science lab, art and music studios, and a rooftop garden.

Summer program. The program runs from mid-June through the end of July for children ages two and up.

Separation. Depending on each child's developmental needs, parents or caregivers are required to work with the school by remaining until their child is ready to say goodbye. Every young child receives a home visit from teachers before the new school year begins. Once children are connected to teachers and peers, as well as to the daily routines, individual plans for saying goodbye are made with each family.

Parent involvement. Parents of each class meet as a group with teachers to discuss curricular and developmental issues. Individual parent conferences are held three times a year or as requested. In addition, the head of school, Ms. Rotter, leads an ongoing bi-weekly series about children and parenting. A group of Studio parents, called Parent Connection, sponsors programs and events to welcome new parents and support returning ones. Parents are also involved in family events and fundraising activities.

Financial. Tuition is non-refundable and is to be paid in full by September 1st. For students admitted during the school year, tuition may be prorated to the trimester. A monthly payment plan and tuition assistance are available.

Transportation. Children come from as far away as Brooklyn, Greenwich Village, Inwood, and the East Side, with the majority of students coming from the Upper West Side. Eligible kindergartners and elementary-grade students receive MTA MetroCards. The school will help arrange a private van or bus service.

Graduates. Have gone on to Beacon, Birth Wathen-Lenox, Bronx Science, Brooklyn Friends, Brooklyn Tech, Fieldston, Friends Seminary, Horace Mann, Hunter, Lab School, LaGuardia, Professional

Performing Arts, Riverdale, Saint Ann's, School of the Future, Stuyvesant and Trevor Day.

Chartered. By the Board of Regents of the State University of New York.

Member. Early Steps, ERB, ISAAGNY, NASAIS, Parent's League.

The West End Collegiate Church Playschool

Ages: 3–5 yrs

Nonsectarian Nursery School

245 West 77th Street
Zip: 10024
(Mailing address:
368 West End Avenue
10024)
Tel: 787-1566
Fax: 721-1411
Web site: www.westendchurch.org/playschool

Established 1964
Gladys Reich, Director
Sangeeta Singh, Administrative Coordinator
Brooke Brodsky, Admissions Director
Nursery enrollment: 60

School year. Mid-September through May.

Ages	*Hours*	*Days*	*Tuition*
3s	9:00–11:45	Mon–Fri	$9,850
4s	12:45–3:30	Mon–Fri	$9,850

Program. Developmental. The environment is designed to help children develop their social, emotional, intellectual, and physical needs in a structured yet flexible setting. The curriculum is based on the child's interests combined with what teachers deem to be important. Activities include group discussions, free-choice time, story time, art and creative movement/music. Problem-solving and creativity are an integral part of the process. The West End Collegiate Church's minister, Kenneth Gorsuch may visit the children during the year to tell stories. Religion is not taught as the school is non-sectarian.

Admissions. The application fee is $45. Inquiries are from September 1st on. Applications should be submitted no later than October 25th for admittance the following school year. Each year there are approximately 25 openings for 3s and a few for 4s. After the application and fee are returned, the school makes appointments for a parent tour and child visit. Notifications are sent according to ISAAGNY guidelines.

Class size. There are two groups each of 3s and 4s with sixteen children in each class. Each class has three teachers.

Staff. All head teachers are New York State-certified, and assistant teachers have training in early childhood education.

Facilities. In the parish house of the West End Collegiate Church. Two rooms are used, one upstairs and one down. The downstairs classroom opens into a large gymnasium with high ceilings and an outdoor courtyard. The gymnasium is well furnished with climbing equipment, sand table, tricycles and scooters. The outdoor play area is on the roof of the Collegiate School.

Separation. In the week before school begins, children receive a home visit and parents attend a parent orientation evening. For the first week of school, the class is separated into two half groups with each group attending the school at different times. During the second week, the complete class attends and the length of the day increases. Parents withdraw gradually but may remain in the classroom or on the premises as needed. Separation is typically completed for all children by the end of the third week. The Pre-Kindergarten is abbreviated only for the first several days of school with all children attending.

Parent involvement. Visits are by appointment. Parents are invited to work on special projects in the classroom and read at circle time. Parents also work in fundraising and accompany classes on field trips. The parent body is a diverse group.

Conferences are held twice yearly, and the school counsels parents on an individual basis regarding ongoing schools.

Financial. The school requires a deposit of $1,500 on acceptance. The remaining payments are made in July, October, January and

March. There is also an eight-month deferred payment plan. Tuition assistance is available.

Transportation. Most children live close by and are brought by parents.

Graduates. Have gone on to a wide range of independent and public schools.

Affiliations. West End Collegiate Church.

Member. ERB, ISAAGNY. The school has no affiliation with the Collegiate School.

West Side Cooperative Preschool

Ages: 2.9–4.8 yrs

Teacher–parent cooperative

165 W. 105th Street
Zip: 10025

Tel: 749-4635

Established 1988
Sharon Flemen, Director
Enrollment: 30

School year. Monday after Labor Day through third week in June. No summer school.

Ages	*Hours*	*Days*	*Tuition*
2.9–4.8	9:00–1:00	Mon–Fri*	$9,400
2.9–4.8	9:00–3:15	Mon–Thurs	$11,610

*Includes one afternoon to 3:30.

Program. Developmental/Eclectic. The school, which is located in the parish house of a landmarked church, balances planned activities and free play, trying to encourage independent thinking. The mixed-age group setting is intended to allow children to work in small groups where peer education and cooperative learning may take place. Daily meetings provide opportunities for idea exchanges, calendar work, listening, and cooperation.

Admissions. There is an application fee of $30. Call for appointments, but many parents begin applying in September. Then they come to an open house. The application deadline is January 13th, but may vary slightly each year. Interviews are held during the fall and winter. Tours last about one hour, and are only for parents. Acceptances are sent by the first week in March.

Class size. There are places for fifteen 3s and fifteen 4s and 5s. Many children remain in the school for two or three years. Both the director, Sharon Flemen, and co-director, Denise La Magna, have masters degrees in early childhood education. There are also one master teacher and three assistant teachers on staff.

Facilities. The classroom is bright and spacious and has a high ceiling, walls with low banks of shelves and cubby-holes, as well as appropriate furniture. Children's artwork and projects decorate the walls. Special areas in the classroom contain a sand table, water table, painting, blocks, and library, and are well organized as well as rich in materials. Dramatic play is also encouraged. Directly across the street is a newly refurbished playground where the children go every morning (weather permitting). Otherwise, children meet on the third floor in the gym (a basketball court), which is stocked with balls, hoops, building blocks, wagons and a trampoline.

Summer program. None.

Separation. Children are introduced to school over a one-week phasing-in schedule. Parents are asked to be available for the week.

Parent involvement. The school is a cooperative, which means that parents are involved and may work with the teachers on a variety of levels. Parents attend five yearly meetings, assist in fund-raising, and volunteer for school support activities, such as publicity.

Financial. Tuition is paid monthly. The first deposit of approximately $1,500 is due by March 15th. At this time, no financial aid is available.

Transportation. Children come from a twenty to twenty-five block radius and must be brought by a parent or caregiver.

Graduates. Children have gone on to Bank Street, Cathedral, Ethical Culture, Hunter, Manhattan Country and public schools.

Member. ISAAGNY, ERB, NAEYC.

West Side Family Preschool

Ages: 16 mos–5 yrs

Nonsectarian Nursery School

63 West 92nd Street (between Central Park West and Columbus Avenue)
Zip: 10025
Tel: 316-2424
Fax: 932-8265
Website: westwidefamilypreschool.org
E-Mail: wesidefam2002@aol.com

Established 1986
Elaine Rosner–Jeria, Director

Enrollment: 30

School year. September through August.

Ages	*Hours*	*Days*	*Tuition (monthly)*
*1s/2s	8:30–12:45	Mon–Fri	$950
1s/2s	8–6	Mon–Fri	$1,495–$1,595
1s/2s	3–5:45	Mon–Fri	$750
3s–5s	8:30–12:45	Mon–Fri	$850
3s–5s	8–6	Mon–Fri	$1,395
3s–5s	8:30–2:45	Mon–Fri	$1,150
3s–5s	3:00–6:00	Mon–Fri	$700

7:30 am drop off by request; modified two- or three-day-a-week, half or full-time schedules, including half-day afternoons are available, check website.

Program. Developmental. The school hopes to serve as an extended family. The program is multicultural and includes small group work with children of the same age, as well as mixed-age activities. Activities centers include a library and reading area. There are small play objects, musical instruments, dramatic play, puppetry, large hollow blocks, arts, cooking, singing, movement, biking and sand and water play.

Music and art classes are available in the afternoons on weekdays. Weekend classes are available at an additional fee.

Admissions. The application fee is $25. Inquire at any time, admissions are on-going. Parents fill out an application before touring, then may arrange to see the school and meet the staff with their children. Acceptances are on a first-come basis. Open houses are held on Wednesdays from 5:45–7:15 PM, check website for specific dates and to download applications. Trial enrollment is offered for those considering the school. It consists of four two-hour sessions scheduled on an individual basis for $160.

Class size. The school is designed to accommodate twenty-seven children at any one time. One large mixed-age group of 10 to 14 is divided appropriately by age for small group activities.

Staff. Staff members have backgrounds in early childhood education, as well as in theater, dance, art and music. All staff members have a working knowledge of Spanish.

Facilities. Housed in a newly renovated brownstone, the center has a kitchen and a sunken, closed sandbox. The rooms have been designed around the children's activities centers. Snacks are provided; children bring their lunches. Additional programs such as gym and pottery classes, at outside facilities, are available at modest fees.

Summer program. A summer program runs through the week before Labor Day. The monthly cost is the same as the regular program for enrolled students, higher for those who enroll as summer students only.

Parent involvement. Parents are encouraged to participate on school committees, help with fund-raising and in the classroom, join in special projects, and accompany the children on field trips. Conferences are twice yearly and whenever staff or parents feel the need. Parents visit by appointment.

Financial. There is an annual registration fee of $500 per child. Contracts are generally for ten or twelve months. A deposit equal to one month's tuition plus an annual materials fee is required on registration, and tuition is payable monthly. Financial aid is available on a limited basis.

Member. Early Childhood Education Council. Proprietorship.

West Side Montessori School

Ages 2.9–6 yrs

Nonsectarian Early Childhood School and Kindergarten

309 West 92nd Street
(between Riverside Drive
and West End Avenue)
Zip: 10025-7213
Tel: 662-8000
Fax: 662-8323
Web site: www.wsms.org
E-Mail: mzemor@wsmsnyc.org

Established 1963
Dr. Marlene Barron,
Head of School
Michelle Zemor,
Admissions Director
Enrollment: 200

School year. September through June.

Ages	*Hours*	*Days*	*Tuition*
3–6	8:30–12:30	Mon–Fri	$15,204
3–6	1:30–5:30	Mon–Fri	$15,204
3–6	9:00–3:00 (12:30 Fri)	Mon–Fri	$19,184
3–6	8:30–5:30	Mon–Fri	$23,704

Children must be 3 by November 1st and must be toilet trained.

Extended hours. Children may arrive at 8:00 and leave at 6:00, at an additional cost.

Program. Montessori. The school was founded in 1963 by five West Side families and a Montessori teacher. Dr. Marlene Barron, a highly qualified expert in early childhood who holds degrees in psychology, education and Montessori education became head of school in 1975. She has written numerous articles and books; some have won awards.

In addition to Montessori activities, the classrooms are richly equipped with open-ended materials such as blocks, Legos, and dramatic play items. Their aim is to support each child's development in reading, math, science, the arts, and, most important, problem-solving strategies. Classroom practices include mixed-age groupings, hands-on active learning, valuing teacher observations and classroom research, and the careful design of the environment and materials. They expose children to a wide range of developmentally appropriate intellectual, physical, and social activities. Their goal is to create communities in which "everyone learns, works/plays, shares, has fun, and celebrates together."

The head of school says the school is a "multi-multi school," that reflects the rich cultural, ethnic, and economic mix of the West Side. The school actively involves parents in their children's education, and serves as a leader in early childhood educational innovation. ERBs are given on the premises, and admissions directors from ongoing schools visit the classrooms each year. Each year four parents meetings are held on "exmissions," two focusing on independent schools, two on public schools.

Admissions. There are four steps to the admissions process: First, parents must observe a class and learn about the school. Second, they submit an application; third, they meet with a member of the admissions committee and fourth, the child visits the school, typically on Friday afternoons in January and February.

Parents also have additional opportunities to visit the school. The head of school hosts several evening forums, and there is also a curriculum night where parents can learn more about the Montessori philosophy and the school. It is not necessary to submit an application before attending either the forums or curriculum night. About 98 children are admitted each year, mostly 3-year-olds. Inquiries begin in August; the deadline for applications is mid-January, and notifications are sent in March.

Class size. There are ten classes of children age 2.9 to 6 years. There are twenty children in each class. Each classroom has two teachers, at least one of whom is Montessori-trained. Longer day classes have three teachers.

Staff. Two social workers or psychologists are available to parents and teachers on a daily basis. Student teachers from New York University, various Montessori teacher education programs, and Teachers College assist. Movement, music, and nature specialists work with the children, half a class at a time. There are extensive professional development opportunities for the staff. Head of School Marlene Barron is head of NYU's Montessori teacher-education program and co-director of the school's accredited Montessori teacher-education program (WSMS-TEP).

WSM has five programs for staff development: there's a tuition grant of $1,500 yearly toward credit-bearing courses, free credits at NYU, a study/travel grant for $2,500 for teachers who have taught at the school for five years, a $150 cultural fund allowance and funds for workshops, and conferences on education.

Facilities. A six-story townhouse. The lower two floors were expanded by 1200 square feet in 1996 and completely air-conditioned and refurbished. The spacious classrooms, running the length of the building, have large windows at the front and back. There is also an institutional kitchen, staff lounge, a variety of small meeting rooms, an informal Parents Room, and administrative offices. The school is "very vertical"; there are no elevators. A well-equipped gym occupies the entire sixth floor. The building is topped by a rooftop play area.

The school provides lunch for a fee or children may bring their own. Lunch is eaten in the classroom.

Summer program. There is an optional 11-week program.

Separation. In June parents attend a "separation" workshop. Over the summer every child receives a postcard from the school, and parents are encouraged to bring their children to visit during the summer. In the fall, families visit the school and meet the teacher before school begins. Teachers also make a home visit before the child begins school. Older children begin classes earlier; younger ones are brought in for shortened sessions during their first week. Parents stay as long as necessary.

Parent involvement. The parent body is very diverse; although most families live on the Upper West Side, some live on the East Side or come from Brooklyn, the Bronx, Queens and, some years, from New Jersey. The school is a dynamic, interactive bustle of adult/child, parent/teacher, social/educational, formal/informal happenings. Activities range from monthly evening workshops led by a social worker, to class events, such as early morning breakfasts, to family weekend events, such as bowling parties. West Side Montessori parents are "super-volunteers." Parents are encouraged to involve themselves in their child's school life by participating in all events. Every year the Parents Association raises significant monies for the Financial Aid fund—through the child-oriented street fair (the Saturday before Mother's Day), auction, and other smaller events. Recently the school raised $300,000, mostly from these events.

Financial. Parents are asked to make the school an $1,000 loan on acceptance. The school has reserve funds of over $5 million. One-third of the children enrolled receive tuition assistance either from the school's Financial Aid fund or from the Agency for Children's Services (ACS).

Graduates. Have gone on to all the independent schools and public schools like Hunter Elementary.

Chartered. By the Board of Regents of the State University of New York.

Members. ACD, AMS, ERB, ISAAGNY, NAIS, NYSAIS, Early Steps.

West Side YMCA Co-op Nursery School

Ages 2.5–5 yrs

Nonsectarian

5 West 63rd Street (between Central Park West and Broadway)	Established 1967
Zip: 10023	Shannon Cussen, Director
Tel: 875-4117	Terri Decker, Admissions Director
E-Mail: tdecker@ymcanyc.org	Enrollment: 120

School year. Mid-September through early June. Summer program available from June through August.

Ages	*Hours*	*Days*	*Tuition*
2s	9:00–11:45	T Th/M W F	$6,075–$7,113
(2.5-2.10)	1:15–4:00	Mon Wed Fri	$7,113
3s	1:00–4:00	Mon Wed Fri	$7,113
3s	9:00–12:00	Mon–Fri	$9,475
4s	9:00–2:00	Mon–Fri	$11,250

Program. The school would prefer to be known as "play-based," not "traditional," despite its emphasis on skills development. Children explore many areas of study in an informal way. Much attention is paid to social development. Activities include blockbuilding, dramatic play, sand and water play, cooking, storytime, manipulatives, art, music and science. Children have access to the facilities at the YMCA which include weekly swim classes. Many classes use Central Park for outdoor playtime as an important resource for learning. Group problem solving, collaborative work and critical thinking skills are emphasized. Teachers work with children individually in various skills areas, evaluating their current level and trying to improve their skills. In prekindergarten children begin more formal work in reading, math, and social studies. Careful records are kept of their progress.

ERB testing is offered on site to enrolled students of the Y.

Admissions. The application fee is $50. Inquiries are from September on. During October and November parents may tour the school before submitting an application. After applying, children are seen in January and February in small playgroups with the admissions director, a teacher and their parents present. The school is interested in finding families who will enjoy the cooperative and make a strong contribution to the school. Notifications are sent according to ISAAGNY guidelines, with optional early notification for siblings and legacies.

Class size. There are three 2s classes of 12 children, three 3s classes of 12–16 children, a 3s/4s class with 16 children and two 4s classes with 18 children. Each class has two to three staff members and a daily "helping parent" volunteer.

Staff. All teachers are licensed with most holding advanced degrees. Specialists in science, music, swimming, and creative movement, and gym work with the children. Two social workers are also available.

There are three staff development training days as well as regular weekly staff meetings at which the director meets with the teaching teams and the children are discussed in depth.

Facilities. The classrooms are spotlessly maintained by the Y, and special classroom maintenance is done by parents as well. Parents bring children directly to their classrooms.

In the fall of 2001, The Co-op Nursery relocated to a new building adjacent to the original West Side YMCA. The nursery is accessible through a security-coded, stroller-friendly entryway. The classrooms are bright and sun-filled, with one classroom on the ground floor, and four more classrooms on the third floor. The children use the Y's pool; additional facilities include a rooftop playground, a newly renovated indoor playspace, a library/resource room, and a family lounge. Large rooms are available for parent meetings and special events.

Summer program. Kinder Camp serves children 4–6 years of age during the months of June, July and August. The camp program includes swimming, sports, arts and crafts and weekly trips. There is a registration process and additional fees are required.

Separation. Both teachers visit each child before school begins. A schedule of short, staggered sessions for small groups lasts about two weeks. Much attention is paid to easing into separation. An orientation evening for parents is scheduled before the start of the school year to introduce parents to each classroom's procedures.

Parent involvement. The director notes that the Co-op provides a strong sense of community, and that parents have the opportunity to learn about their children in a new way, and develop new parenting skills.

Parents must contribute time to committees such as fundraising and playground. They also participate in the classroom on a rotating basis, provide regular help with field trips and swimming, and initiate special classroom projects. Their attendance is required at several meetings per year, including "curriculum night" and a "helping parent" training session. Parents serve on the school's executive committee. Conferences are held twice a year.

Financial. A deposit is due on signing the contract; tuition is payable in June, September and November. Need-based financial aid is available.

Transportation. Children come mostly from the West Side between 48th and 96th Streets. No bus service is available.

Graduates. Have gone on to independent and public schools, with about one-half of the children choosing private schools such as Allen-Stevenson, Calhoun, Cathedral, Dalton, Ethical Culture and Spence.

Affiliations. YMCA. Chartered by the Board of Regents of the State University of New York.

Member. ERB, ISAAGNY.

Tender Care

Ages: 6 mos–5yrs

5 West 63rd Street
Zip: 10023
Tel: 875-4117
Website: www.ymcanyc.org
E-Mail: tdecker@ymcanyc.org

Shannon Cussen,
Director
Terri Decker,
Admissions Director
Enrollment: 85

School year. Twelve-month program.

Ages	*Hours*	*Days*	*Tuition (monthly)*
6 mos–2.6 yrs	8:00–6:00	Mon–Fri	$1,456
2.6–5 yrs	8:00–6:00	Mon–Fri	$1,375

Flexible days and half days available.

Program: Tender Care is a child care center which provides a safe, nurturing and challenging learning environment for young children.

The emphasis of this program is on social development with skill development attended to through the use of open-ended, creative materials and age-appropriate, organized activities. Specials include music, movement, science, and swimming for the older children. There are five bright spacious classrooms on the second floor of the new McBurney Annex of the West Side YMCA.

Admissions: Parents call for an application and are given a small group tour of the facilities. After the tour, the child's name will be placed on a waiting list and the parent will be contacted as soon as there is an available space in the program. (There are periods throughout the year when applications will not be provided because of the length of the waiting list.)

Yaldaynu Center

Ages: 2–5 yrs

251 West 100th Street (corner of West End Avenue)
Zip: 10025
Tel: 866-4993
Fax: 866-1346
Website: www.anschechesed.org

Established 1981
Elaine Anshen Bloom, Director
Enrollment: 50

School year. Eleven-month program. School is closed in August.

Ages	*Hours*	*Days*	*Tuition*
2s	9:00–12:00	5 days	$9,450
	9:00–12:00	3 days	$5,700
	9:00–12:00	2 days	$3,880
3s–5s	8:30–12:30	Tue/Wed/Thurs	$7,825

*Extended hours and other groups are available for an additional fee.

Program. Developmentally oriented. According to the director, "We offer challenging activities, but no child is pushed." Activities include blockbuilding, sand and water play, music, cooking, storytelling, dictation, art, vigorous outdoor play, and play with puzzles and small play objects.

Jewish holidays and Shabbat are celebrated.

Admissions. The application fee is $75. Inquiries may be made at any time, but most come in early winter.

Parents should arrange to visit the center without their children; then they may apply. Acceptances are sent in March.

Class size. Children meet in three groups. There are three teachers in each classroom. A social worker is available regularly.

Facilities. The center occupies two rooms on the third floor of Temple Ansche Chesed and two rooms on the second floor. One is very large, and the second consists of two adjoining areas. There is also a roof playground that younger children use. Older children use the rooftop play area, equipped with a sandbox and climbing and riding toys that the center shares with Purple Circle Day Care and Morningside Montessori, as well as Riverside Park playgrounds. There is access to an indoor playroom for games in inclement weather.

Separation. A parent or caregiver is expected to be available during the first three weeks of school for a phasing-in period which is both gradual and individual.

Parent involvement. Parents are welcome to participate in the classroom. The parents association is active and enthusiastic, and the board consists of parents. Conferences are arranged twice yearly; others are arranged as needed. Family events are planned.

Financial. There is a deposit of one month's tuition on signing the contract. Tuition is payable semiannually. Financial aid is sometimes available.

Graduates. Have gone on to a variety of private and public schools, including Bank Street, Beit Rabban, Calhoun, Ethical Culture, Heschel, Manhattan Country, Ramaz, Rodeph Sholom and Trinity.

Affiliations. ISAAGNY, ERB, BJE, Jewish Board of Family Services.

UPTOWN

Bank Street Family Center

Ages: 6 mos–4.9 yrs

Nonsectarian All-Day Care

610 West 112th Street (between Broadway and Riverside Drive)
Zip: 10025
Admissions tel: 875–4412
Centerbased Early Intervention and CPSE* tel: 875–4573
Homebased Early Intervention and SEIT (Valentina Repola) tel: 875-4572
Fax: 875-4759
Website: www.bankstreet.edu
Click on Family Center link.

Reuel Jordan, Dean of Children's Programs
Amy Flynn, Director/Admissions
Murray Kelley, Special Education
Nicole Geller, Home & Community Services, 875-4683

Enrollment: approximately 45

School year. September through July.

Ages	*Hours*	*Days*	*Tuition*
All	8:00–6:00	Mon–Fri	$26,710

Tuition is pro-rated for 2, 3, or 4 days.

Program. Developmental/interactive. The Center is not formally a part of The Bank Street School for Children, although there are overlapping programs, personnel and history. The Family Center and the School for Children make up the Children's Programs within the Bank Street College of Education. The Center is designed to provide developmentally oriented, culturally sensitive day care and support for families with children six months to four years. The philosophy, and therefore the curriculum, is based on their understanding of how young children learn best. A critical component of the program is providing the opportunity to explore the diversity of the community. Families with alternative lifestyles will feel comfortable here. Family members are encouraged to visit and participate throughout the day. The Center strives to create a welcoming, homelike environment to ensure that both children and adults feel comfortable.

Special education services. The Center also provides early intervention, preschool special education and evaluation services. Children

*Committee on Preschool Special Education

with developmental delays or disabilities are integrated into the classroom. Children with special needs are provided with all appropriate therapeutic services and transportation. In addition, the Family Center provides home and community-based special education services and evaluations. All approved special education services are funded by the New York State Department of Education and Department of Health.

Admissions. The application fee is $50. Call in September or go on-line for an application; submit it promptly. Open houses are held in November, December and January. Interviews with the director are held in January and February. Notifications for the general education program are sent typically in late February. Play sessions are held in March for children applying to the special education program. Admittance to the special education program is based on approval by the Early Intervention System (EIS) or the Committee on Preschool Special Education (CPSE).

Class size. There are three classrooms. Two mixed-aged groups of ten children range from 6 months to 2.8 years. One group of fifteen children ranges in age from 2.9 to 4.0. Children in the Special Education Program range in age from 6 months to 4.9 years in September of the year of admittance.

Staff. Each room has a head teacher, assistant teacher, interns, and student teachers. There is a music teacher, a librarian, and a nurse all available through the Bank Street School for Children.

Facilities. The Family Center is located in the main building of the Bank Street College of Education. It has three fully equipped classrooms with kitchenettes and bathrooms for infant and toddler needs. There are indoor and outdoor play spaces and a library. Individual rooms are available for therapeutic services and napping.

Separation. There is a gradual phase-in process at the beginning of each school year, and the first-week schedule is abbreviated. Parents or others close to the child are expected to take part in the phase-in process.

Parent involvement. Parents are expected to participate on the varying committees and take part in fundraising events. The director says, "We're here as a support and a resource for parents, and they stay in constant touch with us. We're an extension of the family, and we feel strongly that developing partnerships with families is essential to providing quality childcare and education for all children." In addition to daily conversations and written communications, parents and staff meet at least three to five times a year to discuss such issues as siblings, discipline, anti-bias education, etc. Conferences are arranged twice yearly or as needed.

Financial. A $750 deposit is required on acceptance. Sixty percent of tuition is due by July 30, the remainder by January 1. A monthly payment plan is optional. Limited scholarship assistance is available.

Transportation. Transportation is available for children in the special education program.

Graduates. Graduates go on to a variety of programs, other independent schools as well as public pre-K and kindergarten programs, including Bank Street. However, the Center operates independently of the Bank Street School for Children and you must apply separately to each, admission is not automatic.

Affiliations. Bank Street College of Education—Children's Program. Bank Street College graduate students and Liberty Partnership teenagers observe and work with children at the Family Center as part of their professional training.

Bank Street School for Children

Ages: 3–13 yrs

Nonsectarian Nursery and Elementary School

610 West 112th Street
(between Broadway
and Riverside Drive)
Zip: 10025
Tel: 875-4420
Admissions tel: 875-4433
Website: www.bankstreet.edu
Nursery and Kindergarten Enrollment: approximately 50
Total Enrollment: approximately 430

Established in 1918
Reuel Jordan,
Dean of Children's Programs
Marcia Roesch,
Director of Admissions

School year. September through early June.

Ages	*Hours*	*Days*	*Tuition*
3s half day	8:45–11:45	Mon–Thurs, Fri until 1:00	$22,420
full day	8:45–3:00	Mon–Thurs, Fri until 1:00	$24,720
4s	8:45–3:00	Mon–Thurs, Fri until 1:00	$24,720
5s	8:45–3:00	Mon–Thurs, Fri until 1:00	$24,720

Applicants must be 3 by September 1st.

Extended hours. Full-day children, age 4 years and older, may join the after-school program, "Kids, Club" which meets Monday through Friday from 3:00 to 6:00. A session on Friday, 1:00 to 6:00, is available for an additional fee.

Program. Bank Street, a progressive school, has had a profound effect on American education. The school's history is closely connected with the development of this approach. In 1916, Lucy Sprague Mitchell founded the Bureau of Educational Experiments to conduct research into child development. In 1918, the bureau opened its own nursery. It later found a home on Bank Street, expanded its nursery to an elementary school, and took a new name, the Cooperative School for Teachers. In 1950 it was renamed the Bank Street College of Education. The College and the School for Children moved to the Upper West Side in 1970. Bank Street College helped design the national Head Start program and create guidelines for Title IV of the Civil Rights Act of 1965. Its research division is an Early Childhood Education and Research Center for the federal government's Office of Economic Opportunity.

Monitoring the work of New York's Associated Progressive Schools and incorporating the research of psychologists such as Piaget and Anna Freud, the bureau evolved the developmental-interaction approach, now sometimes called "the Bank Street approach." Considered revolutionary in the 1920s, this approach gained broad acceptance. Basically, the child's development is seen as a complex process. The progressive approach recognizes and values each child's unique learning style. Most basic is its conviction that young children learn by doing, and that their most important activity is free-choice play.

Play is seen as each child's method for exploring and integrating his or her rapidly expanding knowledge of properties, connections, and relationships, social experience, notions about reality, and the inner world of fantasy and feeling. Children are not seen as receivers of a curriculum determined by adults, but as discoverers of the value and meaning of their own activities, and as people with strong agendas of their own.

In a Bank Street classroom children are given materials that are flexible and open-ended, able to be used in a variety of ways. The staples are blocks, water, sand, and clay. Generous amounts of work/play time allow the child to choose the kind of play, how it will proceed, where it will lead, when it will stop, and what it will include or exclude. It is the teacher's role to understand the implications of the child's play and to facilitate it.

The core of the Bank Street developmental-interaction curriculum is called social studies (not to be confused with the high-school variety) and is firmly rooted in the child's experience. That is, through various activities, the child explores his or her own experiences of self, family, and neighborhood, re-creating and dramatizing these discoveries through blockbuilding, the arts, dramatic play, and other media. A visit to a firehouse may be examined by talking about it, dictating a story about it, drawing a picture, constructing a replica in blocks, or playing firehouse.

The curriculum responds to and includes the children's interests and daily experiences. Reading, writing, and math are seen as part of the process of finding, organizing, recording, and communicating information. Science and math are presented as methods of inquiry. Music and the arts are also emphasized.

Children's responses to one another are a vital part of the curriculum, and classroom activities are arranged to facilitate these. Older children will construct elaborate buildings in teams, learning to plan, to negotiate, to make decisions, to do research, to compromise, and to work cooperatively on projects.

One 4/5s class, for instance, decides to do a "study" of shoes. They dictate to the teacher a list of various kinds of shoes. Some children are making, and attaching to a chart, cards describing how their shoes opened or closed, with velcro and shoelaces. In one corner of the classroom others set up a shoe store, using their shoes as stock, and busily wait on customers. One child is carefully copying out the word "velcro" for her chart card. Others trace their shoe sizes.

In the developmental-interaction classroom, work centers around blockbuilding. Blocks are seen as remarkably versatile and vital. And they are the major focus for social studies work. By the age of 5, children's dramatic play with blocks is intricate and sophisticated. They have progressed from creating patterns and simple structures, to creating whole cities that mirror their understanding of the world. The cities remain up for a full week or more and become the focus of other activities, such as making signs or props for the buildings, or taking field trips to research and observe. Work with blocks continues until the 7s.

Admissions. The application fee is $40. Inquiries should be made from September on. The application deadline is mid-November for all ages through 6. Since there are a limited number of spaces at each grade level, the admissions office cannot always process all applications received by the deadline.

Once the application has been submitted, the school will arrange an interview for the child. Parent interviews are scheduled after this. Notifications are sent according to ISAAGNY deadlines.

Class size. There is one 3s class of sixteen children, two 4/5s classes of about twenty-one children each, and two 5/6s with about twenty-three children each. The 3s have three teachers, and a part-time graduate student. Older children have two teachers and one or two graduate students. Classes frequently divide in half for music (They use Orff instruments), movement, gym, or visits to the library. An art specialist visits once a week, and the 3's have Spanish introduced once a week.

Staff. The lower school coordinator observes classroom teachers at work and meets with them weekly. The classroom teachers, in turn, supervise Bank Street graduate students and student teachers who work with them. Parent conferences are held twice a year in fall and spring; written reports are sent in February and June.

Summer program. Extended day, holiday, and summer day camp programs are open to the community.

Facilities. The lower school, 3s through 5/6s, is housed on the second floor of the college's handsome, modern building, constructed in 1970. Spacious classrooms with indirect lighting line either side of a wide corridor, often used as additional work space. Puzzles, games, small play objects; books, blocks, woodworking, and cooking equipment; art materials and natural objects; and pets fill up low shelves. Sand and water tables are popular. The blockbuilding space is large, and the constructions are impressive. Ceilings are sound-proofed. Sinks and toilets are child sized. The school is well designed and beautifully maintained. The inner classrooms look out to an extremely large, safety-surfaced play terrace, and their doors open out onto it. It is full of large, hollow building blocks and planks for constructions, as well as a high wooden climbing apparatus.

Lower school children bring their lunches and eat them in their classrooms.

Separation. Separation is considered part of the curriculum, and parents will need to commit themselves to whatever time is necessary for the process. The school believes that even children who may have been in child care from birth will be confronting separation issues in a new way when they enter school as 3s.

Parent involvement. There is an active Parents Association and parents are encouraged to participate in fundraising, organizing lectures, and to join school committees. Scheduled parent visits and contributions to the classrooms are welcome.

Financial. 33 percent of the student body receives tuition assistance.

Affiliations. Bank Street College of Education.

Member. ERB, ISAAGNY.

Barnard College Center for Toddler Development

Ages: 1.7–3.0 yrs

Nonsectarian Nursery and Pre-Nursery Program

3009 Broadway
(at 120th Street)
Zip: 10027
Tel: 854-8271

Website: www.columbia.edu/~bcpsych/toddler/

Established 1973
Dr. Tovah P. Klein, Director
Patricia Shimm, Associate Director
Enrollment: 48

School year. September through April. Spring program: May–June.

Ages	*Hours*	*Days*	*Tuition*
1.7–2.5	9:30–11:45	2 mornings or 1 afternoon	$3,200–$5,600
2.6–3.0	1:30–3:45	2 afternoons	$6,100

Program. The school functions as a part of the Psychology Department at Barnard College. Director Dr. Tovah Klein is trained in psychology and Patricia Shimm, Associate Director, is an early childhood expert and author of *Parenting Your Toddler: The Expert's Guide to the Tough and Tender Years*. The school's aim is to serve the Barnard/Columbia and neighboring communities, to provide Barnard and Columbia students opportunities to observe and work with children, to conduct research in early child development, and to provide a forum for parents to discuss the development of their toddlers. The highly individualized program is based upon active learning through self-discovery. Educational experiences are adjusted to the developmental level of the child to encourage cognitive and socio-emotional development. Activities include sand and water play, puzzles and small play objects, dramatic play, musical instruments, storytime, blockbuilding, arts and crafts, and active play.

Admissions. The application fee is $40. Inquiries begin October 15. Call for an application, which will be sent in December. Admission is based on age and gender. Preference is given to siblings and children of Barnard College and Columbia University faculty and staff. The school welcomes applications from children with developmental disabilities.

Class size. There are two morning groups and two afternoon groups, each with twelve children and six teachers. Each class has a head teacher and five assistants who are all members of the Barnard Department of Psychology. The child/teacher ratio is two or two and a half to one.

Separation. A parent must accompany the child to the program and stay with him or her for the first month.

Financial. Parents pay a $500 deposit on signing the contract. Tuition is payable in August. Scholarships are available.

Affiliations. A division of the Barnard College Department of Psychology.

Bridge Community Nursery School

Ages: 2.9–5 yrs

111 Wadsworth Avenue (near 178th Street)
Zip: 10033
Tel: 928-9741
Fax: 923-3580
Serves 22–24 children
Children are grouped in one class.
Hours: 8:00–6:00 only.

Wanita Anderson, Director
Cost: $80/week

Broadway Presbyterian Church Nursery School

Ages: 2.9–5

Nonsectarian Nursery School

601 W. 114th Street (at Broadway)
Zip: 10025
Tel: 864-6100, ext. 130
Fax: 864-4931

Established 1991
Elizabeth Bergstein, Director
Enrollment: 20

School year. Wednesday after Labor Day to mid-June, with a six-week summer program.

Ages	*Hours*	*Days*	*Tuition**
2.9–5	9:00–12:30	Mon–Fri	$7,620 or $6,090
2.9–5	9:00–2:30	Mon–Fri	$9,920 or $8,400

*Lower figure billed if parent works in the school. Children must be 2.9 as of September and toilet-trained.

Program. The children are not separated by age, allowing each to reach up or down depending on ability. "We try to address where each child is developmentally." The program is very individualized and very child-directed. "We work very much in partnership with parents." Parents may work in the school one morning a week to receive the discounted rate. There are a few partial-week slots. Children bring their own snack and lunch to school.

Admissions. There is an application fee of $25. Parents may begin inquiring for the following year on October 1. After the application is submitted, the parents are asked to come to the school, then parents are contacted to make an appointment for their child. A one-on-one interview is scheduled for after school. Notifications are sent beginning at the end of February. The school gives priority to people connected to the current nursery school class, and to members of the church.

Class size. Twenty places are available. The children are not divided by age.

Separation. There is a two-week phase-in period once the children start school. On the first day, children come in two groups for an hour. By the beginning of the second week, they have begun full classes. Parents are asked to be available during the first few days for their child.

Parent involvement. Involvement includes working in the school, fund-raising, parties, maintenance, publicity, and supplies. There are three or four teachers and one or two parents at the school. Parents help out, but they do not lead, unless they have shown a special aptitude. Parents who don't work in the school are welcome to spend as much time as they can there.

There is one conference in the fall and an optional one in the spring. The board is made up of four church members and three parent members.

Financial. A ten percent deposit is due at the time the contract is signed. Half the tuition is due in August and the remainder in January. There is a $300 participation bond refundable upon request at the end of the year. Limited financial aid is available.

Transportation. No transportation offered by the school. Most students come from a 50-block area around the school, but some have come from other neighborhoods.

Graduates. Most children go to Gifted and Talented, Anderson, or other selective public school programs. Some go to Cathedral and other private schools.

Member. Broadway Presbyterian Church.

Children's Learning Center

Ages: 6 mos–5 yrs

Nonsectarian Child Care Cooperative

90 LaSalle Street	Established 1976
Zip: 10027	Lori Woliner, Director
Tel: 663-9318	
Fax: 663-9326	Enrollment: 50
Website: www.clc-nyc.org	
E-Mail: loriwoliner@clc-nyc.org	

School year. September through June, with an optional July program for the Center's children. Closed in August.

Program hours. Many other schedules are available in addition to those listed below. A minimum of three days a week is required.

Ages	*Hours*	*Days*	*Tuition**
infants	8:30–2:00	3–5 days/wk	$10,900–16,750
	8:30–3:30	3–5 days/wk	$13,430–20,080
	8:30–5:30	3–5 days/wk	$16,510–23,710
2s/3s	8:30–2:00	3–5 days/wk	$9,120–14,000
	8:30–3:30	3–5 days/wk	$11,230–16,790
	8:30–5:30	3–5 days/wk	$12,800–19,820
3/4s	8:30–2:00	3–5 days/wk	$7,400–11,370
	8:30–3:30	3–5 days/wk	$9,120–13,630
	8:30–5:30	3–5 days/wk	$11,200–16,090

*For ten months, varies depending on number of days contracted for.

Program. Developmental. The Children's Learning Center was founded in 1972 by a group of Union Theological Seminary students who wanted to share the responsibility of caring for one another's children in a Seminary apartment while they attended class. In the summer of 2000, the Children's Learning Center moved to Morningside Gardens and is no longer affiliated with Union Theological Seminary. The school believes that children learn best through play, at their own individual rates in a mixed-age group. Teachers encourage children to discover and interpret their world through cooperative and independent play. Art, science, music, social studies, cooking, sand and water play are some of the activities in all three classrooms. A music specialist works with children each week and an educational psychologist is available to teachers, children and parents throughout the year.

The Center places a strong value on the social and emotional development of young children. Language development is one of the Center's strengths; children tend to score far above their peers on verbal assessments.

Admissions. The application fee is $50. Inquiries are accepted throughout the year. Families tour the Center after submitting an application. Notifications are sent out the second week in March with preference given to siblings and affiliates of Morningside Gardens, Jewish Theological Seminary and Barnard College. The center seeks a balance of ages and sexes. It is multicultural and multiracial.

Class size. The children meet in three classes. The infant room has a maximum of 10 children. The 2s room has a maximum of 12 children, and Pre-K has a maximum of 18 children.

Three full-time teachers and an additional college work-study teacher are assigned to each group. A music teacher also works with the children once a week.

Staff. The Center fosters and supports many programs geared to the teachers' professional development. Twice a month the entire staff meets in order to discuss curriculum-building and the teachers participate in out of school or in-house workshops.

Facilities. The Children's Learning Center is located on the ground floor in one of Morningside Gardens' tenant cooperative buildings. The children enjoy the use of two large playgrounds which are located on the premises. The rooms are divided into activity areas with blocks, dramatic play, art activities, table toys and a library. Each room is carpeted and the school is equipped with a full kitchen.

Children bring their own lunches; the school provides snacks.

Separation. Children begin the year with an abbreviated school schedule. Parents are asked to remain in their child's classroom for the first few sessions and then leave the classroom for gradually increasing time periods. The transition period is essential to a successful integration into the life of a classroom.

Parent involvement. The Center is a parent cooperative which depends on parent participation. There is a Parent Board. In addition to a fund-raising commitment, parents must work on a school committee. Two maintenance work days are required each year. Parents are encouraged to bring any special interest or skill to the classroom. There are two parent conferences a year.

Financial. One month's tuition is required at enrollment, along with insurance fees, and an additional month's deposit is due in June. Monthly tuition is payable on the first of each month. There is limited scholarship assistance available.

Transportation. Parents bring their children directly to the classrooms.

Graduates. Have gone on to Bank Street, City and Country School, Dalton, Manhattan School for Children, and PS 25.

City College Preschool

Ages: 2–6 yrs.

Nonsectarian Preschool

Schiff House
133rd and Convent Avenue
Zip: 10031
Tel: 650-8616

LaTrella Thornton, Director

Enrollment: 45

Tuition is $45 per week. The center is open from 7:45–5:30 with evening hours from 4:00–9:00 PM. The school follows the City College calendar, and all students are offspring of City College students. The program is developmental. Children are not assigned to a particular room, and they self-select the rooms in which they are to engage in activities.

The Columbia Greenhouse Nursery School

Ages: 2–5 yrs

Nonsectarian Nursery School

404 West 116th Street and
424 West 116th Street
(between Amsterdam Avenue and Morningside Drive)
Zip: 10027
Tel: 666-4796
Website: columbiagreenhouse.com
E-Mail: cgns@mindspring.com

Established 1919
Vicki Aspenberg, Director

Enrollment: 105

School year. Second week in September through early June. Summer program available through July.

Ages	*Hours*	*Days*	*Tuition*
2s	9:00–11:30	2 or 3 days	$5,000 or $7,500
2s	12:45–3:15	Mon, Tue, Thur	$7,500
2s/3s	9:00–12:00	Mon, Wed, Thur	$7,900
3s	1:00–4:00	Mon–Thur	$8,800
3s–5s	9:00–1:00	Mon–Fri*	$14,350
3s–5s	9:00–2:45	Mon–Fri*	$13,500
		*(Fri until 1:00)	

*Option of an extended day: Monday through Thursday, from 2:45 to 3:45.

Program. Eclectic/Progressive/Developmental. The school emphasizes concrete learning through exploration of materials. Activities like cooking, collaging, blockbuilding, and water play tie in with the rudiments of arithmetic, writing, and reading. Other activities include dramatic play, science, singing, music and movement, active play, storytime, art, and play with small objects, puzzles, and games. The curriculum evolves according to the child's interests and growing skills.

ERB's are given on the premises.

Admissions. The application fee is $30. Inquiries are from mid-September on. Parents will be scheduled for a group tour and a classroom visit after applying. Tours begin in October. Notifications are sent in mid-March. Children are not interviewed. There are openings for 2s, 3s, and 4s. Priority is given to parents affiliated with Columbia and siblings.

Class size. There is one 2s class of ten, a morning 3s class of fifteen, an afternoon 3s class of ten, a 3/4s class of seventeen, and a 4/5s class of twenty-one. Each class has two or three staff members; the 4/5s class has three staff members. Interns also assist, so there are three or four adults in each room.

Staff. Faculty instruction and school operation are in the hands of the director. Five teachers have masters degrees in early childhood education. Most teachers and assistants have been working at the school anywhere from five to twenty-three years.

A specialist teaches music and movement.

Facilities. The school has two locations: a brick townhouse on West 116th Street and the first floor of a nearby residential building also on West 116th Street. Both locations have comfortable classrooms, each well-equipped with sand, water, clay, playdough, blocks, puzzles, games, paints and art materials, books, and musical instruments. The school has two recently renovated outdoor play yards, one with a slide, climbing apparatus, tricycles, large building blocks and sandboxes.

Summer program. Six weeks for 3s–5s. Children need to be previously enrolled in the school.

Separation. A parent/faculty meeting takes place before the school year begins with special attention given to the first weeks of school. Small groups attend shortened sessions at the beginning of the year with parent or caregiver present as needed.

Parent involvement. Each parent is expected to participate on a committee or project, such as the school's newsletter. Parents frequently contribute their talents to the classroom and are invited to observe at any time.

Parent/teacher conferences are held twice yearly. There is an active Parent Association. Seminars on child development issues and ongoing school placement and parenting are offered.

Many of the parents are university students, teaching assistants, professors and administrators.

Financial. A deposit of 20 percent of the tuition is required upon signing the contract. The deposit is a nonrefundable part of the total tuition. The remainder of the tuition is payable on the 1st of June, September and January. Other payment schedules are available upon request. Roughly 10 percent of students receive tuition assistance.

Transportation. None provided.

Graduates. Have gone on to such schools as Bank Street, Cathedral, Columbia Grammar, Dalton, Ethical Culture, Manhattan Country, St. Hilda's and St. Hugh's. Approximately a third of the children attend public schools, including Hunter and Anderson, PS 166, PS 163, and PS 87.

History. The Greenhouse evolved from a playgroup for children of Columbia faculty established in 1919. In 1922 it was offered quarters in a botanical greenhouse belonging to the university. In 1950 parents took responsibility for the school's administration. The program was assessed by consultants from Bank Street and revamped according to the latest research and approaches in the mid-fifties and moved into its present home in 1958.

Affiliations. Columbia University, which supports the school.

Member. ERB, ISAAGNY, NAEYC.

Family Annex

Ages: 18 mos–5 yrs

Nonsectarian Parent Cooperative Day Care Center

560 West 113th Street (between Broadway and Amsterdam Avenue)
Zip: 10025
Tel: 749-3271 or 3540
Website: www.thefamilyannex.org
E-Mail: Thefamilyannex@yahoo.com

Established 1980
Nancy Drescher, Director
Enrollment: 45

School year. September 6th through end of July. Parents contract for the full year.

Ages	*Hours*	*Days*	*Tuition**
18 mos.–5	8:00–5:45	Mon–Fri	$16,000–$18,000 (depending on age and schedule)
18 mos.–5	8:00–12:45 or 1:00–5:45 (8:00–3:30 also available)	2, 3 or 5 days	$8,596–$16,590

*Two or three-day schedules are also available.

Program. The school offers a Reggio Emilia approach, an open classroom curriculum with structured and free time and individual and small group work. Activities include meeting time (discussions, stories, games, and singing), art, learning with small play objects, and physical play. There are also frequent neighborhood outings, yoga and artist-in-residence each week.

Admissions. The application fee is $25. Inquiries are from October on. The director arranges tours for parents. Notification of acceptance is sent as space becomes available or in early March. Children for whom places are not available may be put on a waiting list. Preference is given to children of employees or students at Columbia.

Class size. There is a toddler room for ten children 18 months to 2.6, a nursery room of twelve children from 2.7–3.6, and a prekindergarten room with twelve children 3.7–5. Each room has a teacher and an assistant. The toddlers have three staff members in the morning.

Facilities. Three floors of a brownstone owned by Columbia University. The spacious toddler room opens into a backyard with a sandbox and climbing equipment. The nursery classrooms are on the second floor. The third floor has the prekindergarten room and a full kitchen, and an art studio. Children also use Riverside Park, the grounds of Columbia, and those of St. John the Divine.

Children have the option to bring their lunches, or to order lunch from the school's lunch service.

Separation. Parents and teachers have the option to work out a schedule to accommodate children's needs.

Parent involvement. The director is in charge of the staff and the school's day-to-day functions. Parents elect the board of directors and participate through committees in admissions, hiring, fundraising, budget, and curriculum decisions. Formal parent-teacher conferences are scheduled twice yearly.

Financial. A deposit of one month's tuition is due on signing the contract. Parents contract for the full year. Tuition is payable monthly.

Transportation. Most children come from the Columbia area. No private bus service is available.

Graduates. Have gone on to private schools such as Bank Street, Heschel, and Manhattan Country, as well as to public schools such as Hunter, Anderson, Manhattan School for Children, PS 87, and the Lab School.

Affiliations. Columbia University, ISAAGNY.

Hollingworth Preschool of Teacher's College, Columbia University

Ages: 3–5 yrs

Nonsectarian

Box 170
Teachers College
Columbia University
Zip: 10027
Tel: 678-3851
Website: www.tc.columbia.edu

Established 1983
Dr. Lisa Wright,
Executive Director
Connie Williams Coulianos,
Administrative Director/
Admissions Director
Enrollment: 35

School year. Second week in September through beginning of June.

Ages	*Hours*	*Days*	*Tuition*
3s/4s	8:30–11:30	Mon–Fri	$10,900
3s/4s	11:30–1:00 (optional extended morning)	Mon–Fri	$2,400
4s/5s	11:45–4:00	Mon–Fri	$13,145

Children must be 3 or 4 at the start of the year.

Program. The preschool's curriculum is child responsive with a mission to offer appropriate support to the interests and passions of young learners.

Among the school's goals: "To promote the development of higher-level thinking skills necessary to become critical thinkers and problem solvers"; "To provide children with a conceptual knowledge of the world around them."

Teachers guide the children through a variety of activities most of which the children have chosen.

Past studies have included astronomy, meterology, paleontology and oceanography! Play includes blocks, easel painting, reading, imaginative play, puzzles and games. and music. Problems are viewed as challenges to be embraced with enthusiasm. Children are actively involved in problem-solving.

Admissions. The application fee is $50.

Inquiries are accepted from early September with a deadline for applications in January. Parents call for an application and can attend an evening open house. Parents must have their child assessed by an independent psychologist, at their own expense; the results are reviewed in the admissions process. Next, the school's questionnaire outlining the child's developmental history and present capabilities must be completed and returned with the application fee. The child will then be observed at the school in a small group play session. The school maintains an active waiting list.

Class size. There is one 3s and one 4s class. Each has seventeen children and three teachers.

Staff. The staff includes master teachers as well as assistant teachers who are graduate students at Teachers College.

Facilities. The classroom is a large, sunny room in Horace Mann Hall on the Teachers College campus, which has been renovated and redesigned specifically as a classroom for preschoolers. The school uses various facilities on campus such as the dance studio, and an outdoor lawn on campus for playing. It also has access to the facilities of the Columbia University main campus.

Separation. Individualized. The preschool offers several ways that families begin to connect with the school, starting with a home visit, pictures of teachers, tapes of songs and stories, postcards and a classroom open house.

Parent involvement. Parents are invited to observe at the Pre-School, and participate voluntarily. Parents also help out with all school events. Throughout the year, there are parent-teacher conferences, general meetings, and weekly teacher office hours.

Financial. Tuition can be paid in three installments. A nonrefundable deposit is due on acceptance, which is applied toward the tuition. Scholarship aid is limited.

Transportation. Transportation is provided by parents.

Graduates. Have gone on to Brearley, Cathedral, Chapin, Collegiate, Dalton, Ethical Culture, Fieldston, Horace Mann, Spence, Town, and Trinity, and to public school programs for the gifted. An admissions folder is set up for each child and advice as to ongoing school placement is provided by the Director.

Affiliations. The Hollingworth Preschool is part of Teachers College, Columbia University. However, enrollment is open to all, and college affiliation is not necessary.

The Medical Center Nursery School

Medical Center Campus, Columbia University

Ages: 2–6 yrs

Nonsectarian

60 Haven Avenue (between 169th and 170th Streets)	Established 1957
Zip: 10032	Howard E. Johnson, Director
Tel: 304-7040	Rosa I. Diaz, Assistant Director
Fax: 544-4243	Enrollment: 76
Web site: www.mcns.org	
E-Mail: mcns@mcns.org	

School year. September through late June. Summer program available through August.

Ages	*Hours*	*Days*	*Tuition*
2s/3s	1:30–5:00	Mon–Fri	$8,500
2s/3s/4s/5s	8:30–12:30	Mon–Fri	$9,150
2s/3s/4s/5s	8:00–5:30	Mon–Fri	$16,600

Program. The school provides a secure setting in which children can explore materials, develop relationships with peers and non-parental adults, and participate in learning activities. It cooperates with various departments of Columbia-Presbyterian to permit carefully screened research projects and regular observation of healthy, normal young children.

ERBs are given on the premises.

Admissions. There is a $30 application fee. Inquiries are from September 1st on. The applications deadline is the end of September. Preference is given to children of parents affiliated with New York Presbyterian Hospital or Columbia University. Parents will be called after November 1st to schedule a visit between late November and late February to see the school, and observe a classroom. Notifications are sent in early March.

Class size. Class size ranges from 15 to 23 with three teachers per room. The school has a consulting psychologist, developmental pediatrician and occupational therapist, as well as an educational consultant.

Facilities. The three fully equipped, air-conditioned, spacious classrooms all have expansive views of the Hudson River. There is an additional space for indoor play, a small library, and a kitchen. The outdoor, fenced play area on the terrace, one floor above the school, is equipped with a challenging and dramatic climbing and play structure.

Summer program. End of June through end of August; morning and extended-day programs. Enrollment is by the week.

Parent involvement. Conferences are scheduled regularly, as are schoolwide and classroom parent meetings. Parents are invited to visit the school at any time. Parents voluntarily raise funds for equipment, trips and other projects through a parents association, which meets regularly.

Financial. A deposit of $450 is due on signing the contract. The balance of the tuition is payable monthly, May through April. Extended-hour tuition is payable May through February.

Financial aid is available and must be requested before February 1st. A few children may be funded by ACD.

Graduates. Have gone on to Bank Street, Cathedral, Dalton, Ethical Midtown, Fieldston, St. Hilda's and St. Hugh's, Riverdale Country and District 3 public schools.

Affiliations. Health Sciences Division, Columbia University. Chartered by the Board of Regents of the State University of New York. Accredited by the National Academy of Early Childhood Programs.

Member. ERB, ISAAGNY, Parents League, NYCAEYC, NAEYC.

The Red Balloon Community Day Care Center

Ages: 2–5 yrs

Nonsectarian Parent Cooperative

560 Riverside Drive (between Tiemann Place and 125th Street)
Zip: 10027
Tel: 663-9006
Fax: 932-0190
E-Mail: RBDCC@aol.com
Website: Redballoonlearningcenter.com

Established 1972
Norma Brockman, Director

Enrollment: 49

School year. All year.

Ages	*Hours*	*Days*	*Tuition*
2s	8:00–6:00	Mon–Fri	$1,450 monthly
3–5	8:00–6:00	Mon–Fri	$1,200 monthly

Program. Eclectic. The environment is designed to nurture exploration, independence, self-esteem, and active participation. Teachers prepare a variety of interesting choices which challenge the children and help them develop problem-solving techniques. The program encourages joy in words and books. It also nurtures the children's social and emotional sides; the children learn to value themselves as individuals and as part of a community. According to the director, "When children leave the Red Balloon they are confident, curious, and happy, open to the many possibilities the world has to offer."

Admissions. The application fee is $25. Inquire at any time. The center has a waiting list, so parents should apply as soon as they know they will need care and arrange to visit with their children. Preference is given to members of the Columbia University community.

Staff. The director, three certified head teachers, two assistant teachers, four aides, a cook, and other support staff.

Facilities. Columbia University donates the school space in a faculty building. In addition to three large classrooms arranged into activities areas, there is a large indoor gym, a music room, a small library, a safety-surfaced outdoor play deck and a built-in wading pool.

Breakfast, a hot lunch, and snacks are served family style.

Parent involvement. The school has an open-door policy and encourages parents to spend time in the classroom: to visit, read a story, do a project, and simply come for lunch. An elected Parent Board meets monthly to discuss school policies and daily school functions. Parents are encouraged to join all trips. In addition, the school provides a variety of workshops for parents.

Financial. A deposit of one month's tuition is required on acceptance. Tuition is payable monthly. One-third of the children are funded by ACD.

Transportation. No private bus service is available.

Graduates. Go to public, magnet, and independent schools.

Affiliations. ISAAGNY.

Rita Gold Early Childhood Center

Ages: 6 wks–5 yrs

Box 98, Teachers College	Dr. Leslie Williams,
Room 246, Thorndike Hall	Faculty Co-Director
525 West 120th Street	Dr. Susan Recchia,
Zip: 10027	Faculty Co-Director
Tel: 678-3013	Isabel Belinkie,
	On-site Director

Services are available only to those associated with Columbia University.

The Riverside Church Weekday School

Ages: 2.0–6 yrs

Nursery School and Kindergarten

490 Riverside Drive (between 120th and 122nd Streets)	Established 1930
Zip: 10027	Linda Herman, Educational Director
Tel: 870-6743	Fay Lee, Admissions Director
Fax: 870-6795	
Website: www.weekdayschool-nyc.org	Enrollment: 143

School year. September through June. Summer program, late June and July.

Ages	*Hours*	*Days*	*Tuition*
2.0–2.8	9:00–11:30	Mon/Wed/Fri	$7,600
2.0–2.8	9–11:30	Tu/Th	$5,100
2.0–2.8	12:30–3:00	Tu/Th	$5,100
2.6–6	8:45–12:30	Mon–Fri	$9612
2.6–6	8:45–2:30	Mon–Fri	$10,565
2.6–6	8:45–5:30	Mon–Fri	$13,883

Extended hours. Early drop-off at 8:00 can be arranged, for an additional $950 per year and extra time can be arranged ad hoc, depending on availability, for an hourly fee.

Program. Progressive/academic. The program is child-centered and within a broad framework allows children to explore and experiment with materials and to discover their own potentials and strengths. The curriculum focuses on facilitating social and emotional growth in children as well as on language development and the arts. The "whole language" approach is integrated across the curriculum, with beginning phonics introduced in the 5s program. Children are encouraged to use art to express their thoughts. An art specialist is on staff and the children work in a stimulating art studio. A movement specialist helps develop physical skills through music and movement activities conducted in a spacious movement room. A music specialist develops the children's awareness of sounds, rhythm, and different kinds of musical instruments. Blockbuilding is a significant activity, and every classroom offers a large block area with a spectacular collection of unit blocks.

The school strives to bridge home and school experiences for each child. The basic assumption is that learning occurs best within a context, and new information is best assimilated when based on a child's prior knowledge and experiences. The school's mission reflects the all-inclusive philosophy of Riverside Church and is manifested in the celebration of holidays significant to member families: Christmas, Easter, Succoth, Passover, Hanukkah, Lunar New Year, Kwanzaa, Thanksgiving, Martin Luther King Day. Equally important is each child's birthday celebration in the classroom.

A hot lunch, prepared on site, is served at noon in each classroom. The children eat lunch with their teachers.

Admissions. The application fee is $50. Inquiries are from Labor Day on. Tours are scheduled between October and December. After parents have submitted an application, the school will arrange for them to visit with their children. Notifications are sent in mid-February for kindergarten applicants and in early March for younger children. Preference is given to legacies, church members and siblings. The school strives for a racial, cultural, gender, and economic balance in the classrooms.

Class size. There are ten classrooms: twelve children in the 2s group, fifteen in the 3s, up to fifteen in the 4s, and up to eighteen in the 5s.

Staff. Each classroom has one head teacher and one assistant teacher. Two additional "floating" assistant teachers go where they are needed. Each head teacher has a masters degree in early childhood education.

Facilities. The school's spacious, well-lit, and beautifully maintained classrooms, on the sixth and seventh floors of the church, have breathtaking views of the Hudson River on the west and Morningside Park on the east. There are two large rooftop playgrounds and a full-size gym. The school also has an art studio, movement room, indoor play area, and a charming library.

Separation. In the 2s program, a parent or caregiver stays with the child until both are comfortable separating. 3s begin school in small groups and small sessions which gradually lengthen during the first two weeks. 4s and 5s take only a few days to work up to a full session.

Parent involvement. Parents serve on the advisory administrative board and school committees, and help with social and fundraising events during the school year. They are encouraged to visit their child's classroom to share a skill or talent, or to read a story, participate in circle time, or join the group on a walk to the park. Teachers welcome parents into the classroom so they can learn more about the child's home experiences in order to offer curricular activities that can build on those experiences.

Financial. A nonrefundable deposit of approximately 30 percent is due on signing of the contract. Tuition is payable in five installments. Income from a small endowment fund and from annual fundraising events enables the school to offer limited, need-based tuition assistance.

Transportation. More than half the students come from the Upper West Side, from the 70s through the 120s. Several families come from Washington Heights, the Bronx, and New Jersey. No private bus service is available.

Graduates. Children have gone on to private and public schools such as Bank Street, Brearley, Calhoun, Cathedral, Chapin, Collegiate, Columbia Grammar, Dalton, Ethical Culture, Fieldston, Horace Mann, Manhattan Country, Nightingale-Bamford, Riverdale, Sacred Heart, Spence, St. Hilda and St. Hugh's, Trevor Day, Trinity, UNIS and the Lab School, Manhattan School for Children, PS 9, PS 163, PS 166, PS 75, PS 87, PS 84.

Affiliations. Riverside Church.

Member. ERB, ISAAGNY, NAEYC, ATIS.

Saint Benedict's Day Nursery

Ages: 3–6 yrs

Catholic Nursery School

21 West 124th Street
Zip: 10027

Tel: 423-5715
Fax: 423-5917

Established 1923
Sr. Rose Mary, FHM,
Administrative and
Admissions Director
Sr. Patricia Marie, FHM,
Education Director
Enrollment: 79

School year. The center is open 52 weeks a year.

Ages	*Hours*	*Days*	*Tuition*
3–6	8:00–6:00 only	Mon–Fri	$4,150

Children must be toilet trained.

Program. Traditional. All children participate in daily prayers. The program is highly structured and has a strong skills orientation. Scheduled activities for 4s, for example, include prayers, religion, phonics, math, circle time, free play, storytime, music, social studies, science, holiday shows and free play indoors and outdoors. Art and musical instruction are included in the curriculum.

Admissions. There is a $215 application fee. Call for an application and to arrange a talk with the director and a visit to the nursery school. Afterward an interview will be arranged for the child. Children are accepted on a first-come basis; parents register in the spring for the following September. The school maintains an active waiting list.

Class size. There are six classes: two classes of thirteen 3s, two classes of thirteen 3s and 4s, and one kindergarten class of fifteen. Each class has two in staff.

Facilities. There are six classrooms, as well as a kitchen, office, storeroom, and a well-equipped outdoor playground.

A hot lunch is provided for children in the St. Benedict's Day Nursery and two snacks.

Parent involvement. Parents are active in fund-raising, on school committees, and help on field trips, and with plays and graduation exercises. Conferences are twice yearly, and class parents meet twice yearly. All communications with parents pass through the director's office.

Financial. A registration fee of $215 is required on signing the full-year contract. Payment arrangements vary with parents' needs.

Transportation. Children come from Harlem, the Bronx, and Queens. No private bus service is available.

Graduates. Attend All Saints, St. Aloysius, St. Charles, St. Ignatius, and St. Mark, as well as independent schools.

Affiliations. The school was founded by the Franciscan Handmaids of the Most Pure Heart of Mary and is affiliated with the Archdiocese of New York and Catholic School Board.

St. Hilda's and St. Hugh's School

Ages: 2–13 yrs

Episcopal Early Childhood Program and Primary School

619 West 114th Street (between Broadway and Riverside Drive)
Zip: 10025-7995
Tel: 932-1980
Fax: 531-0102
Website: www.sthildas.org

Established 1950
Virginia Connor, Head of School
Emily Atkinson, Admissions Director
Early Childhood enrollment: 119
Total enrollment: 370

School year. Second week in September through first week of June.

Ages	*Hours*	*Days*	*Tuition*
*2s (Toddlers)	9:00–11:00	*T/Th or M/W/F	$6,500–$8,500
	8:25–12:30	Mon–Fri	$19,000
3–4s	8:25–2:50	Mon–Fri	$23,000
5s	8:25–2:50	Mon–Fri	$25,000

*Children must be 2 as of September 1st for the toddler program.

Extended hours. Parents can arrange for an extended day until 6:30 at an additional cost of $3,500 for the year. Parents may also arrange for an extended day on any afternoon without notice. Costs are pro-rated.

Program. The school is structured and offers a clear academic program. There is a blending of faiths among the students, and concepts of the spiritual and moral world are explored. Daily chapel service begins in first grade.

The curriculum is planned around units of study based on themes. Music, drama, art, foreign language and physical education are emphasized. The toddler program focuses on language development, socialization, and separation in a secure and nurturing environment. Beginning in nursery, students are taught by specialists twice a week for arts, library and physical education.

Junior kindergarten students go to nearby art studios for lessons in technique. Senior kindergarten students have physical education daily in the gym, and go to science lab twice a week. Computer begins in second grade.

Children begin wearing uniforms in first grade.

Admissions. The application fee is $50. Inquiries may be made at any time, but the school requires parents to submit an application before arranging a tour. Parents should call to make an appointment to tour the school. After the school receives the application, the admissions office will call to arrange for an appointment to meet children individually or in small groups. Older children spend either a full- or half-day in a classroom. Applicants to senior kindergarten (5s) must take the ERB. Notifications are sent in February and March.

Class size. The early childhood division includes toddler, nursery, junior, and senior kindergarten classes. Each has two staff members. Toddler classes have three teachers. Children work with specialists in art, music, movement, foreign language, science and library. A full-time nurse is on staff.

Facilities. The school is modern, fully-air conditioned, and beautifully designed. Its centrally located chapel (sometimes used for theater-in-the-round presentations) has a Reiger organ. There are spacious classrooms, a floor of art studios and music studios, three science labs, two technology centers, a full-sized gymnasium/ auditorium (4s/5s receive ballet lessons here), a junior-senior library, a large cafeteria where the children eat and, off the second floor, an enormous outdoor play deck with a slide and swings.

Separation. Varies according to the individual child. The process is not rushed.

Parent involvement. The Parents Association meets monthly. It is active and coordinates fund-raising events and classroom projects; many share special talents, interests, or their cultural heritage both in the classroom and with the school as a whole. Conferences are held twice yearly.

Financial. There is a $3,000 deposit due on signing the contract. Lunch is optional for grades 4 through 8 at an additional cost of $900. Tuition refund insurance (at a cost of 7 percent of tuition) is recommended. Financial aid is available based on need.

Transportation. Children come from the Upper West Side and various other neighborhoods.

Affiliations. St. Hilda's and St. Hugh's was founded by The Community of the Holy Spirit, an Episcopal religious order for women. The school has a full-time chaplain on staff.

Member. ERB, ISAAGNY, NAIS, NAES, NYSAIS.

Tompkins Hall Nursery School and Childcare Center

Ages: 15 mos.–5 yrs

Nonsectarian Parent Cooperative

21 Claremont Avenue	Established ca. 1935
(near 116th Street)	Cynthia Pollack, Director
Zip: 10027	
Tel: 666-3340	Nursery enrollment: 25
E-Mail: TompkinsHall@earthlink.net	Toddler enrollment: 10

School year. September through July 31st.

Ages	*Hours*	*Days*	*Tuition*
Toddlers*	8:30–5:30	Mon–Thurs Fri until 12:30	$21,000
3s	8:30–12:30	Mon–Fri	$11,700
3s and 4s	8:30–2:30	Mon–Thurs (Fri until 12:30)	$13,300
3s and 4s	8:30–5:30	Mon–Thurs Fri until 12:30	$18,200

*Less than full-time available.
Parents who volunteer one morning per week in the classroom receive reduced tuition. Extended days are available for 3s and 4s at an additional fee. Many scheduling options are available at a prorated fee. Call for more information.

Program. Developmental. The school focuses on social skills and emotional development, identifying and talking about feelings, conflicts, choices, relationships, and activities. The day begins with free play, block building, art and imaginative play. Other activities include circle time, music and movement, cooking, and outdoor play. The afternoon program includes more complex activities and field trips.

Admissions. The application fee is $35. Applications begin in October for following year. Call to set time for an individual visit and apply then. Notifications are sent in March. Priority is given to Columbia faculty or staff.

Class size. There is a toddler program of 10 children; the preschool is a mixed age grouping of 25 children in the morning, which is divided by age in the afternoon, twelve in one group, thirteen in the other. After 2:30 all combine into one group.

Facilities. The nursery school occupies an apartment on the ground floor of a Columbia-owned residential building. Visitors are buzzed into a white marble foyer. The door to the nursery school is at the far end. A small room is filled with cubbies and strollers. There is a well-furnished dress-up room, kitchen and snack room, bathroom, office, library, and activities room filled with blocks, toys, a sand table, small climbing structure, small play objects, and a space for large motor activities; a nature and science room, easels, art table, and reading and small motor areas. All the rooms have windows. Half the roof has been fenced in and carpeted to form a play yard. It is equipped with a play house, wooden climbing structures, slides, and a toy shed full of tricycles, wagons, blocks, and other toys. Children bring their lunches; the school provides snacks.

Parent involvement. Parents can elect to work in the classroom. They are obliged to attend monthly parent/staff meetings to discuss curriculum and developmental issues, participate in fundraising and to contribute two work days each year, and to serve on a committee, or take on a school job such as food shopping.

Transportation. No private bus service is available.

Graduates. Have gone on to public and private schools, most recently Bank Street, Dalton, Manhattan School for Children, PS 75, PS 87 and The Anderson Program.

Affiliations. Columbia University.

Washington Heights and Inwood YM-YWHA

Ages: 2.9–5 yrs

Jewish Nursery School and Kindergarten

54 Nagle Avenue
Zip: 10040
Tel: 569-6200
Website: www.ywashhts.org
E-Mail: mgoldman@ywashhts.org

Established 1955
Madlyn Goldman, Director
Enrollment: 45

School year. September through June.

Ages	*Hours*	*Days*	*Tuition*
2.9–5	9:00–11:30 or	Mon–Fri	$450 monthly
	1:00–3:30	Mon–Fri	$400 monthly
2.9–5	9:00–3:30	Mon–Fri	$675 monthly

*Children must be 2.9 by September 1st; family membership is $200 yearly for one child in the nursery program; $225 for more than one child.

Program. "How to share, get along with others and make decisions as a group" is the school's emphasis. Madlyn Goldman brings teaching experience and enthusiasm to her position. In the school's community-based program, children learn about the community they live in, visit several neighborhood shops and have neighborhood leaders visit the class.

Admissions. Y membership fee. Inquiries are from January on. Parents call to arrange to visit the school with their child. Children are accepted on a first-come basis, and parents are notified as soon as possible. Membership in the Y is a prerequisite for nursery school enrollment.

Class size. There is one class of sixteen 3s (3s and young 4s) and one class of twenty 4s and 5s. Each class has three staff members; art, music and rhythm and dance specialists visit weekly. A psychologist is available weekly and for consultations with staff and parents.

Facilities. The school is located in a three-story community center. The children meet in two large, well-equipped classrooms on the ground floor. There is a large indoor play space, a gymnasium, a well-equipped rooftop play area, and a smaller outside playground.

Summer program. Day camp and Nursery camp operates in July and August. Those interested should register in March.

Separation. Children are brought into the program in small groups for short periods of time. The orientation takes about a week. Parents remain in the lobby until needed. Separation is handled individually.

Parent involvement. Parents may visit any time, often joining classroom activities, or accompanying a class on a field trip. The school has a parent committee, which meets every 4-6 weeks with various staff members to discuss special programming, fundraising and other relevant issues. Fundraising events take place in the building. Parents raise roughly $20,000–$30,000 for the school each year. Occasional workshops on parenting issues are organized by a school consultant. Conferences are held twice a year and at parents' request.

Financial. There is a registration fee of $250. Parents pay a deposit of three months' tuition and sign a contract for the school year. Tuition is payable quarterly. Financial aid is available.

Transportation. The school provides transportation for a cost of $200 monthly for round trips, and $125 monthly for one-way trips.

Graduates. Attend community public schools and private schools, including Fieldston, Horace Mann, Riverdale Country, and Yeshiva.

Affiliations and Memberships. Federation of Jewish Philanthropies, YM and YWHA.

DOWNTOWN

The Acorn School

Ages: 23 mos–4 yrs

Nonsectarian Preschool

330 East 26th Street (between First and Second Avenues)
Zip: 10010
Tel: 684-0230
Fax: 696-0514

Established 1966
Jill Axthelm, Director
Helene Daub, Administrator
Enrollment: 115

School year. Early September through early June, with optional June program for enrolled students.

Ages	*Hours*	*Days*	*Tuition and Fees*
23 mos	2:00–3:30	2 days	$3,000
2s	9:00–11:30	2 days	$5,400
2s/3s	9:00–11:30 or 1:00–3:30	3 days	$7,000
3s/4s	8:45–11:45	5 days	$9,600
	or 12:45–3:45	2 days	$2,000–$3,000

Extended hours. There is an early drop-off at 8:30 for $3.00 per day. In addition, an optional extended-day program for 4s is available. A June program for two extended weeks is also available at an additional fee.

Programs.

Stay & Play: For 23 months and older. Headed by a certified early-childhood teacher, a minimum of ten children participate with their parent or caregiver. The children enjoy indoor playground equipment, sing, listen to stories, and explore various activities (easel, sand table, blocks, puzzles, manipulatives) in a classroom setting. A snack is served.

2s: Encourages creativity, exploration, and interaction with a variety of materials (easel, water table, blocks, kitchen area, and many manipulatives) in a nurturing, cheerful, and stimulating environment. The arts are introduced through active participation in singing, listening to stories, cooking, and group art projects. Many children discover the rewards and responsibilities of friendship for the first time. Teachers encourage each child to grow at his or her own pace as they build confidence and independence.

3/4s: Eclectic. Emphasizes self-teaching through independent, active learning planned but not dominated by the teacher. Through an organized, diverse environment, the program seeks to stimulate the child to discover, test, and experience independently his or her rapidly expanding world. All learning experiences encourage each child's cognitive, physical, and socio-emotional development. Three large, attractively designed, and colorful classrooms contain a wide variety of materials. The children are free to choose their own activity and pursue it alone or with others, whether the area be socializing, the sand table, blockbuilding, books, painting. In the large group, each child is encouraged to participate, whether it be the presentation of new materials, the sharing of his/her experiences, singing, or listening to stories. Art, cooking, language arts, and music are all integral parts of the program, encouraging the children to express themselves creatively.

ERBs are given on the premises. The director helps parents choose appropriate ongoing schools for their children.

Admissions. The application fee is $40. Children of all races, creeds, and nationalities are welcome. Call for an application and to schedule a visit. Parent observations begin in the fall, children visit in January or February. The children play, usually in small groups and with parents present. Preference is given to siblings. Notifications are sent by March.

Facilities. The school occupies the ground floor of an apartment building and has several doors opening onto a courtyard through which parents and children enter. The interior is ingeniously divided into classroom areas. There are four main classroom spaces and an indoor play space for music, movement, and rainy-day play. Acorn uses outside, age-appropriate climbing equipment in an enclosed playing area. Weather permitting, all children spend approximately forty minutes a day climbing, running, and playing freely. On cold, rainy days, the children use the all-purpose room for free play. A climbing apparatus, rocking boats, and a slide are provided. Acorn has won over 30 awards for architecture and design and has been chosen by various companies as a testing site for child-related products.

Separation. New children come in small groups for shortened sessions during the first few weeks. Parents may stay in the classroom for this time. The separation program is gradual and flexible.

Parent involvement. Parents serve on the board of directors and are encouraged to become class parents, observe and participate in class activities, and support fund-raising events. Parent-teacher conferences are scheduled in November and March.

Financial. A one-time, $500 nonrefundable reserve fund contribution is required of all new families (the reserve fund is used for capital improvements, e.g., new indoor and outside playground equipment, air-conditioning system, office equipment).

Scholarships are awarded to children residing in Phipps Houses. Potential scholarship students are interviewed by the director in late spring.

Graduates. Have gone on to a variety of public and private schools, including Allen-Stevenson, Birch Wathen-Lenox, Browning, Dalton, Friends Seminary, Grace Church, Riverdale, Spence, Town, UNIS, Village Community School, and PS 40, PS 116 and NEST.

Chartered. By the Board of Regents of the State University of New York.

Member. ISAAGNY, Parents League.

Barrow Street Nursery School/Greenwich House

Ages: 2–5 yrs

Nonsectarian

27 Barrow Street (at Seventh Avenue)	Established 1984
Zip: 10014	Carissa Sachs, Director
Tel: 633–1203	Admissions Director
Fax: 633-1209	Enrollment: 55
Website: www.greenwichhouse.org	

School year. Second week in September through mid June. Camp available in the summer.

Ages	*Hours*	*Days*	*Tuition**
2s	9:00–12:00	Mon,Wed,Fri	$7,800
2s	9:00–12:30	Tue,Thur	$6,700
3s	9:00–1:00	Mon–Fri	$11,300
4–5s	9:00–1:00	Mon–Fri	$11,300

Children must be 2 on entry. An extended day option for children 3–5 years of age is available Monday–Thursday until 2:30, at an additional cost.
*Tuition is subject to change.

Program. A child-centered approach is used. Individual children's special interests and abilities are developed through block building, playing with sand, art materials and dramatic play. The environment is loving and supportive which helps children develop positive self images, confidence and basic social skills.

Admissions. The application fee is $45. Call for applications soon after Labor Day. Tours are scheduled from mid-October until mid-December. Small group play sessions are held in January. Regular ISAAGNY notification dates are followed.

Class size. There is a class of 2s with ten children to two teachers, a class of 3s with 16 children and three teachers, and a class of 4s and 5s with 18 children and three teachers. Specialists teach music, art and gymnastics to each class for an hour each week.

Facilities. The school is located on the third floor of Greenwich House, a Village landmark. Three classrooms are arranged in activities centers. The school has use of Greenwich House's gym and running track (a great runway for tricycles and wheeled toys) and its roof playground, equipped with a climbing structure, toys and blocks.

Separation. Teachers visit each new family before school begins. School starts with a three-day process in which half the group comes for short sessions. Phasing-in can take up to six weeks in the 2s class, depending on how each child handles separation.

Parent involvement. Each class has two class parents. There's an active Parents Association. Parent-teacher conferences are held twice yearly.

Financial. A deposit is required on signing the contract. Scholarship aid and payment plans are available.

Transportation. Most children come from the Village, Soho, Noho, and Tribeca areas. No private bus service is available.

Graduates. Have gone on to Friends Seminary, Grace Church, Little Red School House, St. Luke's, Village Community School, and local public schools. Proprietorship.

Battery Park City Day Nursery

Ages: 1–5 yrs

Nonsectarian

215 South End Avenue,
Battery Park City
(between Albany Street
and Rector Place, south of
World Financial Center)
Zip: 10280
Tel: 945-0088
Fax: 786-1673
Website: www.bpcdaynursery.com

Established 1986
Denise Cordivano,
Head of School
Dana Benzo,
Education Director

Enrollment: 150

School year. September through June.

Ages	*Hours*	*Days*	*Tuition (monthly)*
1–2.11	8:00–6:00	Mon–Fri	$1,400
3–5	8:00–6:00	Mon–Fri	$1,340
1–2.11	8:00–12:00/2:00–6:00	Mon–Fri	$940
3–5	8:00–12:00/2:00–6:00	Mon–Fri	$880

Two and three full- and half-day a week schedules are also available at proportionate rates.

Program. The developmental-interaction model is a primary influence. Activities include dramatic play, painting, drawing, cooking, with puzzles and small play objects, music and dance, poetry, storytelling, blockbuilding, active outdoor play, and reading- and math-readiness for older children.

Admissions. The application fee is $50. Currently parents may call at any time to see if positions are open and to arrange to see the school with their child and talk with the director. The child is invited into a classroom with a parent. Notification of admissions is continuous.

Class size. Toddler/young 2s, 2s and 3s, 3s–4s, and 4s–5s: Each class has a head teacher and two assistant teachers.

Staff. Degreed head teachers and early childhood professionals as assistant teachers make up the staff. The schools also trains interns from local colleges.

Facilities. Seven classrooms on the main floor of a residential building. Each is equipped with a bathroom, learning and play items. There is a backyard with a playhouse, climbing equipment, play cars, carts, etc.

Children bring their lunches. Snacks are provided.

Summer program. A summer program is available in July and August. Enrollment can be weekly or monthly.

Separation. Parents are asked to stay until both child and parent are comfortable.

Parent involvement. Parents may drop in any time. Formal conferences are arranged twice yearly. Informal conferences are held as needed.

Financial. A deposit of one month's tuition is due on signing the contract. Tuition is payable monthly.

Transportation. Most children come from Battery Park City, and Tribeca, or have parents working in the financial district. No private bus service is available.

Member. NAEYC.

Beginnings, Toddler Program and Nursery School

Ages: 18 mos–4.9 yrs

Nonsectarian

130 East 16th Street
(between Irving Place
and 3rd Avenue)
Zip: 10003
Tel: 228-5679
Fax: 228-9907

Established 1983
Sheila Wolper,
Founder
Jane Racoosin,
Director
Claire Zamor,
Admissions Director
Enrollment: 140

School year. Mid-September through May; June and July Program available for children enrolled in the school.

Ages	*Hours*	*Days*	*Tuition*
2s/Toddlers	2:00–4:30	2 days	$6,425
2s	9:30–12:30	2 days/3 days	$6685–10,550
2s/3s	9:00–1:00	3 days	$9,055
2s/3s	8:45–12:45; 2:00–5:00	3, 4 days	$9,055–11,065
4s	1:30–5:00	3, 4 days	$9,710–11,860
4s–5s	8:45–12:45	3, 4, 5 days	$11,655–14,165

Extended hours. For 4/5s, an extended day is available from Monday through Thursday until 2:15 at an additional cost.

Program. Developmental. The school's goals for children are simple: to create a nurturing and stimulating environment, and promote community and personal awareness within a group, to encourage cooperation and problem-solving, and to develop within each child a love of learning. The partnership between teachers and children provides an atmosphere which is rich in possibilities and responds to the unique wonders of each individual child.

Admissions. The application fee is $35. Inquiries are from June through December. There's a lottery for applications dependent on space availability. School visits begin the first week in November. Children visit in small groups on Saturdays and Sundays in January and February. Notifications are sent in early March.

Class size. Children are grouped both chronologically and developmentally. Class size varies with age group. Each class has three or four staff members.

Staff. Head teachers have master's degrees in early childhood education. The school has a part time child development consultant, available one day each week, as well as a music specialist and yoga teacher.

Facilities. The school occupies four floors of a commercial brownstone. The classrooms have access to a sunny play area with a wide range of equipment. Flower gardens and trees provide a welcome respite from city streets. Children bring their lunches and are served healthy and varied snacks (seasonal fruits, cheese, rice crackers, and pretzels).

Separation. The process includes home visits, a separation workshop for parents and caregivers, as well as a modified schedule that gradually builds to the full session. A parent or caregiver remains in the classroom until the child is comfortable.

Parent involvement. Parents coordinate fundraising events, act as class parents, assist on field trips, participate in classroom activities, and help with the school library. Parenting workshops and seminars are offered throughout the year; topics include toilet training, limit setting and sibling issues. Two parent-teacher conferences are scheduled yearly. Parents may visit at any time, join the group to read stories or share a project.

Financial. A deposit of $1,000 is due on signing the contract; tuition is payable in eight installments. Partial financial aid is available.

Transportation. Parents or caregivers bring the children, most of whom come from the East and West Village, Gramercy Park, Tribeca, and Soho.

Graduates. Have gone on to Allen-Stevenson, Brearley, Browning, Buckley, Chapin, City and Country, Dalton, Ethical Culture, Friends Seminary, Grace Church School, Hewitt, Hunter Elementary, Lab School, Packer-Collegiate, Saint Ann's, Spence, UNIS, Village Community School, and The Anderson Program.

Bellevue Educare Child Care Center

Ages: 6 mos–4 yrs

Nonsectarian All-Day Care

462 Second Avenue
(at 27th Street)
Zip: 10016

Established 1971
Sarah J. Maldonado, Executive Director
Delores McCullough, Client Services Coordinator
Enrollment: 41

Tel: 679-2393
Fax: 679-7366

School year. All year.

Ages	*Hours*	*Days*	*Tuition (monthly)*
6 mos–4 yrs	6:00–12	Mon–Fri	*

*Parents must call to inquire about the current fees.

Program. Children and staff are multilingual and multicultural, and emphasis is placed on interpersonal, self-evaluation, and verbalization skills. The curriculum is based on the High/Scope Educational Approach. The center uses a variety of preschool key experiences that allow a child to assess a situation and make independent choices. The school has an open classroom setting which incorporates different areas that include a library, blocks, music, house corner, science, art and computers.

Admissions. The registration fee is $100. Inquire at least six months in advance. Admission availability is based on the age of the child. Tours are arranged at a mutually convenient time.

Class size. The class size is presently 10 infants, 10 toddlers, and 21 preschoolers. Due to the extended hours option, sometimes the center can accommodate more children.

Staff. Volunteers and interns occasionally augment the staff. Nurses, pediatricians, and social workers are available through Bellevue Hospital.

Facilities. Located within Bellevue Hospital Center, accessible through a staircase and elevators. Educare consists of one large area, divided imaginatively into three classrooms with interconnecting activities areas. Lockers are available for belongings. Activities areas include blockbuilding, library, dramatic play, music and movement, science, art, and table toys. The facilities are modern and inviting, imaginatively designed and well-maintained and equipped.

Children are given breakfast, lunch, and an afternoon snack.

Separation. Parents bring the children and stay for the first day. Parents are asked to be accessible when it is felt the children need them. There is an open door policy.

Parent involvement. Many parents are on the staff of Bellevue Hospital. There are monthly evening meetings of the board, staff, and parents (child care is provided) on subjects chosen by the parents. Parents are members of the board of trustees. Parents also help with fund-raising and assist in the classroom. Field trips are organized by the parents association. Parents may visit whenever they choose, but they should call if they plan to spend a half or full day. Parent/teacher conferences are twice yearly or at the parents' request.

Financial. There are different measures of eligibility for enrollment. Parents can call the center for specific information.

Transportation. Parents are required to escort their children to and from the center.

Graduates. Attend both private and public schools.

Affiliations. Bellevue Hospital Center.

Bellevue South Nursery School

Ages: 2.10–5 plus yrs

Nonsectarian

10 Waterside Plaza (at 25th Street and East River)
Zip: 10010
Tel: 684-0134
Website: bsnurseryschool.org
E-Mail: bsns10@aol.com

Established 1970
Caroline Mechanick, Director
Estelle Hofstetter, Educational Director
Enrollment: 30

School year. Early September through Early June.

Ages	*Hours*	*Days*	*Tuition*
2.10–3.8	8:45–11:45	Mon–Fri	$8,800
3.9–5	12:45–3:45	Mon–Fri	$8,800

Program. Eclectic. At Bellevue South Nursery School, the children are given a great deal of freedom to explore in a noncompetitive atmosphere. Teaching is informal and based on the child's interest. The director plays the piano and sings with the children daily. There is a combination of full group, small group, and individual activities which include art, water and sand play, blockbuilding, dramatic play, small play objects (beads, puzzles), daily music and movement, art projects, cooking, science and nature, reading, math, and computer-readiness.

Admissions. The application fee is $35. Inquiries are from mid-September on. Parents should call for information. They will be invited to attend the school's open house. A parent guide will answer questions. Parents are active in the school's operation and can serve in the classroom once a month. The school wants prospective parents to have a clear idea of what is involved. Interested parents are given an application form after the open house.

An appointment is made to meet the child, usually in a group with four other applicants, while school is not in session. During this time, the director will talk with the parents individually. Parent guides are also available to answer more questions about parent involvement in the school.

The school tries to balance the age range in the classes. Notifications are sent in March.

Class size. There are usually fifteen children in the morning class and fifteen children in the afternoon. There are two head teachers, the director, and a parent in the classroom. The afternoon program offers young 5s a chance to mature for kindergarten.

Facilities. The school is on the plaza level of the southernmost Waterside Plaza building. The 25th Street pedestrian bridge goes right to its door. One large, well-windowed room is divided into activities centers by low bookshelves filled with brightly colored plastic baskets containing small play objects and blocks. An adjoining room contains a climbing loft, workbench, a slide, a play kitchen, dress-up and puppet theater. There is a child-sized bathroom. The children also use the playground in the Waterside complex.

Separation. Seen as a developmental process and a great deal of attention is paid to it. Parents are informed during the application process that they or their caregiver will need to make a two-week commitment when school starts and they are encouraged to stop by before school opens to familiarize their child with the location. Teachers visit new children at home; there is a parents' orientation meeting to explain the phasing-in process.

The children start in small groups with shortened hours, leading up to the full session and full group. Parents or caregivers remain in the classroom during this period, and their withdrawal is gradual.

Parent involvement. Parents are active in nearly every facet of the school. They constitute the board of directors, handle the school's payroll, bookkeeping, communications and legal matters, and help coordinate admissions, oversee fund-raising, and serve as parent of the day. Parents organize a dinner with a silent auction in the spring and in the fall. In addition, there are frequent workshops on such issues as reading- and math-readiness, child development, and ongoing schools.

Financial. A $900 nonrefundable deposit is due on acceptance and applied toward tuition. Tuition is payable quarterly.

Transportation. No private bus service is available.

Graduates. Have gone on to Claremont, Collegiate, Brearley, Browning, Dalton, Friends Seminary, Hewitt, Horace Mann, Manhattan Country, Town, and UNIS, Village Community School, as well as local public schools and Gifted and Talented programs, including PS 158, and PS 116, NEST and Hunter.

Member. The Early Childhood Education Council, ERB, ISAAGNY, ATIS.

Borough of Manhattan Community College Early Childhood Center

199 Chambers Street
Zip: 10007
Tel: 220-8250
Fax: 748-7462
E-Mail: cjordan@bmcc.cuny.edu

Claudette Jordan,
Assistant Administrative Director

For BMCC students' families only. Serves children ages 2 years through kindergarten. The family day care network serves children from two months through 12 years of age.

Brotherhood Synagogue Nursery School

Ages: 2.4–5 yrs

Jewish Nursery School

28 Gramercy Park South
(at 20th Street)
Zip: 10003
Tel: 995-9867
Fax: 420-9512
Web site: www.brotherhoodsynagogue.org

Established 2001
Merril Feinstein-Feit,
Director
Enrollment: approximately 42

School year. September through June.

Age	*Hours*	*Days*	*Tuition*
2.4–3.0	9:00–11:45	Mon–Wed–Fri	$9,200
3s	8:50–12:30	Mon–Fri	$12,600
4's	8:50–2:00 (Fri until 12:30)	Mon–Thurs	$14,000

Program. Developmental. Special attention is paid to a child's individual needs by teachers and the director. Children are encouraged to participate in both large and small group activities that include language development, social skills, free play, circle time, science, snack, outdoor play, story time, music, dramatic play, block building, art and sand play.

Jewish traditions, values and experiences are central to the program, through the celebration of Shabbat and other Jewish holidays.

Admissions. The application fee is $60.

Parents may call the school to schedule a visit, and request an application. An informational meeting for parents with the director is held along with a tour of the school.

Class size. In the two's group there are approximately twelve children to three teachers, the three's and four's will have roughly fifteen children and three teachers.

Staff. Teachers hold masters degrees in early childhood education and/or have extensive experience working with young children. Regular workshops are held with teachers and outside professionals. There is an early childhood consultant on staff along with a music and movement specialist. Membership to a variety of early childhood organizations and associations is also provided. The director meets weekly with the staff.

Facilities. Located in a historic former Friends Meeting House, the new addition has three large classrooms and a private outdoor playground on the premises.

Separation. Children are gradually expected to separate from their parents or care givers. The school provides support to families throughout the process and does home visits and maintains frequent communication between home and school.

Parent involvement. The Parents Association is an active group of parents who volunteer for a variety of activities.

Graduates. Attend a variety of independent, public and Jewish day schools including: Village Community School, Heschel, Solomon Schechter, Buckley, Ethical Culture, Little Red School House,

Birch Wathen-Lenox, PS 116 Gifted and Talented Program, NEST, PS 40 and PS 41.

Affiliations. Brotherhood Synagogue.

Buckle My Shoe Nursery School

Ages: 3 mos–5 yrs (Worth Street)
21 mos–5 yrs (West 13th Street)

40 Worth Street (at the junction of Church and Thomas Streets)
Zip: 10013
Tel: 374-1496
Fax: 577-9678
Website: www.Bucklemyshoe.org
E-Mail: kflynn@bucklemyshoe.org

Linda Ensko, Director
Preschool enrollment: approximately 100

230 West 13th Street (between Greenwich Street and Seventh Avenue)
Zip: 10011
Tel: 807-0518
Call 374-1496 for inquiries

Preschool enrollment: approximately 30

School year. Parents contract for September through June. A summer program is offered for July and August.

Ages	*Hours*	*Days*	*Tuition*
Infants/toddlers	8–6	Mon–Fri	$2,000
2s		Mon–Fri	$1,950
3s–5s		Mon–Fri	$1,800

Toilet training. Not required for admission. Regular toileting time is incorporated into the day's schedule, and children between 2 and 3 are encouraged to sit on the child-sized toilets as they are ready. Students of all ages have a change of clothes on hand.

Program. The school follows the Reggio Emilia approach, requiring strong parental involvement and documentation of learning experiences. The curriculum focuses on a monthly theme, e.g., our families, the seasons, sea life, transportation. Children learn through hands-on, inquiry-based methods with an emphasis on decision-making and socialization. Activities include circle and story time, art, science, math with manipulatives, dramatic play, sand and water play, music, blockbuilding, computer, cooking, and gymnastics. Specialists offer French, Italian, movement, music, yoga, art and theater. Children from the 3s on take monthly field trips to pick apples, visit farms, the American Museum of Natural History and the Bronx Zoo.

Admissions. Registration begins with a sign up list. Parents attend a scheduled tour and meet with the director.

Class size. *Worth Street:* The child to adult ratio for infants and toddlers is 3:1; for 2s, 5:1; and for 3/4s, 7:1.

West 13th Street: There are three groups: 2s, 3s, and 4s.

Staff. Head teachers hold or are working toward a masters degree in early childhood education and have Reggio Emilia training.

Facilities. *Worth Street:* The downtown school's vast (10,000 square feet) ground-floor space boasts high ceilings and light streaming in from two walls of windows. Low partitions divide the space into individual classrooms and play areas. Surfaces are colorful and clean, and the equipment is up to date. A roomy, cushioned gym is equipped with apparatus for tumbling and climbing as well as swings. A new art space, or atelier, offers children a hands-on creative arts experience. An expanded block area completes this project. Children use nearby Washington Market Park and Hudson River Park; as well as other community venues such as theaters, libraries, etc.

West 13th Street: The school has three rooms on the ground floor of a carriage house. While the classes rotate to share certain facilities such as the sandbox, water table, and mat-lined climbing area, each group is based in a classroom of its own. Books, math manipulatives, art materials, and puzzles are available on accessible shelves in activity areas. A large carpeted room that includes an upstairs loft playhouse and a piano is available to the 4s. The children use nearby playgrounds.

Separation. Depends on the individual child. Parents of 2s are encouraged to stay until the child is comfortable. To ease separation, parents may schedule play dates at the school for their child before school begins.

Parent involvement. Potluck dinners at the beginning and end of the year; a parents' advisory board addresses school-wide issues, planning, and fundraising. Parents volunteer for class trips and participate in classroom activities. Two parent-teacher conferences are scheduled yearly, more if requested. Parents may visit at any time.

Financial. A deposit of $1,000 is due on signing the contract and applied to the last month's tuition. There is a yearly insurance fee of $550, and a $400 specialist fee. Tuition is payable monthly or quarterly. A 20 percent discount is offered on a sibling's tuition. Limited scholarship aid is available.

Graduates. Have gone on to private and public schools including, City and Country, Corlears, Ethical Culture, Friends Seminary, Hunter Elementary, Little Red School House, Packer Collegiate, Trinity, Village Community, and PS 6, 124, 234, 41, and 3 as well as NEST, Hunter and other gifted and talented programs.

Member. NAEYC.

Chelsea Day School

Ages: 2–5 yrs

Nonsectarian Nursery School

345 West 14th Street (between 8th and 9th Avenues)
Zip: 10014
Tel: 675-8541
Fax: 675-8385

Established 1981
Jean Rosenberg, Director

Enrollment: 110

School year. Second week in September through second week in June.

Ages	*Hours*	*Days*	*Tuition*
2s	9:00–12:00	3 days	$6,600
3s	9:00–12:00	Mon–Fri	$11,000
3s–5s	9:00–3:00	Mon–Fri	$16,500

Extended days available weekly to 3 PM, at an additional fee. There is an insurance fee of approximately $300. Toilet training is not required.

Program. Developmental. Chelsea Day School was founded by its current director, Jean Rosenberg, who has taught children two to eighteen years of age. The school prefers to be known as the one that follows "the principles of child development," rather than one with an "eclectic" program. The curriculum stresses play and uses projects to encourage learning, intellectual growth and build community. Ongoing projects are planned to bring families together. Religious rituals are not observed, but the "Celebration of Light" is. "The yearbook is a particular favorite of mine," says Mrs. Rosenberg. The children's photographs and pictures are a fine example of preschool art work.

Staff. The 2s classes have ten children in each session with two teachers; the 3s have fifteen each with three teachers; the 4s have sixteen with two teachers. Each class has specialists in art and music twice a week. There are two classes at each age level. There is a teacher's enrichment fund of $20,000 that is used for conferences, staff development workshops and grants. Individual grants of $500 must be board-approved.

Facilities. The school moved in 1996 to a newly designed facility on the third floor of a three-story building on 14th Street. There are six classrooms, a large central meeting room, a room rented out to Music Together, and a roof playground and garden above the third floor.

Summer program. Runs for seven weeks at a per day cost of $55 until 1:00, $65 until 3:00.

Parent involvement. Parents may visit at any time without an appointment. They serve on school committees, run the library, help with admissions tours, tend the garden, and run the Auction and Winter Fair. The school is closed twice a year for parent-teacher conferences, and parents are encouraged to request additional conferences whenever they feel the need.

Financial. A non-refundable deposit of $1,000 is required upon signing of contract for the school year. Half of the remaining tuition is due on September 1, the balance on December 1. A non-interest bearing loan of $1000 per family is required. Financial aid is available.

Transportation. About 90 percent of the children come from the Chelsea and upper Greenwich Village neighborhoods. Public bus service is available on the M 14-Crosstown bus, M 11-Ninth Avenue bus or by subway on the A, C, E, 1, 2, 3, 9 trains or the Path train to 14th Street. No private bus service is available.

Graduates. Have gone on to City and Country, Corlears, Dalton, Ethical Culture, Friends Seminary, Grace Church, Little Red School House, Midtown West, Saint Ann's, Village Community School, as well as PS 3, 11, 41, 89, and 234.

Chartered. By the Board of Regents of the State University of New York.

Member. Downtown Early Childhood Association, NAEYC and ISAAGNY.

The Children's Garden at General Theological Seminary

Ages: 2 mos–3 yrs

175 9th Avenue (between 20th and 21st Streets)
Zip: 10011
Tel: 243-5150, 924-9266
Fax: 727-3907
Website: www.gts.edu
E-Mail: admissions@gts.edu

Susan Stein, Director

Nursery enrollment: 37

School year. Year-round.

Ages	*Hours*	*Days*	*Tuition (monthly)*
Infants to 2.0	8:00–6:00	Mon–Fri	$1,525
Toddlers (2s)	8:00–6:00	Mon–Fri	$1,525
Preschool (3s and 4s)	8:00–6:00	Mon–Fri	$1,525

Program. Developmental. The child's interests abilities and experiences determine the curriculum for all age groups, with a special emphasis on encouraging social and verbal skills. The twos and preschoolers daily activities are open-ended and include art, music, dramatic play, block building, sand, water play, reading, math-readiness projects and games and cooking. A music and movement specialist comes once a week to work with all three classes and there is a strong emphasis on daily outdoor activity.

Admissions. There is no application fee. Inquiries are at any time. Parents should call the director to arrange to visit the school. Families of all religious traditions are welcome. Siblings and legacies have priority admissions.

Class size. The infant room has eight children, the twos have fourteen and the preschool has thirteen. Each classroom has three full-time teachers, one of whom is licensed, and part-time teachers.

Facilities. One of the best-kept secrets in Chelsea, this small preschool nestles on the grounds of an 1830s seminary, its stone and brick church and buildings set amid grassy, tree-shaded lawns. The school has a large playground with swings, slides, a sandbox, and wooden climbing equipment. Children also ride trikes and scooters on the enclosed paths. They cultivate a garden along the playground fence. The preschool feels like a little house filled with amiable clutter. On campus, there is one small and one large room joined by a long bathroom and child-sized facilities. A third classroom is located on West 20th Street in a seminary-owned building.

Separation. Parents remain in the classroom for the child's first two days, leaving for increasing periods of time. Separation is an individualized process. Children usually take a week or two to separate.

Parent involvement. Parents can visit at any time, and come along on trips. Two parent-teacher conferences a year are supplemented by informal monthly meetings of parents and teachers where developmental issues and classroom activities are discussed.

Financial. There is a non-refundable registration fee of $250. The school requires one month's tuition payment, which is placed in an escrow account, in advance. There is a separate fee for a weekly music/movement program.

Affiliations. General Theological Seminary.

The Children's International Workshop at Union Square

Ages: 2–5 yrs

17 East 16th Street (between Union Square West and Fifth Avenue)
Zip: 10003
Tel: 691-8964

Established 1976
Jacquelyn Marks, Director
Enrollment: 60

School year. September through June. A summer program is available in July and August.

Ages	*Hours*	*Days*	*Tuition (monthly)*
All	8:00–12:00	3 days	$750
	8:00–12:00	Mon–Fri	$950
	12:30–5:30	3 days	$750
	12:30–5:30	Mon–Fri	$950
2s	8:00–4:00	Mon–Fri	$1,600
3s/4s	8:00–6:00	Mon–Fri	$1,600

There is an added charge for diapers. Flexible hours available for full day program.

Program. The main emphasis is on the arts (painting, drama, music), along with a full readiness program for the 3s, which introduces children to the alphabet and numbers from 1 to 20. The readiness program relies on manipulatives as well as games and stories. Group play is also important, allowing young children to learn how to work out their fears and anxieties by role playing. Every other week the children take trips. The 3s visit the neighborhood police and fire stations, the deli, park, and farmer's market. Threes and 4s go to locations that complement their art and readiness programs, such as museums, the Empire State Building, the Fashion Institute of Technology, and parks. There is an annual exhibit of the children's artwork to which parents and friends are invited. There are no computers in school in accordance with the school's philosophy.

Admissions. There is no application fee. Applications are on a rolling basis. Parents are asked to tour the school and the children are observed informally.

Class size. The student-teacher ratio is 5:1 for 2s, 6:1 for 3s to 5s.

Staff. The teachers have degrees in the fine arts and/or early childhood.

Facilities. According to the director, "We feel that nursery school children, especially those living in Manhattan, need space, light, and a warm feeling in their environment. The Children's Workshop is situated in a 2,000-square-foot loft with an emphasis on light and space. We purposely keep a home-like atmosphere and stay away from the classroom-like environment which your child will have from kindergarten through college."

Separation. Handled on an individual basis. Usually the child begins with an abbreviated schedule and parents stay on the premises as long as necessary.

Financial. A deposit of one month's tuition is required upon entrance. Tuition is due monthly.

Graduates. Have gone on to Friends Seminary, Grace Church, Little Red School House/Elizabeth Irwin and UNIS.

Chinatown Day

Ages: 2–5 yrs

35 Division Street
Zip: 10002
Tel: 431-3845
Serves 150 children

Gary Wen,
Director

Chinatown Garment Industry Day Care Center

115 Chrystie Street, 2nd floor
Zip: 10002
Tel: 219-2286
Union Local 22325 members' children only.

City and Country School

Ages: 2–13 yrs

Nonsectarian Nursery and Elementary School

146 West 13th Street (between 6th and 7th Avenues)
Zip: 10011
Tel: 242-7802
Total enrollment: 290
Website: www.cityandcountry.org

Established 1914
Kate Turley, Principal
Lisa Horner, Director of Admissions
Nursery enrollment: 105

School year. Second week of September through mid-June.

Ages	*Hours*	*Days*	*Tuition*
IIs AM	9:00–11:30	Mon–Fri	$14,420
IIs PM	1:00–3:30	Mon–Thurs	$13,380
IIIs AM	9:00–12:50	Mon–Fri	$16,920
IIIs PM	1:30–4:50	Mon–Fri	$15,600
IVs	9:00–3:00	Mon–Fri	$21,020
Vs	9:00–3:00	Mon–Fri	$22,180

By 3, children should be toilet trained.

Extended hours. 3:00–5:45 for IVs–VIIs, at an additional cost. Children may be dropped off at 8:40. Early morning drop-off begins at 8:00 AM for an additional fee.

Program. Progressive. One of the city's leading progressive schools, it was founded by Caroline Pratt in 1914. Her brilliant work and that of innovative educators associated with her was closely studied by the Bureau of Educational Experiments (later Bank Street) and was influential in the development of progressive education. Pratt's book, *I Learn from Children,* describes the experimenting through which the programs originated and reflects the respect for children that the method embodies.

The core of the preschool program is blockbuilding and dramatic play. Children create increasingly complex structures out of blocks that represent their world. Then they explore the social roles connected with the world they have created. Preschool activities include painting, collage and clay work, science, library and story time, music, woodworking (3s–5s) and movement, play with small objects and vigorous outdoor play. Middle-school children have real jobs, in the school post office, store, and printshop. A strong sense of community develops here.

Another distinctive feature of City and Country is the absence of the usual dramatic play (housekeeping or dress-up corner) that most nursery schools have. C&C maintains that props channel a child's imagination too narrowly and often separate the boys and girls.

Both boys and girls participate equally in blockbuilding. Children do not congregate around "boys" or "girls" activities, commonplace behavior in many nursery schools, where boys monopolize the blocks, Legos, and the workbench, and girls use the housekeeping corner. A C&C member noted that both sexes show equal interest in blocks and woodworking. Teachers assist children to discover how to work as a group.

Admissions. The application fee is $50. Inquiries are from October on. The admissions process is informal. Parents observe the school in operation, escorted by the admissions director. Then 2s and 3s, accompanied by parents, are seen in small groups in a play setting. Older children are invited to join a classroom session for a full day. Interviews are conducted only when places are open. Notifications are sent by March, according to ISAAGNY guidelines.

Class size. There are three 2s classes of ten each, and two morning classes each of 3s, 4s, and 5s, and an afternoon class of 3s, each with at least two staff members. Teaching assistants are usually graduate students in early childhood education who come to this unique school for training. Specialists working with the children include a psychologist, rhythms teacher, learning specialist and librarian.

Facilities. Children and parents are buzzed through a windowed door into an airy reception room directly on street level. The school takes up four floors of three interconnected remodeled brownstones that have been sound-proofed and child-proofed. As the school has grown, City and Country also occupies a three-story building joined by the school's outdoor yards, on West 12th Street. The rooms are large and many windowed, with high ceilings. They have open central spaces available for blockbuilding and dramatic play, rather than the strongly defined activities areas found in traditional schools. The furnishings are sturdy and well maintained.

In every nursery area there are shelves of the building blocks designed by the school's founder and now a staple in most nursery schools. The degree to which a school is progressive is almost measurable by the amount of space and time devoted to building with these blocks. More space and time are devoted to them here than in any school in the city.

City and Country has a smaller range of materials than many other schools, and they are simple, open-ended ones which the school believes will avoid overstimulation. Many of the toys are made by the children.

Commercial or adults' artwork is not displayed in the nursery rooms. Pinned to classroom walls are portfolios of each child's often vibrant and expressive art. Children do not take it home daily to show their parents; they are not doing it for parental approval. It is their work.

A large backyard play area, augments the school's rooftop play area and rainy-day playroom. The gymnasium, used in the school's innovative rhythms program, has a high, wood-beamed ceiling.

In the outside play areas there are sturdy green crates, large enough to hold several children, lightweight aluminum hanging ladders for climbing into and out of, miniature sawhorses, planks for construction, and the large hollow blocks from which the older children construct their miniature cities.

Summer program. The optional six-week program is open to the 4s through 7s.

Separation. The 2s, 3s and 4s are visited by their teachers before school begins. Parents are requested to give whatever time they are able to the separation process, which may take anywhere from a week to several months. When school begins, children are brought into the class in small groups for short sessions. Parents remain with them in the classroom, withdrawing gradually to stand by in the foyer if needed. It is in that same foyer that the 2s see their parents off each morning.

Parent involvement. The school attracts families from all five boroughs and New Jersey. There's a broad range of parents whose professions range from the arts to the more traditional occupations of medicine, law and investment banking. There are frequent parent-teacher get-togethers above and beyond the twice-yearly academic conferences. Evening lectures are held at which teachers explain their methods and work, or in which an outside professional speaks. The board of trustees is composed mainly of alumni, parents, staff and friends.

Financial. A deposit of $2,500 is due by February 15 or according to the contract date for those who enroll later. The balance of tuition and fees is payable in five installments. A 10-installment plan is available as well. Both plans begin April 1st. A $400 enrollment fee, and $900 building fee for nursery years and a $1,400 annual building fee thereafter are required. Many parents make additional financial contributions to the school's Annual Fund.

Graduates. Have gone on to Art and Design, Bronx Science, Brooklyn Friends, Calhoun, Dalton, Dwight, Elizabeth Irwin, Fieldston, Friends Seminary, Horace Mann, Marymount, Music and Art, Nightingale-Bamford, Saint Ann's, Stuyvesant, Trevor Day, UNIS, and many others.

Member. ERB, ISAAGNY, NAIS, NYSAIS.

The Children's Aid Society/ The Philip Coltoff Center at Greenwich Village

Ages: 2–5 yrs

Nonsectarian

219 Sullivan Street
Zip: 10012
Tel: 254-3074
Fax: 420-9153
Web site: www.childrensaidsociety.org
Total Preschool Enrollment: 242

Rochelle Miller,
Director
Ellen Cerniglia,
Admissions Director

School year. Beginning September to beginning June, extended day programs until 6 PM with speciality classes (pottery, art, dance, etc.) available. Summer program in July and August for children ages three to seven.

Ages	*Hours*	*Days*	*Tuition*
2–3	9:00–12:00 or 1:00–4:00	T,Th, or M,W,F or M–F	\$3,780–\$8,240
3s–4s	9:00–1:00 or 12:30–3:30	M,W,F or M–F	\$5,930–\$8,240
4s–5s	9:00–2:00	Mon–Fri	\$9,705

Toilet training not required.

Program. Developmental/Eclectic. Focuses on development of social skills and hands-on exploration of the environment. The school uses materials such as blocks, sand and water, and paint. Arts, crafts, movement and working on group and as well as individual projects are emphasized, along with manners and sharing. Children make up stories in a group or summarize neighborhood trips. Pre-K children had turned their room into a forest with wall paintings and paper mâché birds. A teacher read to children sitting up, lined along a wall. There are no computers or worksheets. Children are not taught the alphabet, but children are given admissions counseling for on-going schools. Classes tend to work on themes: building a block of New York City, for example, or studying space and the solar system or Antarctica. Each class has outdoor time on the school's playground.

Admissions. Currently-enrolled children are given priority. Call or log onto the website for details. The school advises applicant families to make appointments for visits during September through December. The visit and application should have been made by the beginning of January in order to ensure a place for the following year. Each application must be accompanied by a nonrefundable \$50 registration fee. For the year, 2007–08 the school has a new, tiered lottery system in place. In years past, parents were known to spend the night camping outside the school because applications ran out so quickly.

Class size. The 2s classes have ten children and two teachers; three 3s classes have 16 children and two teachers; and the 4s have 18 children and two teachers.

Facilities. Located in the heart of Greenwich Village, a block south of Washington Square, two large buildings joined by an extensive soft surface playground with colorful climbing equipment and a separate water play area that's used during summer camp. The preschool building was redone in 1993. Rooms vary in shape, size and number of windows. They are spacious, bright and clean, with care taken to admit daylight. Rooms are divided into eight different activity areas. Children use the adult-size, windowed gym/auditorium with a low stage at one end and an adjacent mirrored dance room on the other. There's a large, clean fully-equipped kitchen with three refrigerators. The school supplies a snack. Children bring their lunches.

Separation. There is a gradual phase-in scheduled over the course of the first week. When parents first leave the room they are asked to stay at the building while children convene in half groups for half the class time. The easing-in period continues for the second week with the whole group, or individually as needed.

Parent involvement. The school ensures parents tons of communication: including newsletters, E-Mails, parent/teacher conferences and notes. There is a library committee, a book fair, and carnivals, a benefit, and fall harvest fest and more. Each class has two class parents who assist teachers. The school hosts seminars for parents through the parents committee, and invites parents to share books, and lead projects or volunteer ideas.

Financial. The school holds fundraisers to raise money for the program and also a special benefit for scholarships that go to families in need.

Graduates. Have gone on to City and Country, Corlears, Friends Seminary, Grace Church, UNIS, Little Red School House, Village Community School, PS 3 41, NEST, and other Gifted and Talented programs.

Corlears School

Ages: 2.6–9 yrs

Nonsectarian Nursery and Elementary School

324 West 15th Street (between 8th and 9th Avenues)
Zip: 10011
Tel: 741-2800
Fax: 807-1550
Web site: www.corlearsschool.org
E-Mail: office@corlearsschool.org

Established 1968
Thya Merz, Head of School
Rorry Romeo, Admissions Director

Nursery enrollment: 32
Total enrollment: 140

School year. Mid-September through the second week in June. Summer program from mid-June through the end of July.

Ages	*Hours*	*Days*	*Tuition*
2s/3s	9:00–12:00	Mon–Fri	$15,012
2s/3s/4s/5s	9:00–3:00	Mon–Fri	$19,226
6s–9s	9:00–3:00	Mon–Fri	$21,768

Extended hours. Early drop-off (8:00) and after-school care are available for children age 4 years and older at a modest fee. In addition, after school specialty classes for 4s and up include drama, chess, sports, and chess.

Program. Developmental. The core curriculum consists of social studies and science. Preschoolers learn through direct observation and hands-on activity. Teachers pay close attention to socialization and emotional development. Language arts evolve through listening and responding to storybooks, dictating stories, verbal problem solving and the writing process. Science is begun through cooking, daily observations about the weather, seasonal changes, planting seeds, water experiments. Observations, such as "What floats/What sinks," are recorded on wall charts. Math (one of this school's great strengths) begins as play with multi-colored Cuisenaire rods, which encourage abstract thinking and problem-solving.

Children's varied artwork—figurative and abstract—has a free, exuberant look reflecting each child's unique style. Children write stories with illustrations. Teachers assemble their own materials.

Admissions. The application fee is $50. Interested parents may attend the autumn open house. The application deadline is December 1st. ERB scores are not required. The director of admissions interviews parents. Children applying participate in small playgroups. Notifications are made according to ISAAGNY guidelines.

Class size. Both twos and threes classes are limited to sixteen children. There are eighteen to twenty in the older classes.

Staff. Each classroom has a head teacher and one assistant. There are specialists in art, music, movement, physical education, science, library, and Spanish.

Facilities. Two five-story Chelsea brick townhouses provide spacious classrooms, each with three large windows. Classrooms provide a loft for reading, a large block space, a place for dramatic play, carpeted meeting and reading area, plus stations for cooking, washing-up and science. All ages visit the 14,000 volume library. Every day, children will spend time in the large back yard. There is also a gym, and an art studio in the basement. Full-day children bring their lunch. 6s and up use computers in their classrooms.

Summer program. Four weeks in June and July for nursery school-age children and children up to 6 years old.

Separation. "It's a gentle weaning," according to Rorry Romeo, admissions director. Children begin the year with small groups and partial days. The younger children take a week or two to adjust. Parents leave the classroom when they and the children are ready.

Parent involvement. Parents serve on the school's board, and run fundraisers such as the Spring Fair and Auction. 96 percent of parents give to the annual fund. Parent-teacher conferences are scheduled twice-yearly, in addition to two curriculum meetings led by a head teacher. Parents may visit classrooms by appointment.

Financial. A tuition deposit of $4,000 is due with the contract. The balance is due in equal installments May 1 and September 1. Each family makes a non-interest bearing, one-time loan of $1,000 per child, payable in three installments. The annual building and equipment fee is $600, $360 for the second child, none for the 3rd child.

Thirty percent of students receive financial aid, with an average grant of $5,000. To promote economic and ethnic diversity, Corlears participates in Early Steps. According to the admissions director, the school is also committed to its middle-class families.

Transportation. Private bus transportation can be arranged.

Graduates. Graduates have gone on to Allen-Stevenson, Berkeley-Carroll, Brooklyn Friends, Browning, Calhoun, Friends Seminary, Hewitt, Little Red School House, Nightingale-Bamford, Poly Prep, St. Luke's, UNIS and Village Community School.

Chartered. By the Board of Regents of the State University of New York.

Member. ERB, ACD, NAEYC, ISAAGNY, NAIS, NAEYC, NYSAIS.

Downing Street Playgroup Cooperative

32 Carmine Street
Zip: 10014
Tel: 924-2557

Kerry Holbrook,
Director
Enrollment: 18

The Downtown Little School

Ages: 2–5 yrs

Nonsectarian Nursery School

15 Dutch Street
Zip: 10038
Tel: 791-1300

Website: www.downtownlittleschool.com

Established 1974
Kate Delacorte,
Co-Director
Meredith Gary,
Co-Director
Enrollment: 80

School year. September through mid-June.

Ages	*Hours*	*Days*	*Tuition*
2s	9:00 – 11:30 or	Mon–Thurs	$9,000
	1:00 – 3:30		$8,500
3s	8:45 – 11:45 or	Mon–Fri	$9,000
	1:00 – 4:00		$8,500
4s	9:00 – 12:00	Mon–Fri	$9,000
	9:00 – 2:30	2 days	$11,500
4s/5s	9:00 – 2:30	Mon–Fri	$14,000

Extended day options available for an additional fee.

Program. Major stated goals of the school are "to have the children feel comfortable in an educational setting, to stimulate their curiosity, to give them the opportunity to explore materials and social relationships." The school offers interrelated experiences that emphasize language skills, the exploration of feelings, dramatic play and blockbuilding, and include science, art, music, water play, and cooking.

Admissions. The application fee is $40. The school accepts applications right after Labor Day and has at least one open house in the fall. Parents may schedule a visit at any time. Acceptances are sent by the ISAAGNY deadline, which is usually in early March. Parents must reply in two weeks. A waiting list is maintained.

Preference is given to siblings. The school seeks diversity.

Staff. Head teachers have completed or are close to completing a masters degree in early childhood education.

Facilities. There is one ground floor area with a rooftop playground.

Summer program. The summer program runs for six weeks.

Separation. Parents stay as long as they are needed.

Parent involvement. Conferences are held twice a year and as requested by parents or teachers. Parents are welcome in the classroom.

Financial. A tuition deposit of $1,000 is required when parents register. The balance is payable in four installments. Some financial aid may be available.

Graduates. Have gone on to a wide range of private and public schools.

CP Kids

Ages: 2.9–5 yrs

Nonsectarian

The Field House at Chelsea Piers
Pier 62
23rd Street and Westside Hwy
Zip: 10011
Tel: 336-6500 ext. 6573
Fax: 336-6515
Website: www.chelseapiers.com/fh
E-mail: backeb@chelseapiers.com

Established 2005
Betsey Backe, Director

Enrollment: 14

School year. September through June.

Age	*Hours*	*Days*	*Tuition*
2.9–5	9–3	5/3/2 days	$1020/$795/ $665 per month
2.9–5	8–6	5/3/2 days	$1385/$1075/ $850 per month

Program. Developmental. The guiding philosophy of the program at CP Kids is that optimal development takes place in an environment that gives balanced, attentive care to the whole child. The school works to support, nurture and encourage children to grow in three basic areas: physically, through careful attention to the child's health, fitness and nutrition; socially, by building strong relationships characterized by trust, respect and love; and cognitively, through active learning, which forms the basis for all other activities.

Admissions. The application fee is $35.
Parents can call anytime to arrange a tour of the preschool. Priority

in admissions is given in the following order of affiliation: Chelsea Piers employees, tenants of Chelsea Piers, clients of Chelsea Piers, community members.

Class size. The class is made up of 12 to 15 children with two full-time teachers.

Staff. Head teachers are New York State certified. Assistant teachers have previous experience with preschoolers, a high school diploma and 60 college credits.

Facilities. CP Kids is located in the Field House at Chelsea Piers. The school features a new, sunny and spacious classroom. The school also has access to the facilities within the Field House and parks located nearby.

Summer program. The summer program runs during June, July and August. It follows the curriculum of the regular school year with more time devoted to outdoor activities.

Afterschool program. Parents may request additional hours at a rate of $13.50 per hour or may sign up for the extended day program from 8–9 am and 3–6 pm.

Separation. Parents spend two full days in the classroom with the child, participating in activities and helping the child adjust to the new environment.

Tuition assistance. Discounts are given to Chelsea Piers employees and Chelsea Piers tenants.

Transportation. Chelsea Piers is not far from the 23rd Street stop of the C and E subway lines. The M23 bus makes stops in the Chelsea Piers complex.

The Educational Alliance Preschool

Ages: 2–4 years

Jewish Nursery

197 East Broadway (between Jefferson and Clinton Streets)
Zip: 10002
Tel: 780-2300 ext. 429
Web site: www.edalliance.org

Established 1970
Leslie Klein Pilder, Director

Enrollment: 75

School year. Early September through early June.

Ages	*Hours*	*Days*	*Tuition*
2s	8:30–11:30 or 12:30–3:30	2, 3, 5 days	\$3,300–\$7,020
2s	8:30–3:00	2, 3, 5 days	\$5,175–\$9,000
3s	8:30–11:30 or 12:30–3:30	Mon–Fri	\$3,300–\$7,020
3/4s	8:30–3:00	Mon–Fri	\$9,000
3/4s	8:30–6:00	Mon–Fri	\$9,000 plus \$300/month

Early drop-off and extended day options are available for roughly an additional \$100/month.

Program. The Educational Alliance Preschool provides students with child-centered classrooms based on NAEYC (National Association for the Education of Young Children) guidelines. Each classroom offers children a mixture of individual, self-directed play and group activities led by teachers. Every room contains learning centers which provide children the opportunity to interact freely with the environment and each other, developing cognitive, social, emotional, and physical skills. Each classroom contains a reading corner, a sand table, an art area, a dramatic play corner, and block center (as mandated by law). Teachers provide small group and whole class experiences for the children, engaging youngsters in activities not easily experienced on their own. Art, cooking, science, literacy and cultural lessons often occur in group settings.

The Torah Tots classrooms include direct instruction in Judaism, but all classrooms are grounded in its ethical teachings in a multicultural context.

Admissions. The registration fee is $125. Inquiries are from mid-September on, though registrations occur in January and February. Parents should call to arrange to visit the school. Parents are notified in March. Children of all faiths are welcome.

Class size. In accordance with regulations of the New York City Department of Health; typically for 2s classes there is one adult for five children; for 3s and 4s the ratio is one adult to seven children.

Staff. All group teachers are certified by the New York City Department of Health.

Facilities. The school is located on the third floor of the Educational Alliance, a community center and settlement house. In addition to its large classrooms, the school has two play roofs equipped with climbing apparatus, tricycles, wagons, and toys. On rainy days, children use the gym. Children bring their own lunches. Snacks are provided.

Summer program. Weekly summer programs/sessions are available from June to early August and there are multiple session options.

Parent involvement. There is an active Parent Association which raises money for the school, plans special activities (such as holiday parties), and helps create a state of the art preschool experience. Parents are encouraged to share their talents both in and out of the classroom. Seminars for parents on topics of interest are offered. Teacher conferences are held twice yearly, and are available at any time upon request. Parents are encouraged to stay with their children during the early transition weeks.

Financial. A registration fee is payable with the application. First and last month tuition installments are due at contract-signing. The remainder is payable monthly (Credit cards are accepted.) Partial scholarships are available. There is a 10 per cent discount for siblings and a special early bird discount of 5 per cent of the tuition, excluding the registration fee if the entire tuition is paid by April 3rd.

Transportation. Most of the children come from the nursery's immediate neighborhood: the Lower East Side, Tribeca, Soho, and the Village. The school is close to public transportation.

Graduates. Have gone on to Beth Jacob, Manhattan Day School, Mesivta Tifereth Jerusalem, Ramaz, St. James and St. Joseph's, The Town School, and UNIS, as well as Earth School, P.S. 234, 130 and 110.

Affiliations. UJA Federation of New York which also provides some of the school's scholarship money, JCC Association, United Neighborhood Houses, United Way.

Member. Downtown Early Childhood Association, Jewish Early Childhood Association of the Board of Jewish Education.

FedKids
Imagine Early Learning Center

Ages: 2 mos–5 yrs

26 Federal Plaza, Rm110
NY, NY 10278
Tel: 212-264-4277

Bente Slotwiner,
Director
Total enrollment: 77

School year. year-round

Ages	*Hours*	*Days*	*Tuition*
2 mos–2 yrs	7:30–6:00	Mon–Fri	Federal Emp. $1090 Non-Fed Emp. $1365
3 yrs–5 yrs	7:30–6:00	Mon–Fri	Federal Emp: $786 Non-Fed Emp: $1208

Toilet Training is not necessary. Optional part-time schedule, 2 days or 3 days.

Program. FedKids provides a stimulating and nurturing environment in which infants, toddlers, and preschoolers can thrive. Teachers plan and implement a developmentally appropriate curriculum for all areas of development. Each child is encouraged to actively participate and learn through self-discovery and expression. The program is tailored by age groups with emphasis placed on the individual needs of each child.

Admissions. The admissions are ongoing as space becomes available, it is best to inquire as far in advance as possible. Fees are payable on a monthly basis, with one month's pre-payment on signing of the contract.

Class size. Infant rooms have a ratio of one adult to three children; there will be three teachers to eight children. The one-year-old rooms have three teachers and ten children. The two-year-old rooms have two teachers and ten children. The preschool room has two teachers and around fifteen children.

Facilities. The center is located on the lobby floor of 26 Federal Plaza, a federal building. Classrooms are beautiful open spaces which are very well maintained by the federal government. There are two outdoor playgrounds on the premises, plus an indoor gym.

Parent involvement. All Imagine Early Learning Centers have an open-door policy, with parents encouraged to visit whenever possible. Parents are invited on all field trips. There are potlucks, a monthly newsletter, and a curriculum board with the day's schedule and activities of focus in each room. There are two parent-teacher conferences a year, and a Parent Advisory Board that meets every few months.

Financial. ACD vouchers are accepted and there are discounted rates for federal employees.

Graduates. Graduates go on to New York public and private schools.

First Presbyterian Church Nursery School

Ages: 2.3–5 years

12 West 12th Street (between Fifth and Sixth Avenues)	Established 1952
Zip: 10011	Ellen Ziman, Director
Tel: 691-3432	Enrollment: 103
Website: www.fpcns.org	
E-Mail: fpcns@aol.com	

School year. Monday after Labor Day through mid-June.

Ages	*Hours*	*Days*	*Tuition*
young 2s	9:00–11:30	Tues Fri	$5,360
older 2s	1:00–3:30	Mon Wed	$5,360
older 2s	9:00–11:30	Mon Wed Thurs	$7,280
3s	1:00–3:30	Mon–Thurs	$7,390
	8:45–11:45	Mon–Fri	$10,610
4/5s	8:45–11:45	Mon–Fri	$10,610
	8:45–2:15	Mon–Thurs, Fri until 1:15	$12,480

Children need not be toilet-trained on entry.

Program. Developmental. The approach is based on the principle that learning occurs through interaction with peers and adults and also through hands-on involvement with carefully chosen materials in a responsive environment. Children are encouraged to make choices and solve problems in a setting that includes a variety of work areas: blocks; sensory and art materials; music, movement, cooking, dramatic play; and caring for plants and animals. Language skills are developed through conversation, literature, and storytelling. Age-appropriate curriculum evolves from the children's interest both as a group and as individuals. Interests are pursued in the classroom through discussion, books, and investigations; and outside the classroom through trips in the building and neighborhood. Large motor activity takes place daily, on the roof playground or indoors during inclement weather. There is a twice-a-week afterschool program offered in six-week segments and focusing on special interests such as printmaking, gardening, etc.

ERBs are administered on the premises.

Admissions. The application fee is $30. Applications are mailed in September. Call in September after Labor Day to request an application. Returned applications are entered into an admissions lottery. Appointments are made to see the school for those whose applications were drawn in the lottery. Tours and open houses are held in October and November. There are 30 openings for 2s each year, 10 for 3s, and typically a few for 4/5s. Children's visits follow in January and February and consist of a 30-minute classroom playtime with a few other children. Parents remain with their children during the visit. Notifications are sent in accord with ISAAGNY guidelines, in early March. Early notification is given to siblings, church members, and children of former students. Early notification status does not guarantee admission.

Class size. Ten to eleven 2s, fifteen 3s, twenty or twenty-three 4/5s.

Staff. Each class has a head teacher and assistant teacher, an aide, student teachers, and specialists. Head teachers have a masters degree/certification in early childhood education; assistant teachers have a bachelor's or associate's degree in early childhood with professional experience. There are specialists for woodworking, music, and movement. A consulting psychologist meets with teachers or parents every week.

Facilities. The school is located on the fourth floor of the church house. The school's modern, well-equipped facilities include four spacious classrooms with tall windows overlooking the church garden and 12th Street, a circulating library of children's and adult books, a woodworking room, and a room set up for movement and indoor play in inclement weather. There is also a fenced-in, rubber-padded roof playground with a playhouse, climbing equipment, riding toys, big blocks, balls, etc. Children bring their own lunches; snacks are provided.

Separation. A parent meeting is held to explain the separation process which may be adjusted to individual abilities and needs. For young 2s, a parent consultant assists parents through the phasing-in period, when schedules build incrementally from a shorter day with half groups to a full session with full groups. The goal is for children to be in school without their parents as soon as they are able to be in a group and rely on the teachers for support.

Parent involvement. There are parent-teacher conferences twice a year as well as ongoing dialogue with parents about their children. The school holds an open school night to discuss curriculum and an ongoing schools night to help parents plan their search for their child's next school. In addition, the school offers occasional parenting workshops as well as a seminar series on parent issues such as communication, discipline, and siblings.

Parents participate in classes on school birthdays, act as trip chaperones, and share their talents, jobs, and memories with the children. They also volunteer in the parent-run library and in various fundraising activities such as the bake sale, puppet show, and the annual auction. Parent fundraising supports the scholarship fund.

Financial. A $1,000 deposit applicable toward tuition is required with the signed contract. The balance of tuition is paid in three installments; a monthly payment schedule can also be arranged; tuition assistance is available based on need.

Transportation. Children come from Greenwich Village, the East Village, Soho, Tribeca, Chelsea, Gramercy Park, Stuyvesant Town, and are brought by their parents or caregivers.

Graduates. Have gone on to Allen-Stevenson, Brearley, Brooklyn Friends, Buckley, Calhoun, Chapin, City and Country, Corlears, Dalton, Dwight, Ethical Culture, Epiphany, Friends Seminary, Grace Church, Little Red School House, Packer Collegiate, St. Ann's, St. Luke's, Spence, Trinity, UNIS, Village Community, as well as Hunter Elementary, the Lab School, PS 3, PS 41, PS 116 and other public schools.

Affiliations. First Presbyterian Church.

Member. Downtown Early Childhood Association, ERB, ISAAGNY, ATIS.

The Gani Early Childhood Center Sol Goldman YM-YWHA of the Educational Alliance

Ages: 2–6 yrs

344 East 14th Street

Zip: 10003
Tel: 780-0800 x 238/266
Web site: www.edalliance.org
E-Mail: caroleweber@14.streety.org

Established 1984
Carole Weber, Director
Enrollment: 70

School year. Mid-September through beginning of June. Summer program available.

Ages	*Hours*	*Days*	*Tuition**
2s/3s/pre-K	8:30–12:30	2, 3, 5 days	$5,815–14,040
2s/3s/pre-K	8:30–3:00	2, 3 days	$5,815–14,040
2s/3s/pre-K	9:00–6:00	5 days	$5,815–14,040
	9:00–3:00	5 days	$5,815–14,040

*Members receive a discount for certain programs.

Extended hours. An 8:30–6:00 schedule is available for an additional charge.

Program. Developmental. Gani's experienced early childhood staff provides a warm, nurturing environment, helping young children grow socially, emotionally, and educationally while gaining self-confidence and exploring new concepts. The curriculum includes a variety of activities, including imaginative play, language arts, block building, sand and water play, art, music, fine and gross motor activities, and storytelling. The program provides children with a thematic approach to learning. Topics of interest are chosen by the children in the class and are investigated in the classroom learning centers. Children always use manipulative materials when learning math and science. Jewish holidays and Shabbat are observed and celebrated through stories, songs, dance, games, and cooking projects. There is physical activity on the outdoor rooftop playground and gym.

The Russian Early Childhood Center is a two-day program offered in the Russian language for children two to four years old. As a component of the Gani school, this program emphasizes the same developmental philosophy and Jewish programming. Families of all backgrounds are welcome. This program can be supplemented with three days in the Gani Preschool.

Admissions. The application fee is $50. Parents may call to request a visit and an application. A time will be scheduled for parents to meet with the director with their children informally.

Class size. Ranges from 10 in the 2s class, to a maximum of 20 in Pre-K with a minimum of two teachers in each class.

Staff. The school provides staff with a range of professional development opportunities.

Facilities. The school occupies an entire floor of a four-story Jewish Community Center. The floor has been divided into five extremely large classrooms. A large indoor gymnasium and a rooftop playground that provides excellent space for gross motor activities.

Summer program. June through mid-August.

Separation. Parents are asked to be available until the child adjusts.

Parent involvement. The Gani Early Childhood Center has an active Parents Association. The school believes it is the extension of the family and strives for parent involvement to enhance child development. The Parenting and Family Center offers classes and activities in all areas of family life: support, guidance, parenting tips and education. Topics of workshops and classes include parenthood, prenatal care, Mommy and Me, single parenting, working moms, Me and My Dad, and more. The combination of Parenting and Family Center with the Gani Early Childhood Center provides families with extensive and innovative educational, social, and cultural experiences.

Financial. A deposit of $2,000 is due on signing the contract; the remainder of tuition is payable in two installments, September 1st and December 1st. Financial aid is available.

Transportation. No private bus service is available.

Graduates. Gani graduates have been accepted at many private schools including City and Country, Corlears, UNIS, Friends Seminary, Grace Church, Saint Ann's, the Abraham Joshua Heschel School, Little Red School House, Ramaz and Ethical Culture. Public schools include neighborhood schools, NEST and Hunter College Elementary School.

Affiliations. The Sol Goldman Y is a program of the Educational Alliance.

Member. Downtown Early Childhood Association, ERB, BJE, Parents League.

Imagine VetsKids

3 mos–5 yrs

Dept. of Veterans Affairs
New York Medical Center
423 East 23rd Street
Zip: 10010
Tel: 951-3435
Fax: 951-6827
Website: imagineelc.com
E-Mail: jennifer@imagineelc.com

Jennifer Hohl,
Director

Preschool Enrollment: 18
Total Enrollment: 48

School year: Year round.

Hours: Monday through Friday, 7:30 AM – 6:00 PM. There is a maximum of nine hours per day, 5 days a week, available for full-time enrollment; and a minimum of two nine hour days for part-time enrollment.

Fees: Infants and Toddlers $1,453* monthly. Preschoolers $1,170* monthly.

Program. Eclectic. All learning occurs through play; there are no work sheets or academic time tables. Children are exposed to reading, writing, and math with attention paid to an individual child's readiness. Name writing, for instance, is introduced in the 4s, but if a child cannot write his or her name, it's okay. However, the older 4s/5s class follows a standard Pre-K curriculum to better prepare the children for kindergarten.

Admissions. As with other Imagine Early Centers, children enroll throughout the year as places become available. It is advisable to call by December if a child will be attending school the following autumn. Upon admission and the signing of the contract, a deposit of one month's tuition must be made. This will be credited to the last month of enrollment. Deposits carry over from year to year. Fees are paid monthly.

Facilities. The building is new and air-conditioned. When you enter through the front door of the Veteran's Hospital a security guard

*A fee of $10 is charged for every 10 minutes a child remains after six. Snacks are provided, children bring their lunch. Toilet training is not required. Children keep a change of clothes at school.

will direct you to the center. There are two classrooms, both long rectangles, with bright yellow walls and blue cabinets. The toddler room, with six large windows, can be divided to accommodate an older and a younger group.

Separation. The process takes about a week. Initially, the children attend for a shorter day (two hours for infants and toddlers, three hours for preschoolers) in the company of a parent, grandparent or sitter. Adult accompaniment varies with the individual.

Parent involvement. There is an open door policy. Parents are welcome at any time. There are two parent-teacher conferences yearly. The parent advisory board serves as liaison between the administration and parents.

Financial. Licensed to take ACD vouchers.

Jack and Jill School

Ages: 2.6–5 yrs

Nonsectarian Nursery School

209 East 16th Street (between 3rd Avenue and Rutherford Place)
Zip: 10003
Tel: 475-0855
Web site: jackandjillschool.com

Established 1949
Mrs. Jean Leshaw, Director

Enrollment: 55

School year. Mid-September through June 4.

Ages	*Hours*	*Days*	*Tuition*
young 3s	9:00–12:00 or	Mon–Fri or	$9,270
	9:00–12:00	Tues, Wed, Fri	$7,600
	1:00–4:00	Mon–Thurs	$7,450
young 4s	8:45–12:15	Mon–Fri	$9,870
	8:45–2:30	Mon–Fri	$10,600
4s/5s	8:45–3:00	Mon–Fri	$10,800

Children must be 2½ when they enter and must be toilet trained. Early morning drop-off at 8:15 AM may be arranged for a fee.

Program. Traditional. The school, though it eschews workbooks and worksheets and focuses strongly on social development, also includes a structured reading- and math-readiness program and many activities with a strong cognitive focus. Activities include cooking, science, dramatic play, blockbuilding, carpentry, arts and crafts, storytime, and work with small play objects. The 3s focus on social adjustment and self-care, seasonal observations and celebrations, and simple concepts. The 4s and 5s have more defined study units and take many field trips. An integrated curriculum allows exploration through varied activities. Special classes are offered in Spanish and music/movement.

ERBs are given on the premises. Some ongoing school admissions directors visit to observe applicants in a classroom setting.

Admissions. The application fee is $40. Inquiries are from October on. The applications deadline is January 15th. Parents should call for an applications kit and ask for the date of the school's open house. Tours are given weekly in the fall. After submitting an application, parents arrange an interview with the director during November or December. The child is observed in January or early February. Notifications are sent by March. Preference is given to children of parish members and siblings.

Class size. There are two 3s classes of eleven, one young 4s class of twenty, and one 4s/5s class of twelve to fourteen children. The 3s classes have two teachers, the young 4s have three teachers and the 4s/5s class has a head teacher and an assistant.

Facilities. The school is located on the ground floor of St. George's Parish House. The entrance is down a flagstone-paved drive and off the church's tiny courtyard. There are three comfortable classrooms, two of which look out on the play yard facing 16th Street. The yard has an imaginative climbing structure. The classrooms are well equipped and divided into small activities centers for dramatic play, blockbuilding, woodworking, storytime, and so on. On rainy days, the school uses the flagstoned church chantry as a play space. Mats cover the floor. A hall in the church is used for weekly music and movement classes.

Summer program. Three weeks in June and a July camp.

Separation. Teachers visit children at home before school begins. Children are introduced in small groups for shortened sessions.

Parents may remain in the classroom, especially the first week, but are encouraged to wait in the hall after that.

Parent involvement. Parents are involved in raising funds. There are occasional evenings with outside experts speaking on child development, and breakfasts devoted to ongoing schools selection and the ERBs. Parents are welcome in the classroom. Conferences are held twice yearly.

Financial. A tuition deposit of $1,200 is due on signing the contract. The balance is payable in two installments in June and November or in nine monthly payments, June through February. Some scholarship aid is available.

Graduates. Have gone on to Allen-Stevenson, Birch Wathen, Brearley, Browning, Buckley, Chapin, Collegiate, Convent of the Sacred Heart, Corlears, Dalton, Epiphany, Ethical Culture, Family School, Friends Seminary, Grace Church, Greenwich Village Neighborhood, Heschel School, Hewitt, Horace Mann, Lenox, Little Red School House, Marymount, Nightingale-Bamford, Park East Eshi, Rudolf Steiner, St. Ann's, St. Bernard's, St. David's, St. Hilda's and St. Hugh's, St. Joseph's, St. Luke's, Spence, Town, Trinity, UNIS, and Village Community School.

Affiliations. St. George's Episcopal Church. Chartered by the Board of Regents of the State University of New York.

Member. ERB, Downtown Schools Association, ISAAGNY, NAEC, Parents League.

Kid's Korner

Ages: 20 mos–5 yrs

247 West 24th Street
(between Seventh and Eighth Avenues)
Zip: 10011
Tel: 229-9340
Fax: 414-5745
Website: www.thekidskornerpreschool.com

Established 1992
Yolanda Contrubis, Director
Jennifer Denza, Education Director
Enrollment: 38

School year. September through June. A July and August summer program is optional.

Ages	*Hours*	*Days*	*Tuition*
2s	8:00–6:00	2 to 5 days	$6,200–$9,900
	8:00–4:00	2 to 5 days	$6,200–$9,900
	8:30–11:30 or 2:00–5:00	2 to 5 days	$6,200–$9,900
3s	8:00–6:00	2 to 5 days	$8,100–$12,359
	8:00–4:00	2 to 5 days	$8,100–$12,359
	8:00–11:30 or 1:30–4:30	2 to 5 days	$8,100–$12,359
4s/5s	8:00–6:00	3 to 5 days	$9,000–$11,556
	8:00–3:00	3 to 5 days	$9,000–$11,556
	8:00–11:30 or 2:00–5:00	2 to 5 days	$9,000–$11,556

Further flexibility of schedule is available, with a minimum of 2 days required for 2s and 3s, and a minimum of 3 full days (8:00–3:00) for 4s/5s. Lunch is available for an additional fee.

Program. Developmental. Kid's Korner strives to give children a warm, accepting environment where they will develop confidence, self-esteem, inner discipline, and increasing independence. The children explore and discover their world through structured and free-play activities, which enable each child to learn at his or her own pace.

Admissions. The application fee is $35. Applications are accepted throughout the year. Preference is given to siblings of past and present children.

Class size. There are three classes. The 2s have six children, the 3s and the 4s/5s have a maximum of twelve each.

Staff. Each class has a full-time teacher and assistant teacher as well as an intern. An optional music, dance, and gymnastic program is offered at an additional fee.

Facilities. The school occupies two floors in a brownstone in Chelsea. The 2s room is adjacent to a private playground equipped with a sandbox, two climbers, and assorted riding toys. Both the 3s and 4s/5s rooms are arranged into centers focusing on science, blocks and puzzles, computer, housekeeping, art, drama, music, and a reading corner.

Parent involvement. Parents and teachers keep in touch about a child's development through informal and scheduled conferences. The school encourages parents to participate in as many school events as their busy schedules allow. Parents are often invited to speak about or show the children any special skills or interests. Parents also help to raise funds for the school's scholarship fund.

Financial. One-quarter of the year's tuition is required upon enrollment. The balance is payable in three installments, due in June, August, and October. Other payment schedules are available upon request. There is a $275 fee for materials, siblings receive a 10% discount.

Graduates. Have gone on to City and Country, Corlears, Dalton, Epiphany, Hunter, Little Red School House, Our Lady of Pompeii, St. Luke's, UNIS and Village Community School, as well as The Anderson Program, Lower Lab and public schools in the area.

Learning, the Arts, and Me Nursery of Third Street Music School Settlement

Ages: 2*–5 yrs

*Must be 2 by March 15th before school starts.

Nonsectarian

235 East 11th Street (between 2nd and 3rd Avenues)
Zip: 10003
Tel: 777-3240
Fax: 477-1808
Website: www.thirdstreetmusicschool.org
E-Mail: kbooth@thirdstreetmusicschool.org

Established 1979
Karen J. Booth, Educational and Admissions Director
Enrollment: 86

School year. Mid-September through mid-June.

Ages	Hours	Days	Tuition
2s	9:00–11:00/30	Tu and Wed	$3,200
	11:30–1:30/2:15		
3s	1:00–4:00	Th and Fri	$4,000
3s–4s	9:00–12:00 or	Mon–Fri	$8,790
	1:00 to 4:00		$6,830
3s–4s	9:00–12:00	M, T, W	$6,480
3s–4s	1:00–4:00	M, T, W	$6,480

"Lunch Bunch," a group that meets for lunch and playtime, $700–$1,008, (2 or 3 hours).

Children must be toilet trained on entry. Full and partial scholarships are awarded based on need.

Program. Developmental. The Third Street Music School Settlement was founded in 1894, "to provide arts instruction to the children of the Lower East Side, regardless of their ability to pay." It is the oldest community music school in the country. LAM (Learning, the Arts and Me) is the nursery program. It emphasizes fostering creativity and social development. Learning is through exploration. Music, art, creative movement, early language and math are all part of the curriculum. Third Street was the prototype for settlement schools throughout the country and has provided artistic training for thousands of children.

There are many group projects which encourage children to cooperate, share ideas and plan work together. The warm relationships teachers foster with the children creates a relaxed, respectful and cheerful tone which allows children to feel comfortable and truly express themselves. The arts are integrated into the math, language arts, science and social studies curriculum.

Nearby resources, such as St. Mark's farmer's market are visited. In the fall, groups often choose to study apples or pumpkins, discovering how the produce got to the city, how it grows and how it is harvested. Children walk to the market, interview farmers, look at all the different wares and make purchases. After returning to school, children talk or create books about their experiences, and have cooking projects that have yielded apple crisp and apple sauce. One math activity has children taste-testing different color apples, red, green and yellow, and graphing the results based on favorites.

Orff Instruments are introduced in the LAM program; children meet once a week with an Orff-trained music specialist as well as a creative movement specialist. Classes also visit the dance studios to see a flamenco demonstration or to listen to a musician play the cello, drums or flute. There are also dance performances and concerts that classes may attend.

Admissions. The application fee is $25. Inquiries are from August on. The application deadline is January 15th. Parents call for an application packet and make an appointment to see the school. A group play interview will be scheduled for the parent and child once an application has been received. Notifications are sent according to ISAAGNY guidelines.

Class size. Six classes of fifteen each (thirteen in the 3s class), with two teachers per class. Classes are grouped by age, (young 3s, 3s–4s, and 4s).

Staff. Most LAM teachers are fully certified, and are active professionals in their fields. There is an active development program, and teachers have extensive experience in early childhood education. A child consultant visits regularly to work with teachers.

Facilities. Located in the spacious facilities of the Third Street Music School, which include a 300-seat auditorium, 35 studio/practice rooms equipped with pianos, one dance studio, a kiln room, and special classrooms used for art workshops and the nursery school classes. The school's music library houses over 10,000 records, books, libretti, and scores. The LAM program has its own library and there is a parent's lending library.

Summer program. A five-week fun, relaxed program for children 3 to 6 years-old with a strong creative focus. Open to children not enrolled in LAM.

Separation. Separation is gradual and based on the individual needs of the child. There is a classroom visit in the fall and an orientation evening for parents. School starts with a modified schedule that gradually builds up to a full schedule. Parents or caregivers may stay in the classroom until the child feels comfortable. Teachers work closely with parents and children to facilitate a smooth separation process.

Parent involvement. The Parents Association is composed of class representatives and other parent volunteers who sponsor special events and projects. The LAM nursery hosts an auction, a book fair, and an art fundraiser each year. Parents coordinate social events such as a dinner before Curriculum Night.

Parent-teacher conferences are held twice a year, and a weekly parent discussion group which focuses on child development, child rearing, and how children learn. The school holds an annual fundraising luncheon at the Pierre Hotel as well as theater parties.

Financial. A deposit of $750–$1,250 is required along with a $30 registration fee. Fifteen to twenty percent of students receive financial aid.

Affiliations. The Third Street Music School Settlement is a member of the National Guild of Community Schools of the Arts, the Downtown Early Childhood Association, ERB, ISAAGNY, and the Parents League.

Additional programs. The Third Street Music School offers year long programs for children in traditional or Suzuki string instruction, Suzuki piano, guitar, and musicianship modern dance (age 3 and 4 years and older), children's chorus, art, and ballet (age 5 years and older). There are also creative movement classes for toddlers and older 2s, a "Paint and Play" class, and other art and movement classes for prenursery children two hours a week.

Graduates. Have gone on to Friends Seminary, Grace Church, Dalton, Spence, Marymount, Village Community School, Little Red School House, Saint Ann's, St. Luke's, UNIS, as well as PS 41, Ps 40, PS 3, PS 116, Hunter, Anderson, NEST, the Neighborhood School, Earth School and the Lab school.

Sara Curry Preschool at Little Missionary Day Nursery

Ages: 2–6 yrs

Nonsectarian

93 St. Mark's Place	Established 1896
Zip: 10009	Eileen Johnson,
Tel: 777-9774	Director
Fax: 777-2655	Enrollment: 39

School year. Beginning of September through end of June. A summer program is available.

Ages	*Hours*	*Days*	*Tuition (monthly)*
2s	8:30–3:00	Mon–Fri	$860
3s–4s	8:30–3:00	Mon–Fri	$735
	8:30–6:00	Mon–Fri	$610
2–6	*3:00–6:00	Mon–Fri	$50–60 per day
	*(afterschool program)(3–5 day option)		

Three- and four-day programs are also available at a prorated cost; after-school tuition varies based on the number of days and hours.

Program. Developmental. The goal of the program is to help each child grow, on a social, emotional, physical, and intellectual level. School is seen as having two main functions: helping children learn how to learn, and aiding them in an understanding of what it means to be part of a social group. Through the use of simple, open-ended materials like blocks, clay, cloth, water, and paint, the children are encouraged to bring their experience of the world into the classroom and share and build on it. The teachers, acting as guides, spur the children on to ask questions, to seek out more information on subjects that interest them. Children work with a movement and a music specialist once a week and make frequent field trips to the nearby parks, a community garden, the library, and other locations inside and outside the neighborhood. The school regards the diversity of its Lower East Side community as one of its greatest strengths; "We seek to reflect and celebrate this asset."

Admissions. There is no application fee. The application process for the following September begins in January. Families must attend an open house, complete an application, and come in for an individual visit with their child. The school seeks to keep all its classrooms balanced in terms of gender, age, and to reflect to the diversity of the community.

Class size. In the 2s classroom there are ten children with three teachers. The 3s classroom has fifteen children with three teachers and in the afterschool program there are twelve children with three teachers.

Facilities. The school is located in the ground and first floors of a brownstone owned by the school; it has a front garden and a rear play yard. Outdoor play also takes place in Tompkins Square Park playgrounds and play spaces, other local parks, and the community garden at 6th Street and Avenue B. Children bring their own lunches, but healthy snacks (whole-grain crackers, fruits and vegetables, juice) are served at regular points during the day.

Summer program. There is a six week summer program available for children two to six years of age.

Separation. Separation is based on the needs of the individual child and family. Parents/caregivers are encouraged to stay until both they, and the child, feel comfortable at school and are welcome in the classrooms as long as their behavior is consistent with the program's aims.

Parent involvement. Parents/caregivers serve on the board of directors and its related committees. Families are extremely active in fundraising, and construction projects. Their understanding is that schools function best by creating and developing a partnership between educators and families, one that takes into account and serves the needs of children and the people who care for them. Parent workshops are presented monthly in collaboration with The New York Psychoanalytic Society's Parent Child Center. These workshops provide a safe and open environment for parents to discuss parenting issues under the guidance of experienced professionals. This is a free service to parents.

Financial. Tuition is due at the beginning of each month. Some financial assistance is available. ACD vouchers and other child care subsidies are accepted.

Graduates. Generally go on to alternative public schools in District 1 and some private schools.

Little Star of Broome St. Day Care Center

Ages: 2.0–6 years

131–51 Broome Street
Zip: 10002
Tel: 673-2680
Fax: 777-7971

Michelle Huang,
Director

Early childhood enrollment: 75

School year: Open all year.

Hours: 8:00–6:00, depending on individual needs of families.

Facility: The school is located in a one story building with four spacious classrooms, a large library, kitchen and an outdoor playground with an area for gardening and apple trees for picking.

Financial: Licensed to take ACD vouchers.

Affiliation: Chinese-American Planning Council

Manhattan Kid's Club

Ages: 3 mos–5.8 yrs

Nonsectarian All-Day Care

21 East 13th Street
Zip: 10003
Tel: 741-3774
Fax: 989-7897

(Second Location)
629 East 14th Street
Zip: 10009
Tel: 533-1977

Established 1996
Beth Garcia,
Executive Director
Bouasavanh Rathamany,
Educational Director
Vicki Novak,
Executive Director
Enrollment (13th Street): 89
Enrollment (14th Street): 136

School year. Year round.

Ages	*Hours*	*Days*	*Tuition (monthly)*
3 mos–9 mos	7:30–6:00	Mon–Fri	$1,400
10 mos–24 mos	7:30–6:00	Mon–Fri	$1,400
2–3.8 yrs	7:30–6:00	Mon–Fri	$1,400
3–5.8 yrs	7:30–6:00	Mon–Fri	$1,400

The monthly tuition is pro-rated for fewer days per week and includes snacks, lunch, and diapers.

Program. The Manhattan Kid's Club is a full time, child care center that encourages social interaction and exploratory play while nurturing positive self-esteem. The program is child-centered and activity-oriented, providing youngsters with a varied environment to explore at their own pace and according to their individual cognitive abilities. The school believes, "childhood should be a journey . . . not a race." All families are welcome; children can learn to recognize what they have in common while respecting and enjoying the diversity that makes each of them unique.

The daily activities include both individual and group time, free choice and structured activity, as well as quiet and active periods. The space is divided into areas offering creative art activities, dramatic play, books, cognitive games, and small- and large-muscle activities.

The most important goal of the curriculum is to help children become enthusiastic learners. This means encouraging them to be active, creative explorers who are not afraid to try out their ideas and think their own thoughts.

Admissions. The application fee is $100. Children may be enrolled at any time throughout the year. Tours are given by appointment only. If a class is at capacity, parents may place their child on a waiting list.

Class size. The Infants and 1s classes have eight children each with three teachers, the 2s have ten children each with two teachers and the 3s and 4s have eighteen children with two to three teachers in each class.

Facilities. The space is newly renovated. There are eight classrooms, an indoor gymnasium, kitchen, staff area, and business office. The children use Washington Square and Union Square Parks for outside play time.

Separation. Before entering, families and children are encouraged to visit for a few hours to become familiar with the teachers and students. Because each child is different, the staff works with the parents and child to make the transition as easy as possible.

Parent involvement. Parents are welcome at all times to observe, visit, or eat lunch with their children, as well as to volunteer to help in the classroom (volunteers must have a PPD/Mantoux tuberculosis test yearly). All communication between the staff and the families is based on the concept that parents are and should be the principal influence in children's lives. Parents are invited to two parent-teacher conferences each year and are encouraged to speak with the staff about any concerns or questions they have about their child with regard to the program. A Parents' Club meeting is held monthly. In addition, parents are asked to volunteer for school cleanings, held on two separate weekends.

Financial. One month's tuition is required as a deposit. Tuition is paid monthly by the 5th of each month.

Transportation. Most families live or work in the neighborhood and the children are brought by their parents or caregivers. No private bus service is available.

Manhattan Nursery School

Ages: 15 mos–5 yrs

Christian Day Care and Nursery School

38 West 32nd Street, Suite 306	Established 1996
(between Fifth Avenue and Broadway)	Sinok Park,
Zip: 10001	President
Tel: 631-0543/0547	Kyeongsook Rim,
Fax: 244-8077	Director
E-Mail: contact@manhattannurseryschool.com	Enrollment: 93

School year. All year.

Ages	*Hours*	*Days*	*Tuition (monthly)*
15 mos–2 yrs	8:00–7:00	Mon–Fri	$1,200
2–3 yrs	8:00–7:00	Mon–Fri	$1,020
3–5 yrs	8:00–7:00	Mon–Fri	$980

Tuition is pro-rated for two-, three-, and four-day-a-week schedules. Flexible hours are available for all ages. A 10% sibling discount is available.

Program. Developmental. The program is based on Christian values and offers various educational activities, which include art, dramatic play, table games, puppetry, read-alouds, songs, poems and musical games. Breakfast, lunch, and snack are provided.

Admissions. Parents call for an appointment to tour the facility and are required to submit an application. The school maintains an active waiting list.

Class size. There are five classes. The toddler class has a maximum of twelve, the pre-K a maximum of fifteen.

Staff. Each class has a head teacher and assistant teacher.

Facilities. Classrooms are large, colorful, bright, and very cheerful. Various learning areas focus on library, reading, housekeeping, puzzles, blocks, drama, art and music, and computer. The school is fully air conditioned and carpeted and features a well-equipped indoor playground.

Parent involvement. Parents are closely involved in the school's day to day activities. There are two parent-teacher conferences each year.

Financial. A registration fee of $50 as well as a half-month's tuition deposit are required upon registration. In addition, a $10 materials fee is payable each month. The half month tuition deposit is returned to the parent upon the child's departure from school.

Transportation. Most parents bring their children directly to the classrooms.

Mei Wah Day Care/ Chinese Methodist Center Corporation

Ages: 3–5 yrs

Methodist All-Day Care

69 Madison Street
(at Catherine Street)
Zip: 10002
Tel: 349-2703
Fax: 349-0702
E-Mail: cmcc@cumc-nyc.org

Established 1975
Mey Joy Choy, Director

Enrollment: 20

School year: All year.

Ages	*Hours*	*Days*	*Tuition (monthly)*
3–5 yrs	8:30–6:00	Mon–Fri	$400
3–5 yrs	8:30–12:30 or 2:30–6:00	Mon–Fri	$300

Children must be toilet-trained.

Program. Developmental. The program is bilingual and bicultural and offers an early childhood curriculum.

Admissions. There is no application fee. Parents may call at any time of year to see if vacancies are open and to arrange to visit the school. Children are accepted on a first-come basis. If no spaces are available, children will be put on a waiting list.

Class size. There is one group of 20 children with two staff members.

Facilities. The classroom is fully equipped and there is an indoor gym. Snack, lunch, and supper are homemade and provided daily.

Parent involvement. There is an orientation meeting in which the Center's regulations are discussed. Parents are involved in fundraising and assist at holidays and on field trips. Visits are by appointment only.

Financial. There is a $50 non-refundable registration fee. Tuition is payable monthly or in advance. ACD vouchers are accepted.

Transportation. No private transportation.

Graduates. Attend public and parochial schools.

Affiliation. Chinese United Methodist Church.

Montessori School of Manhattan
Tribeca Campus and Wall Street Campus

Ages: 2–6 yrs

Montessori School

54 Beach Street (between
Hudson and Greenwich Streets)
Zip: 10013
Tel: 334-0400
Fax: 334-0483

2 Gold Street (between
Maiden Lane and Platt Street)
Zip: 10038
Tel: 509-1400

Website: www.montessorimanhattan.com
E-Mail: montessorimanh@aol.com

Established 2003
Mrs. Bridie L. Gauthier,
Head of Schools
Ms. Kristin Ramey,
Director of Education/Admissions
Ms. Sharahn McClung,
Director of Administrative Affairs,
Tribeca Campus
Ms. Cecelia Fernandez,
Director of Administrative Affairs,
Wall Street Campus
Enrollment:
Tribeca–250 capacity
Wall Street–300 capacity

School year. September–June

Ages	*Hours*	*Days*	*Tuition*
Toddlers (2s)	12:45–3:45	T, Th	$8,950
Toddlers	12:45–3:45	M, W, F	$10,950
Toddlers	8:45–11:45	M–F	$14,950
Toddlers	12:45–3:45	M–F	$14,950
Toddlers	8:45–3:45	M–F	$19,950
3–6 yrs	9:00–12:00	M–F	$13,950
3–6 yrs	1:00–4:00	M–F	$13,950
3–6 yrs	9:00–4:00	M–F	$18,950

*Children stay for lunch. They must be toilet trained on entry.

Program. Montessori. The environment and curriculum are designed to provide children ages 2 to 6 with a life-long love of learning. The Montessori-certified teachers are specially trained in using Dr. Montessori's methods and materials to successfully guide each child in developing unique abilities within a carefully planned curriculum. Using learning materials designed to be responsive to a wide range of interests and skills, children are encouraged to explore a world of ideas, information and creativity. The Montessori curriculum stresses an interdisciplinary approach to learning.

Supported by one-on-one guidance from teachers, students work both independently and in small groups with other children. Parents and community resources contribute to and enrich the learning partnership.

Admissions. Parents should contact the school (334-0400) to request an application packet. When a completed application is received, the admissions department will contact the family to schedule a classroom observation. The head of school reviews all applications and makes admissions decisions. Parents receive a contract after children have been accepted. Admissions is complete when the school receives the signed contract and specified fees. Priority is given to siblings and alumni families.

All children must be toilet-trained, with the exception of the toddlers (2-year-old children). Children who qualify by age for the local public school Kindergarten program, will be considered for Kindergarten at the school after consultation between teacher and parents.

Class size. Toddlers: 10 children, 2 teachers; Preschool: 16 Children, 2 teachers.

Staff. Teachers are Montessori certified and have New York State Department of Education certification.

Facilities. The Tribeca campus consists of four toddler classrooms and five preschool classrooms on three floors. The beautifully renovated facility is all natural wood, with natural lighting in each classroom. There is a playroom on each floor where students have music, yoga, drama, performing arts and movement classes and an art studio where they have weekly art lessons.

The Wall Street campus consists of four toddler classrooms and five preschool classrooms on a single floor. This facility is also all natural wood, with natural lighting in each classroom. There is a full gymnasium where students have music, yoga, drama, performing arts and movement classes and an art studio where they have weekly art lessons.

Summer program. Part-time and full-time programs are available. The MSM Summer program follows the same daily schedule as the one followed during the academic year with a greater emphasis on cultural studies and physical development. During the summer the children spend more time enjoying swimming, on outdoor activities, music and movement, sports and arts and crafts projects. The Montessori Summer Program places an emphasis on cultural and language lessons, including individual and group lessons. The staff conducts all summer classes. The program is based around a theme, such as the study of a specific continent, and all lessons and activities grow from that common theme.

After School. Optional after-school classes are offered at the Tribeca campus from 4:00–4:45 PM once per week. These classes include, but are not limited to: Spanish, French, Mandarin, ballet, cooking and music.

The Wall Street campus offers early drop-off and late pick-up for those families requiring an extended school day. Students in the Extended Hours Programs enjoy a variety of art, music and group activities, as well as snack, story time and free play. Children may be dropped off as early as 8:00 AM and picked up as late as 6:00 PM. The Extended Hours Programs are available for both occasional and regular use.

Separation. New children take part in a gradual phase-in in which children first meet in smaller groups for a one-hour block of time. During the phase-in days, parents should be prepared to remain at or close to the school. If a child shows a willingness to allow parents to leave the classroom they are encouraged to do so. Other children may experience greater difficulty in separating from parents and need them to remain in the classroom for a longer period of time. Each child's separation needs are accommodated.

Parent involvement. Parents are encouraged to join the Parents Association, take part in educational workshops and volunteer in classrooms. The Parents Association meets with the head of school regularly throughout the school year. One of the major goals of this group is to provide activities and events that will enrich the lives of the student body. The PA sponsors student activities, arranges teacher appreciation week activities, helps to promote and faciliate parent education nights, plans and implements annual fund raisers as takes part in other enriching activities.

Workshops on a variety of toppics are offered by staff and guest presenters two or three times each year and all MSM families are encouraged to participate in these events. Parents are also encouraged to be involved in their children's classrooms in a variety of ways, including, sharing their expertise and talents, and helping supervise on class trips.

Financial. The Tribeca campus offers full and partial tuition assistance. Application forms are available upon request.

Transportation. Tribeca Campus: 1, A, C, E trains; Wall Street Campus: 2/3 4/5/6 N/R trains.

Graduates. Have attended a variety of public and private schools, including Spence, Packard, Saint Ann's, PS 234, Nightingale-Bamford, Horace Mann, St. Luke's, PS 89, Friends Seminary, Lycée Francais, Claremont, PS 41, Little Red School House, The Anderson Program, Brooklyn Heights Montessori and Calhoun.

Member. AMS; ATIS.

Nazareth Nursery

Ages: 2–6 yrs

Catholic

214–16 West 15th Street
(between 7th and 8th
Avenues)
Zip: 10011-6501
Tel: 243-1881
Web site: www.nazarethnursery.com

Established 1901
Sister Lucy Sabatini,
Director

Enrollment: 55

School year. September through July.

Ages	*Hours*	*Days*	*Tuition (monthly)*
2–6	8:00–5:30	Mon–Fri	$695

*Child must be toilet trained.

Program. Nazareth Nursery is a Montessori school with a Catholic emphasis. The day includes supervised play and work periods during which children can work with materials previously demonstrated.

Admissions. Inquiries are year round. Parents should call and arrange to visit the school. Children of all faiths are welcome.

Class size. There are three multi-age groups with three staff members in each group.

Facilities. The school has three comfortable classrooms and a backyard play area. Lunch, morning and afternoon snacks are served.

Parent involvement. Four to six parents meetings each year are devoted to child safety and health, parenting, and child development. Parents are involved with fund-raising, as classroom aides, on school committees, and with special classroom projects and field trips.

Financial. Payments are made quarterly or monthly. There are some preliminary fees before a child is admitted. A loan of $165 is required per child, and a $250 per child payment to the building fund is required. The loan is refunded if all obligations have been fulfilled.

Transportation. The school does not provide transportation. The children come from Chelsea and Greenwich Village, from other Manhattan neighborhoods, and the outlying boroughs.

Graduates. Have gone on to Guardian Angel, St. Bernard's, St. Francis Xavier, St. Joseph's and P.S. 11, 41, and to public and parochial schools in Brooklyn, the Bronx, Staten Island and New Jersey.

Affiliation. The school is affiliated with the Archdiocese of New York.

Member. North American Montessori Teachers Association.

Our Lady of Pompeii Elementary School

Ages: 3–13 yrs

Catholic

240 Bleecker Street
Zip: 10014
Tel: 242-4147
Fax: 691-2361
Website: www.LadyofPompeii.org

Established: 1931
Sr. Colleen Therese Smith, ASCJ, Principal

School year. September through June.

Ages	*Hours*	*Days*	*Tuition (monthly)*
3s	8:30–2:00	Tu W Th	$3,400
4s	8:30–2:00	Mon–Fri	$4,900
Kindergarten	7:50–2:30	Mon–Fri	$3850

Enrollment. There are places for sixteen 3s, twenty 4s and twenty-four kindergartners.

After-School Program: Is available.

Affiliation. Archdiocese of New York and Middle States Association of Schools and Colleges.

Our Lady of Sorrows Elementary School

Ages: 3–13 yrs

Catholic

219 Stanton Street
Zip: 10002
Tel: 473-0320
Fax: 420-0285

Mrs. Mary George,
Principal

Enrollment. Serves twenty-four 3s and 4s as well as twenty-five 5s.

Affiliation: Archdiocese of New York.

The Park Preschool

Ages: 2.2–5 yrs

Nonsectarian Nursery School

275 Greenwich Street
(one block south of Chambers between Greenwich and West Broadway)
Zip: 10007
Tel: 571-6191
Fax: 732-5256
Website: www.theparkpreschool.org

Established 1989
Ellen Offen and Kevin Artale,
Directors

Enrollment: 92

School year. September through June, and a six-week summer camp.

Ages	*Hours*	*Days*	*Tuition*
All	8:30–5:30	2,3,5	$6,700–14,650
All	8:45–3:30	2,3,5	$6,300–13,600
All	8:45–1:00	2,3,5	$5,450–11,500
2–3.5	8:45–11:45	2,3,5	$5,000–11,400
All	1:00–4:00 or 5:30	2,3,5	$5,000–11,500

There is an enrollment fee of $150 and a supply fee ranging from $150 to $275. Children need not be toilet-trained.

Program. Progressive. The school has a relaxed, welcoming atmosphere. Teachers help children develop social skills, independence, and self-esteem. Learning is tailored to each child's developmental level and emotional needs. The school believes that children "think by doing." The program gives them opportunities to experiment, discover, and express their original ideas. "We give them freedom, let them try, let them fail, encourage them, let them succeed, and rejoice with them," says the director. Groups are mixed age: younger children model appropriate social and academic strategies by watching the older children; the older children reinforce concepts they have already learned by teaching the younger ones.

Each room has areas for science, math, language arts, art, manipulatives, and puzzles, with a library and listening center. Walls display the children's artwork.

Admissions. Appointments for a visit and interview may be made throughout the year. To hold a child's place for September, parents send in a non-refundable deposit consisting of the enrollment fee, supply fee and one month's tuition. The enrollment process begins in mid-February.

Class size. There are three mixed-age classrooms, including two 2s–3s classrooms with 12 students, two teachers and one assistant teacher and one 3s–5s class with 18 students, two teachers and one assistant teacher.

Staff. Music and movement specialists visit once a week.

Facilities. Entry at street level takes you past the director's office and into a large room with wide storefront windows. The older children occupy this space. Downstairs, the two classrooms are windowless but brightly-lit with clean, off-white walls. The newly-renovated basement also includes a gym. Here, the 4s were observed with their movement specialist, dancing in the dark with flashlights. Children use the playground of Washington Market Park, half a block away.

Summer program. A summer program is offered from the end of June to early August. Children may attend two, three, or five days a week, with a minimum of two weeks.

Separation. All students are phased in. Parents are welcome to stay or not, depending on the child's readiness. Phase-in takes about a week, after which separation is tailored to the individual child's needs.

Parent involvement. Parental involvement is encouraged. On occasion, parents teach a special class to the children, accompany children on field trips, or cook a special holiday treat.

Financial. Financial aid is not available.

Transportation. Most families come from within walking distance in Battery Park City and Tribeca.

Graduates. Have gone on to Berkeley Carroll, Brearley, Chapin, City and Country, Corlears, Grace Church, St. Luke's, UNIS, Village Community School, PS 3, 89, 234, Early Childhood Center, and the Lab School.

San José Day Nursery

Ages: 1–6 yrs

Catholic

432 West 20th Street
(between 9th and
10th Avenues)
Zip: 10011
Tel: 929-0839
Fax: 924-0891

Established 1921
Sister Trinidad Fernandez,
Director

Enrollment: 57

School year. September through July. School is closed during the month of August. No summer program.

Ages	*Hours*	*Days*	*Tuition*
All	8:00–5:00*	Mon–Fri	$185 weekly

*Beginners need not be toilet trained. Some students stay until 6:00 PM.

Program. The school blends Montessori and progressive methods. Religious activities are part of the curriculum.

Admissions. The application fee is $175
Inquiries are year 'round. Call during the year for an application and to arrange a visit. Notifications are sent promptly, depending on when an application is filed.

Class size. There are four classes which include eight 1s, thirteen 2s, seventeen 3s, and twenty 4s and 5s. Each group has two in staff. The majority of the staff is fluent in Spanish.

Facilities. The school is located on three floors of a brownstone directly opposite General Theological Seminary. It has an outdoor playground equipped with climbing apparatus, and a spacious yard for outdoor meals in good weather.

Parent involvement. One or two evening seminars are offered on child-rearing and developmental stages. Parents may visit any time. They arrange fund-raising events and help out during shows and holiday social events.

Financial. A contract or deposit is not required. No financial aid is available. There is a supplies fee of $50.

Transportation. About half the children live in the neighborhood; the rest have parents working close by. Bus service is not available.

Graduates. Have gone on to Guardian Angel and St. Columbia Grammar schools, as well as independent schools.

Affiliations. Archdiocese of New York, Catholic Charities of Greater New York.

Tenth Street Tots Childcare Center

Ages: 2–4 yrs

Nonsectarian

297 East 10th Street
Zip: 10009
Tel: 982-8701
Fax: 982-8701
Website: www.tentots.com

Established 1983
John Touhey, Founder
April Gore, Director
Enrollment: 15

School year. September through July.

Ages	*Hours*	*Days*	*Tuition (monthly)*
2–4	8:30–3:00	Mon–Fri	$850
2–4	8:30–3:00	3 or 4 days	$700–750

Program. Developmental. Play is seen as the child's work. Social skills are stressed. Activities include blockbuilding, sand and water play, dramatic play, cooking, storytimes, play with puzzles, games, small play objects, and a heavy emphasis on arts, crafts, and music.

Admissions. Inquiries are ongoing. Applications are accepted whenever positions are open. Parents will be asked to visit the center and meet the director. Children are observed in groups with the parents present or they may join in school activities. Parents are notified of acceptance on an ongoing basis.

Class size. There are five 2s, 3s, and 4s and three staff members; with a 5 to 1 student/teacher ratio.

Facilities. The ground floor of a residential brownstone on the northern edge of Tompkins Square Park. It consists of one large room and a front yard. Children us Tompkins Square Park for outdoor play. They bring their lunches.

Parent involvement. Parent visits are welcome any time, and there are social get-togethers once or twice a year. Parents serve on the board of directors and help arrange social events. Families come from the East Village, and the parent body is extremely diverse.

Financial. A deposit of $200 and three month's tuition is required on signing the contract, refundable only if the school is given sufficient notice and can find a replacement. Tuition is payable on the first of every month. There is a charge of $10 if a child is picked up late. Financial aid is available.

Transportation. No private bus service is available.

TriBeCa Community School

Ages 2–5 yrs

22 Ericsson Place
Zip: 10013
Tel: 226-9070
Fax: 226-9073
Website: www.tribecacommunityschool.com
E-Mail info@tribecacommunityschool.com

Established 2006
Ayala Marcktell, CEO and Founder
Zvia Dover, Pedagogical Director
Enrollment: TriBeCa Community opened in 2006.

School year. September–June. A summer program is being developed.

Ages	*Hours*	*Days*	*Tuition*
2–5	9–12 noon or 1–4 pm	5 days	$15,225
2–5	9–12 noon or 1–4 pm	4 days	$15,000
2–5	9–12 noon or 1–4 pm	3 days	$11,550
2–5	9–12 noon or 1–4 pm	2 days	$8,500

Program. The TriBeCa Community School is inspired by the Reggio Emilia approach to early childhood education, which is based on nurturing a child's sense of self-esteem and competency. Children are engaged in experiences that are tailored to their natural curiosity about the world using such tools as music, art, theater, science and the surrounding neighborhood. Programs are designed to cultivate students' cognitive, intellectual and social skills through long-term inquiries based on the children's and teachers' interests. These investigations emphasize collaboration, documentation of the children's work, problem-solving and the involvement of parents and the community. Emphasis is placed on open-ended materials and imaginative play is encouarged.

Admissions. Application fee is $50

Parents are asked to attend a one-hour introductory session, and submit an application after deciding that the school is the appropriate choice for their family. Siblings of currently enrolled children and alumni have priority. Admission is on-going until places are filled. TriBeCa Community School does not test children nor interview families.

Class size. 2 yrs: up to 10 children, with two collaborating teachers. 3 yrs: up to 15 children with two collaborating teachers. 4 yrs: up to 18 children with two collaborating teachers.

Staff. Teachers are certified by New York State in early childhood Education and participate in ongoing training throughout the year. Teachers work in teams.

Facilities. The Tribeca Community School is located in the newly-renovated Ice House building. It was designed with children in mind, affording ample opportunities for play and exploration. Classrooms offer lots of open space and are designed with familiar elements to create a home-like environment, and foster a feeling of belonging. A central atelier (art studio), offers access to materials for inspiring and engaging children in creative projects.

Summer program. The summer program is being developed.

Separation. There is a separation-transition period during which parents are encouraged to stay in the classroom with their child. Once the child is ready, parents move to a comfortable sitting area.

Parent involvement. The school has an open door policy. Parents are viewed as partners in the educational experience and are encouraged to be involved in constructive ways. The school provides a parents' sitting area where parents can learn more about their children's activities and the school in a comfortable setting. Parents are also encouraged to attend parent workshops sponsored by the school, and volunteer as needed.

Financial. 10% of tuition is due with the application and thereafter: 30% by March 1st, 30% by May 1st, 30% by July 1st. No financial aid is available at this time (2007).

Transportation. Nearest subway stations: Franklin and Canal Streets, 1 and 9 lines.

Member. NAEYC, NAREA (a Reggio Emilia organization).

Trinity Parish Preschool and Nursery

Ages: 6 mos–5 yrs

Episcopal Nursery School

68 Trinity Place (directly behind Trinity Church)
Zip: 10006
Tel: 602-0829 or 0802
Fax: 602-9601
Web site: www.trinitywallstreet.org

Established 1982
Linda Smith, Director
Enrollment: 127

School year. All year. No contract required.

Ages	*Hours*	*Days*	*Tuition (monthly)*
6 mos–3 yrs	8:00–6:00 only	Mon–Fri	$1,625
3–5 yrs	8:00–6:00 only	Mon–Fri	$1,435*

*Nonrefundable registration fee of $250

Program. Traditional. In addition to an emphasis on social skills and verbalizing, there is strong, individualized skills preparation in prereading, premath, science, music, art. The program provides an academic curriculum which stresses learning geared to individual growth. Children are encouraged to communicate, share their thoughts and ideas, and to respect the rights of others. The classroom environment is designed to enhance the development of each child physically, emotionally, socially intellectually and spiritually. Children attend a weekly chapel service. The school also holds an annual Christmas pageant.

Admissions. No application fee.
Inquiries are at any time. Parents should arrange to visit the school. Children of all faiths are welcome.

Class size. There are eight infants or ten toddlers and twelve to twenty preschool children with three staff members.

Staff. The forty-four full- and part-time staff members. Eleven are state-certified with degrees in early childhood education. The remainder either have degrees in childcare or are enrolled in college. A pediatrician and a consulting psychiatrist are available.

Facilities. The preschool and nursery occupies eleven large rooms on two floors of a large, well-maintained office building occupied by Trinity Church. The babies have a separate crib and toy-filled room and regularly use a nearby room and an adjoining, carpeted lounge that is climate controlled and air conditioned. Older children use the indoor gymnasium.

Separation. Parents are asked to pick up their child early during the first two weeks to ease the child's transition to school.

Parent involvement. Lunch and Learn workshops are held each year on parenting issues. Conferences are held three times a year and as parents request them.

Financial. A deposit of $250 is due for registration, and tuition is payable monthly.

Transportation. This is a commuter school. A large number of children live outside Manhattan but have parents working in the financial district. No private bus service is available.

Graduates. Have gone on to many schools within New York City, including Chapin, Dalton, Grace Church, Hewitt, Trinity, and UNIS.

Affiliations. Trinity Episcopal Church.

Member. ERB, ISAAGNY, NAEC.

University Plaza Nursery School, Inc.

Ages: 2–5 yrs

Nonsectarian Parent Cooperative

110 Bleecker Street (between LaGuardia Place and Greene Street)
Zip: 10012
Tel: 677-3916
Fax: 471-1700
Website: www.universityplazanursery.com
E-Mail: info@universityplazanursery.com

Established 1967
Leyann Beausoleil, Director

Enrollment: 29

School year. Mid-September through mid-June.

Ages	*Hours*	*Days*	*Tuition*
2.6–5	9:00–2:00	Mon–Fri	$8,800

An afterschool program is available from 2:00-4:30 PM at an additional cost.

Program. Activities include free play, blockbuilding, art, cooking, writer's workshop, music and nature study. A music and movement teacher visits weekly. Children bring their own lunch and parents take turns providing snacks.

Admissions. The application fee is $35 Applications are accepted September through December. Parent tours are given in November while school is in session. Notification is sent in March. Preference is given to the children of faculty, staff and students of New York University.

Class size. There are eleven children in the 3s class and seventeen children in the 4s/5s, each with two full-time teachers, and a third, part-time special education teacher or "AmeriReads" tutor.

Staff. Each classroom has a certified teacher and an assistant. New York University provides AmeriReads students weekly.

Facilities. Two well-equipped rooms in NYU's Silver Towers building with an adjoining playground, and use of the Key Park in Washington Square Village.

Summer program. A six-week summer program is available.

Separation. The school year begins with a transition schedule that includes home visits, shortened days and smaller groups. Parents are encouraged to stay in the classroom until their child is comfortable.

Parent involvement. Parents help run the school. Each parent performs a job that requires approximately four hours of services each month. (They may buy exemption from these duties if they wish.) There are monthly board meetings and general meetings two times a year. Conferences are scheduled twice a year and as necessary.

Financial. A non-refundable deposit is due on signing the contract. Tuition aid is available for eligible families.

Transportation. Close to A C E, F/V, 4, 5, 6, N R, Houston Street buses, Broadway buses.

Graduates. Have gone on to private schools such as Friends Seminary, Grace Church, Little Red School House, St. Anthony's, St. Luke's, Village Community School, as well as Hunter, PS 3, 11, 41, 89, 116, 234 and Nest, Saint Ann's, Gifted and Talented programs and The Neighborhood School.

Member. Downtown Early Childhood Association, NAEYC, ERB, Parents League, Parent Cooperative Preschools International.

Village Kids Nursery

Ages: 2–5 yrs for nursery school (Parent-Child Classes for ages 12–24 mos.)

244 West 14th Street 2nd Floor (near 8th Avenue)
Zip: 10011
Tel: 337-2587
Fax: 337-2588
Website: www.villagekidsnursery.com
E-Mail: info@villagekidsnursery.com

Established June 2006
Molly Malone, Director
Enrollment: 56

School year. Mid-September through the end of May. There is also a six-week summer program for two weeks in June and four weeks in July.

Ages	*Hours*	*Days*	*Tuition*
Pre-separation (12–24 mos)	1 1/2	2	$40/class
2s (1.11 yr–2.11)	3 hrs/day	2/3/5	$8,200/$9,200/ $11,900
3s and 4s (2.11 yrs–5 yrs	4 hrs/day*	5	$13,000

*optional 1 1/2hr extension for 3s and 4s

Program. The program of Village Kids Nursery is based on the premise that kids growing up in downtown Manhattan have rich lives full of various kinds of stimulation, unique in both quantity and quality. These children deserve a school experience that helps them make sense of their world.

The purpose of Village Kids Nursery is to provide a safe, stimulating, creative, respectful and nurturing environment for students, families, and teaching staff. Children become part of a community and are encouraged to try new things, ask questions, explore ideas and discover themselves.

Teachers with diverse styles are encouraged to bring their creativity to the classrooms and engage in a process of developing themselves through explorations with children. They are fostered like artists, not supervised like technicians. Children are encouraged to create, experiment, and explore their world. The overriding belief is that authority should be based on respect, not power. Compassion and acceptance are cornerstones of this philosophy. Diversity is encouraged within an individualized curriculum designed to accommodate children who fall outside the spectrum of typical development.

Admissions. There is a $50 application fee. Families are given individual tours. Tours are generally for adults only but exceptions are made at the parents' request. Families may choose to apply before or after touring. (If the tour schedule becomes overbooked, applications are required before touring.) Applications are due in January. Small group play dates are scheduled for February. (Play dates are not used for admissions purposes.) Placement letters are sent in March.

There is also a January start program. Applications are taken year round and placement letters are sent out in November. Priority is given to siblings and students enrolled in the Pre-separation program. (No application is necessary for Pre-separation classes.)

Class size. The 2s class has eight children and two teachers. The 3s has 10–12 children and 2–3 teachers. The 4s has 16 children and 2–3 teachers.

Staff. Head teachers have New York State certification and are trained to work with their age group. Assistant teachers have bachelors degrees or significant experience with preschool age children. Specialists in music, art and gymnastics have appropriate training.

Facilities. Features five classrooms located on the second floor. There is also an 800-square-foot gym with big, sunny skylights.

Summer program. The program, which is mornings only, runs two weeks in June and four weeks in July. Mixed-age classes are generally composed of children who attend the regular school. Some new children are accepted as space allows.

Afterschool programs. Various specialty classes are offered in the afternoons. Classes for 3s and 4s run from 1:30–2:30 pm. (Children in the 9–1 pm program have a short rest time between the morning and the after-school.) Classes are open to children from other schools as well. After-school classes are offered school-age children from 3:30–4:30 pm.

Separation. Separation is very gradual. Teachers conduct home visits before school starts. Children begin in half groups with shortened days. Parents or caregivers remain in the classroom. Gradually the day becomes longer, the half groups merge, and parents move out of the classroom into the hall, down the hall, and eventually out of the school. The process is individualized for each family as needed.

Parent involvement. Parents have a voice in many of the decisions made in the school, and organize all the fundraising (generally an annual auction which helps fund scholarships, capital improvements, and a professional development fund for teachers). Parents and teachers are encouraged to be in contact, providing mutual feedback, sharing observations and learning from each other. The school works to build a community of learners among children, teachers and parents, based on reflection and respect.

Tuition assistance. The school offers limited financial assistance based on financial need. It will also consider barter arrangements and individualized payment plans. Those seeking financial assistance are asked to submit a recent tax return and letter describing their financial circumstances.

Transportation. The school is located very near the A/C/E trains, the L train and 8th Avenue and 14th Street buses. The 1/2/3 trains and 7th Avenue buses are less than a block away.

Graduates. Many graduates have gone on to Village Community School, Little Red School House, Saint Ann's, City and Country, PS 3, PS 41, PS 234 and PS 89. Others attend Friends Seminary, St. Lukes, Grace Church, Corlears, Packer, Ethical Culture, Ideal, Hunter and Anderson. Some students apply to non-public schools for children with special needs such as Churchill, Gateway, Gillen Brewer, Mary McDowell and McCarten.

Member. Parents League.

Village Preschool Center

Ages: 2–5 yrs

Nonsectarian

349 West 14th Street
(between 8th and 9th Avenues)
Zip: 10014
Tel: 645-1238
Fax: 645-0129
Website: www.villagepreschoolcenter.com

Established 1977
Suzette Burdett and Jeffrey Ramsay, Co-Directors
Enrollment: 115

School year. September through May. Summer program, June to mid-August.

Ages	*Hours*	*Days*	*Tuition (monthly)*
2s/3s	9:00–11:50	2–5 days	$535–$1,095
3s/4s/5s	9:00–2:10 or	3–5 days	$1,040–$1,550
	12:45–4:15	2–5 days	$630–$1,170

Early drop-off (8:30-9:00 AM) for morning children is an additional $7.00 per day. Children do not need to be toilet trained.

*For 2s/3s, there is a minimum schedule of two days for both morning and extended day hours.

**For 4s/5s there is a minimum schedule of three days for the morning classes and two days for the afternoon.

Program. Montessori and Bank Street-oriented. French language lessons. The school provides a warm, supportive, family atmosphere for a child's first separation from home where each child is special and where learning and play are integrated. There is a strong but unpressured academic component. Activities include outdoor play in the private play yard, computer skills, sand and water play, music, sing-a-longs with a guitar, puppetry, Montessori materials, art, cooking, dramatic play, stories, reading-readiness games, phonics (from age 2 on), introduction of the alphabet, colors, shapes and numbers, hands-on science projects, including caring for pets. A small group activity is always available for the children to join, but children are never forced to join any activity. Social skills and relationships are stressed.

Twos are introduced to French through songs, stories and common expressions; there are formal French lessons daily for the threes and fours.

The school is committed to charitable work, including support for a land mine removal, disaster relief, and a Haitian orphanage.

Admissions. There is no application fee Based on a parent-child visit, admissions are ongoing. Call for information and to schedule a one-on-one visit with your child. Applications are available upon completion of the family visit.

Class size. There are twenty-five 2s/3s divided into two classrooms, and twenty in the 4s/5s group. The children meet in three mixed-age groups. For the 2s/3s the staff/child ratio is 1:3.5; for the 3s/4s/5s the ratio is 1:5.

Staff. Full time staff members include specialists in reading, French, woodworking, science, drama, music, and puppetry.

Facilities. The school, which is located on the second floor of a commercial building, has three rooms and access to a private outdoor courtyard with climbing apparatus, safety floor mats and a vegetable/flower garden. Snacks are served.

Separation. Parents or caregivers may stay until the child feels happy and at home with teachers and classmates.

Parent involvement. The school encourages parent involvement. The directors are available day and night for parents and will help with any crisis. Parents often give lessons on special holidays such as Chinese and Indian New Year, on weekly themes, talking about work, and play music as part of the Instrument of the Week program. Families participate in the charitable activities. Conferences are held once yearly and as necessary.

Financial. The school does not require a contract. There is a registration fee of $425, not applicable towards tuition, and a deposit of the first and last months' tuition is due upon enrollment. Tuition is payable quarterly, and monthly for special situations.

Graduates. Have gone on to Calhoun, City and Country, Collegiate, Ethical Culture, Dalton, Friends Seminary, Grace Church, Little Red School House, Packer, Poly Prep, Saint Ann's, St. Luke's, Trevor Day, Trinity, Village Community School, as well as The Anderson Program, Lab, Hunter, NEST, PS 3 PS 41 and PS 150.

Affiliations. The directors are members of the AMS and NAEYC

The Washington Market School

Ages: 1.6–4.0 (Duane Street)
2.6–6.0 (Hudson Street)

Nonsectarian Montessori Nursery School

55 Hudson Street	Established 1976
Zip: 10013	Ronnie Moskowitz,
134 Duane Street	Head of School,
Zip: 10013	Maggie Morris,
Tel: 406-7271 (Duane Street)	(Hudson Street) Site Director
Tel: 233-2176 (Hudson Street)	Joan McIntee,
	(Duane Street) Site Director
	Aida Torres-Schneider,
Website: www.washingtonmarketschool.org	Administrator
E-Mail: administration@washingtonmarketschool.org	Enrollment: 300

School year. Mid-September through mid-June.

Ages	*Hours*	*Days*	*Tuition*
1.6–5.6	9:00–12:00 or 1:00–4:00	Mon Tues, or Wed–Fri, or Mon–Fri	$5,500–$13,807
2.6–5.6	1:00–6:00	Mon–Fri	$14,400
2.6–5.6	9:00–3:00	Mon–Fri	$16,100
2.6–5.6	9:00–6:00	Mon–Fri	$20,200

Program. Montessori. Ronnie Moskowitz, head of school, founded the Washington Market School about thirty years ago. Her first class of twelve children has grown and this is considered to be one the finest early childhood programs in Manhattan. She is the "often unseen eyes in every classroom," and knows every child. The school is supported by local artists, entertainment industry executives, celebrities and neighborhood pioneers and has become an integral part of the TriBeCa community. The program aims to offer a creative educational experience within the structure of a Montessori curriculum. Teachers encourage each child to fulfill his/her own developmental needs, encourage individual freedom and provide social experiences using Montessori materials and age-appropriate activities. Washington Market is noted for its programs in science, aroma and chess. The goals of the school are the development of each child's self-esteem, independence and an inherent interest in learning and creativity in a non-racist, non-sexist and non-elitist community.

Admissions. The application fee is $40. Inquiries are from September on. Applications may be cut off in January. Call to arrange a visit. After observing in the classroom, parents meet with several other parents and the director for a question-and-answer period. Notifications are sent in March. Preference is given to minority children and siblings, although because of limited space, siblings cannot always be accepted.

Class size. The youngest half-day classes have ten children, with three in staff. The older groups have fifteen to twenty children, with two to three staff members each.

Staff. Eleven of the thirty staff members have masters degrees in early childhood education. Volunteers include teaching interns from NYU, Borough of Manhattan Community College, and Pace College's "City-as-School."

Facilities. *Duane Street*: the ground floor in a Tribeca co-op with a gym. *Hudson Street*: two floors in a Tribeca co-op with a gym/recreation area.

Summer program. An eight-week summer camp for 2s–6s is offered at the Hudson Street school, limited to enrolled students.

Separation. *Duane Street*: For the first two weeks, the youngest children meet in half classes for 90 minutes and parents are asked to stay for these shortened periods. *Hudson Street*: Four new children are introduced into a classroom each day. Parents may stay in the classroom for about twenty minutes for several days.

Parent involvement. Parent seminars are given monthly by the school's consulting psychologists. Recent topics have included sleep disorders, aggression, limit-setting, and other developmental issues. Parents are involved in fundraising: potluck suppers, the annual gala, bake sales, and the like; they also arrange social events and go on field trips. Conferences and classroom observations periods are arranged twice yearly and upon request.

Financial. A refundable building fund deposit of $300 is required on signing the contract. Tuition is payable in four installments, in June, August, October, and December. About 5 percent of students receive partial scholarships.

Transportation. No private bus service is available.

Graduates. Have gone on to Brearley, Collegiate, Convent of the Sacred Heart, Friends Seminary, Grace Church, Little Red School House, Nightingale-Bamford, Packer Collegiate, Saint Ann's, St. Luke's, Village Community School, and to public schools and programs for the gifted at Hunter, and PS 3, PS 11, PS 41, PS 124, and PS 234.

Chartered. By the Board of Regents of the State University of New York.

Member. AMS, Downtown Early Childhood Association, ERB, ISAAGNY, NAEYC, Early Childhood Council of NYC, Parents League, Child Care, Inc.

West Village Nursery School

Ages: 2.8–5 yrs

Nonsectarian Parent Cooperative

73 Horatio Street (between Greenwich and Washington Streets)
Zip: 10014
Tel: 243-5986
Fax: 243-6121
Web site: www.westvillagenurseryschool.org
E-Mail: wvns@hotmail.com

Established 1962
Paula Kaplan, Director

Enrollment: 48

School year. Mid-September through early June. Summer program available in June and July.

Ages	*Hours*	*Days*	*Tuition*
2s (with parent)	two afternoons a week	M/W or T/Th for 27 weeks	$2,900
3s/4s	9:00–12:00	Mon–Fri	$8,100
4s	9:00–2:00	Mon–Fri*	$9,380

Children must be 2.8 in September for 3s group. *Until noon on Fridays.

Program. Developmental with an emphasis on socialization. The school was founded in 1962 by a group of neighborhood parents; some taught at the school for many years. The school has had only four directors, the current director, Paula Kaplan, is a former parent and sent her three children to the school from 1969 to 1979. She has been director for seventeen years and holds a masters degree in Early Childhood Education from Bank Street College. The program does not have an academic orientation. The curriculum includes arts and crafts, blockbuilding, dramatic play, music and movement, and cooking. Every year the maple tree in the school's backyard is tapped, the sap collected and boiled down to make syrup. Based on children's interests and abilities, themes are developed that incorporate the skills that form a basis for reading and math.

Special programs. Parents/2s workshops begin a three-year sequence. These groups have a maximum of eight children and meet twice a week for 1½ hours.

Admissions. The application fee is $35
Inquiries are from September on. Open houses are held in November. Parents visit the school in January for individual interviews and informational tours given by members of the admissions committee. Brief group play sessions for children applying to the 3s and 4s classes are held with parents present. Notification is sent in early March; siblings and children of alumni are given preference. WVN seeks diversity and encourages applications from families of all backgrounds.

Class size. The 3s class consists of fifteen children, the 4s, of eighteen. At least three adults- the teacher, parent-teacher and assistant teacher, and one or two parents staff each class. Occasional teaching interns assist. There is also a music specialist and a yoga instructor.

Staff. Class meetings are held once a month to discuss how and what the children are learning. The teacher also meets twice a year, or more often if necessary, with parents for private conferences. Teachers' enrichment is available through workshops, seminars and course work in early childhood.

Facilities. The school is occupies two floors of a West Village brownstone owned by the co-op. Its safety surfaced, backyard playground is well equipped for 3s and 4s and has a summer wading pool.

Summer program. The summer program runs for six weeks in June and July. (Monday through Friday in June, and Monday through Thursday in July, from 9:00-1:00).

Separation. Children in the 3s group are introduced in small groups for short periods with a parent present as needed. The process normally lasts from two to three weeks. Parents do not assist in the classroom for the first month of school.

Parent involvement. The school is closely knit and family oriented. It is owned and operated by the parents and they are unusually and deeply involved in all aspects of the school. The Staff has full responsibility for the educational program. Parents share all other tasks, contributing their professional skills and creative talents. Parents take on a variety of administrative tasks, including fundraising. Many are on the board. They serve in the classroom on a rotating basis, averaging two times a month, and commit a half-day to refurbishing the classroom during the two weeks before school begins. Through parent-teacher workshops the school fosters a strong parent support program so families share the experience of raising children. Lifelong friendships are made among parents and children.

Financial. The school does not have an endowment but they own the building that they are in, 73 Horatio Street, and also have some rental income. Interest from a reserve fund helps keep tuition rates low as well. A deposit of $1,000 is due on signing the contract, the balance is due in September, and in January. Partial tuition aid is available with priority given to families already in the school.

Transportation. No private bus service is available. Children come predominantly from Greenwich Village, Chelsea, Tribeca, and Soho.

Graduates. Have mainly gone on to City and Country, Corlears, Friends Seminary, Grace Church, Little Red School House, St. Luke's, Village Community, and PS 3 and 41.

Chartered. By the New York State University Board of Regents of the State University of New York.

Member. Downtown Early Childhood Association, NAEYC, ISAAGNY, Parents League.

Your Kids "R" Our Kids

Ages: 3 mos–5 yrs

30 West 15th Street
Zip: 10011
Tel: 675-6226
Fax: 675-2094
Website: yourkidsourkids.com
E-Mail: info@yourkidsourkids.com

Established 1993
Suzie Shapiro,
Education Director
Irwin Silver,
Executive Director

Total enrollment: 56

School year. Year-round program.

Ages	*Hours*	*Days*	*Tuition (monthly)*
All	7:30–6:00 PM	5 days (full time only)	$1,100

*Breakfast, a hot lunch and afternoon snacks are provided.

Program. Based on the Bank Street (Progressive/Developmental) model, much attention is paid to individual growth. There is some structure and stability, and each group has a schedule, but there is flexibility. A typical day's schedule is well-organized; it includes free play (with puzzles and blocks), creative movement, art and singing as well as "learning time." Academic skills grow out of children's interests; math, reading and language are a natural extensions of these interests.

Admissions. Registration is open all year, but parents should apply at least three to six months in advance to secure a start date. To schedule a tour, call or visit the website. A registration fee and a one-month advance payment are required at time of enrollment. Fees are paid monthly.

Class size. Infant/Toddlers have a 4–1 teacher/child ratio; preschoolers, 7:1. Children move on to the next group depending on readiness, not chronological age.

Staff. Certified for early childhood education. Each preschool class has a teacher with a BA or comparable early childhood education qualifications. There are also weekly specialists in music, art and French.

Facilities. An air-conditioned, clean and freshly painted floor-through loft of the ground floor of a residential building off of Fifth Avenue, in the Flatiron District. There are five play/classrooms with age appropriate equipment and furnishings. The bathrooms have child-sized fixtures. Video cameras and release-buzzed doors are the security at the main entrance. In good weather, children play in the Union Square playgrounds, a block and a half away, as well as visiting libraries and child-friendly shops.

Separation. The majority of children at Your Kids have working parents and the school takes this into account by accommodating the individual needs of the child during the initial transition period. Children and parents visit the facility before the child begins school. The child starts with a shortened day; however, the staff will cuddle and build a bond with a child immediately.

Parent involvement. The doors are open to parents to observe without an appointment. Since the school is not a non-profit entity, parents don't have to fund-raise. The school arranges some family days on weekends and there are parent-teacher group meetings (by classroom) at least three times a year. Individual parent-teacher conferences are made by request and progress reports are sent home twice yearly. Parents are encouraged to attend field trips.

Graduates. Have gone on to Friends Seminary, Grace, St. Joseph's, UNIS, Village Community School, and PS 41, among other schools.

Affiliations. Member, NAEYC. Proprietorship.

Additional Ongoing Schools with Pre-Kindergarten and Kindergarten Programs

For families who have children in an ongoing school or are alumni, or legacies, an ongoing independent (private) school with a nursery program is a very attractive choice. It eliminates the onus of going through the admissions process for kindergarten when the competition for places is most fierce.

There are a handful of ongoing schools that offer nursery programs beginning with pre-Kindergarten in addition to their elementary and/or middle and high school programs, that are not included in this book, mainly because they do not have a focus on the education of younger children. A more complete description of these ongoing schools and their programs can be found *The Manhattan Family Guide to Private Schools,* 5th edition, Soho Press.

Below are some ongoing schools that are not included in this book, but that offer nursery programs.

Children's Storefront

70 East 129th Street
New York, NY 10035
Tel: 427-7900
Fax: 289-3502
Web site: www.thechildrensstorefront.org
E-mail: kathyegmont@thechildrensstorefront.org
Total enrollment: 168 (Pre-kindergarten through 8th grade)

Ethical Culture

33 Central Park West
(at 63rd Street)
New York, NY 10023
Tel: 712-6220 (main number)
Tel: 712-8451 (admissions)
Fax: 712-8444
Main Website: www.ecfs.org
Total enrollment: Approximately 500 (Pre-kindergarten 4s through 5th grade)

Grace Church School

86 Fourth Avenue
(at 14th Street)
New York, NY 10003
Tel: 475-5609
Fax: 475-5015
E-Mail: mhirschman@gcschool.org
Website: www.gcschool.org
Total enrollment: 394 (Junior Kindergarten 4s through 8th grade)

Little Red School House and Elisabeth Irwin High School LREI

Lower and Middle Divisions
272 Sixth Avenue (Bleecker Street)
New York, NY 10014
Tel: 477-5316 ext 210
Fax: 677-9159
Website: www.lrei.org
Total enrollment: 560 (Pre-kindergarten 4s-12th grade)

Manhattan Country School

7 East 96th Street
New York, NY 10128
Tel: 348-0952
Fax: 348-1621
E mail: admissions@manhattancountryschool.org
Web site: www.manhattancountryschool.org
Total enrollment: 180–190
(4/5s Pre-kindergarten/kindergarten through 8th grade)
4/5s places: 18

Saint David's School

12 East 89th Street
New York, NY 10128
Tel: 369-0058
Fax: 289-2796
Web site: www.saintdavids.org
Total enrollment: 375 (Pre-kindergarten 4s through 8th grade)
Pre-kindergarten places: 16; kindergarten places: 45

St. Luke's School

487 Hudson Street
New York, NY 10014
Tel: 924-5960
Fax: 924-1352
Web site: www.stlukeschool.org
Total enrollment: 200 (Junior kindergarten 4s* through 8th grade)
Junior kindergarten places: 18; kindergarten places: 5–10

St. Patrick's Catholic Elementary School

Ages: 4–14 yrs

233 Mott Street
Zip: 10012
Tel: 226-3984
Fax: 226-4469

Dr. Stephen, Principal
Total enrollment: 146

3s, 4s, 5s are broken up into different groups; 20 children enrolled.

Affiliation. Archdiocese of New York.

*(by Oct 1st)

RESOURCES AND NURSERIES FOR CHILDREN WITH SPECIAL NEEDS AND LEARNING DISABILITIES

Nursery school directors can often identify children who have either a developmental lag, behavioral and/or psychological issues, or learning disabilities as soon as they enter their first Mommy and Me class as toddlers. Early intervention really makes a difference. Parents no longer have to wait until their child is struggling in elementary school to seek the appropriate programs. Remediation, testing, evaluations and counseling can be started when children are as young as two years old. Children who might not have been able to keep up in a normal classroom and would suffer from feelings of low self esteem can be taught how to overcome and deal with their learning issues in these specialized early childhood programs and then possibly move on to a mainstream school.

If you are concerned that your child may have a learning issue don't be afraid to ask the teacher if she thinks that it's a good idea to have your child evaluated; if the answer isn't satisfactory ask your nursery school director. Your child's school should be apprised of any testing you do outside, and provided with the results so it can best work with your child. It's best to test early and then re-test every three years (or as often as every year if necessary). Medication is sometimes prescribed for children with attention disorders to help them settle down and acclimate.

The Parents League can provide a complete listing of schools for children with developmental and learning disabilities with classes that are small in size and highly structured. They vary in size from about six to twelve students per class with a head teacher, an assistant and a variety of specialists who work with children one-on-one. Often, these schools will have mixed age groupings of children because many learning disabled children learn at rates that do not correlate with their ages.

Here are some of the resources in the New York City area that educate children with learning disabilities and other issues. Many children with learning disabilities have gone on to wonderful colleges (including the Ivy League) and have successful careers and happy and productive lives.

The New York Branch of the International Dyslexia Association

71 West 23rd Street, Suite 514
Zip: 10010
Tel: 691-1930
Fax: 633-1620
Website: www.nybida.org
E-Mail: info@nybida.org

The New York branch of the International Dyslexia Association (NYB-IDA) is a not-for-profit organization that provides information, referrals, training and support to professionals and families with respect to the impact and treatment of people with dyslexia. It offers a free telephone referral service; as well as training and workshops for professionals and peer support groups for adults, parents and teens. The NYB-IDA also sponsors an annual conference on dyslexia and related topics. Annual memberships are available.

The Learning Disabilities Association of New York City Telephone Referral Service

Tel: 645-6730
Fax: 924-8896
Website: www.LDANYC.org
E-Mail: LDANYC@LDANYC.org
Open weekdays from 9 AM to 5 PM

This nonprofit organization is an affiliate of the Learning Disabilities Association of America. Trained counselors will explain how to recognize symptoms, and offer referrals to community based agencies in the New York City area. The Learning Disabilities Association also provides printed material and conducts monthly workshops and adult support groups.

The Parents League of New York, Inc.

115 East 82nd Street	Patricia Girardi,
Zip: 10028	Executive Director
Tel: 737-7385	Alice Goldman,
Fax: 737-7389	Diana Fisher,
Website: www.parentsleague.org	Learning Disability Advisors

The Parents League sponsors a workshop and provides information and referrals about learning disabilities to member parents. Mrs. Alice Goldman, an advisor with the Parents League, is particularly knowledgeable about which schools specialize in which type of LD. Please refer to page 383 of this directory for more information about The Parents League of New York.

Resources for Children with Special Needs

116 East 16th Street
Suite 5th floor
Zip: 10003
Tel: 677-4650

Resources for Children is a nonprofit information, referral, advocacy, training and support center for programs and services for children (from birth to age twenty-one) with learning, developmental, emotional or physical disabilities. It publishes a family support guide listing camps and summer programs for children with special needs.

Advocates for Children of New York, Inc.

151 West 30th Street, 5th floor
(between 6th and 7th Avenues)
Zip: 10001
Tel: 947-9779
Fax: 947-9790
Website: www.advocatesforchildren.org
E-Mail: info@advocatesforchildren.org

Advocates for Children works to protect and extend the rights of children with learning and /or developmental disabilities in public schools.

National Dissemination Center for Children with Disabilities

Ages: Birth to 22 yrs

PO Box 1492
Washington, DC
Zip: 20013-1492
Tel: (1-800) 695-0285 or (202) 884-8200
Fax: (202) 884-8200
Website: www.nichcy.org
E-Mail: nichcy@aed.org

The A.D.D. Resource Center, Inc.

215 West 75th Street
Zip: 10023
Tel: (646) 205-8080
Fax: (646) 205-8080
E-Mail: addrc@mail.com

Executive Director:
Harold R. Meyer

Established in 1989. Seminars, courses, workshops and services for parents and children that focus on Attention Deficit Hyperactivity Disorder.

The National Center for Learning Disabilities

381 Park Avenue South, Suite 1401
Zip: 10016
Tel: 545-7510/toll free: 888-575-7373
Fax: 545-9665
Web site: www.NCLD.org

NCLD is a voluntary, not-for-profit organization founded in 1977 by Carrie Rozelle. It operates a national information and referral service and is the nation's only central, computerized resource clearing-house committed solely to the issues of LD.

AMAC Children's House

2.6–5 years

25 W. 17th Street
Zip: 10011
Tel: 645-5005
Fax: 645-0170
Web site: www.amac.org
E-Mail (Available through the website)

Established 1961
Frederica Blausten,
Executive Director
Enrollment: 70 families

School year. All-year

Age	*Hours*	*Days*	*Tuition*
2–5	8:30–1:30	Mon–Fri	N/A

Program. The center uses the Applied Behavior Analysis (ABA) method, the only scientifically-based and state-approved treatment for autistic spectrum disorders. It seeks to eliminate the frustrating and time-consuming splintering of services that families of special-needs children often face. This method relies on intensive behavioral programming to teach targeted skills and behaviors.

The program looks at the family system as a whole, paying particular attention to the interaction of emotional, cognitive and language development in the child. AMAC participates in the Universal Pre-K program. The organization also has a school serving children 5–15-years-old as well as after-school and weekend programs.

Admissions. Enrolled children have difficulties ranging from autism to emotional problems. Most children have average intelligence and potential for mainstream programs. Parents call, are screened and an appointment is made for a full-team screening at the preschool.

Applications are taken throughout the year, and the center urges parents to apply as soon as they identify a need. Acceptances are based on the openings available. The center attempts to balance ages and abilities. Private and public funding is available.

Tests. An evaluation from an outside source is helpful. If this has been done, it should be furnished, but is not required. The center has experts in specialized assessments.

Class size. Children are placed in small mixed age groups of six, eight or ten children. Each group is assigned one special education teacher and at least two assistant teachers. In addition, the center has on staff two speech and language specialists, a part-time consulting staff including occupational therapists, a psychiatrist, and psychologists who work with and participate in team conferences with the children and their families.

Separation. Teachers and a social worker will meet the family and child two or three times before school begins. When school begins, parents may remain until children are comfortable or as their schedules permit.

Parent involvement. There are informal and formal gatherings with other parents and family members, as well as special school outings and holiday celebrations. The school encourages the entire family to visit. Seminars and classes are given on subjects of interest to the parents. Parents can visit at any time, and staff members are always available.

Transportation. Children come from all over the metropolitan New York area, and are brought by parents or by NYC Department of Education buses.

Graduates. Many of the children who graduate from the school can be mainstreamed into educational programs for normal children or less restrictive educational programs. Others go on to special education programs.

Affiliations. Association for Metroarea Autistic Children.

ADDITIONAL LISTINGS

The listing below is incomplete and programs change frequently. Parents should call the Early Childhood Direction Center (see page 376) for guidance.

Child Development Center

Ages: 2–5 years

120 W. 57th Street
Zip: 10019
Tel: 632-4733, 582-9100
Website: www.jbfcs.org
Click on "Programs and Services,"
enter: Child Development Center
Serves 35 children in the Therapeutic Nursery School

Marian Davidson-Amodeo, Director

The center serves children with developmental, behavioral, emotional or organic handicapping conditions. In the Therapeutic Nursery School, two teachers work with each group of eight to ten children. There are classrooms, an outdoor rooftop playground, kitchen, workshops, and a resource room. Therapy is available for parents. The center also includes an outpatient mental health clinic for children and/or families. An early intervention group for 2-year-olds with simultaneous parent guidance serves five families. The center also serves as a consultant to many day care centers and nursery schools. The center is a program of and is located in the offices of the Jewish Board of Family and Children's Services, Inc.

Columbia Presbyterian Hospital/ Therapeutic Nursery at Babies Hospital

622 W. 168th Street (between Broadway and Ft. Washington Ave.)
Zip: 10032
Tel: 305-9042

Dr. Daniel Schechter, Medical Director

Council Center for Problems of Living

1727 Amsterdam Avenue
Zip: 10031
Tel: 694-9200

William Witherspoon,
Director

East River Schools

577 Grand Street (between Madison Avenue and the FDR Drive)
Zip: 10002
Tel: 254-7300

Steve Berman,
Director

Preschool program for children with a full range of developmental disabilities, ages 2 to 5 years.

The Gillen Brewer School

410 East 92nd Street
Zip: 10128
Tel: 831-3667
Fax: 831-5254
Website: www.gillianbrewer.com
Preschool enrollment: 24

Established: 1993
Donna Kennedy,
Head of School
Milt Sleeter,
Assistant Head of School
School age enrollment: 60

The Gillen Brewer School began as an early childhood program and evaluation site, and now extends up through the elementary grades. Parents are very pleased with the school. The program serves children who have a wide variety of severe and often multiple language, emotional, developmental, learning and health-related disabilities, including cerebral palsy, seizures, asthma, ADHD, feeding issues, cancer, heart problems, profound deafness, mobility issues, severe allergies, and autism.

The program spans a 12-month year that follows the New York State learning standards while meeting each student's needs individually. The preschool program serves children from just under 3-years old to 5 years-old. The school age program serves children 5 to 10-years-old who are classified as either learning disabled, emotionally disturbed, speech or health impaired.

Kennedy Child Study Center

151 East 67th Street
Zip: 10021
Tel: 988-9500
Fax: 327-2601
Website: www.kenchild.org
E-Mail: info@kenchild.org

Kathrin Criveau,
Human Resources Director
Peter Gorham,
Executive Director

The center serves hundreds of families annually, providing services for slowly developing and retarded children who may also have multiple handicaps. Services include diagnostic evaluations, educational assessments, infant and preschool special education, infant stimulation and therapeutic intervention and family services, including education and Saturday Respite.

Northside Center for Child Development, Inc.

Early Childhood Center

1301 5th Avenue (at 110th Street)
Zip: 10029
Tel: 426-3400
Fax: 410-7561
Website: www.northsidecenter.org

Dr. Thelma Dye,
Director
Dr. Roseann Harris,
Director, Early Childhood Center

A therapeutic nursery for children with developmental difficulties.

Rusk Institute Preschool and Infant Development Programs

Ages 1–5

Therapeutic preschool

400 E. 34th Street — Meryl Kantrowitz, Director
Zip: 10016 — Stephen Lorigan, Coordinator/Early intervention
Tel: 263-6045
Fax: 263-7771
Website:
www.med.nyu.edu/rusk/services/pediatric/outpatient/educational.html

Rusk's Preschool and Infant Development programs provide individualized educational and early intervention services for children under five.

Hours of operation: Monday–Friday, 8:30–2:00, Sept–June; 6-week summer program.

Staff. In a nursery setting, experienced certified teachers of special education work with children.

Episcopal Social Services Therapeutic Nursery

Therapeutic Nursery School

2289 5th Avenue — Celeste Gordon, Special Education Director
Zip: 10037
Tel: 283-3100

United Cerebral Palsy of New York City Manhattan Children's Center

122 E. 23rd Street — Stuart Zavin, Director
Zip: 10010 — Enrollment: 53
Tel: 677-7400 ext. 400
Fax: 982-5268
Website: www.ucpnyc.org

Multi-service center providing early intervention, special education preschool, rehabilitation therapy services, and day care is offered for children 2- to 3-years of age.

PARENTING and OTHER RESOURCES

Information Sources and Referral Agencies
Parenting Centers and Parent–Toddler Programs
Support Groups and Workshops and Seminars

INFORMATION SOURCES AND REFERRAL AGENCIES

Agency for Child Development

66 John Street
4th floor
Zip: 10038
Telephone Advisory Service:
718-367-5437 (or dial FOR-KIDS)

Head Start
Website: www.nyc.gov
click: Administration for Children's Services, Head Start Info.

ACD is responsible for funding and monitoring all public day care programs in New York City.

Parents may call ACD's telephone advisory service to obtain a listing of all licensed nursery schools and family or center-based day care programs in the metropolitan area. ACD counselors will provide limited information, including the names and addresses of several programs in the caller's residential or work neighborhood, ages of children served, cost of care, and hours of operation.

ACD partially or fully funds care for children whose parents meet its financial guidelines at participatory nursery schools and center-based or family day care programs. Parents wishing to take advantage of this financial aid must apply to the agency and be screened at one of its regional offices. ACD also administers the federally sponsored Head Start program which serves 3 to 5-year-olds.

Child Care, Inc.

322 Eighth Avenue (at 26th St)
4th Floor
New York, New York: 10001
General Telephone: (212) 929-7604
Parent Services: (212) 929-4999
Fax: (212) 929-5785
Web site: www.childcareinc.org
E-Mail: Info@childcareinc.org

Nancy Kolben,
Executive Director

New York City's largest child care resource and referral (CCR&R) agency, Child Care, Inc. is a nonprofit organization serving parents, early childhood professionals, early learning and school age programs. Parent Services has trained counselors that provide telephone consultations and child care referrals to over 4,000 parents annually. Families can obtain information on finding early care as well as school age and summer programs for children age birth through twelve. The service also includes information on how to access child care subsidies, tax credits and resources for children with special needs. Parent Service provides publications that are step-by-step guides for parents with respect to each child care option.

Child Care, Inc. also offers training to child care program staff and child care providers. A corporate membership program offers child care consultations, referrals and workplace lunchtime seminars for employees.

New York City Association for the Education of Young Children

66 Leroy Street, St. Luke's Place (near 7th Avenue below Grove Street)
Zip: 10014
Tel: 807-0144
Fax: 807-1767
E-Mail: office@nycaeyc.org
Website: www.nycaeyc.org

Meredith Lewis, President
Jorge Saenz De Viteri, President-Elect

This is the largest membership group in New York City specifically concerned with the education of young children (from infancy to age eight). Through the state and national organizations, NYC-AEYC is part of a network of thousands of people actively working on programs, research, legislation, teacher training, and other issues affecting young children. The national organization, NAEYC, is located in Washington, DC (www.naeyc.org); in New York State, NYSAEYC is located in Albany (www.nysaeyc.org). NYC-AEYC sponsors workshops, an annual conference, discussion groups, and publishes a newsletter and other materials. It is located in the Early Childhood Resource and Information Center (page 376).

The New York City Department of Health, Division of Day Care

Website: www.nyc.gov

This city agency shares responsibility for all New York City child care with the Agency for Child Development. The division of day care licenses programs and provides training for new providers.

The agency will mail to inquirers an address and telephone listing of all currently licensed early childhood programs in the metropolitan area.

All programs listed in this directory are licensed, and each is inspected twice and sometimes three times a year. Each must be relicensed every two years and those caring for children under 2 years old must be relicensed every year. Licensing covers minimum standards for physical space, equipment, program/group size, teacher/child rations, staff credentials, health examinations and immunization schedules for staff and children, food service and admissions policies.

Schools and centers are allowed to enroll two children per room above the number for which they are licensed, because attendance varies so greatly among preschoolers. Each classroom where there are children age 2 and older must have at least one state-certified teacher. Minimum child/staff rations require that there be one teacher and an assistant for 2s groups with six to ten children, 3s groups with 11 to 15 children, 4s groups with 13 to 20 children, and 5s groups with 16 to 25 children. All faculty and staff must be fingerprinted. Children must have health examinations yearly and at least 90 days before entering school. Infants and children under age 3 must be examined 30 days before and twice yearly. School and center personnel are forbidden to administer medication to children unless it is specifically labeled with adequate documentation. Each program must also receive approval from the Buildings and Fire departments.

Educational content and play equipment are not specified beyond the dictum that they be "appropriate and adequate."

To find licensed school listings on-line at the DOH website, go to www.nyc.gov. Under the "City Agencies" heading, click on "Health and Mental Hygiene," then "Search Bureau of Day Care." On the "Bureau of Day Care" page, click on "Research Group Day Care Facilities," click on "Manhattan" (or another borough), search listing alphabetically or by zipcode. Listings include school name, address, and status of license.

Early Childhood Direction Center New York Hospital Presbyterian Hospital

435 E. 70th Street #2A — Marilyn Rubinstein, Director
Zip: 10021
Tel: 746-6175
E-Mail: mrubinst@nyp.org

Established in 1982. Provides free neutral information and referral to parents, professionals and agencies looking for services for children with known or suspected special needs. Children must be between newborn and five years of age. Staff can provide information about early intervention programs, preschool special education services, day care, Head Start, summer programs, home care, respite programs, parent education, support groups, counseling, advocacy, financial and legal assistance.

The center is funded by the New York State Education Department, the New York State Office of Mental Retardation and Developmental Disabilities, and New York Presbyterian Hospital.

Early Childhood Resource and Information Center Division of New York Public Libraries

66 Leroy Street, St. Luke's Place
(near 7th Avenue
below Morton Street)
Zip: 10014
Tel: 929-0815
Website: www.nypl.org

The center is located on the second floor of the attractive old Carnegie building. Downstairs there is room for stowing strollers. Upstairs is the collection of materials on early childhood education and parenting and a parent/child area, equipped with blocks, toys, a storytime nook, rocking horses and rocking chairs, a small slide, playpens, tumbling and resting mats, housekeeping corner, and records. Free workshops and seminars presented by educators cover a wide variety of topics related to early childhood. To receive a monthly schedule, send a self-addressed, stamped envelope.

Early Steps

540 E. 76th Street
(between York Avenue and
the FDR Drive)
Zip: 10021
Tel: 288-9684
Fax: 288-0461

Jacqueline Y. Pelzer,
Executive Director

Early Steps provides counseling, guidance and referral services to families of children of color as they apply to independent schools for kindergarten and first grade whether they need financial aid or not.

THE ERB
The Educational Records Bureau

220 East 42nd Street
(The Daily News Building)
Suite 100
Zip: 10017
Tel: 672-9800
Fax: 370-4096
E-Mail: isaagny@erbtest.org
Website: www.erbtest.org

Sharon Spotnitz,
Executive Director

Although the ubiquitous "ERB," is an IQ test and developmental scale that is required for admission to most of Manhattan's elite private kindergartens is not supposed to be a measure of success, it is. If your child scores well, it's truly a good thing. When scores fall below above average, admission to the best private schools becomes an uphill battle.

The ERB has been under contract with ISAAGNY (Independent Schools Admissions Association of Greater New York) for over forty years. The ERB administers a variety of intelligence and developmental tests to children of all ages. According to the ERB, all of the examiners are at least master's level, many are doctoral level candidates, some are clinical psychologists or even PhD's. There are roughly sixty examiners employed at the ERB during the admissions season and they are all experienced. If your child's nursery school is a member of ISAAGNY then your child will probably be tested at his or her nursery school; if not you can bring your child to the ERB offices for testing.

Having a central testing agency administer one test for kindergarten admissions to all children is intended to "eliminate repetitive testing and thus minimize the strain on children and parents." Prior to the selection of the ERB, parents used to take their children for formal testing at each ongoing school to which they applied. However, many ongoing schools still require up to an hour of their own "informal testing," so you can still expect your child to be thoroughly scrutinized everywhere he or she goes. It seems to parents that it is the strain on the ongoing schools and their admissions offices that has mostly been alleviated since they can now see many more than one child at a time.

Children are compared with others their age; there is no advantage in holding off testing with the idea that your child will "know more." In fact, children are expected to do more as they become older; in some cases the younger child might have a slight edge. More children are now being tested in spring; in many instances those tested early score higher. Also, the later in the year it is, the more likely your child may have a cold or other illness. If your nursery school director thinks that your child is ready and "your child is four-years-old by May 1st and, will separate readily" testing in the spring often proves better. Each report is individually written, carefully reviewed and mailed in the order of the test date. Remember to schedule well in advance of school deadlines. It usually takes three to four weeks to receive the ERB report.

At some nursery schools, the fall semester of the four-year-old group is like "Stanley Kaplan" for the ERB. Children are given worksheets for practicing matching skills, copying geometric shapes and tracking mazes. They are drilled in their colors, taught to write their names and play with parquetry blocks (for spatial relations). Some children even bring Weekly Readers home to work on.

The cost is $400 but there is an ISAAGNY Fee Waiver Program for families who require financial aid. Parents must fill out a form requesting that the test results be sent to the ongoing schools to which the parent has applied. There is a minimal additional charge for each school in excess of six. Be sure to follow up with the schools to make sure that they received the results. The test determines strengths and weaknesses and where along the developmental scale a child falls; it was not devised as an admissions test, it is an evaluation of a child's development in language and visual/motor skills. The test is composed of four verbal and four nonverbal (or performance) sections. Children do not have to read or write to take this test. Like all standardized tests, it is a snapshot of the child's development taken on one day.

Parents are sent a full copy of the confidential ERB report. You can discuss the results with your nursery school director or you may schedule a private consultation with the ERB, or both. It is common belief that some of the very selective ongoing schools admissions directors have a cut-off score below which they will not admit a candidate. This is simply not true, there are children with astronomical scores who have not been admitted and children with scattered scores who have been.

Do not prepare or coach your child for this test, for it will probably be discovered. One four-year old blurted out "I forgot it all," as he walked into the tester's office. The testers are looking for how spontaneous a child is when responding to questions that have never been heard before, for their problem-solving strategies and other levels of information. The author of this directory thinks that it can be counter-productive to tutor your child for the test. However, anxious parents who feel that they must do something to prepare their child, may stop into Toys 'R Us, Barnes and Noble, Comp USA, The Wiz or even a well stocked pharmacy for games and activities that you can enjoy doing together. Remember there's no substitute for experience and a trip to a museum, lollipop concert, a farm, the children's zoo, the bakery and the grocery store, can all be opportunities for learning and will increase your child's general knowledge.

It's a good idea to let your child know that they are going to do "special work" with a teacher who would like to see how much they know. Let them know that there will be some new things and that he'll get a chance to learn. It's important that your child knows that you'll be in the waiting room if you bring him or her to the ERB's offices; the child should be comfortable if he or she takes the test at a familiar nursery school. Some schools even have special rooms designated just for ERB testing. If your child has separation issues it may be best if your spouse or caregiver brings him or her to ERB's offices.

ERB will not test an unhappy or reluctant child; the anticipation of a pleasant experience is the best preparation for being tested and, of course, a little luck.

Head Start

Tel: 232-0966
Website: www.nyc.gov, city agencies, Department of Health and Mental Hygiene, Division of Day Care, research group day care facilities

Independent Schools Admissions Association of Greater New York (ISAAGNY)

Website: www.isaagny.org

Founded in 1965, and composed of admissions directors and heads of early childhood programs, ISAAGNY meets on a regular basis to simplify and coordinate the admissions procedures among independent schools in the New York Metropolitan area. It is now composed of approximately 150 member schools. ISAAGNY contracted with the Education Records Bureau to administer uniform admissions testing. In addition, ISAAGNY schools have the same admissions notification and parent reply dates. These guarantee that families have at least two weeks in which to decide what school to accept. The dates vary each year, depending on how weekends fall on the calendar.

Board of Regents of the State University of New York

Tel: 518–474-5922
Fax: 518-486-1385
Web site: www.nysed.gov

Above and beyond New York City's day care licensing, many nonpublic nursery schools and kindergartens are voluntarily registered by the Board of Regents of the State University of New York, which, through regulations set by the State Department of Education, has more stringent standards than the city. In addition to meeting the board's requirements for classroom size, location, construction, eating, rest, sanitary facilities, equipment, outdoor play space, and fire and safety regulations, the classrooms must include activities centers for block-building, dramatic play, water play, creative arts, painting, clay, collage, science and nature study, cooking and music, as well as adequate books, pictures, puzzles, games, and small manipulatives. Outdoor equipment must include well-anchored climbing and play structures, plus wheel toys, tricycles, wagons, trucks, building equipment, ladders, sawhorses, and a place to store portable equipment.

Child/teacher ratios are at eight to one for 3s, ten to one for 4s (with a maximum of twenty children per class) and fifteen to one for 5s (with a maximum of twenty-two children per class. These class sizes are based on the availability of 35 square feet of indoor space per child.

Class sizes are based on the availability of 35 square feet of indoor space per child. Each school must show evidence of developmentally appropriate curriculum and early education programs adapted to ages, interests, and needs of the children. Children must also have the opportunity to choose and become involved in manipulation of various materials, objects, and textures, dramatic play activities, arts, large motor play, discussions and games, literature, music, science, and field trips. Schools must also show positive parent collaboration in the education of their children, including conferences, parent workshops, newsletters, and participation in program planning and decision making.

OTHER NYC GOVERNMENT-RUN REFERRAL ORGANIZATIONS

New York City Child Care Resource Center and Referral Consortium

Tel: 888-469-5999

NYC Department of Health and Mental Hygiene

(Licenses Childcare Facilities)
Tel: 280-9253 or
(718) 676-2444

NYC Early Intervention Program

If you believe your child has a developmental delay or disability call for referrals and evaluations.

Tel: (888) 577-BABY or
219-5580

Day Care Council of NYC Inc.

Tel: 206-7836

Child Development Support Corp

Tel: (718) 398-6738

ADVISORY SERVICES

Aside from this book and the director of your nursery school, there are other useful resources in Manhattan to help you choose the right ongoing independent school for your family. Keep in mind that the best source of information is always the school itself. Ask the school you are interested in if it has spring tours. Perhaps you can rule it out or take a second look in the fall when you apply. Once the fall admissions process gets rolling you will usually not be able to take another look until your child is accepted to the school. Advisory services (or educational consultants) help parents approach the independent school admissions process in an organized manner and provide reassurance and advice to apprehensive parents.

Parents, whether you choose to use a consultant or not, please be advised that some independent schools admissions officers have informed us that they do not look kindly on applicants who use the services of consultants. So if you choose to use one, obviously don't broadcast it anywhere.

All of the services listed below require a fee and the range, which is vast, is from about $200 to $5,000, or more.

1. The Parents League of New York, Inc.

115 East 82nd Street
Zip: 10028
Tel: 737-7385
Web site: www.parentsleague.org

Patricia Girardi,
Executive Director

Annual membership fee: $115 for one year or $275 for three years
Only members of the Parents League can participate.

The Parents League was founded in1913 and is a nonprofit organization of parents and independent schools. It offers a school advisory service for member parents who need advice about the process of applying to schools and information about the schools. Please call for an appointment. The advisors now have broad experience with respect to independent schools as educators, admissions directors, heads, financial aid officers, board members and parents' association representatives.

The Parents League distributes the *New York Independent Schools Directory*, published by the Independent Schools Admissions Association of Greater New York (ISAAGNY). Anyone may purchase this book for an additional $20.00 at the office, $23.00 by mail or online. *Please be aware that the entries in this book are written by the schools themselves.*

The Parents League sponsors Independent School Day, held in the fall, at which parents can pick up printed material, including brochures and applications, from various city independent schools, that primarily serve grades K–12. Representatives from the independent schools are available to answer *brief* questions. Be prepared for a mob scene, but it will save you countless phone calls.

The Parents League sponsors forums on admissions, at which admissions directors from five or six independent schools speak and then answer questions from the audience about the admissions process. It offers a summer advisory service and a special education advisory service.

---

2. Penny Miskin, MS

167 East 82nd Street, Suite 1B
Zip: 10028
Tel: 396-1062

Ms. Mishkin has been in private practice for 15 years; her specialty is fine motor skills, visual-spacial perception and occupational therapy.

---

3. Lana F. Morrow, Ph.D.

350 Central Park West
Suite 1Q
Zip: 10025
Tel: (646) 338-7676

Dr. Morrow administers neuropsychological evaluations and remediates children who have learning disabilities. She advises families as to which independent school will be best suited for their child and offers talks and strategies on organization and cognitive, and academic planning.

4. Schools & You

328 Flatbush Avenue — Sarah D. Meredith
Suite 372
Brooklyn, New York
Zip: 11238
Tel: 718 230-8971
Web site: www.schoolsandyou.com

Ms. Meredith provides information and consultations on Manhattan and Brooklyn school choices from nursery through eighth grade for both public and private schools. She will consult by phone, internet or in your home, workplace, or another convenient location. Resource materials accompany every consultation.

5. Smart City Kids

251 East 77th Street — Roxana Reid
Suite 3D
Zip: 10019
Tel: 979-1829
Website: www.smartcitykids.com

Fees are approximately $150.00 an hour.

Ms. Reid, a former kindergarten teacher with a masters in social work, specializes in nursery and kindergarten admissions. Smart City Kids holds workshops and private sessions that prepare parents and children for every aspect of the admissions process: how to handle interviews, testing, skill requirements, applications and essays. They also offer a caregiver workshop that suggests activities for caregivers and their three and four-year-old charges.

6. Robin Aronow, Ph.D

155 Riverside Drive
Suite 12C
Zip: 10024
Tel: 316-0186 or (917) 685-1549
E-mail: dragnet@tuna.net

Fees range from $60 for 15 minutes to $195 for 1 hour; many billing options are available.

Dr. Aronow, a social worker not a psychologist, works individually with families considering both public and private schools on all aspects of the admissions process from nursery school through upper grades. She does not provide or believe in professional coaching for the ERBs or Stanford-Binet IQ tests.

---

7. Manhattan Private School Advisors

360 Central Park West — Amanda Uhry
Zip: 10025
Tel: 280-7777
Web site: www.privateschooladvisors.com
E-mail: info@privateschooladvisors.com

Fees start at $7,500.

Amanda Uhry, an alumna of Fieldston, University of Pennsylvania, and Columbia Graduate School of Journalism, owned a successful public relations firm for a decade before opening her advisory firm. MPSA works with families on every aspect of the admissions process for all grade levels, including college and boasts a 100% success rate and offers unlimited meetings, calls, E-Mails and consultations.

8. Madden & Warwick, LLC

1112 Park Avenue
Zip: 10128
Tel: 831-3272
E-mail: Mam1750@aol.com; jwarwick25@aol.com

Mary Madden,
Jane Warwick

Mary Madden and Jane Warwick advise families about the private school admissions process from nursery through middle school. Rates vary according to need.

PARENTING CENTERS AND CLUBS, PARENT-TODDLER PROGRAMS*

Free To Be Under Three

Ages 6 mos–32 mos

Nonsectarian Parent-Child Program

1157 Lexington Avenue
Tel: 998-1708
Website: www.freetobeunderthree.com

Program: Singing, group activities, dance and free play.

Facilities: Held in the downstairs classrooms of All Souls

School Year. Late Sept–Mid May

Summer Program: 8 weeks June and July.

	Hours	*Tuition*
Fall Spring (12 wks)		
	45 minute classes	$425
	1 hr classes	$525
	1 hr 15 min classes	$575
Summer (8 wks)		
	45 minute class	$325
	1 hr	$375

*See also La Escuelita pre-school program, p. 175, *supra,* and Village Kids Nursery parent-child classes, p. 344, *supra.*

Madison Playgroup

Ages: 2.3–3 yrs

325 East 65th Street
Zip: 10021
Tel: 879-9161

Established 1980
Susan Beatus
and
Gretchen Lengyel,
Co-Directors
Judy Jay,
Director of Admissions
Total enrollment: 40

Ages	*Days*	*Tuition*
2.3–3 yrs	2, 3 days (AM, or AM and PM)	$9,400–10,500

Madison Playgroup is a pre-nursery program that helps children learn how to separate, play with others, and in many instances gives them an edge in their nursery school interview. Children need to be 2.4 years of age to attend. Separation is a gentle process. The playgroup occupies the first floor of a Brownstone. The space is divided into interest areas plus a reception area. Classrooms are equipped with toys and child's furnishings, rocking and climbing equipment, and a lounge area. Children are not required to be toilet trained upon admission; however, the process should have begun. After an application is received, a visit is arranged for parents and children during the fall/winter.

74th Street MAGIC at Epiphany Community Nursery School

Ages: 6 mos–3 yrs

510 East 74th Street
(off York Avenue)
Zip: 10021
Tel: 737-2989
Web site: www.74magic.com
E-Mail: info@74magic.com

Llana Shipley,
Director

Tuition: From $530 for the 17 week session. Costs vary by choice of activity and number of classes.

Program. 74th Street MAGIC offers a preschool alternative program and "on my own" classes for 2s/3s. Other classes available include music, art, gymnastics, science, cooking, and dance.

Class size. Eight children, eight parents/guardians. One to 1½ hour sessions in music, art, cooking, and science (for 2s and 3s). Children ages 6 months to 3 years must be accompanied by a parent or caregiver who should be prepared to participate. For children ages three through fourteen years, there is no parent or caregiver participation.

ACT Programs at the Cathedral of St. John the Divine

Toddler program ages: 18–36 mos
Nursery program ages: 2.3–4.5 yrs

Nonsectarian

Preschool/Universal Pre-K*
Cathedral of St. John the Divine
1047 Amsterdam Avenue (at 112th Street)
Tel: 316-7530
Fax: 316-7569
Web site: www.stjohndivine.org/ACT

Established 1971
Marie Del Tejo, Director of Programs
José V. Torres, Executive Director

Program. Encourages individuality through variety and choice in activities within a guided structure. There are two programs, one for children 12–36 months old and their caregivers, the other a two-day-per-week nursery for children ages 2.3–4.5 years. The toddler program features gym in a well-equipped indoor playground, singing, storytelling. Weather permitting, older toddlers play outside and garden on the cathedral campus.

The nursery curriculum concentrates on development of interactive skills, pre-reading activities, and enjoyment of learning. Instructors communicate daily with parents about children's progress and families are informed of program changes, concerns, and interesting events outside of ACT.

---

*Universal Pre-K is a federally subsidized program.

So Glad We Waited Network
Claremont Children's School

Ages Infant–elementary yrs

235 West 71st Street — Lois Nachamie, Director
Doctor's Suite 2
Zip: 10023
Tel: 866-5620
Web site: www.sogladwewaited.com
E-Mail: sogladwewaited@aol.com

The director, Lois Nachamie, a parent educator since 1990, and an award winning author whose books include *Big Lessons for Little People So Glad We Waited, A Hand Holding Guide for Over 35 Parents,* and *Big Lessons for Little People: Teaching Our Children Right from Wrong While Keeping Them Healthy* is often consulted as an authority on parenting after 35. The network offers on-going support groups for over-35 parents of infants through elementary school age children. Individual and couples' counseling is available along with long- and short-term counseling for parenting and other family issues.

The fee is $70 per session, semester. Groups register in September and January.

Discovery Programs/The Toddler Center

251 W. 100th Street — Stella Moon, Director
Tel: 749-8717
E-Mail: discovery251@yahoo.com
Web site: www.discoveryprograms.com

A variety of parent/toddler classes are offered for children between 12 and 36 months, including gym, pre-ballet, art, and music-dance-and-storytime. Classes are directed to the child's developmental needs. The classes change seasonally, so ask for a recent catalogue. In addition to parent/toddler classes, there are gradual separation classes for two-year-olds, and classes for 3 year-olds and up without their parents.

Early Childhood Development Center

Ages: 4 wks–3 yrs

Nonsectarian Parent/Child Programs

163 E. 97th Street
(at 3rd Avenue)
Tel: 360-7803
Fax: 348-7253

Established 1969
Becky Thomas,
Director

Program hours. Varied, September through July.

Program. The center arranges a 20-week series of hour-long discussion groups of eight to ten parents (usually mothers) with their children and infants. Most parents who join with infants remain for the full three years and become a strong support system for one another. The groups are led by a professional in the child care field and a trained parents facilitator. Topics cover developmental issues, family relations, schooling, problems of city living and so on.

Admissions. Call to find out if a group is available. Acceptances are on a rolling basis.

Enrollment. The center may have as many as 19 groups operating at once.

Cost. $450 for twenty sessions.

Facilities. The center occupies a ground-floor corridor in a well-designed, modern brick high-rise. It is appropriately decorated and well-maintained. Two meeting rooms, on either side of an observation room equipped with one-way windows and headphones for trainees in child development are opposite a playroom for older children staffed by teachers. Infants and toddlers remain with their parents; the rooms are equipped with individual bassinets. There are additional conference rooms and offices, as well as a comfortable lounge area.

Staff. The staff includes a child psychiatrist, psychologist, specialists in child development, a social worker and a pediatrician. There is also a program for individuals wishing child development and parent education training. The school's training consists of a nine month course, including observation and analysis with a curriculum developed by the center.

Publications. The center also publishes three books by Dr. Nina Lief, Dr. Mary Ellen Fahs and Becky Thomas, the school's founding directors, that are available in book stores: *The First Year of Life*, *The Second Year of Life*, and *The Third Year of Life*.

Sackler Lefcourt Center for Child Development

Ages: Infancy–3 yrs

Parent/Child Programs

17 East 62nd Street
(between Fifth and
Madison Avenues)
Zip: 10021
Tel: 759-4022
Fax: 838-7205
Website: www.sacklerlefcourtcenter.com

Established: 1982
Ilene Sackler Lefcourt,
Director

Program year. September through June

Ages	*Hours*	*Tuition*
Mother/Baby 2–12 mos	1 hr/wk	$3105
Mother/Toddler 13–18 mos	50 min/wk	$5,960
Mother/Prenursery 19–30 mos; Prenursery	1 hr 2/3 days/wk	$7,847

Programs. The Center's programs include playgroups for children with discussion groups for mothers. Groups are designed to promote development and to provide information to parents about early childhood issues and the evolving parent-child relationship.

The play groups enable babies, toddlers and young children to learn through play. With mothers present, children play independently, join in group activities and interact with peers. Activities include: manipulative toys, water and sand play, and symbolic play materials.

Mothers groups meet weekly at the same time children play. While observing and interacting with their children, mothers discuss parenting, development and other experiences. There are six children and their mothers in each group. All groups are led by two professionals trained in early child development.

A new program called REACH is for mothers and their children 16–36 months old who are receiving early intervention services. REACH groups promote peer interaction and parent-child communication for children with special needs.

Group size. There are six children in a playgroup and two playgroup leaders; six mothers in a discussion group and a discussion leader.

Admissions. Enrollment begins in the spring; groups begin in fall. Parents should call to arrange an individual visit. Waiting lists are maintained.

Facilities. Located on the ground floor level of a townhouse on a quiet street, the center's small offices are attractively designed and furnished. There are two small playrooms, the director's office and a waiting area. The sunny pre-nursery playroom looks out on a courtyard and adjoins a small room where mothers' discussion groups are held. The rooms are well-equipped with age-appropriate materials. Other rooms are also bright and spacious. Coffee and tea are served.

The Parenting Center at the 92nd Street Y

1395 Lexington Ave.
(at 92nd Street)
Zip: 10128
Tel: 415-5611
Website: www.92Y.org

Sally Tannen,
Director

The Parenting Center is entirely independent of the Y's nursery school. Parents should call for a seasonal catalogue. The center offers an extensive selection of 12–16-week courses for parents and children, newborn to age 4. These include courses for parents-to-be and activities for parents and children to share, such as cooking, art, science, and movement. There are also workshops and seminars on such matters as sleep, setting limits, separation, and other issues and aspects of the parent-child relationship.

Parents who join the center will receive priority registration with a discount on class fees, free entry to the New Parents Get Together and Toddler Seminar, and use of the Y's library. Scholarship aid is available.

CLUBS

Citibabes

477 Broadway
3rd floor
Zip: 10013
Tel: 334-5440
Web site: www.citibabes.com
E-mail:

A lunch spot, gym, and play area in which parents may entertain themselves and their toddlers. Classes, guest speakers, books, and child minding are some offerings for the downtown set.

Divalysscious Moms

136 East 55th Street
Suite 6P
Web site: www.divalyssciousmoms.com
Tel: (917) 601-0068

An organization that encourages mothers' networks for a wide vary of activities from spa treatments, to interesting speakers, supporting charities, school admissions, personal issues, dining and entertainment.

New York University School of Continuing Education Center for Career Education and Life Planning

Office of Admissions,
145 Fourth Ave
Room 201
Zip: 10003
Tel: 998-7200
Website: www.scps.nyu.edu

A family care provider education program for people who want to start their own day care center.

Parent Guidance Workshops

180 Riverside Drive
Zip: 10024
Tel: 787-8883
Fax: 787-9029
Website: www.samalin.com
E-Mail: samalin@aol.com

Nancy Samalin, M.S., Director

Introductory and advanced workshops for parents of toddlers through teens are offered. Nancy Samalin also gives lectures and seminars at schools and institutions locally and nationally.

St. Luke's-Roosevelt Parent Family Education

Roosevelt Hospital — Jo Leonard, R.N., M.A., FACEE, Director
1000 10th Avenue
Room 11-A–28
Zip: 10019
Tel: 523-6222
Web site: www.wehealnewyork.org

Offers more than 20 classes, including pre-conception and lamaze, childbirth classes and provides infant/child CPR, first aid instruction, classes in parenting of toddlers, sibling preparation, and other programs for children of all ages and parents.

YWCA Health Promotion

610 Lexington Avenue
(at 53rd Street)
Zip: 10022
Tel: 755-4500

Parent/toddler swim programs (6 mos–3 yrs). Children 3 years and older can swim without their parents. Children must be toilet trained or wear rubber pants. Swim caps required. Programs available for children with disabilities who are accompanied by caregivers or parents.

Index of Schools and Programs

Alphabetical Index

Index of All-Day Programs (with starting age)

East Side

West Side

Index of Parent-Toddler Programs

Index of Schools/Programs for Children with Special Needs

Website Index

Abraham Joshua Heschel School, *www.heschel.org*
ACT Programs at the Cathedral of St. John the Divine, *www.stjohndivine.org/ACT*
Advocates for Children of New York, Inc., *www.advocatesforchildren.org*
AMAC Children's House, *www.amac.org*
Bank Street Family Center, *www.bankstreet.edu*
Bank Street School for Children, *www.bankstreet.edu*
Barnard College Center for Toddler Development, *www.columbia.edu/~bcpsych/toddler*
Barrow Street Nursery School/Greenwich House, *www.greenwichhouse.org*
Basic Trust Infant/Toddler Center, *www.basictrust.org*
Battery Park City Day Nursery. *www.bpcdaynursery.com*
Bellevue South Nursery School, *bsnurseryschool.org*
Board of Regents of the State University of New York, *www.nysed.gov*
Brick Church School, The, *www.brickchurch.org*
Brotherhood Synagogue Nursery School, *www.brotherhoodsynagogue.org*
Brownstone School and Daycare Center, *www.brownstoneschool.com*
Buckle My Shoe Nursery School, *www.Bucklemyshoe.org*
Caedmon School, The, *www.caedmonschool.org*
Calhoun School, The, *www.calhoun.org*
Central Synagogue May Family Nursery School, *www.centralsynagogue.org*
Chabad Early Learning Center, *www.chabadwestside.org/celc*
Child Care, Inc., *www.childcareinc.org*
Child Development Center, *www.jbfcs.org*
Children's Aid Society/The Philip Coltoff Center at Greenwich Village, *www.childrensaidsociety.org*
Children's All Day School and Pre-Nursery, *www.childrensallday.org*
Children's Garden at General Theological Seminary, The, *www.gts.edu*
Children's Learning Center, *www.clc-nyc.org*
Children's Storefront, *www.thechildrensstorefront.org*
Children of Today, Ninos de Hoy, *www.hometown.aol.com/childtdy/myhomepage/index.html*
Christ Church Day School, *www.christchurchnyc.org*
Citibabes, *www.citibabes.com*
City and Country School, *www.cityandcountry.org*
Claremont Children's School, *www.claremontschool.org*
Columbia Greenhouse Nursery School, The, *www.columbiagreenhouse.com*
Columbus Park West Nursery School, *www.cpwn.org*
Columbus Preschool and Gym, *www.columbuspre-school.com*
Convent of the Sacred Heart, *www.cshnyc.org*
Corlears School, *www.corlearsschool.org*
CP Kids, *www.chelseapiers.com/fh*

Creative Playschool, *www.5as.org/sections/playschool.asp*
Discovery Programs/The Toddler Center, *www.discoveryprograms.com*
Divalysscious Moms, *www.divalyssciousmoms.com*
Downtown Little School, The, *www.downtownlittleschool.com*
Early Childhood Resource and Information Center, *www.nypl.org*
Educational Alliance Preschool, The, *www.edalliance.org*
Educational Records Bureau, The, (ERB), *www.erbtest.org*
Epiphany Community Nursery School, *www.74magic.com*
Ethical Culture, *www.ecfs.org*
Family Annex, *www.thefamilyannex.org*
First Presbyterian Church Nursery School, *www.fpcns.org*
43rd Street Kids Preschool, Inc., *www.43rdstreetkids.org*
Free To Be Under Three, *www.freetobeunderthree.com*
Gani Early Childhood Center, *www.edalliance.org*
Garden House School of New York, *www.gardenhouseschool.org*
Gillen Brewer School. The, *www.gillianbrewer.com*
Grace Church School, *www.gcschool.org*
Headstart, *www.nyc.gov* click: Administration for Children's Services, Head Start Info or *www.nyc.gov*. city agencies, Health and Mental Hygiene, Bureau of Day Care
Hollingsworth Preschool of Teacher's College, Columbia University, *www.tc.columbia.edu*
Horace Mann School Nursery Division, *www.horacemann.org*
House of Little People, *www.thehouseoflittlepeople.com*
Imagine VetsKids, *www.imagineelc.com*
Independent Schools Admissions Association of Greater New York (ISAAGNY), *www.isaagny.org*
International Preschools, the, *www.ipsnyc.org*
Jack and Jill School, *www.jackandjillschool.com*
JCC in Manhattan, The Saul and Carole Zabar Nursery School, The, *www.jccmanhattan.org/nurseryschool*
Kennedy Child Study Center, *www.kenchild.org*
Kid's Korner, *www.thekidskornerpreschool.com*
La Escuelita, *www.laescuelitanyc.org*
La Scuola d'Italia "G. Marconi", *www.lascuoladitalia.org*
Learning Disabilities Association of New York City Telephone Referral Service, The, *www.ldanyc.org*
Learning, the Arts, and Me Nursery of Third Street Music School Settlement, *www.thirdstreetmusicschool.org*
Le Jardin a L'Ouest, *www.lejardinalouest.com*
Little Dreamers of NYC, *www.littledreamersofnyc.com*
Little Red School House, *www.lrei.org*
Lycée Francais de New York, *www.lfny.org*
Lyceum Kennedy French International School, *www.lyceumkennedy.org*
Madison Avenue Presbyterian Day School, The, *www.mapc.com*
Mandell School, The, *www.mandellschool.org*
Manhattan Country School, *www.manhattancountryschool.org*

Manhattan Private School Advisors, *www.privateschooladvisors.com*
Marymount School of New York, *www.marymount.K12.ny.us*
Medical Center Nursery School, The, *www.mcns.org*
Memorial Sloane-Kettering Cancer Center, Children's Center, *www.brighthorizons.com*
Metropolitan Montessori School, *www.mmsny.org*
Montessori School of Manhattan, *www.montessorimanhattan.com*
Montessori School of New York International, *www.montessorischoolny.com*
Morningside Montessori School, *www.morningsidemontessori.org*
National Center for Learning Disabilities, The, *www.NCLD.org*
National Dissemination Center for Children with Disabilities, *www.nichcy.org*
Nazareth Nursery, *www.nazarethnursery.com*
New York Branch of the International Dyslexia Association, The, *www.nybida.org*
New York City Association for the Education of Young Children, *www.nycaeyc.org*
New York City Department of Health, Division of Day Care, The, *www.nyc.gov*
New York University School of Continuing Education Center for Career Education and Life Planning, *www.scps.nyu.edu*
92nd Street YM-YWHA Nursery School, *www.92y.org*
Northside Center for Child Development, Inc., *www.northsidecenter.org*
Nursery School at Habonim, The, *www.habonim.net*
Our Lady of Pompeii Elementary School, *www.LadyofPompeii.org*
Parenting Center at the 92nd Street Y, The, *www.92y.org*
Parent Guidance Workshops, *www.samalin.com*
Parents League of New York, Inc., The, *www.parentsleague.org*
Park Avenue Synagogue Early Childhood Center, *www.pasyn.org*
Park Preschool, The, *www.theparkpreschool.org*
Philosophy Day School, *www.philosophyday.org*
Purple Circle Day School, *www.purple-circle.org*
Rabbi Arthur Schneier Park East Day School, *www.rasped.org*
Ramaz School, *www.ramaz.org*
Red Balloon Community Day Care Center, The, *www.Redballoonlearningcenter.com*
Resurrection Episcopal Day School, *www.redsny.org*
Rhinelander Nursery School, The, *www.rhinelandercenter.org*
River-Park Nursery School and Kindergarten, *www.riverparknurseryschool.com*
River School, The, *www.theriverschool.com*
Riverside Church Weekday School, *www.weekdayschool-nyc.org*
Riverside Montessori, *www.twinparks.org*
Rocking Horses Nursery School, *www.rockinghorsenurseryschool.org*
Rodeph Sholom School, The, *www.rodephsholomschool.org*
Roosevelt Island Day Nursery, *www.ridn.org*
Rudolf Steiner School, The, *www.steiner.edu*

Rusk Institute Preschool and Infant Development Programs, *www.med.nyu.edu/rusk/services/pediatric/outpatient/educational.html*
Sackler Lefcourt Center for Child Development, *www.sacklerlefcourtcenter.com*
Saint David's School, *www.saintdavids.org*
St. Bartholomew Community Preschool, *www.stbarts.org*
St. Hilda's and St. Hugh's School, *www.sthildas.org*
St. Ignatius Loyola Day Nursery, *www.saintignatiusloyola.org*
St. Luke's-Roosevelt Parent Family Education, *www.wehealnewyork.org*
St. Luke's School, *www.stlukeschool.org*
Schools & You, *www.schoolsandyou.com*
74th Street MAGIC at Epiphany Community School, *www.74magic.com*
Smart City Kids, *www.smartcitykids.com*
So Glad We Waited Network, *www.sogladwewaited.com*
Stephen Wise Free Synagogue Early Childhood Center, *www.swfs.org/ecc*
Studio School, The, *www.studioschool.org*
Temple Emanu-el Nursery School, *www.emanuelnyc.org*
Temple Israel Early Childhood Learning Center, *www.templeisraelnyc.org*
Temple Shaaray Tefila Nursery, *www.shaaraytefilanyc.org*
Tender Care, *www.ymcanyc.org*
Tenth Street Tots Childcare Center, *www.tentots.com*
Town House International School, *www.townhouseinternationalschool.org*
Town School, The, *www.thetownschool.org*
Trevor Day School, *www.trevor.org*
TriBeCa Community School, *www.tribecacommunityschool.com*
Twin Parks Park West Montessori School, *www.twinparks.org*
Trinity Parish Preschool and Nursery, *www.trinitywallstreet.org*
United Cerebral Palsy of New York City Manhattan Children's Center, *www.ucpnyc.org*
University Plaza Nursery School, Inc., *www.universityplazanursery.com*
Vanderbilt YMCA, *www.ymcanyc.org*
Victoria Goldman, *www.victoriagoldman.net*
Village Kids Nursery, *www.villagekidsnursery.com*
Village Preschool Center, *www.villagepreschoolcenter.com*
Washington Heights and Inwood YM-YWHA, *www.ywashhts.org*
Washington Market School, *The,www.washingtonmarketschool.org*
West End Collegiate Church Playschool, The, *www.westendchurch.org/playschool*
West Side Family Preschool, *www.westsidefamilypreschool.org*
West Side Montessori School, *www.wsms.org*
West Village Nursery School, *www.westvillagenurseryschool.org*
William Woodward Jr. Nursery School, *www.woodwardns.org*
Yaldaynu Center, *www.anchechesed.org*
York Avenue Preschool, *www.yorkavenuepreschool.org*
Your Kids "R" Our Kids, *www.yourkidsourkids.com*

PROPHECY IN THE NEW MILLENNIUM

PROPHECY IN THE NEW MILLENNIUM

A FRESH LOOK AT FUTURE EVENTS

JOHN F. WALVOORD

Kregel Publications
Grand Rapids, MI 49501

Prophecy in the New Millennium: A Fresh Look at Future Events

Published by Kregel Publications, a division of Kregel, Inc., P.O. Box 2607, Grand Rapids, MI 49501. Kregel Publications provides trusted, biblical publications for Christian growth and service. For more information about Kregel Publications, visit our web site: www.kregel.com.

Library of Congress Cataloging-in-Publication Data
Walvoord, John F.
Prophecy in the new millennium: a fresh look at future events / John F. Walvoord.
p. cm.
1. Bible—Prophecies—End of the world. 2. End of the world—Prophecies. I. Title.
BS649.E63 W355 2001 236—dc21 2001029019
CIP

ISBN 0-8254-3967-1

Printed in the United States of America

2 3 4 5 / 05 04 03 02 01

CONTENTS

INTRODUCTION

As the twenty-first century begins, it is understandable that the new millennium has sparked renewed interest in prophecy. The crises at the close of the twentieth century focused on whether the end of the age is approaching.

One significant event causing this interest in prophecy was the Gulf War, because all of the church creeds—whether Protestant, Roman Catholic, or Greek Orthodox—have statements to the effect that Christ is coming again to judge the world. Even the secular press was conscious of the fact that this war might be a token of the Second Coming. Widespread publicity resulted, with long articles appearing in the secular press on the question of whether the Gulf War should be associated with Armageddon. But, as the Gulf War subsided, it became particularly clear that Armageddon will be a totally different war than the Gulf War.

Actually, the Scriptures say nothing about the war that occurred in the Gulf. However, the fact is that the nations of the world, first in the oil crisis of 1973 and then in the Gulf War, became vitally interested in the Middle East to the extent that they assembled their armies there to stop further aggression. It created a climate of prophetic fulfillment, even though some of it was misguided and without scriptural support.

Predictions of the Rapture of the church picture the first

major event of the end time. The Rapture has long been considered an imminent event; that is, as far as scriptural revelation is concerned, it could occur anytime. For this reason, the Thessalonian church expected the Lord's coming in their lifetime. Frequently in the history of the church, people have attempted in vain to date the coming of the Lord, thus keeping expectancy alive. One must clarify, however, that imminence does not necessarily mean that the Lord is coming soon, so the question remains whether any evidence exists that the Rapture of the church could be soon.

In a survey of the history of prophetic fulfillment in the following exposition, some interesting facts emerge. First, some people have made misguided efforts to date creation and the period between Adam and Abraham, based on the genealogies that Scripture furnishes, but because these genealogies are demonstrably not complete and skip many generations, most intelligent scholars avoid any attempt to date the period before Abraham. Although conservative scholarship rejects the millions of years advanced by the evolutionist, it is entirely possible that creation took place somewhere between 5,000 and 10,000 B.C. This estimation would give time for the events that occurred in this period (which would include the Flood) and for Noah and his descendants to repopulate the world after the Flood.

From Abraham on, however, one can fairly safely set up a chronology and tentatively date the various events. The period between Abraham and Moses was approximately five hundred years, and from Moses to Christ was approximately fifteen hundred years. Now that the world has gone on for another two thousand years since the time of Christ, it would seem normal, in God's direction of human history, that the time factor is in favor of a soon return of Christ.

The twentieth century has witnessed some amazing events

that relate to prophecy. As explained in the text, the three major areas of prophecy are the nations, Israel, and the church. Since World War II, major changes have occurred in all three of these areas. Israel is back in the land, the United Nations was formed as the embryonic concept of a world government, and the church has fulfilled its special character as the body of Christ, beginning on the Day of Pentecost. The world church movement, represented by the harlot on the scarlet beast in Revelation 17, seems clearly to be an anticipation of the world church, which will be completely apostate in the days before the Second Coming.

All three of these major areas of prophecy have seen significant changes that seem to harmonize with what the Scriptures describe at the time of the Rapture. This fact certainly provides some evidence that the Rapture could be very soon. In addition, the peaceful situation between the major nations in Europe also makes possible the fulfillment of the revived Roman Empire, which in Scripture often is pictured as a background for the days immediately following the Rapture.

In addition to these major elements, apostasy, both theological and moral, is clearly overtaking the professing church, and although unusual interest in prophecy now exists, it has not brought revival to the church or resulted in large numbers of people coming to Christ. All of this fits precisely the background of the time when the Rapture will occur.

As our world changes rapidly, some very important questions are posed. For example, how long will Israel be able to stay in the Promised Land without being overpowered by the Palestinians? How long will it be before the United Nations becomes more powerful? How long will it be before the church becomes completely apostate, which will occur only after the Rapture?

When all of these factors are evaluated, there now exists

what can be called a window in which the world situation is precisely what the Bible describes at the time of and immediately after the Rapture. Because of the changes that occur daily, this window will not continue to be the same as it is today, and it would seem necessary for the Rapture to occur before the world situation becomes less in harmony with what the Bible pictures for the time of the Rapture.

Considering all of these issues, a need exists for both a renewed study of prophecy to see exactly what the Bible predicts and practical exhortation for people to be saved and to fulfill God's plan for their individual lives.

To assume that the twenty-first century will witness some tremendous fulfillment of Bible prophecy is not unreasonable. But this assumption hinges on the question as to when the Rapture will occur; therefore, a renewed study of all of the factors for the end of the age seems appropriate in light of the new millennium. The following exposition is offered with a prayer that it will help people understand the intricacies of prophecy and alert them to the proper response of our hearts to the truth, that is, to be ready when Christ returns.

CHAPTER 1

PROPHECIES FULFILLED IN THE TWENTIETH CENTURY

In the centuries of human progress since Adam, the twentieth century deserves its own unique place as an era of unusual prophetic fulfillment that is unequaled in history, except possibly in the first century. As many scholars have noted, about one-fourth of the Bible was predictive when it was written. In the author's book *Every Prophecy of the Bible* (formerly titled *Prophecy Knowledge Handbook*), he noted that approximately one thousand prophetic passages are found in the Scriptures, some of them contained in one verse and others in extended passages. As was demonstrated in that book, approximately half, or about five hundred, of such passages have already been fulfilled literally.

History answers the most important question in prophetic interpretation, that is, whether prophecy is to be interpreted literally, by giving five hundred examples of precise literal fulfillments. The commonly held belief that prophecy is not literal and should be interpreted nonliterally has no basis in scriptural revelation. Undoubtedly, a nonliteral viewpoint is one of the major causes of confusion in prophetic interpretation.

Some prophecies that are in figurative language have to be interpreted, such as some in Daniel, Ezekiel, and Revelation. But in many cases, the meaning is clearly understood and seldom is the symbol left unexplained in the Bible. A solid record emerges of fulfillment of prophecy in the past and an anticipation that each prophecy will have that same literal fulfillment in the future.

The hundreds of prophecies that are in the Bible can be grouped under three major headings:

1. prophecy concerning the nations, especially as illustrated in Daniel;
2. prophecy concerning Israel, a constant theme in the Old Testament; and
3. prophecy concerning the church, revealed only in the New Testament.

Even prophecies concerning the angels are linked somewhat to these prophecies.

Remarkably, the twentieth century has set the stage for the preparation for prophecies to be fulfilled in the future. Foundational to all of these fulfilled prophecies are the prophecies of Daniel.

FULFILLED GENTILE PROPHECIES IN THE BOOK OF DANIEL

Daniel 2 describes the vision that God gave to Nebuchadnezzar and that Daniel interpreted. In the vision, a large statue with a head of gold represented Babylon. The chest and the arms of silver represented the next empire of Medo-Persia. The belly and thighs of bronze symbolized Greece. And the legs of iron and the feet of iron and clay stand for the empire of Rome (vv. 32–33). The first three empires are named in Daniel 7–8.

In Nebuchadnezzar's vision, the image is struck by a rock that was cut out without a hand and that destroys the image.

The rock, in turn, becomes a huge mountain that fills the whole earth (2:34–35). This image anticipates prophetically the second coming of Christ, the destruction of gentile power, and the establishment of Christ's kingdom in the world. This prophecy is subject to complete fulfillment at the Second Coming.

The body of the image represented the second and the third empires, that is, the Medo-Persian and Greek empires, both of which have been completely fulfilled. The fourth empire is a climax that is represented by the legs of iron and the feet of iron and clay. The fourth empire is not named in the passage, although the preceding empires are named in Daniel 8:20–21. The Roman Empire, the fourth empire, was the greatest of all empires, and although it is not named, it obviously followed the Grecian empire historically. What the legs represent has already been fulfilled in the history of the Roman Empire. The feet, consisting of an iron-clay mixture, are prophetic of the final revival of the Roman Empire, which yet awaits fulfillment. The whole image will be destroyed at the second coming of Christ, as revealed in the summation of the four kingdoms (2:44–46).

Daniel had four visions in his later years. The first vision gives additional information about the prophecy of the four kingdoms. In Daniel 7, the four empires are represented as beasts: Babylon as a lion (v. 4), Medo-Persia as a bear (v. 5), Greece as a leopard (v. 6), and Rome as a terrifying and powerful beast (v. 7).

As the first three empires have already been fulfilled, prophetic interest centers on the Roman Empire in its final form, described here as a ten-nation empire, with the ten horns of Daniel 7:7 representing ten kingdoms (v. 24).

Additional revelation is given, however, concerning the final state of these ten countries that represent the Roman Empire. Daniel 7:8 describes a conqueror who controls first three of the countries and then, eventually, all of them, resulting in a world empire (v. 23). The fourth empire is described thus: "It will be different from all the other kingdoms and will devour the whole earth, trampling it down and crushing it" (v. 23).

Special attention is directed to the final king, the future Antichrist, who will conquer first the three kings of the ten-nation group and then all ten nations. He will have supreme power, although he is described as wielding it for only "a time, times, and half a time" (v. 25). This phrase is commonly interpreted to mean three and a half years, that is, one plus two plus a half. At the second coming of Christ, he will be destroyed and Christ will bring in the everlasting kingdom (vv. 26–27).

But the book of Daniel in its prophecy does not take into consideration the entire present age from Pentecost to the Rapture; its revelation presents the Roman Empire as continuing to the time of its ultimate destruction. This view is consistent with a principle of the Old Testament, namely, that prophecy from the Old Testament will frequently describe, in much detail, events that are prophetically fulfilled up to the first coming of Christ, including the first coming, but then skip from that almost immediately into end-time prophecy, describing the Great Tribulation and the events that climax in it. Although often ignored in prophetic interpretation, this lack of prophecy concerning the present age in the Old Testament has been observed even among those who do not recognize the whole program of prophetic fulfillment.

Obviously, in this period between the first coming of Christ and the events leading up to the Second Coming, which is the church age, a great many events have taken place that help to set the stage for the end-time events leading up to the Second Coming. Of considerable interest are the events of the twentieth century that conclude almost two thousand years of human history since Christ's first coming.

Although the United States of America is not recognized in prophetic history, it is one of the remarkable powers that emerged in the twentieth century. It is recognized today as the world's leading force politically, militarily, and economically. Great Britain, which once was both the dominant naval power in the world and a possessor of many colonies, reached its peak and has declined considerably in the twentieth century. So Britain is no longer a major factor in world politics, although it often supports the United States in various political decisions.

The twentieth century also witnessed two great world wars that eclipsed anything else that history had considered and that climaxed centuries of conflict between Great Britain, Germany, and other European countries. But now a prophetically significant situation has arisen. For centuries, the European nations have fought each other, but after World War II, a sudden change occurred. Instead of arming for the next conflict as they had done many times before, they adopted a peaceful solution to their differences and attempted to solve them in what was called the Common Market, more recently named the European Union. No longer are they preparing to fight each other. The obvious reason is that all of these nations possess atomic weapons and have the capability to annihilate other nations. Another world war would be suicide for all of the countries involved.

The situation thus establishes, at least on the surface, a peaceful relationship between these major countries. This is a necessary prelude to the revival of the Roman Empire as prophesied in the Bible. Even secular sources are predicting an eventual United States of Europe, united politically in a way that is similar to what the Bible prescribes for the end of the age. The revival of the Roman Empire as a ten-nation group is prominent in the context of the Rapture or whenever the scene unfolds after the Rapture.

The condition of Europe today, with peace between the

major countries, is a primary factor in supporting the concept that the Rapture of the church, which has always been imminent, is now also predictably soon. (See chapter 4 for further discussion.) Another noteworthy feature of the twentieth century has been the rise of Japan and China. Japan, of course, was the principal adversary of the United States in the eastern hemisphere in World War II, and although she was defeated, somewhat deflated, and encountered economic problems, she nevertheless recovered and now is an important factor in the whole Asian situation.

Even more important than the recovery of Japan, however, has been China's coming of age. With its population of approximately 25 percent of the world's peoples, China obviously is growing militarily and financially and is destined unquestionably for a much larger role in the future of the world than it had in the twentieth century. It is impossible to predict either the extent of this influence or the possible outcome of occasional clashes between Russia and China.

The twentieth century has also witnessed tremendous changes in the Middle East. World War II brought with it the revival of Israel and the growth of Russia. Central in all of this, of course, is Israel, poised as it is between Syria, Egypt, and Jordan and in the middle of all of the tension of the Middle East situation.

The whole Middle East came to life during the Gulf War, which followed the previous energy crisis of 1973, and raised worldwide the question of whether this was the final war of prophetic fulfillment. Although it soon became clear that this war was not Armageddon, for the first time the entire world was focused realistically on the military situation in the Middle East, which is a powder keg that could explode at any time.

Syria and Egypt also have continued to grow in power. Although they are not like other ancient countries of world history, they still share important roles in the Middle East situation.

The twentieth century also witnessed the tragic fulfillment of the predictions of Scripture that things will become worse morally as time progresses. The alarming prophecy of 2 Timothy 2 speaks of terrible times in the last days when morality will be forgotten. This lack of regard for honorable conduct has spread also to the church, and its departure from the faith is outlined in 2 Peter 2.

Taken as a whole, the prophecies concerning the nations in both the Old and New Testaments are in harmony with the Scriptures, as they portray the time that the Rapture of the church will occur. No further fulfillment is necessary. No change in the world situation is required for the tremendous event of the Rapture of the church.

ISRAEL IN PROPHECY

Predictions concerning the future of Israel form a major portion of Old Testament prophecy, beginning with Abraham and continuing through Malachi. Almost every book of the Old Testament deals with Israel's prophecy or has it as a background for its revelation. The theme is continued in New Testament prophecy, which traces Israel into eternity future.

THE ABRAHAMIC COVENANT

The basis for much of Israel's prophetic future lies in God's promises to Abraham, as recorded in Genesis 12. Most significantly, only eleven chapters of Genesis deal with the thousands of years from the beginning of the creation to the time of Abraham. By contrast, the record of Genesis chapters 12–50 is devoted entirely to Abraham, Isaac, Jacob, and Joseph. This emphasis on Israel in the very beginning of the Bible makes clear that Israel is very important in carrying out God's eternal purposes.

The Abrahamic covenant was revealed in connection with Abraham's leaving his homeland and traveling to the Promised Land. According to Genesis 11, Abraham and his parents lived in Ur of the Chaldeans, a place not too far from Babylon in Mesopotamia. Their physical circumstances included an advanced civilization with two-story buildings and lovely public parks. From this comfortable background, Abraham was called to a life of a nomad, living in tents.

The command of God was unmistakable. God said to him, "Leave your country, your people and your father's household and go to the land I will show you" (Gen. 12:1). In recognition of Abraham's willingness to obey God, he was given the Abrahamic covenant, which consisted of three major promises:

1. Abraham himself was promised a great name (v. 2);
2. Abraham was assured that he would be the progenitor of a great nation (v. 2); and
3. all people on the earth, regardless of their racial background, would be blessed through Abraham (v. 3). In keeping with this the most extensive promise is God's promise to bless those who bless Abraham and to curse those who curse him (vv. 2–3).

These promises, of course, have largely been fulfilled. Abraham is still a household name, even though he lived four thousand years ago. Not only was he the progenitor of Israel but also many other descendants were born to him. Through Abraham's posterity the prophets came, the Scriptures were written, the twelve apostles were chosen, and, supremely, the Savior, Jesus Christ, came and provided salvation through His death and resurrection. The Abrahamic promises continue to provide background for the history of our present and future world.

Abraham's obedience was somewhat limited, however, because as a result of the customs of the times, even though he was an old man, he still was subject to his father's direction. When his father heard of God's call to Abraham, he told Abraham that he would go with him and also instructed him to take his nephew Lot.

In addition to the Abrahamic covenant, the most important promise given to Abraham was that his posterity would inherit the Holy Land. According to Genesis 12:7, "The LORD appeared to Abram and said, 'To your offspring I will give this land.'" The promise of the land is one of the most important prophecies of the Old Testament. Throughout the Old Testament, this promise is repeated and unfolds as a major theme of both the Major and the Minor Prophets. The ultimate possession of the land, in spite of the fact that the Israelites were dispossessed several times, remains an important central factor in prophetic fulfillment. It will come to its climax after the second coming of Christ, when Israel is permanently placed in the Promised Land, as prophesied in Ezekiel 47–48.

The confusion that this promise of the land has produced is most unfortunate. Following the faulty concept that prophecy is not literal, amillenarians interpret, without any scriptural support whatever, that the land is simply another title for heaven. In this way, they derail all of God's promises to Israel of their ultimate triumph and prosperity in the millennial kingdom, thereby enabling them to deny also that the millennial kingdom will ever eventuate. Accordingly, the interpretation of Genesis 12:7 becomes the background for massive division in the interpretation of prophecy, a division that continues even today. Whenever the word *land* is mentioned in the Old Testament, the context always relates it to the physical land that today we call the Holy Land.

Genesis records the struggles of Abraham when no son was given to him and God refused to recognize either Ishmael or Eliezer of Damascus, his servant, as the inheritor of the promise. Miraculously, when Abraham and Sarah were both beyond normal childbearing age, Isaac was born. Although Abraham became the father of many others in the years to follow, none of them qualified as the promised seed to inherit the land.

Genesis also records the account of Isaac's wife not bearing children until his old age, but eventually Jacob and Esau were born. God chose Jacob, the younger of the twins, to be the progenitor of the race of Israel. His twelve sons headed the twelve tribes of Israel and became the basis for Israel's prophecy throughout the Old and New Testaments.

The Old Testament records the amazing history of Israel as it continues after Abraham. From Genesis 12 to the book of Malachi, the narration deals with God's government of the people of Israel. As the Old Testament continues, all the books deal in some way with the progress of Israel in their country, their fulfillment of prophecy, and the revelation that God gave them through the prophets. In view of the massive character of these Scriptures, it is difficult to understand how any biblical scholar concludes that God has no eternal purpose for Israel and somehow distort or misinterpret the Scriptures that speak of Israel's future even today.

Much of the doctrine of grace is derived from God's dealing with Israel, even though the Mosaic system is basically legalistic. Apart from His grace, it would have been impossible for God to deal with the failure of Israel and their leaders. His dealings include the chastening of the Assyrian captivity; the Babylonian captivity and the place of Israel in the empires of Babylon, Medo-Persia, Greece, and Rome; and their scattering after A.D. 70. A temporary regathering of a portion of Israel is occurring today to form a government in Israel, a major element in the contemporary scene. Through it all, Jerusalem, the city of God, continues to play a major role in international movements, and the current tensions between Israel and the Palestinians are reminders that there will be no peace on earth until Jesus Christ reigns in His millennial kingdom.

THE CHURCH IN PROPHECY

The Old Testament, while it provided for the salvation of the Gentiles, did not anticipate the revelation of the New Testament that God would create a new people, with Jews and Gentiles being merged into one spiritual body. In connection with Christ's conversation with Simon Peter, the important statement is given that "on this rock I [Christ] will build my church" (Matt. 16:18). How this would be accomplished would not be revealed until the Epistles were written and the full truth of the church in the purpose of God was revealed.

It is very important in prophecy to distinguish sharply between God's purposes for Israel and God's purpose for the church. The entire present age is a period of God's dealings with the human race in a way that the Old Testament did not anticipate. His purpose for the church in both the present age and the future is distinct from what He has promised and will fulfill for the nation Israel. Those who confuse the church and Israel do so at the expense of confusing prophecy as a whole, leaving in question so many prophecies regarding both Israel's future and that of the church.

Properly understood, the church as a separate entity from the human race began on the Day of Pentecost when the Holy Spirit came to indwell every believer. They were baptized into the body of Christ, an entirely new entity, composed of both Jews and Gentiles on an equal basis. Before Pentecost, believers were born again, but they did not universally enjoy the indwelling of the Holy Spirit or the baptism of the Spirit. The baptism of the Spirit is summarized in 1 Corinthians 12:13: "For we are all baptized by one Spirit into one body—whether Jews or Greeks, slave or free—and we were all given the one Spirit to drink."

Additional revelation is given concerning the baptism of the Spirit in Acts 10, in connection with the gospel's being preached to Cornelius and his household. Until that time, the apostles had not comprehended that God had a purpose for the Gentiles and that salvation in Christ for them is the same as it is for the Jews. As a result of Peter's preaching to Cornelius and his household (detailed at length in Acts 10), the Holy Spirit was poured upon the new Gentile believers. Peter understood for the first time that they were genuinely saved. Acts 10:46–48 records, "For they heard them speaking in tongues and praising God. Then Peter said, 'Can anyone keep these people from being baptized with water? They have received the Holy Spirit just as we have.' So he ordered that they be baptized in the name of Jesus Christ. Then they asked Peter to stay with them for a few days."

Peter's fellow Jews criticized his actions, and his defense is recorded in Acts 11:15–17 as follows: "As I began to speak, the Holy Spirit came on them as he had come on us at the beginning. Then I remembered what the Lord had said: 'John baptized with water, but you will be baptized with the Holy Spirit.' So if God gave them the same gift as he gave us, who believed in the Lord Jesus Christ, who was I to think that I could oppose God?" The text goes on to say in verse 18, "When they heard this, they had no further objections and praised God, saying, 'So then, God has granted even the Gentiles repentance unto life.'" This extension of the gospel to the Gentiles forms the basis for the whole missionary effort of Paul and others who preached the gospel throughout the Mediterranean world.

The subsequent history of the church records the persecutions that the believers faced in the first and second centuries. When sometime later the church was recognized as a legal entity, the organized church of the early centuries emerged and achieved considerable power in a time when much of the political scene was in disarray. The growth of the church in power and numbers continued until the division of the Roman and Greek churches in the beginning of the second millennium.

Centuries later, the Protestant movement arose as a protest against the Roman Catholic Church and its departure from the Word of God. Protestantism became a major movement, resulting in many more bodies or denominations with increasing organizational fragmentation of the church.

In the years following World War II, however, a world church movement that had its beginning even before World War II emerged to unite. This movement climaxed in the establishment of the World Council of Churches in 1948. Although on the surface its members agreed about the necessity of the central character of Christ in Christianity, many people who adhered to the world church actually no longer held to orthodoxy. Christianity and the world church movement has largely been captured by liberals and radicals. The result is that many of the churches that have remained true to the biblical faith are not a part of this ecumenical movement.

IS PROPHECY BEING FULFILLED TODAY?

Often overlooked in the study of prophecy is the fact that significant prophecies are fulfilled today. The Word of God is full of promises that are, in effect, prophecies of what will happen when certain conditions are met. Prophecies also exist and are being fulfilled today that are inevitable and absolutely certain in the power and will of God. God is continuing today to demonstrate His supernatural power in many respects.

One of the most evident factors in the fulfillment of prophecy is that people are saved by trusting in Christ. The gospel, as it is preached, is a conditional gospel. If people will believe, they will be saved. Each person who is saved is a fulfillment of the prophecy that is involved in the gospel message.

The Word of God also promises in Galatians 5:16, "So I say, live by the Spirit, and you will not gratify the desires of the sinful nature." As this verse is translated more literally in the NKJV, "Walk in the Spirit, and you shall not fulfill the lust of the flesh." This verse indicates that a believer who is victorious in his life needs to walk moment by moment in dependence on the Holy Spirit. Such enablement from God is supernatural, and again the promise finds prophetic fulfillment.

Frequently in Scripture, Christians are exhorted to pray with the assurance of answered prayer, as is stated in 1 John 5:14: "This is the confidence we have in approaching God: that if we ask anything according to his will, he hears us." It is a common experience of Christians to see answered prayers, and each answer, of course, is a fulfillment of prophecy.

An outstanding illustration of contemporary fulfillment is found in the declaration of God that Israel will continue as a nation as long as the sun, moon, and stars endure. According to Jeremiah 31:35–36, Israel will continue as a nation throughout human history: "This is what the LORD says, he who appoints the sun to shine by day, who decrees the moon and stars to shine by night, who stirs up the sea so that its waves roar—the LORD Almighty is his name: 'Only if those decrees vanish from my sight,' declares the LORD, 'will the descendants of Israel ever cease to be a nation before me.'"

The fact that Israel has retained its national identity to the present hour is a remarkable evidence of the power of God. Other nationalities and races soon become absorbed, mixed and indistinguishable, as is the case in the United States, where the various national and racial backgrounds lose their distinctiveness in intermarriage in this new world. Israel, in spite of the fact that the nation has been scattered over the world for thousands of years, is clearly an identifiable race with an identifiable future prophetic fulfillment. Every time a person recognizes a Jew, he is seeing prophecy being fulfilled.

In the sweeping prophecies of Daniel predicting the six empires (Egypt, Assyria, Babylon, Medo-Persia, Greece, and Rome) that will precede the ultimate kingdom of God on earth, it is significant that no such empire has emerged since the Roman Empire. The world awaits the revival of the Roman Empire to fulfill its destiny before the second coming of Christ.

As was mentioned earlier, the Scriptures make clear that the world, instead of improving through the preaching of the gospel as postmillenarians teach, will become progressively worse. Second Peter 2:1–22 outlines the widespread apostasy from the truth. This apostasy had already begun in the first century. Second Timothy 3 details the increasing sin of the human race in history. Paul wrote,

> But mark this: There will be terrible times in the last days. People will be lovers of themselves, lovers of money, boastful, proud, abusive, disobedient to their parents, ungrateful, unholy, without love, unforgiving, slanderous, without self-control, brutal, not lovers of the good, treacherous, rash, conceited, lovers of pleasure rather than lovers of God—having a form of godliness but denying its power. Have nothing to do with them. They are the kind who worm their way into homes and gain control over weak-willed women, who are loaded down with sins and are swayed by all kinds of evil desires. (vv. 1–6)

The world has always been wicked and has departed from God throughout its history. But in the present situation—with the Word of God readily available to all people, translated into many languages, and broadcast on television and radio—the tragic fact is that in spite of the truth's being preached in churches in many of our cities, our country (and the world as a whole) continues to be desperately wicked, fulfilling the Scriptures that predict this situation.

The fact that prophecy continues to be fulfilled exactly as the Bible anticipates is another confirmation that prophecies that are yet future, which will have their fulfillment in the new millennium, are in our immediate view. Many indications exist that human history is reaching its climax in end-time events. This evidence is part of the substance of prophetic revelation in the Bible.

With almost two thousand years elapsing since the first coming of Christ and predictions concerning the future of Israel, the church, and the nations, the question still naturally arises concerning the fulfillment of prophecy in the new millennium.

The Bible does not give specific prophecies relating to the new millennium, except that prophecies that are not fulfilled at its beginning could very well find fulfillment early in the new millennium. Accordingly, a careful search of prophecies that are yet to be fulfilled and the evidence of their imminence remains a practical activity.

CHAPTER 2

THE RAPTURE: THE FIRST PROPHETIC EVENT OF THE NEW MILLENNIUM

Although the church at large has greatly neglected the Rapture as a theological prophecy, for those who accept the Bible as the Word of God and interpret its prophecies literally, it remains a most important prediction for the future. Although no anticipation of a Rapture and no prophecy of the church as the body of Christ is given in the Old Testament, once the New Testament was written, it became a major expectation of the future.

THE RAPTURE NOT REVEALED IN THE OLD TESTAMENT

The second coming of Christ is mentioned in both the Old Testament and Matthew 24–25, but the Rapture was not revealed until the night before the Crucifixion in John 14:1–3. The prophecy fell on deaf ears, however, because the disciples were expecting Christ to fulfill the promise concerning His Second Coming, including the establishment of a kingdom on earth in which they had been assured that they would have prominent parts in its government (Matt. 19:28). They did not understand the necessity of Christ's first dying on the cross and the time interval between the two comings of Christ. Therefore, Christ did not enlarge on this revelation, and it was left to the apostle Paul, through special revelation from God, to reveal later in 1 Thessalonians and the other Epistles the basic doctrine of the Rapture.

THE RAPTURE AS A MAJOR PROPHETIC EVENT

A number of central passages, beginning with John 14:1–3, deal with the Rapture of the church in the New Testament. As was mentioned in the preceding paragraph, the disciples did not realize the difference between the first and second comings and merged the two events; therefore, they were unprepared to understand that Christ was about to leave them. The discourse from the Upper Room was very upsetting to them because Christ predicted both that one of their number was going to betray Him and that He was going to leave them. This prophecy did not fit at all into their expectations of Christ's bringing in the prophesied millennial kingdom, in which they would have prominent places of authority.

In answering their problems, Christ revealed for the first time the wonderful fact of the Rapture in John 14. All other preceding mentions of the coming of the Lord refer to the Second Coming. In this passage, He promised to come back and take them to the Father's house: "In my Father's house are many rooms; if it were not so, I would have told you. I am going there to prepare a place for you. And if I go to prepare a place for you, I will come back and take you to be with me that you also may be where I am" (vv. 2–3).

Christ did not attempt to explain this statement because the disciples had no background to understand it, confusing as they did the first and second comings of Christ. This lack of explanation added to their consternation rather than quieting their hearts. As the passage indicates, the Rapture is a movement of believers from earth to the Father's house in heaven.

Further revelation was given in Paul's epistles to the Thessalonians. After Paul's conversion, he needed additional revelation from God and was taught the doctrine of the grace of God and the purpose of God in forming Jews and Gentiles into a new entity—the church. Accordingly, Paul had two basic messages in his missionary journeys. First, Christ had died and risen again, offering salvation and forgiveness to all who would trust in Him. Second, Christ is coming again to take believers from earth to heaven.

While His death is a matter of history, His coming for the church is presented as an imminent hope for which they could live expectantly. It is quite apparent in the Thessalonian passages that they were expecting this momentarily as something that could occur at any time. Therefore, when some of their members who had just come to faith in Christ died, it raised a new question in their minds as to when they would be reunited with the deceased.

When Timothy was sent to Thessalonica to investigate for Paul, he encountered a number of theological questions that were only natural in view of the brief time that Paul had been there. One question concerned when they would see their deceased loved ones. If the Lord came for those who were living, would they have to wait for some future time before their loved ones would be resurrected? How much they understood about the Rapture's being followed by a time of great trouble and then the second coming of Christ is unclear. They possibly thought that the resurrection will take place at that time. In answer to that question, we have a major passage in 1 Thessalonians 4:13–18, in which Paul revealed what the Rapture is and how it relates to those who have died.

He explained, first, how the Rapture is designed to give us hope and help in times of the loss of loved ones: "Brothers, we do not want you to be ignorant about those who fall asleep, or to grieve like the rest of men, who have no hope" (v. 13). The certainty of their faith is mentioned in verse 14: "We believe that Jesus died and rose again and so we believe that God will bring with Jesus those who have fallen asleep in him." What Paul meant is that the Thessalonians believed in the death and resurrection of Christ—the essential truths of the gospel—and that the Rapture was just as sure to be fulfilled in the future as the death of Christ was fulfilled in history. Throughout the Old Testament, the death of Christ was predicted and was a matter of prophecy. But now, it is more than just prophecy; it is history.

Then he mentions that the souls of those who have died in Christ will come with Christ at the time of the Rapture; that is, "God will bring with Jesus those who have fallen asleep in him." A detailed picture of what will occur at the Rapture follows. He declares that those living at the time of the Rapture will not have to wait for those who are resurrected: "According to the Lord's own word, we tell you that we who are still alive, who are left till the coming of the Lord, will certainly not precede those who have fallen asleep" (v. 15).

THE RAPTURE DESCRIBED

In 1 Thessalonians 4:16–17, Paul explained further exactly what will happen:

> For the Lord himself will come down from heaven, with a loud command, with the voice of the archangel and with the trumpet call of God, and the dead in Christ will rise first. After that, we who are still alive and are left will be caught up together with them in the clouds to meet the Lord in the air. And so we will be with the Lord forever.

In other words, their fears of having to wait to see their loved ones at the time of the Rapture are ungrounded. As a matter of fact, they will be resurrected from the graves just a moment before living Christians will be caught up to meet the Lord. The expression "will be caught up together" (v. 17) is where we get the word *rapture* since it can be translated "caught up," "snatched up," or "raptured." The promise is that once Christians meet the Lord, they will be with Him forever and no more separation will occur. Then the final message of the chapter, "therefore encourage each other with these words" (v. 18), is a practical application of this truth to their expectations.

Another number of transparent observations can be made in this discussion. First, quite clear is the fact that this is a real event and not symbolic in character. The prophecies of this section will be fulfilled literally. Second, one should observe that no preceding events are described and the Rapture is described as the next event or one that is imminent. Quite clear is the fact that the Thessalonians regarded it thus, and that is what God intended. In the chapter that follows, understanding is given that when the Rapture occurs, the Day of the Lord will begin. This period of God's immediate judgment is discussed in more detail later.

FOUR ASPECTS OF THE RAPTURE

In examining what happened to the church at the time of the Rapture, one can note the following four stages of prophetic fulfillment.

1. Believers in Christ will receive a new body when the Lord comes. This fact is indicated in the resurrection of those who have died. Later revelation given to the Corinthians indicates that living Christians will be changed instantly like those who are raised from the dead and will have bodies suited for heaven:

> Listen, I tell you a mystery: we will not all sleep, but we will all be changed—in a flash, in the twinkling of an eye, at the last trumpet. For the trumpet will sound, the dead will be raised imperishable, and we will be changed. For the perishable must clothe itself with the imperishable, and the mortal with immortality. (1 Cor. 15:51–53)

Therefore, the first phase of the Rapture is one of resurrection and translation.

2. The Rapture will begin a new relationship to Christ in the symbolism of marriage. Christ is presented in 2 Corinthians 11:2 as the husband of the church, which is His bride, and the Rapture is the occasion when Christ will claim His bride as His own.

At the time of Christ, the tradition of marriage involved three stages. The first stage was the dowry stage, when the parents of the bridegroom paid the parents of the bride a dowry that signified the legal marriage. The second stage is illustrated in Matthew 25 in the parable of the virgins. The bridegroom and his friends claimed the bride by going from the home of the bridegroom to the home of the bride. She knew that he was coming and was ready with her maiden friends to join the procession, going from her home to the bridegroom's home. This symbolic event is fulfilled, of course, at the time of the Rapture. The third stage was the wedding feast that came after the marriage and speaks of the fellowship that those in heaven will experience.

The church already is married to Christ because He died for her on the cross and paid the dowry. But the Rapture is when the bridegroom will claim His bride, and from that point, as is stated in 1 Thessalonians 4:17, "we will be with the Lord forever."

3. The third phase in God's plan for the Christian is the judgment seat of Christ, which is the subject of the next chapter, when believers will be evaluated as to the eternal value of their life on earth. This evaluation is not a matter of judgment of salvation or of sin but rather of value or the eternal worth of what they accomplished in life.

4. In connection with the judgment seat of Christ, a reward is promised, as stated in 2 Corinthians 5:10: "For we must all appear before the judgment seat of Christ, that each one may receive what is due him for the things done while in the body, whether good or bad." The nature of the award is not mentioned in Scripture, but it could very well be in the form of privileged service and position before God in eternity. As believers have been faithful in this life, God will give them appointments of doing something for Him in heaven. Believers will have the passion to show their love for Christ and will eagerly want to do something for Him. A place of privileged service will be a vehicle for satisfying this desire.

This fourth phase of the believers' relationship to Christ extends into eternity when they will dwell forever in the new heavens, the new earth, and the New Jerusalem (Rev. 21:22). Understandably, Christians who believe what the Scriptures teach on this subject should be eagerly awaiting the Rapture of the church and praying for its fulfillment.

In addition to the Scriptures discussed herein, other references to the Rapture are found in the Bible. In Titus 2:11–14, for example, the truth of the Rapture is described as a blessed hope:

> For the grace of God that brings salvation has appeared to all men. It teaches us to say "No" to ungodliness and worldly passions, and to live self-controlled, upright and godly lives in this present age, while we wait for the

> blessed hope—the glorious appearing of our great God and Savior, Jesus Christ, who gave himself for us to redeem us from all wickedness and to purify for himself a people that are his very own, eager to do what is good.

The fact that at the Rapture we will see Christ in His glory is an incentive to live a godly and pure life.

The final revelation of the Rapture is found in the book of Revelation. The final book of the Bible is primarily a revelation of the second coming of Christ rather than the Rapture, but those living in the church in the present age nevertheless have this expectation. The church in Thyatira, which in some respects had drifted into apostasy, nevertheless had some true believers. Revelation 2:25–26 states, "Only hold on to what you have until I come. To him who overcomes and does my will to the end, I will give authority over the nations."

In connection with the church in Philadelphia, which was true to the Lord as an illustration of a godly church, the following promise is given: "Since you have kept my command to endure patiently, I will also keep you from the hour of trial that is going to come upon the whole world to test those who live on the earth. I am coming soon. Hold on to what you have, so that no one will take your crown" (Rev. 3:10–11).

Obviously, this statement implies a pretribulation Rapture because they are promised to be kept from the future hour of trial that would be fulfilled on earth before the Second Coming. The Scriptures are explicit that the Philadelphia church will be kept *from*, not *through*, the Tribulation. As will be revealed later, nowhere in the book of Revelation is any mention of a Rapture of the church occurring either in the process of the Tribulation itself or at the time of the Second Coming.

THE RAPTURE: THE FIRST OF IMPORTANT UNFULFILLED PROPHECIES

As important as it is, the Rapture, which is the beginning of world-shaking events that are predicted for the future, could very well take place early in the new millennium. Accordingly, the Rapture can be designated as the first of the following prophetic events.

1. Immediately following the raptured church's going to heaven is the judgment seat of Christ, which will recognize the quality and value of every believer's life on earth.
2. Although not clearly designated as occurring before or after the Rapture, one of the major events of the new millennium may well be the revival of the Roman Empire in what secular Europe is describing as "the United States of Europe." The exact date is not revealed for its formation, but evidence exists that it will be in existence right after the Rapture.
3. The emergence of the Antichrist occurs, variously designated in the Scriptures as the little horn of Daniel (Dan. 7:8), "the man of lawlessness" (2 Thess. 2:3), "the ruler who will come" (Dan. 9:26), the king who "will do as he pleases" and who "will exalt and magnify himself above every god" (Dan. 11:36), and "one of the heads of the beast" (Rev. 13:5). He will first be manifested in history when he conquers three of the ten nations of the revived Roman Empire (Dan. 7:8) and then the remaining seven.
4. The beginning of the Day of the Lord (1 Thess. 5:1–12).
5. The covenant of Daniel 9:27, covering the last seven years leading up to the second coming of Christ and completing God's program for Israel at that time.

6. The invasion of Israel by six nations prophesied in Ezekiel 38–39. This prophecy probably will be fulfilled in the first half of the last seven years, leading up to the Second Coming.
7. A world government in fulfillment of Daniel 7:23 and Revelation 13:1–18. This event will be Satan's substitute for the millennial reign of Christ and will occur in the Great Tribulation, the last three and a half years before the Second Coming.
8. The persecution of Israel and all Christians, including all who oppose the Antichrist (Rev. 12:13; 13:15; cf. Zech. 13:8). The period is designated in Scripture as "a time of distress" (Dan. 12:1), "a time of trouble for Jacob" (Jer. 30:7), a time of "great distress" (Matt. 24:21), and "the great tribulation" (Rev. 7:14). The first prophecy of this coming time of distress is found in Deuteronomy 4:26–28. Jeremiah speaks at length of this in Jeremiah 30:5–7. Other references include Daniel 7:7–8. The period involving the Great Tribulation is three and a half years, or forty-two months (Rev. 11:2; 13:5), or 1,260 days (Rev. 12:6). The period is climaxed with a great world war, described in Daniel 11:36–45 and Revelation 16:13–16.
9. A major event is the judgment of the Gentiles in Matthew 25:31–46 in preparation for the millennial kingdom. Those who are described as goats, that is, the unsaved, are eliminated. The righteous, designated as the sheep, are qualified to enter the millennial kingdom.
10. Resurrection takes place for the righteous who have not already been raised, including the Old Testament saints (Dan. 12:2–3). The martyred dead of the Tribulation are also raised to enter the millennial kingdom (Rev. 20:4–6). The judgments, anticipated in Matthew 24–25, will also be fulfilled in preparation for the millennial kingdom.

11. The second coming of Christ is a climactic event that completes these tremendous events. It is described as a movement from heaven to earth with Jesus Christ as the glorious King followed by the armies of heaven, including all of the saints and angels who will accompany Christ as He sets up His kingdom on earth for a thousand years as prophesied.
12. The judgments of that period include the destruction of the armies gathered against Christ (Rev. 19:13–21), including the capture of the world ruler, the Antichrist, and the False Prophet, who are both cast alive into the lake of burning sulfur (v. 20).
13. The millennial kingdom, which follows the Second Coming, fulfills the many prophecies of the Old Testament concerning a kingdom on earth as well as the brief description given in Revelation 20.
14. The final doom of Satan and the wicked dead (Rev. 20:7–15), including Satan's being cast into the lake of burning sulfur and the casting of all of the wicked whose names are not in the Book of Life from hades, a temporary place for the wicked dead, into the lake of burning sulfur (vv. 11–15).
15. The creation of the new heaven, the new earth, and the New Jerusalem is the climax of God's prophetic program (Rev. 21:1–22:21).

Each of these important future events will be discussed in the following chapter.

THE IMPORTANCE OF LITERAL INTERPRETATION

In understanding the imminence of the Rapture, as well as prophecy as a whole, it is most important to follow consistently the literal interpretation of prophecy. The Rapture is a movement of the church from earth to heaven and is in sharp contrast to the church's return with Christ at the Second Coming, which occurs more than seven years later as a movement from heaven to earth. Those who compromise the interpretation of prophecy by interpreting the Bible as teaching correctly a premillennial return of Christ but incorrectly a posttribulational Rapture, do so because they depart from a literal interpretation of prophecy of the Tribulation and the contrast of the heavenly movement at the time of the Rapture with the movement from heaven to earth at the Second Coming. Posttribulationism requires a departure from a literal interpretation of the tribulation period that precedes the Second Coming. For those who interpret prophecy literally, the Rapture remains the most important doctrine to be fulfilled, and the fact that it is imminent makes it all the more important.

THE RAPTURE AN IMMINENT EVENT

As far as Scripture revelation is concerned, the Rapture could have occurred in the first century, as even the Thessalonians were expecting it in their lifetime. The centuries that have passed have not changed the fact that the Rapture is imminent, but they have raised the issue of how soon it will occur.

Obviously as the years pass, the Rapture grows nearer. After almost two thousand years, it would seem appropriate for our present world to see fulfillment of this important event that leads to the great climaxes of prophecy in the Bible. The references to the Rapture in the Bible do much to bring this assumption into proper perspective.

The Rapture as presented in the Bible is always an imminent event, as indicated in references throughout the New Testament (e.g., John 14:2–3; 1 Cor. 15:51–58; 1 Thess. 4:13–18; 2 Thess. 2:1–5; Titus 2:11–14; Rev. 2:25; 3:10–11). Never in the many references to the Rapture is any event predicted as occurring before the Rapture. No signs are given. The Rapture itself is anticipated, as in Titus 2:13, where believers are described as waiting for "the blessed hope—the glorious appearing of our great God and Savior, Jesus Christ." Never is the church told to look for the Antichrist or the Tribulation. Much evidence exists in both contemporary history and the description of the world situation that would indicate that the time is ripe for the Rapture. As will be noted in the following discussion, the present world situation is precisely what the Bible predicts for the time of the Rapture.

THE RAPTURE IN RELATION TO THE SECOND COMING

In modern Christianity, considerable debate has occurred in many works published on the question as to whether the Rapture is before end-time events, beginning with the appearance of the Antichrist conquering the revived Roman Empire, occurs somewhere in the middle of the period, or is merged with the Second Coming itself. The arguments both pro and con are intricate and complicated. They are resolved once the revelation of the events leading up to the second coming of Christ, which are referred to in the Bible as the beginning of the Day of the Lord (1 Thess. 5:1–2), are examined carefully.

The approach to this complicated problem will be to present, first, what the Bible teaches about the period leading up to the second coming of Christ, asking the question as to whether any evidence exists that the Rapture occurs in this entire period. The pretribulation Rapture view holds that the Rapture occurs first. The posttribulation view usually merges the Rapture with the Second Coming. Other views place the Rapture in the middle of the period. Obviously, this issue is one of the most important decisions to be made in establishing the prophetic program of God. Therefore, when the facts of the period leading up to the Second Coming have been fully explored, the question will then be raised as to where the Rapture fits into this prophetic picture. The extensive nature of this theological discussion is illustrated in the author's book *The Rapture Question*, which attempts to analyze the problem completely in three hundred pages.

THE ORDER OF EVENTS CONCERNING THE RAPTURE

In the reconstruction of the end times in the fifteen major events, the scenario may be summarized as follows. After the Rapture, the Roman Empire, revived in the form of ten nations, is conquered by the future Antichrist, who first gains control of three countries and then of all ten nations. This event is revealed in Daniel 7:7–24.

The Man of Sin, the little horn of Daniel 7:8, who is the future Antichrist, having conquered the ten countries, enters into a seven-year covenant (9:27), which he observes for three and a half years. This covenant introduces the seven years leading up to the Second Coming. However, at the end of the first three and a half years, the Antichrist has reached such power that he proclaims himself dictator over the whole world. This declaration precipitates what the Bible refers to as the Great Tribulation (Dan. 12:1; Matt. 24:21; Rev. 7:14), the time of unprecedented trouble that leads up to the second coming of Christ.

The Antichrist will be revealed at the beginning of the Day of the Lord when he conquers all ten countries of the ten-nation kingdom, which event occurs more than seven years before the Second Coming. Then follows the seven-year covenant of Daniel 9:27. His full revelation will occur at the beginning of the Great Tribulation when he claims to be God. Of course, this view refutes the post-tribulational and midtribulational views of the Rapture because he obviously is going to be revealed after the Rapture and before the Tribulation. Paul argues in 2 Thessalonians 2:1–5 that they were not in the Day of the Lord because the Antichrist had not yet been revealed. This revelation will be one of the first events in the fulfillment of the Day of the Lord. We will consider Paul's discussion of the Day of the Lord and its events later.

In contemplating what the twenty-first century might bring, one naturally can assume that the Rapture could very easily take place soon. Many changes will take place in the twenty-first century that might remove some of the evidences that the Rapture is soon. It seems natural to conclude that a window now exists for the Rapture to occur, and this window will not exist forever, especially not throughout the whole twenty-first century. Accordingly, although we have no basis for date-setting, we have every reason to believe that the Rapture of the church is very soon, as a later discussion of the signs of the times will support.

CHAPTER 3

THE JUDGMENT SEAT OF CHRIST

One of the central texts in the exhortation of the Scriptures in regard to preparation for the Rapture is 1 Corinthians 15:58: "Therefore, my dear brothers, stand firm. Let nothing move you. Always give yourselves fully to the work of the Lord, because you know that your labor in the Lord is not in vain."

THE PROSPECT OF REWARD

The rationale behind the instruction that we should give ourselves fully to the work of the Lord is that our labor is not in vain. This reasoning holds before the believer the prospect that after the Rapture of the church there will be an accounting that the Bible calls the judgment seat of Christ. The central passage on this topic is 2 Corinthians 5, where this prediction is part of a passage referring to the characteristics of our ministry, and it is summarized in verses 6–10:

> Therefore we are always confident and know that as long as we are at home in the body we are away from the Lord. We live by faith, not by sight. We are confident, I say, and would prefer to be away from the body

> and at home with the Lord. So we make it our goal to please him, whether we are at home in the body or away from it. For we must all appear before the judgment seat of Christ, that each one may receive what is due him for the things done while in the body, whether good or bad.

In a word, this passage expresses the fact that, while we are waiting for the coming of the Lord, we should be living for Christ because after the Rapture we will appear before the judgment seat of Christ, a judgment for Christians only. This judgment of believers will be in regard to whether our works have been good or bad. These works are not moral issues but value issues. In other words, what we have done with our life will be graded as to whether it is good and in the will of God or bad and worthless.

SALVATION NOT THE ISSUE

The issue of what our judgment will be when we get to heaven has sometimes been confused with the way of salvation. The Bible is clear that salvation is by grace because of the death of Christ and is not based on any works on the part of believers. But there is the biblical expectation that if they are saved, they are "God's workmanship, created in Christ Jesus to do good works, which God prepared in advance for us to do" (Eph. 2:10). A believer is not only forgiven of his sins but also justified, that is, declared righteous (Rom. 5:1), which means that God sees him in the perfect righteousness of Christ. Accordingly, he is not only forgiven but also declared to be righteous as far his position before God is concerned.

Therefore, at the judgment seat of Christ, the issue is not salvation but whether our works after we are saved were either good or bad. Everyone at the judgment seat of Christ has been saved and justified by faith and is assured of his eternal existence with Christ. It is a time, however, of accountability because salvation is not only a work of God but also an act of trust in which God has committed to us the possibility of serving Him effectively. The question is going to be whether we have accomplished this expectation.

ILLUSTRATION OF A BUILDING

The Scriptures use several illustrations to make this plain. First Corinthians 3:10–15 offers the illustration of the construction of a building. The foundation is Christ, as Paul indicated in verse 10: "By the grace God has given me, I laid a foundation as an expert builder, and someone else is building on it. But each one should be careful how he builds."

Some people have taken this statement as a picture of a local church, which it could be, but it is also a picture of the individual Christian.

In verses 11 and following, revelation is given that various materials can be used to build on this foundation. Paul states, "If any man builds on this foundation using gold, silver, costly stones, wood, hay, or straw, his work will be shown for what it is, because the Day will bring it to light. It will be revealed with fire, and the fire will test the quality of each man's work" (vv. 12–13).

The significance of the materials is not indicated, but in Scripture gold is usually used in reference to the glory of God, silver to redemption (Lev. 27:1–8), and costly stones to all sorts of other work. According to 1 Corinthians 3:15, when the building that is made of wood, hay, and stubble—which represent different levels of value, as far as this world is concerned, but are equally subject to destruction at the judgment seat of Christ—is tested by fire, it will burn up. Gold, silver, and precious stones obviously will survive the fire because they are not combustible. Accordingly, Paul writes, "If what he has built survives, he will receive his reward. If it is burned up, he will suffer loss; he himself will be saved, but only as one escaping through the flames" (vv. 14–15).

As this passage makes plain, the issue of salvation is not considered here because every believer is saved, but rather it is a question of what he has done after his salvation that is regarded as worthwhile before God. Christians who understand the judgment seat of Christ will have a pointed reminder that life is a trust that should be fulfilled by faithful service. This fulfillment will be revealed at the judgment seat of Christ.

ILLUSTRATION OF RUNNING THE RACE

A second illustration is in 1 Corinthians 9:24–27, where a Christian's life is pictured as a race. In the city of Corinth, athletic events were very important, and running a race was a common experience. In the traditions of that time, the person who won the race was given a crown of leaves, which was a temporary token of his victory. This passage reminds us that in the race of life, Christians also will get a crown, but our crown will be permanent and indestructible.

> Do you not know that in a race all the runners run, but only one gets the prize? Run in such a way as to get the prize. Everyone who competes in the games goes into strict training. They do it to get a crown that will not last; but we do it to get a crown that will last forever. Therefore I do not run like a man running aimlessly; I do not fight like a man beating the air. No, I beat my body and make it my slave so that after I have preached to others, I myself will not be disqualified for the prize.

In the races at Corinth, only one person could win the race. By contrast, in life every Christian can win because he is not running in competition with somebody else but is competing only with himself. The exhortation, of course, is to run the race and win. As the passage points out, running a race has rather obvious rules.

First, the runner lays aside all heavy clothing that would hinder his running and puts on a lightweight track suit and spiked shoes that grip the ground and prevent his slipping. The runner lines up at the starting line. When the starter fires his pistol, signaling the beginning of the race, the runner immediately charges from the starting blocks. In my observation of athletic contests, I have never seen a runner turn around to the starter and say, "Do you mean me?" In the Christian life, however, we often tend to ignore God's commands to us. We often act like Moses, wanting our Aaron to do the job for us. The first law of winning the race is to get out of the starting blocks as soon as the starter's pistol fires.

In the nature of a race, we do not run aimlessly; we stay on course. If the runner runs off the track or out of his assigned lane, he is disqualified. Winning the race is the most important thing to the serious runner. He does not stop to pick flowers. He does not take time to wave at the grandstand and show how great he is. Instead, he concentrates on making his body exert the energy necessary to win the race and gain the prize. Paul speaks of beating his body, in other words, forcing himself to do what God wants him to do, so that he will not be disqualified and fail to receive the prize.

One of the most amazing facts of this illustration is that everyone can win. It is not a matter of trying to beat somebody else, but of living up to the potential of what the grace of God can do in us.

ILLUSTRATION OF A TRUST

We find a third illustration in Romans 14:10–12. Paul raises the question of judging each other in connection with the judgment seat of Christ:

> You, then, why do you judge your brother? Or why do you look down on your brother? For we will all stand before God's judgment seat. It is written: "As surely as I live," says the Lord, "every knee will bow before me; every tongue will confess to God." So then, each of us will give an account of himself to God.

The judgment seat of Christ reminds us that we have not been appointed as judges of our fellow Christians. It is true that any preacher or exhorter has to recognize sin as sin and recognize good works as good works. But it is not our responsibility to evaluate the extent to which a Christian brother is serving the Lord. In raising the question of why we judge our brothers, so often we obviously are judging others in an effort to make ourselves look better, which, of course, is wrong. Instead, as Paul points out, we are to be subject to God's judgment seat.

Paul predicts that every knee will bow to God and that every tongue will confess to God. This point, of course, is true in eternal judgment. The sad fact is that if a person does not do it in this life, it will be too late to do it in the life to come. The exhortation, of course, is that we should bow the knee *now* and yield our heart and tongue to the Lord.

The matter is summarized in verse 12: "So then, each of us will give an account of himself to God." This verse means that our life is a trust, and, as is the nature of a trust, we have to give an account to God of what we have done with what He has entrusted to us. No two of us have exactly the same responsibilities, the same gifts, or the same opportunities. Each person will be judged on the basis of what he did with what God has given him. Therefore, as the Scriptures state, we should not judge our brothers but rather ourselves and seek to please God in everything that we do. This truth is a great equalizer because it gives every Christian an equal opportunity to win.

As the Scriptures reveal concerning the judgment seat of Christ, those who serve the Lord effectively receive a reward. The Scriptures do not specify what that reward is. Our reward might be in the form of privileged service to God in heaven.

In heaven, Christians will realize more than we possibly can while on earth how wonderfully God dealt with us in grace in saving us and bringing us to Himself. This realization will cause us to love the Lord because He first loved us. Accordingly, our major desire in heaven will be to express in some way our love for Him.

It is entirely probable that God will give each Christian a different sphere of activity and service for Himself, although the Scriptures are very limited in what they indicate we will be doing. Second Timothy 2:12 states, "If we endure, we will also reign with him." Apparently, in the Millennium, Christians will have assignments of duties in connection with the millennial reign of Christ. In the eternal state, Scripture states simply, "his servants will serve him" (Rev. 22:3). Apparently, our reward will be in the area of assigned tasks and responsibilities in keeping with our faithfulness in this life.

A major motivation in our service should be our love for Christ, as is stated in 2 Corinthians 5:14–15: "For Christ's love compels us, because we are convinced that one died for all, and therefore all died. And he died for all, that those who live should no longer live for themselves but for him who died for them and was raised again." A Christian who is walking in fellowship with God will be serving God, not simply for the hope of reward, but for the opportunity we have of showing the Lord that we love Him and want to serve and honor Him in our life and ministry.

The facts contained in the doctrine of the judgment seat of Christ support the concept that prophecy is primarily a practical subject that tells us what is going to happen in the future to prepare us for the events before they happen. As God has revealed the future in the Scriptures, He clearly wants us to study and know exactly what His plan and purpose for us is so that our lives will be in keeping with what He has promised to accomplish for us in the future.

The wonderful future that is promised at the Rapture emphasizes how important it is for us to realize that the Rapture could be very near and that what is now prediction will have its complete fulfillment in God's plan and purpose. The Rapture could very well be fulfilled in the twenty-first century.

CHAPTER 4

THE UNITED STATES OF EUROPE AS THE NEW EUROPE

As the twenty-first century begins, prophecies unfulfilled at the close of the twentieth century obviously will have their fulfillment in the millennium that follows. Most important, however, is the question of how soon such fulfillment will occur in the new millennium.

One of the significant events that has occurred is the dramatic changes in Europe. These changes seem to harmonize with what the Bible predicts for the climax of the times of the Gentiles; therefore, the Scriptures relating to it merit close attention and careful interpretation. The prophet Daniel was given a significant role of not only tracing the history of Israel in Daniel 9:24–27 but also of predicting gentile prophecy. (This was mentioned earlier in chapter 1.) The details of this point are important in evaluating the present situation.

THE IMAGE OF NEBUCHADNEZZAR

In answer to Nebuchadnezzar's question as to the meaning of his dream, Daniel told the king what he had seen:

> You looked, O king, and there before you stood a large statue—an enormous, dazzling statue, awesome in appearance. The head of the statue was made of pure gold, its chest and arms of silver, its belly and thighs of bronze, its legs of iron, its feet partly of iron and partly of baked clay. While you were watching, a rock was cut out, not by human hands. It struck the statue on its feet of iron and clay and smashed them. Then the iron, the clay, the bronze, the silver and the gold were broken to pieces at the same time and became like chaff on a threshing floor in the summer. The wind swept them away without leaving a trace. But the rock that struck the statue became a huge mountain and filled the whole earth. (Dan. 2:31–35)

In chapter 2, in the image of Nebuchadnezzar's dream, four empires were described that can be identified as the king of Babylon as the head of the image, the Medes and the Persians as the upper part of the image, Greece as the lower parts of the image, and the Roman Empire as the legs and feet. The stone made without hands is obviously the kingdom of God that eventually will destroy gentile power. Details, including the names of the first three empires, are added in Daniel 7–8. The empires are Babylon (7:3–4), Medo-Persia (v. 5), and Greece (v. 6). The fourth empire (v. 7), which is not named but which is the greatest empire of all four, is obviously fulfilled in history in the Roman Empire. It is described as a great beast that devoured all previous kingdoms.

Although Daniel did not understand what he was recording, history has made clear that all of the prophecies of the first three empires and almost all of the prophecies of the fourth empire have been fulfilled. As described in Daniel and elsewhere in the Old Testament, the Roman Empire as the symbol for gentile power was to be brought to conclusion by the second coming of Christ. Characteristically, the Old Testament skips the whole present church age, although it describes in detail events up to the first coming of Christ. It then concentrates on the few years leading up to the Second Coming.

As far as the Old Testament is concerned, there is no interruption of Roman power. History records, however, that the Roman Empire died. Although many centuries elapsed from its founding and apex of power to its final departure from history, for all practical purposes, the Roman Empire does not survive today.

THE FINAL STAGE OF THE ROMAN EMPIRE

After describing the tremendous power of the fourth kingdom that has been fulfilled in history, however, Daniel 7:7 says that it "had ten horns." This final stage of the Roman Empire has never been fulfilled, although many scholars have tried to find something that would correspond to it. As is the case in the use of symbols in the Bible, frequently they are explained in the context. In Daniel 7:24, for example, the ten nations are declared to be kings: "The ten horns are ten kings who will come from this kingdom." In other words, when the Roman Empire is revived to fulfill this prophecy, it will exist in the form of ten units joined in a political union.

The ten-nation stage of the Roman Empire, as yet unfulfilled, predicts a revival of the Roman Empire in the form of ten countries. Although the names of the nations are not given nor their territories defined, one can assume, from the fact that the Roman Empire was largely a European empire, that the revived Roman Empire will be in the form of a United States of Europe. In light of this prediction, a remarkable sequence of events has confirmed that such a union is entirely possible in the near future.

In the history of Europe, the major nations of Great Britain, France, and Germany experienced centuries of conflict, usually climaxing in a war in which one side or the other won. Immediately after peace was achieved, however, they would start arming for the next war, a situation that resulted in constant warfare in Europe with no hope of a unified political state.

After World War II, however, a remarkable change took place. Great Britain, France, and Germany are no longer arming to fight each other today, simply because all three of these nations possess the atomic bomb with the means of completely destroying the other nations. Accordingly, a war would result only in the destruction of all three nations rather than supremacy by one nation. With this in view, the European nations formed an economic bloc called the Common Market by which they joined forces and adopted an economic strategy to meet the current needs.

Conferences have been held about and major steps have been taken toward achieving a unified Europe. A common currency and credit have been devised. Although many problems exist because some of the nations, particularly Great Britain, are reluctant to give up their sovereignty, now even the secular world is predicting that it is just a matter of time until these European nations are joined into a United States of Europe. This unification would provide a fulfillment of Daniel 7:7 and other passages that imply such a union.

From the standpoint of the fulfillment of other prophecies, such as the Rapture, this development is highly significant because although the Rapture itself has no signs, the scene after the Rapture is frequently described as consisting of a ten-nation political unit (Rev. 12:3; 13:1–7; 17:3–16). The Scriptures are not clear as to whether the ten nations will be formed before or immediately after the Rapture. But in the events that follow the Rapture and leading up to the Second Coming, the ten-nation group becomes prominent.

THE ANTICHRIST: THE LITTLE HORN

In this context, further prophecy is given in Daniel 7:8, in which a little horn is mentioned: "While I was thinking about the horns, there before me was another horn, a little one, which came up among them; and three of the first horns were uprooted before it. This horn had eyes like the eyes of a man and a mouth that spoke boastfully." The little horn is obviously a man who conquers three of the ten countries and then apparently becomes the ruler of all ten nations, although the Scriptures never explain how this expansion takes place.

The rest of Daniel 7, beginning in verse 9, gives the context for the whole situation, first providing a vision of heaven (vv. 9–10). There follows a prediction that the beast who has ten horns will be destroyed and brought to an end at the Second Coming (v. 11; Rev. 19:17–21), in contrast to the three preceding gentile empires that for a time continued, at least in part in their successors (Dan. 7:12). The second coming of Christ is also described in Daniel 7:13–14 with the universal triumph of God in the political situation of the world.

When Daniel wanted to have information about this, he was reminded that the four beasts of chapter 7 are the four kingdoms that were revealed earlier in chapter 2 (7:23–27). When he asked about the fourth beast, the Roman Empire is described. The ten horns are ten kings. The little horn, after conquering the ten countries, eventually expands until the whole earth is under his power. Daniel 7:23 explains this little horn's rise to power: "The fourth beast is a fourth kingdom that will appear on earth. It will be different from all the other kingdoms and will devour the whole earth, trampling it down and crushing it." Daniel 7:11–12 describes the ultimate destruction of the kingdom of gentile power. The millennial kingdom will be fulfilled before the final everlasting kingdom comes to pass.

Although Daniel 7 is the major passage, many references to these ten nations are made throughout Scripture. Revelation 13 summarizes the final world empire of the Antichrist and its place in future prophecy, as the ten horns are mentioned frequently (Rev. 13:1). Revelation 12:3 refers to "an enormous red dragon with seven heads and ten horns and seven crowns on his heads." In Revelation 17:3, the ten horns are mentioned again, along with the seven heads, and described as a scarlet beast on whom the woman sits. This woman is symbolic of the final world church movement. The seven heads and ten horns are also mentioned in Revelation 17:7, 16.

THE COVENANT OF DANIEL 9:27

When all of these Scriptures are combined, they portray a scene of ten nations ruled by the little horn of Daniel 7:8. This little horn eventually becomes the Antichrist and world ruler, beginning with his control of all ten countries. From that position of power, he is able to fulfill Scripture, such as Daniel 9:27, which describes his entry into a seven-year covenant supposedly to bring peace to the Middle East.

In the seventy sevens of Daniel 9:24–27, Israel's major role in prophecy unfolds. In verse 27, the final seven years are described thus: "He will confirm a covenant with many for one 'seven.' In the middle of the 'seven' he will put an end to sacrifice and offering. And on a wing of the temple he will set up an abomination that causes desolation, until the end that is decreed is poured out on him."

The person who makes the covenant is described as "the ruler who will come" (v. 26) whose people—the Romans—earlier destroyed Jerusalem in A.D. 70. He is, therefore, connected with them because he is the Roman ruler. Obviously, the covenant is an attempt to bring peace to the Middle East, but a sudden change emerges in the middle of that seven years.

THE GREAT TRIBULATION

As the Scriptures indicate in Revelation 13:7, the ruler, who is the Antichrist, takes control of the whole earth, begins the Great Tribulation, and, as ruler, persecutes Israel, desecrating their temple and putting an end to the sacrifices, much as Hitler persecuted the Jews in Germany. This event is referred to again in Daniel 12:11–12, which refers to the abolition of the sacrifice, the desecration of the temple, and the emergence of the period of 1,335 days, which is the time between the second coming of Christ and the beginning of the millennial kingdom. In this period of judgment, the situation will be used to prepare the way for the rule of Christ on earth.

Putting all of these facts together makes the probable emergence of a United States of Europe in the immediate future highly significant in prophecy and a definite token of the fact that the Rapture of the church could be very soon. As our world situation cannot remain in this present order very long and is rapidly changing, it would seem that the Rapture of the church must occur before too many other changes take place. The situation today is exactly in keeping with Scripture if the Rapture will occur soon.

CHAPTER 5

ISRAEL IN THE NEW MILLENNIUM

In terms of extended passages in the Bible, few subjects are treated more extensively than prophecy concerning Israel. This fact makes it all the more remarkable that such confusion exists about prophecy concerning Israel. As in other prophetic problems, the difficulties stem once again from the fact that many people do not take prophecy literally. An important aspect of this is the fulfillment of the Abrahamic covenant, previously discussed in chapter 1.

THE PROMISED LAND

Israel has already demonstrated literal fulfillment of prophecy concerning their movement from the Promised Land to Egypt; in the Exodus, their return to the Promised Land; in the Assyrian captivity of the ten tribes; and ultimately in the Babylonian captivity of the two remaining tribes. In all of these instances, prophecy has been fulfilled literally.

One of the major problems is the question of the Promised Land that we discussed earlier. Part of the Abrahamic covenant was God's revelation to Abraham of the promise and prophecy that "to your offspring I will give this land" (Gen. 12:7). With absolutely no evidence or proof in support, opponents of premillennialism have declared that "the land" is merely a reference to heaven. In fact, not one verse in the Old Testament uses the word *land* in reference to the eternal state.

Under the influence of nineteenth-century postmillennialism, the concept of the land's being heaven became very popular in both hymnology and exegesis. Common in their hymnology is the idea, again with no scriptural support, that the Jordan River is a type of the death of the believer. This view leads to the idea that at a Christian's death, he is received into the Promised Land and in a nonliteral way fulfills the promise of a millennial kingdom on earth.

Typology is not a basis for scriptural doctrine, but if typology is used, the proper interpretation is that the Jordan River is a type of the death of Christ, not the death of a believer. Through His death on the cross, it is possible for a Christian to go into the area of a life of faith, our present life, where in a spiritual sense God allows Christians to claim by faith every foot of the Christian experience that is possible for them. Our present experience as Christians is typical of Israel's experience in the Promised Land—with its successes and failures, and sins and shortcomings, none of which harmonize with the picture of heaven.

The wrong doctrine of the church's fulfilling the promise of the Millennium is a major departure from literal interpretation. The question of Israel's inheritance of the Promised Land is repeated in so many hundreds of passages that it is mind boggling that interpreters of the Bible can ignore it. It is the main theme of the major prophets and the minor prophets, and Israel is constantly asking questions of when they will possess the Promised Land.

ISRAEL'S CURRENT POSSESSION OF THE LAND

In history, it is obvious that while the Jews have been in and out of the Promised Land, they do not now permanently possess it. Prophetically significant is the fact that after the destruction of Jerusalem in A.D. 70, they were scattered worldwide as prophesied in Deuteronomy 28:64–68:

> Then the LORD will scatter you among all nations, from one end of the earth to the other. There you will worship other gods—gods of wood and stone, which neither you nor your fathers have known. Among those nations you will find no repose, no resting place for the sole of your foot. There the LORD will give you an anxious mind, eyes weary with longing, and a despairing heart. You will live in constant suspense, filled with dread both night and day, never sure of your life. In the morning you will say, "If only it were evening!" and in the evening, "If only it were morning!"—because of the terror that will fill your hearts and the sights that your eyes will see. The LORD will send you back in ships to Egypt on a journey I said you should never make again. There you will offer yourselves for sale to your enemies as male and female slaves, but no one will buy you.

A portion of the Jewish population of the world, now numbering millions, is back in Israel and is organized as a political state. Prophecy indicates that this return would be in unbelief, as far as Jesus Christ is concerned, and very few Christian Jews are in the Holy Land today. The prophetic purpose of their being there, however, is to make possible the covenant of Daniel 9:27, the seven-year covenant made by the Antichrist that climaxes at the second coming of Christ. It is impossible to have a covenant with a people that are not politically organized but Israel is now organized as a political state, thus making the covenant possible.

ISRAEL IN THE GREAT TRIBULATION

This is the first phase of the ultimate regathering of Israel, but, as Matthew 24:15–22 reveals, at the beginning of the Great Tribulation, Israel will find it necessary to avoid the persecution of the Antichrist by fleeing to the mountains of Judea:

> So when you see standing in the holy place "the abomination that causes desolation," spoken of through the prophet Daniel—let the reader understand—then let those who are in Judea flee to the mountains. Let no one on the roof of his house go down to take anything out of the house. Let no one in the field go back to get his cloak. How dreadful it will be in those days for pregnant women and nursing mothers! Pray that your flight will not take place in winter or on the Sabbath. For then there will be great distress, unequaled from the beginning of the world until now—and never to be equaled again. If those days had not been cut short, no one would survive, but for the sake of the elect those days will be shortened.

This event is an incident of considerable prophetic importance because it implies that the current occupation of Israel in the Holy Land will continue until the beginning of the Great Tribulation, a time that, according to pretribulational interpretation, will be after the Rapture of the church. In other words, the prediction of some prophecy interpreters that Israel will be driven out of the land by the Palestinians before the Rapture is not supportable by this Scripture reference. Also clear is that the current occupation of Israel in the Holy Land is not the permanent occupation that is promised to Abraham and the prophets.

During the time of the Tribulation preceding the Second Coming, Israel will suffer greatly at the hands of the Antichrist, and many catastrophes will affect the entire population. According to Zechariah 13:8, two-thirds of the Israelites in the land will perish. Only one-third will survive until the Second Coming.

ISRAEL AT THE SECOND COMING

The Second Coming will occur on the very day that there will be house-to-house fighting in Jerusalem. Zechariah 14:1–6 indicates that in the final world war, at the second coming of Christ, the armies that have been fighting each other for power will unite to oppose the army of heaven, which is why Satan has assembled the various armies (Rev. 16:13–14).

As Revelation 19:15 indicates, a word from Christ destroys them all, as detailed in Revelation 19:17–21. It will be an awful slaughter of multiplied millions of men and beasts assembled to fight it out for power but now united in opposition to the army of heaven. It is in connection with the second coming of Christ that Israel comes to the fulfillment of their promises concerning the Promised Land. The Scriptures are both abundant and very specific in declaring that Israel will be regathered in the last days.

Ezekiel 20:33–38 predicts clearly Israel's final regathering at the Second Coming, the purging of the unsaved, and the placing of the saved in the Promised Land.

Jeremiah 30:5–11 predicts that Israel will survive the Tribulation.

> This is what the LORD says: "Cries of fear are heard—terror, not peace. Ask and see: Can a man bear children? Then why do I see every strong man with his hands on his stomach like a woman in labor, every face turned deathly pale? How awful that day will be! None will be like it. It will be a time of trouble for Jacob, but he will be saved out of it.
>
> "In that day," declares the LORD Almighty, "I will break the yoke off their necks and will tear off their bonds; no longer will foreigners enslave them. Instead, they will serve the LORD their God and David their king, whom I will raise up for them.
>
> "So do not fear, O Jacob my servant; do not be dismayed, O Israel," declares the LORD. "I will surely save you out of a distant place, your descendants from the land of their exile. Jacob will again have peace and security, and no one will make him afraid. I am with you and will save you," declares the LORD. "Though I completely destroy all the nations among which I scatter you, I will not completely destroy you. I will discipline you but only with justice; I will not let you go entirely unpunished."

David their king will be resurrected and they will serve the Lord after being regathered (Ezek. 34:23–24; 37:24–25). Jeremiah 31 is another graphic prophecy concerning their being gathered from all over the world to be under the rule of Jesus Christ in the millennial kingdom:

> This is what the LORD Almighty, the God of Israel, says: "When I bring them back from captivity, the people in the land of Judah and in its towns will once again use these words: 'The LORD bless you, O righteous dwelling,

> O sacred mountain.' People will live together in Judah and all its towns—farmers and those who move about with their flocks." (vv. 23–24)

Israel will also be treated graciously, as indicated in the new covenant of Jeremiah 31:31–37. Verses 33–34 summarize this treatment thus:

> "This is the covenant I will make with the house of Israel after that time," declares the LORD. "I will put my law in their minds and write it on their hearts. I will be their God, and they will be my people. No longer will a man teach his neighbor, or a man his brother, saying, 'Know the LORD,' because they will all know me, from the least of them to the greatest," declares the LORD.

ISRAEL'S FINAL REGATHERING

The details of these prophecies are confirmed in Ezekiel 39:25–29, which predicts that Israel will be regathered from all over the world and that unbelievers will be purged out, but that righteous Israel—apparently those Jews who have accepted Christ as Savior—will be brought into the land that Abram was promised. Ezekiel 39:25–29 states specifically that all of the Jews will be gathered and none will be allowed to be dispersed in the entire world.

Ezekiel 47:13–48:29 divides the land into twelve parcels, with a tribe assigned to each parcel. Israel will thus possess the Promised Land, in keeping with the promise to Abraham, until the earth is destroyed at the end of the millennial kingdom. Ezekiel closes with a description of the city of Jerusalem (48:30–35).

In contemplating the changes that undoubtedly will take

place in the new millennium, the fact becomes increasingly clear that the present state of Israel in the Holy Land is exactly what one would expect if the Rapture is about to take place. It is also, from a human standpoint, necessary to recognize that the status quo of Israel and the Palestinians is very unstable and cannot continue in this state indefinitely.

From a human standpoint, apart from Scripture, that the Palestinians ultimately will prevail and secure their goal of making Jerusalem their capital city and driving out the Jews would seem probable. This view is supported by the various forms of worldwide anti-Semitism today. Only the Bible, with its chart of future events that picture Israel still in their present land until the beginning of the Great Tribulation, gives the viewpoint that Palestinian triumph will be delayed until that time.

Although the church is not Israel, the sequence of Israel's prophetic fulfillment is such that if God is now dealing once again with Israel after no prophetic progress has been evident since Pentecost, it would seem that the time for the church in the present age is about over, and we can reasonably expect the Rapture to occur any day. The rapid changes that characterized the end of the twentieth century undoubtedly will continue into the new millennium, and what has been revealed would support an early fulfillment of the Rapture.

ISRAEL'S PLACE IN THE MILLENNIUM

The future of Israel is an important part of the doctrine of the Millennium that will be considered later. In general, however, once Israel is reassembled and installed in their land at the second coming of Christ, they will enjoy the blessings of being a special nation in God's plan, a special blessing throughout the thousand-year reign of Christ.

As will be brought out in the discussion of the Millennium, Christ is going to reign in Jerusalem, Israel, and over the entire world. The Scriptures indicate the Millennium to be a time of unusual spiritual blessing that God graciously brings upon Israel, not because they deserve it, but because He is the God of grace, fulfilling the new covenant of Jeremiah 31.

At the beginning of the Millennium, only believers will be allowed in this period. As the Millennium progresses, no doubt there will be a growing group of unbelievers, as there will be in the gentile world, which will be judged at the conclusion of the thousand-year kingdom described in Revelation 20:8–9.

As will be brought out in the discussion of the new heavens and the new earth following the millennial kingdom, Israel will have a prominent place in the eternal plan of God, as indicated by their names on the twelve gates of the city and the fact that God has throughout history recognized them as a people who are specially blest.

The New Jerusalem will include the saints of all ages, but each will retain the identity derived from his historical background. Israel will remain Israel and thereby be distinguished from both the church and the saints of gentile nations.

CHAPTER 6

THE ANTICHRIST AND THE COMING WORLD GOVERNMENT

In the great conflict between God and Satan, which has characterized the entire history of the world, God clearly has permitted Satan to rebel against and oppose Him and, in many respects, to be temporarily successful. Satan's program as a whole is one of imitation of and opposition to the work of God. In the revelation of Satan's downfall in Isaiah 14:12–15, he indicates his original sin when he says, "I will make myself like the Most High" (v. 12). We find a further description of Satan's downfall in Ezekiel 28:12–15. God, however, permits Satan to have great power and to oppose Him throughout history, always, however, within the limits of God's will. Accordingly, we can expect Satan in every way to try to imitate God's program. This imitation becomes especially evident in prophecy when Satan raises up a human individual to be the Antichrist.

The Bible never calls this character the Antichrist. The term *antichrist* is mentioned four times in the New Testament, indicating in human history that there will be many called antichrists (1 John 2:18, 23; 4:3; 2 John 7). The use of the prefix *anti-* indicates that this individual will be against Christ and also a substitute for Christ. Accordingly, the term *antichrist* is used as a synonym for the man of lawlessness and other titles for the Antichrist that appear in the Scriptures.

THE INTRODUCTION OF THE ANTICHRIST IN PROPHECY

Because the Antichrist is part of the satanic purpose to imitate Jesus Christ, that he should be involved in the final history of the four world empires of Daniel is only natural.

As was mentioned earlier, the four empires have been fulfilled in history in Babylon, Medo-Persia, Greece, and Rome. With all of the prophecies concerning these empires having been fulfilled (except for the latter stage of the Roman Empire), the last days of the Roman Empire will be in the form of the ten-nation league in the revival of the Roman Empire in the end times. The ten horns of the Beast are said to be ten kingdoms, a political union of nations from a portion of the ancient Roman Empire (Dan. 7:24).

The Antichrist was introduced in Daniel 7:8: "While I was thinking about the horns, there before me was another horn, a little one, which came up among them; and three of the first horns were uprooted before it. This horn had eyes like the eyes of a man and a mouth that spoke boastfully."

The Antichrist is depicted as a little horn, an eleventh horn, that uproots three of the ten horns (nations) and then apparently gains control of all ten nations. The eleventh horn is obviously an individual of great political power who becomes the head of the ten-nation group. This event becomes very significant in determining when the Antichrist will appear and be identifiable and provides the main facts concerning the end times.

Scripture does not indicate the exact time of the formation of the ten nations. The Rapture itself does not have any signs, but it is described as occurring in a certain historical context, and the ten-nation group is a part of that context. The ten nations will no doubt be formed either before or right after the Rapture. The conquering of the ten nations, however, occurs after the Rapture, as it involves the identification of the Antichrist which will not occur until after the Rapture. The identification of the Antichrist is at the beginning of the Day of the Lord and will make clear that the Day of the Lord has begun in its major events. This will be confirmed by the declaration that there will be a restrainer, “the one who now holds it back will continue to do so until he is taken out of the way” (2 Thess. 2:7), which involves the Rapture of the church and the removal of the Holy Spirit from indwelling the saints. The situation with the Holy Spirit returns to what it was before Pentecost.

The national connection of the Antichrist has been the subject of considerable speculation. The Bible seems to identify him only as a Roman, which means that he has to originate from one of the Roman Empire nations. Beyond this, the Scriptures do not give us specific information, although some obscure references are sometimes cited, trying to prove that he belongs to one or more countries. The fact to be remembered is that the national origin is not important, except that he apparently arises from a nation in the former Roman Empire. His racial connection is not important; his political power is the main subject of biblical revelation.

THE SEVEN-YEAR COVENANT OF THE ANTICHRIST

Once the Antichrist gains control of the ten countries, he is in a position of power and is able to execute that to which Daniel refers in Daniel 9:27, the last seven years of Israel’s prophetic future before the Second Coming. Daniel 9:24–27 outlines the broad scope of Israel’s prophetic future. Of the 490 years involved in this prophecy, 483 years are fulfilled by the time of the death of Christ referred to in verse 26: "the Anointed One will be cut off and will have nothing." The last seven years of this 490 years, which climaxes at the Second Coming, is still future and has, of course, never been fulfilled, as is demonstrated by the fact that the Second Coming has not been fulfilled. This passage gives chronology that is specific at that time concerning God's plan for the end times.

Daniel 9:27 indicates that in the middle of the seven years will come a sudden change: "In the middle of the 'seven' he will put an end to sacrifice and offering. And . . . he will set up an abomination that causes desolation, until the end that is decreed is poured out on him."

The Antichrist, of course, will have identification when he makes that seven-year covenant, and additional identification is revealed in the middle of the seven years, when he takes over and assumes power over the whole world. Daniel 7:23 predicts that he will "devour the whole earth, trampling it down and crushing it."

In Daniel 8, Antiochus Epiphanes, the ruler of Syria (175–164 B.C.), in many ways anticipated the character and work of the Antichrist. He desecrated the temple and set himself up as God. Before eventually dying of natural causes, Antiochus killed thousands of Jews, trying to impose pagan religion upon them. But even before his death, the temple was restored and the Jewish faith was renewed. Because Antiochus in many respects is an antichrist, some people think that Daniel 8:23–25 is a specific prophecy of the Antichrist. It is more probable that it is a description of Antiochus Epiphanes, who is an amazing illustration of what the Antichrist will do.

The Antichrist appears again in prophecy in Daniel 11:36–45: "The king will do as he pleases. He will exalt and magnify himself above every god and will say unheard-of things against the God of gods" (v. 36).

He is further described in verse 37: "He will show no regard for the gods [Elohim] of his fathers or for the one desired by women, nor will he regard any god, but will exalt himself above them all." Interpreters have had difficulties in regard to the expression "he will show no regard for the gods of his fathers," and some of them have taken it to mean that he is a renegade Jew. However, the Scriptures here use the Hebrew word *Elohim* for God, which is a general word, not *Jehovah* or *Yahweh* ("Lord"), which is the normal expression for the God of Israel. The Scriptures seem to go out of the way to indicate that he is not a Jew but rather the final ruler of the Gentiles who claims deity.

He is further described as having no regard "for the one desired by women" (v. 37). Many explanations of this phrase have been given, probably the best of which is that he is disregarding the desire that women have to be the mother of Messiah. In other words, he disposes of the whole messianic concept that Jesus is the Messiah of Israel.

We find further description of him in verse 37: "nor will he regard any god," indicating that he will "exalt himself above all of them" (and, as 2 Thess. 2:4 mentions, proclaim himself to be God). Actually, he is an atheist empowered by Satan.

The Antichrist is further described as one who "will honor a god of fortresses" (Dan. 11:38). This statement seems to indicate that he recognizes the power of war and the uses of gold, silver, and other wealth to enable him to wage war. Daniel 11 goes on to describe the Battle of Armageddon, in which the armies fight back and forth across the land of Israel in their efforts to establish themselves politically. In the midst of this war the second coming of Christ will occur, and the armies on earth will forget their differences and unite to fight the heavenly army.

The Second Coming occurs 1,260 days (forty-two months)

after the beginning of the Great Tribulation. The destruction of the Antichrist and his army seems to take thirty days after the Second Coming, and the thirty days are added to the 1,260 days to make the 1,290 days of Daniel 12:11. Another forty-five days are added to make the 1,335 days of Daniel 12:12, which is accompanied by the judgment of the nations (Matt. 25:31–46) and Israel (Ezek. 20:33–38). Involved also are the resurrections of the Old Testament saints (Dan. 12:1–2) and the martyred dead of the Tribulation (Rev. 20:4–6). The millennial kingdom will begin after all of these major events have been fulfilled.

The exact chronology of the end times has been subject to incorrect interpretation. As 2 Thessalonians 2:1–12 indicates, the Man of Sin, the Antichrist, is fully revealed at the middle of these last seven years before the Second Coming. When all of the Scriptures are applied to the situation, it becomes clear that he is identified when he conquers the ten nations of the revived Roman Empire more than seven years before the Second Coming. In the events that follow, he continues to be identified as the one who makes the covenant (Dan. 9:27). When he assumes the role of world dictator and claims to be God at the middle of the last seven years, his identification is complete, thus fulfilling 2 Thessalonians 2:3, when the full events "come" at the beginning of the Great Tribulation.

A major New Testament passage concerning the Antichrist is Revelation 13, a chapter that interrupts the prophetic program of the book of Revelation to speak of two principal characters, that is, the Beast and the False Prophet, referring to the Antichrist and his assistant as described in this chapter.

The background is again the revived Roman Empire, which has been conquered by the Antichrist, as stated in Revelation 13:1: "And I saw a beast coming out of the sea. He had ten horns and seven heads, with ten crowns on his horns, and on each head a blasphemous name." He is described as one who continues the political power of the three preceding empires in this final revival of the Roman Empire. We learn also that "the dragon gave the Beast his power and his throne and great authority" (v. 2). In Revelation 12:3, 7–9, the Dragon is identified as Satan.

One of the mysteries of the Antichrist is found in Revelation 13:3: "One of the heads of the beast seemed to have had a fatal wound, but the fatal wound had been healed. The whole world was astonished and followed the beast." Some people have taught that the Antichrist died and will be resurrected, and, on that basis, they have developed a whole series of suggestions as to how someone from the past (such as Judas Iscariot, Nero, or another person) will be resurrected to be the Antichrist. A flaw in this argument, however, is that Satan does not have the power to resurrect anyone from the dead.

Of the several other explanations given to this passage, the most probable is that the Antichrist suffers an assassination attempt and receives a wound that normally would be fatal. Satan, however, has the power to heal, and apparently the seemingly fatal wound is healed, giving the Antichrist the character of being supernatural and leading to his worship as indicated in Revelation 13:4: "Men worshiped the dragon because he had given authority to the beast, and they also worshiped the beast and asked, 'Who is like the beast? Who can make war against him?'"

Revelation 13:5 indicates that the extent of his worldwide reign is forty-two months: "The beast was given a mouth to utter proud words and blasphemies and to exercise his authority for forty-two months." This period is equivalent to the Great Tribulation, mentioned in Daniel and by Christ and also earlier in Revelation (7:14). It consists of 42 months of 30 days each, 1,260 days in all. The Antichrist is allowed to blaspheme

God and continue for the 42 months of rule over the world and martyr thousands of those who come to Christ at that time. "He was given power to make war against the saints and to conquer them. And he was given authority over every tribe, people, language and nation" (13:7).

We find a second character associated with him in Revelation 13:11–17, which refers to "another beast coming out of the earth" (v. 11). In contrast to the Antichrist, with his political character claiming to be God, this person is an associate of a more religious character and his work is to cause people to worship the Antichrist. This passage reveals that he is to have great power and is one who performs miraculous signs.

In Revelation 13:11–13, John recorded the following:

> Then I saw another beast, coming out of the earth. He had two horns like a lamb, but he spoke like a dragon. He exercised all the authority of the first beast on his behalf, and made the earth and its inhabitants worship the first beast, whose fatal wound had been healed. And he performed great and miraculous signs, even causing fire to come down from heaven to earth in full view of men.

In his power to perform miracles, he creates the image of a beast and apparently deceives people by giving it the appearance of life:

> Because of the signs he was given power to do on behalf of the first beast, he deceived the inhabitants of the earth. He ordered them to set up an image in honor of the beast who was wounded by the sword and yet lived. He was given power to give breath to the image of the first beast, so that it could speak and cause all who refused to worship the image to be killed. (vv. 14–15)

This passage also introduces the situation in which he forces people to worship the image and they are unable to buy or sell unless they do, as is described in Revelation 13:16–17: "He also forced everyone, small and great, rich and poor, free and slave, to receive a mark on his right hand or on his forehead, so that no one could buy or sell unless he had the mark, which is the name of the beast or the number of his name."

The situation is such that he requires people who want to buy or sell any product to have a mark on their foreheads or on their hands, indicating that they are worshiping the Antichrist. This requirement puts any believer in Christ under terrific pressure to submit, acknowledging that the Beast is God.

A final problem exists in that the number of the Beast is given. Revelation 13:17–18 states, ". . . so that no one could buy or sell unless he had the mark, which is the name of the beast or the number of his name. This calls for wisdom. If anyone has insight, let him calculate the number of the Beast, for it is man's number. His number is 666."

The question, of course, is what "666" means. Endless speculation exists, and this question is frequently treated at length in commentaries on the book of Revelation. In many languages, letters also have numerical meanings. In Latin, for instance, a *V* is a five, an *X* is a ten, a *C* is one hundred, and an *M* is one thousand. Letters in Hebrew and Greek also have numerical significance.

Accordingly, people have made many attempts to analyze the names of the historical characters of the past and reduce the letters of their names to their numerical equivalents. One familiar attempt concerns Kaesar Nero, spelled Kaisar Neron, using Hebrew endings in this analysis of Nero's name. The *K* is considered to equal one hundred, *S* equals sixty, *R* equals two hundred, *N* equals fifty, *R* equals two hundred, *O* equals six, and *N* equals fifty. The numerical value of the name adds up to

666. Almost endless speculation continues, and the same method is used to analyze all kinds of other names.

The many attempts to identify the Beast illustrates that none of the methods being used is right. As a matter of fact, the Man of Sin cannot be identified until after the Rapture, and then it would refer to a future or present individual and not to a personality from history.

The number 666 might reflect the humanity of man in that it is short of the perfect number, 777. God, in giving him that number, acknowledges his prominence and temporary power but is demonstrating that, in spite of his spectacular and miraculous signs, he is only a man.

It is possible that at the time when all of these events occur, further insight as to what all of this means will be given. Fortunately, none of this affects our Christian hope, the blessing of the Rapture of the church or the nature of our salvation. These events will occur only while Christians are in heaven.

The Antichrist, of course, is involved in the great struggle at the time of the second coming of Christ. When Christ returns and performs His judgments on the world, however, one thing that will occur is that the Beast and the False Prophet will be cast into the lake of fire, as stated in Revelation 19:20:

> But the beast was captured, and with him the false prophet who had performed the miraculous signs on his behalf. With these signs he had deluded those who had received the mark of the beast and worshiped his image. The two of them were thrown alive into the fiery lake of burning sulfur.

Subsequent to this event, Satan will be bound for a thousand years. At the end of the Millennium, he, too, will join the Beast and the False Prophet in the lake of fire (20:10). In the end, God is triumphant.

CHAPTER 7

THE IMPENDING DAY OF THE LORD

The general character of the Day of the Lord is introduced in the study of the timing of the Rapture in 1 Thessalonians 5. The Day of the Lord begins when the Rapture occurs, even though the major events of the Day of the Lord will occur much later. If the Rapture itself is imminent, then the Day of the Lord, with all of its dramatic features, is also pending and could begin at any time.

The Day of the Lord is a familiar term in the Old Testament when God dealt with Israel in judgment. When they strayed from Him, He would bring in an opposing army or would impose drought or some other disaster upon them to bring them back to the proper worship of God. Such a time of judgment might be relatively short, or it could be long.

The book of Joel is largely devoted to the subject of the Day of the Lord with prophecies that have been fulfilled and are scheduled to be fulfilled in the future. Joel 1:15–18 and 2:1–2 describe the Day of the Lord as it is experienced in the Old Testament:

> Alas for that day! For the day of the LORD is near; it will come like destruction from the Almighty. Has not

> the food been cut off before our very eyes—joy and gladness from the house of our God? The seeds are shriveled beneath the clods. The storehouses are in ruins, the granaries have been broken down, for the grain has dried up. How the cattle moan! The herds mill about because they have no pasture; even the flocks of sheep are suffering. . . .
>
> For the day of the LORD is coming. It is close at hand—a day of darkness and gloom, a day of clouds and blackness.

Some of these prophecies had partial fulfillment in the Old Testament. The Day of the Lord, as described in Joel, goes far beyond anything that Israel had ever experienced. Joel 2:30–32 states,

> I will show wonders in the heavens and on the earth, blood and fire and billows of smoke. The sun will be turned to darkness and the moon to blood before the coming of the great and dreadful day of the LORD. And everyone who calls on the name of the LORD will be saved; for on Mount Zion and in Jerusalem there will be deliverance, as the LORD has said, among the survivors whom the LORD calls.

Isaiah 13:9–16 likewise predicts the details:

> See, the day of the LORD is coming—a cruel day, with wrath and fierce anger—to make the land desolate and destroy the sinners within it. The stars of heaven and their constellations will not show their light. The rising sun will be darkened and the moon will not give its light. I will punish the world for its evil, the wicked for

> their sins. I will put an end to the arrogance of the haughty and will humble the pride of the ruthless. I will make man scarcer than pure gold, more rare than the gold of Ophir. Therefore I will make the heavens tremble; and the earth will shake from its place at the wrath of the LORD Almighty, in the day of his burning anger. Like a hunted gazelle, like sheep without a shepherd, each will return to his own people, each will flee to his native land. Whoever is captured will be thrust through; all who are caught will fall by the sword. Their infants will be dashed to pieces before their eyes; their houses will be looted and their wives ravished.

As the Day of the Lord includes the Millennium, the predictions of the Day of the Lord also describe the earth's being renewed, as in Joel 2:18–27. Many other passages about the Day of the Lord are found in the Old Testament (Isa. 2:12–21; 16:9–16; 34:1–8; Joel 3:9–12; Amos 5:18–27; Obad. 15–17; Zeph. 1:7–18).

In the New Testament definition of the Day of the Lord, however, it becomes apparent that it will be a major chronological period, characterized by immediate judgment of sin and rebellion in one way or another, in contrast to the present age of grace.

THE DAY OF THE LORD IN 1 THESSALONIANS

First Thessalonians 5 discusses, immediately after the revelation of the Rapture in chapter 4, the time of the Rapture. Verse 1 states, "Now, brothers, about times and dates we do not need to write to you, for you know very well that the day of the Lord will come like a thief in the night."

According to 1 Thessalonians 5:3–4, the Day of the Lord

is a time of sudden disaster: "While people are saying, 'Peace and safety,' destruction will come on them suddenly, as labor pains on a pregnant woman, and they will not escape. But you, brothers, are not in darkness so that this day should surprise you like a thief." This time of sudden destruction describes very accurately the Great Tribulation.

This contrast between the Tribulation and the age of grace is brought out in that the Day of the Lord is actually a time of spiritual night for unbelievers in contrast to the day of grace in which believers are living today. As 1 Thessalonians 5:5 states, "You are all sons of the light and sons of the day. We do not belong to the night or to the darkness." This verse teaches that the church is in a different time period that precedes the Day of the Lord, and this view is confirmed by 1 Thessalonians 5:9: "For God did not appoint us to suffer wrath but to receive salvation through our Lord Jesus Christ." Our appointment is a period of grace, and their appointment is of a period of suffering, tribulation, and affliction.

THE DAY OF THE LORD AS A DIVISION OF PROPHETIC HISTORY

Although a number of dispensations are taught in the Old Testament, the major contribution is the dispensation of the Law under the Mosaic code when Israel was given more than six hundred laws to govern their behavior. This code constituted a major revelation of God's dealing with Israel and the human race before New Testament times.

In the present age, the church is enjoying what is known as the age of grace, in which God is not dealing directly with human sin. The subject of grace as a matter of salvation is introduced plainly in the New Testament not only with the coming of Christ but also as a rule of life in which God deals graciously with those who trust Him, reckoning to them the righteousness of Christ. The transition from the Law of Moses to the day of grace is briefly stated in John 1:17: “For the law was given through Moses; grace and truth came through Jesus Christ.” So far in history, the dispensation of the Law and the present dispensation of grace constitute the major chronological divisions of God’s dealings with man.

The third and final chronological division of history and prophecy is designated the Day of the Lord, including the whole period following the Rapture of the church and continuing throughout the whole millennial kingdom, a period of more than a thousand years. The period is characterized by God’s dealing directly with human sin as in the tribulation period leading up to the Second Coming. In the millennial kingdom, He rules with a rod of iron and deals with flagrant sin immediately. As the opening events of the Day of the Lord cover a multitude of prophetic details, one is wise to consider it under three major subdivisions.

1. The Day of the Lord as a Period of Preparation

As was pointed out earlier, the Day of the Lord as a time period begins at the Rapture, but its major prophetic events are fulfilled later. Accordingly, there is a time period before the tremendous earth-shaking event occurs in the fulfillment of prophecy leading up to the second coming of Christ. As was mentioned earlier, this period of preparation ushers in the revival of the Roman Empire. The Antichrist will gain control of all ten countries, as Daniel 7 indicated. Scripture does not reveal the length of the period of preparation, but by implication it is relatively short, allowing the Antichrist to consolidate his gains and become the outstanding political leader of the end times.

2. *The Day of the Lord as a Period of Peace*

Daniel 9:27 indicates that once the Antichrist gains a place of power, he enters into a seven-year peace treaty that climaxes chronologically at the second coming of Christ.

Daniel 9:24–27 is a major prophecy concerning the 490 years of Israel's prophetic future. The last seven years are mentioned in verse 27: "He will confirm a covenant with many for one 'seven.' In the middle of the 'seven' he will put an end to sacrifice and offering. And on a wing of the temple he will set up an abomination that causes desolation, until the end that is decreed is poured out on him."

The one who makes the covenant, as described in verse 27, is the Antichrist, related as the Roman ruler, whose people earlier destroyed Jerusalem. The seven-year peace treaty is interrupted at midpoint when he takes over as world governor and stops the sacrifices and offerings in the temple that has been built.

The original purpose of the covenant is to bring peace to the Middle East, especially in the relationship between Israel and the other nations. Actually, from the point of the view of the Antichrist, it is a period during which he wants to consolidate his political power.

A major feature of the first three and a half years of the seven years is an invasion of the land of Israel from the north that is described in detail in Ezekiel 38–39. In these two chapters, six nations undertake an invasion of the land of Israel, namely, Magog, Persia, Cush, Put, Gomer, and Beth Togarmah (38:1–6).

Interpreters of this passage have arrived at widely different conclusions concerning when this invasion will take place. Because of the reference to Gog and Magog in Revelation 20:7, some people want to identify it as the final struggle at the end of the millennial kingdom. But good reasons exist for rejecting this view because the prophecy of Ezekiel 38–39 indicates that, unlike the description given in Revelation, life goes on for a considerable period. Other explanations seem more appropriate for the use of the terms *Gog* and *Magog*.

Some interpreters want to place the invasion at the beginning of the millennial kingdom, but because the adult population at that time is composed entirely of Christians, it is doubtful whether any of them would attempt an attack on Israel, and the circumstances do not coincide.

Another possibility is to link the invasion with Armageddon. But a close study of Ezekiel 38–39 demonstrates that this war is cut off at its beginning when armies have reached only the northern part of Israel, which is contrary to the description of Armageddon, in which house-to-house fighting is occurring in Jerusalem on the very day of the Second Coming, as Zechariah 14 states. Only six nations are participating in the war here, in contrast to the number of nations at Armageddon, which includes the majority of the nations of the world.

Although such interpretations are always debatable, it seems best to picture the invasion as occurring within the first three and a half years of the seven-year period, leading up to the second coming of Christ, a time when Israel is at peace, as is described in Ezekiel. The invasion of Israel is pictured as something that God Himself encourages as a means of bringing Israel back to dependence on Him. Ezekiel 38:4 speaks of God on these terms in relation to Magog: "I will turn you around, put hooks in your jaws and bring you out with your whole army—your horses, your horsemen fully armed, and a great horde with large and small shields, all of them brandishing their swords."

Considerable speculation has occurred about the nature of their armor, referred to as shields, and their swords and horses.

Some people have thought that these symbolize that their invasion involves modern weapons but that the description is written in language that would make sense at the time this prophecy was given. As the description continues, however, the weapons of the battle are pictured as wood that is used for kindling. This picture does not fit the idea of weapons of modern warfare.

The Bible itself does not answer these questions, but it is possible that in the end time there will be a peace movement in which the nations of the world will disarm, as far as modern weapons are concerned. Accordingly, airplanes, tanks, and other forms of modern warfare might not exist at that time. If an invasion of Israel becomes suddenly desirable, they would need to arm the invading armies with weapons that are easily made of wood and correspond to the weapons that the enemies against them might have. Although this view does not solve the problem completely, it is best not to speculate at length on matters about which the Bible itself is not clear; rather, we should accept the more important conclusion that this invasion is a disaster for the invaders, as the Scriptures describe.

Some people have attempted to link Meshech and Tubal with portions of Russia, but most scholars do not interpret the passage that way. The country of Magog is located in the southern part of what was formerly the Soviet Union, and the other nations are generally located there, although some of them are more distant from this area. Without going into great detail, one can conclude that this invasion is a sneak attack upon Israel that penetrates her northern border.

Ezekiel 38:10–13 records the thinking of the invaders:

> This is what the Sovereign LORD says: On that day thoughts will come into your mind and you will devise an evil scheme. You will say, "I will invade a land of

> unwalled villages; I will attack a peaceful and unsuspecting people—all of them living without walls and without gates and bars. I will plunder and loot and turn my hand against the resettled ruins and the people gathered from the nations, rich in livestock and goods, living at the center of the land." Sheba and Dedan and the merchants of Tarshish and all her villages will say to you, "Have you come to plunder? Have you gathered your hordes to loot, to carry off silver and gold, to take away livestock and goods and to seize much plunder?"

Noteworthy in this description is the fact that Israel is living in peace and not suspecting an attack, which is very unusual because most of the time Israel is in a controversy with her neighbors and perpetually prepared for attacks. This description seems to point to the first half of that last seven years when Israel is basking in the supposed protection of the Antichrist, who has promised to protect them from their enemies and is prospering financially. It does not fit Israel during the Great Tribulation when they will be fleeing for their lives.

The fact that some of the invaders are described, as in Ezekiel 38:15, as coming from the far north and attacking Israel on its northern borders is significant: "You will come from your place in the far north, you and many nations with you, all of them riding on horses, a great horde, a mighty army." This view is also confirmed in Ezekiel 39:2, which speaks of them as coming from "the far north," apparently indicating the involvement of at least some of the states of the former Soviet Union, which are mostly Islamic and therefore would want to attack Israel.

Because the invasion is unexpected, no time exists for an army to interpose to protect the people of Israel. But as the Scriptures make plain, God Himself intervenes and, in a series of supernatural acts, destroys the invading army.

Earlier, in Ezekiel 38, God indicated that He was going to condemn them:

> This is what the Sovereign LORD says: I am against you, O Gog, chief prince of Meshech and Tubal. I will turn you around, put hooks in your jaws and bring you out with your whole army—your horses, your horsemen fully armed, and a great horde with large and small shields. (vv. 3–4)

In Ezekiel 38:18–23, God reveals His great wrath against them and, in a series of disasters, destroys the invading army. These disasters include a great earthquake (vv. 18–20). Apparently, the armies are disorganized and start fighting each other, as Ezekiel 38:21 indicates: "Every man's sword will be against his brother." In addition, God pours a plague upon them. There is a flood with "torrents of rain" and hailstones and burning sulfur, which implies fire from heaven (v. 22).

In Ezekiel 39:2–6, further destruction of the army occurs. It says that all of the armies will be destroyed, eaten by vultures and wild animals, and that God will also bring fire on Magog's homeland as a judgment. Ezekiel 39:7 states the conclusion: "I will make known my holy name among my people Israel. I will no longer let my holy name be profaned, and the nations will know that I the LORD am the Holy One in Israel."

The climax is a battle in which the armies are totally destroyed. Ezekiel 39:4 describes it thus: "On the mountains of Israel you will fall, you and all your troops and the nations with you." As a result of the battle, many thousands of people are killed; it will take the survivors seven months just to collect the dead bodies and bury them in the land (v. 12), and the debris of the battle in the form of wood will be enough for seven years' use (v. 9).

The fact that the debris will burn for seven years has influenced some interpreters to state that this event occurs more than seven years before the Second Coming. But, of course, seven years of the burning of fuel is not a prophetic event, and they will need fuel in the millennial kingdom as well as before. Accordingly, the amount of fuel being burned does not date the period. The battle probably takes place somewhere toward the end of the first three and a half years, leading up to the Second Coming. Apart from this war, the period seems to be predominantly a time of peace for three and a half years, the first half of the seven years preceding the Second Coming.

3. The Day of the Lord as a Time of Persecution

The attack on Israel by these forces is also an attack on the Antichrist because he is supposed to protect Israel. It is an attempt to challenge his political control. When the attack fails, it will probably result in the Antichrist's being exalted to a position of even greater power and his enemies' destruction. This situation is the platform on which the last three and a half years, leading up to the second coming of Christ, is introduced as the Great Tribulation, the time of unprecedented trouble.

According to Christ, the last three and a half years begins with a very sudden change. Overnight, the Antichrist takes over as ruler of the whole earth, desecrates the temple, and begins the persecution and attempted elimination of the nation Israel. This fact is clearly indicated in Matthew 24:15, where Christ urges the Jews to flee Jerusalem and go to the mountains of Judea to escape their persecutors. Christ described the severe hardships that will occur at that time when people will have to leave their homes with nothing but the clothes on their backs. It will be a difficult time for nursing mothers and pregnant women, as the forces of the Antichrist pursue and destroy them as far as possible. Christ summarizes the situation in Matthew 24:21–22: "For then there will be great distress, unequaled from the beginning of the world until now, and never to be equaled again. If those days had not been cut short, no one would survive, but for the sake of the elect those days will be shortened."

A number of Old Testament passages can be brought to bear upon this aspect of the Day of the Lord (e.g., Deut. 4:26–28; Isa. 2:12–21; 13: 9–16; 34:1–8; Jer. 30:5–7; Dan. 7:23–25; 12:1, 11–12; Joel 1:15–2:11; 2:28–32; 3:9–21; Amos 5:18–20; Obad. 15–17; Zeph. 1:7–18). The book of Revelation, however, provides the major description.

After John, the author of Revelation, is shown the vision of heaven, he is introduced to the scroll that he sees in the hands of Christ (5:6–7). The scroll is a rolled-up parchment that has seals on the edge and that is placed such that, as the scroll is unrolled, the seals are broken successively. Although this picture is presented symbolically, obviously each of these seals represents a major event of the time of the Great Tribulation. Many expositors extend this event over the entire seven years. But obviously the events speak largely of the Great Tribulation period. The first seal introduces a rider on a white horse, which symbolizes victory, that speaks here of the Antichrist, holding a bowl and having a crown but no arrow. Plainly, the Antichrist comes into power as the dictator of the entire earth, not by war peacefully. This power grab occurs at the midpoint of the last seven years before the Second Coming.

War, however, follows because the second seal describes war. The third seal speaks of famine, which is a natural result of war, with a man laboring all day for one quart of wheat, enough for one day's food for a family. Cheaper grain such as barley would provide more food, but there is not enough money left to buy oil and wine, which usually accompanies a meal.

The fourth seal is a devastating judgment. It pictures a pale horse with a rider named Death and Hell, and, according to Revelation 6:8, "They were given power over a fourth of the earth to kill by sword, famine and plague, and by the wild beasts of the earth." Any understanding of this in its ordinary language would lead to the conclusion that nothing like this has ever happened, and the clear statement that a fourth of the world's population would be destroyed makes impossible any concept that the church is going through this time of tribulation, as the posttribulationists teach. The fourth seal, however, is not the end. It is followed by the fifth seal, which speaks of a multitude of martyrs who will be killed because of their faith.

The sixth seal talks about disruption in the heavens, with the moon turning into blood, the stars falling to the earth, and mountains and land being disturbed by an earthquake. The destruction is worldwide and so obvious that the kings of the earth and the leaders hide in the caves, hoping to escape the wrath of God and saying, "'Fall on us and hide us from the face of him who sits on the throne and from the wrath of the Lamb!' For the great day of their wrath has come, who can stand?" (Rev. 6:16–17). This event is clearly the Great Tribulation.

Although this passage is a combination of literal and symbolic revelation, it is very obvious that if the ordinary words of this passage are allowed to carry their normal meaning, they teach a time of trouble such as the world has never experienced. The blessed hope will keep the church from the wrath of God by being fulfilled before this period begins.

The seventh seal, recorded in Revelation 8, introduces a second series of seven that are the content of the seventh seal. Most of the judgments deal with a third of the earth and destroy the earth and the trees; turn the seas into blood; and turn to darkness a third of the stars, the sun, and the moon. This judgment is declared to be only the beginning, as recorded in Revelation 8:7–13. There follows the fifth trumpet, which seems to speak of demonology, although the demons are described as locusts that look like horses. Nothing in our experience enables us to comprehend this scene, but clearly they will torment the people on earth for five months (9:10). This judgment is pronounced as the first of three woes.

The second woe is the release of demons who inflict plagues on the human race with the result that one-third of mankind is killed (9:18). If one takes simply the fourth seal, when one-fourth of the earth is destroyed, and the sixth trumpet of Revelation 9:18, which speaks of one-third being destroyed, it is clear that already in the terrible catastrophes of the end times at least half of the earth will be destroyed. The seventh trumpet that follows reveals another series of seven (11:15–19; 16:1–21).

The bowls of the wrath of God are similar to the trumpet judgments, but in contrast to the trumpets, the bowls seem to extend to the entire world. The first bowl brings terrible sores upon the unsaved. The second bowl turns the seas into blood and destroys shipping with resulting famine. The third bowl destroys water in the streams (Rev. 16:4–7). The fourth bowl changes climates and causes increased heat. Revelation 16:9 says, "They were seared by the intense heat and they cursed the name of God, who had control over these plagues, but they refused to repent and glorify him." It is amazing how often in the book of Revelation—in spite of the demonstration of the power of God and the necessary condemnation of the sins of the human race—that there is still so little evidence of repentance.

The fifth bowl plunges the world into darkness temporarily and causes people to suffer physical pain (vv. 10–11). The sixth bowl is a tremendous further development that describes the Euphrates River as being dried up in preparation for a great military invasion from the east. Whether this drying up is done by divine action or by the dams that have already been built across the Euphrates is immaterial. The point is that the

Euphrates River is not allowed to stand in the way of millions of men crossing from the east to the west to engage in what the Bible calls Armageddon.

Clearly, Satan has inspired the world to follow the Antichrist and to recognize him earlier in the end-time events. Now it declares that the spirits of demons are going to entice the whole world to come to the Holy Land to oppose Christ, as stated in Revelation 16:13–14:

> Then I saw three evil spirits that looked like frogs; they came out of the mouth of the dragon, out of the mouth of the beast and out of the mouth of the false prophet. They are spirits of demons performing miraculous signs, and they go out to the kings of the whole world, to gather them for the battle on the great day of God Almighty.

Scripture states that the nations will gather in a place that is called in the Hebrew tongue Armageddon. This area is Mount Megiddo in northern Israel, which stands at the head of a great valley to the northeast of Jerusalem.

Armageddon is the central marshaling place for the armies. Clear from other Scriptures, such as Daniel 11:40–45, is the fact that this gathering of millions of troops for the great end-time war covers the whole land of Israel, perhaps two hundred miles north and south and from the Mediterranean Sea in the west all of the way to the Euphrates River in the east. In this context, the final bowl of wrath is poured out (Rev. 16:17–21). A severe earthquake will level the cities of the Gentiles but apparently not hurt Israel. Verse 19 declares that the great city is divided into three parts. Some people believe that this refers to Jerusalem, but more probably it refers to Babylon, as described in Revelation 18. Jerusalem is described as remaining intact, although it is under attack in Zechariah 14. The prediction is that "the cities of the nations collapsed" (Rev. 16:19), describing the huge earthquake and its destruction of all buildings in the world.

Simultaneously, islands and mountains disappear, and the destruction is completed by huge hailstones, weighing a hundred pounds each, falling on the earth. If a secular writer was attempting to describe a picture of horror, it would be impossible for him to describe a scene more tremendous than this scene.

When the seventh bowl of wrath is poured out, it brings us chronologically to the second coming of Christ. But other events are also occurring. Revelation 17 describes the world church movement as a harlot riding a scarlet beast. This description apparently portrays the organized church as joining with the Antichrist to conquer the world and martyr the true saints. This event occurs in the first half of the last seven years. Before the chapter ends, however, the ten-nation group destroys the woman to prepare the way for the worship of the Antichrist in the last three and a half years (vv. 16–17).

Chapter 18 describes the city of Babylon as being completely destroyed. Because the description pictures Babylon as a commercial city, some people believe that it will be the capital of the world government of the Great Tribulation and will be greatly rebuilt beyond what exists now. As such, it will fulfill the many prophecies of the Old Testament that picture Babylon's ultimate destruction, which Isaiah predicted but that has not yet occurred:

> Babylon, the jewel of kingdoms, the glory of the Babylonians' pride, will be overthrown by God like Sodom and Gomorrah. She will never be inhabited or lived in through all generations; no Arab will pitch his

> tent there, no shepherd will rest his flocks there. But desert creatures will lie there, jackals will fill her houses; there the owls will dwell, and there the wild goats will leap about. Hyenas will howl in her strongholds, jackals in her luxurious palaces. Her time is at hand, and her days will not be prolonged. (13:19–22)

Likewise, Jeremiah devotes two long chapters (chaps. 50–51) to Babylon's destruction. The tremendous destruction of Babylon is a prelude to the second coming of Christ, which is described in chapter 19.

At the beginning of the twenty-first century, it is clear that if the Rapture occurs the events described herein may well be fulfilled in the early part of this new millennium. Obvious in Scripture is the fact that tremendous impending world events call for individuals to examine their trust in God, their personal salvation, and their manner of life as they seek to serve the Lord.

CHAPTER 8

THE SECOND COMING OF CHRIST

Obviously, inasmuch as the first coming of Christ occupied four Gospels, as well as extensive portions from the Old and New Testaments, the second coming of Christ is likewise a major doctrine. All of the church creeds—whether Roman Catholic, Greek Orthodox, or Protestant—recognize it, stating that Christ is coming again to judge the world. Not surprisingly, therefore, the second coming of Christ is a prominent subject of the Old Testament and the major subject of the last book of the Bible, the book of Revelation.

The term *second coming* is not precisely scriptural. It is based upon many verses, including Hebrews 9:28, which states, "Christ was sacrificed once to take away the sins of many people; and he will appear a second time, not to bear sin, but to bring salvation to those who are waiting for him." In contrast to His first coming—in which He suffered, died on the cross, and rose in triumph before ascending into heaven—the Second Coming has to do with His rule over all of the earth, the subduing of His enemies, and His judgment upon the wicked. It also involves the whole doctrine of the kingdom of God as presented in the Bible.

THE DESCRIPTION OF THE SECOND COMING IN THE OLD TESTAMENT

The most dramatic picture of the Second Coming in the Old Testament is found in the vision that Daniel had of heaven and the return of Christ:

> As I looked, thrones were set in place, and the Ancient of Days took his seat. His clothing was as white as snow; the hair of his head was white like wool. His throne was flaming with fire, and its wheels were all ablaze. A river of fire was flowing, coming out from before him. Thousands upon thousands attended him; ten thousand times ten thousand stood before him. The court was seated, and the books were opened.
>
> Then I continued to watch because of the boastful words the horn was speaking. I kept looking until the beast was slain and its body destroyed and thrown into the blazing fire. (The other beasts had been stripped of their authority, but were allowed to live for a period of time.)
>
> In my vision at night I looked, and there before me was one like a son of man, coming with the clouds of heaven. He approached the Ancient of Days and was led into his presence. He was given authority, glory, and sovereign power; all peoples, nations and men of every language worshiped him. His dominion is an everlasting dominion that will not pass away, and his kingdom is one that will never be destroyed. (7:9–14)

The Second Coming, of course, is implied in every Scripture passage where it speaks of Christ's reigning on earth, of which there are many that support the whole idea that God reigns supreme. Daniel 7:26–27 also summarizes the reign of God at the time of the destruction of the Antichrist at the Second Coming:

> But the court will sit, and his power will be taken away and completely destroyed forever. Then the sovereignty, power, and greatness of the kingdoms under the whole heaven will be handed over to the saints, the people of the Most High. His kingdom will be an everlasting kingdom, and all rulers will worship and obey him.

THE DOCTRINE OF THE KINGDOM

The rule of God over the earth is a frequent subject of Scripture and has many subdivisions. As the Creator, God is omnipotent and obviously controls and rules the entire natural world. This role is described in many passages (e.g., 1 Chron. 29:11–12; Pss. 47:8; 93:1–2; 97:1; 99:1; 146:10; 103:19). Psalm 103:19 is very explicit: "The LORD has established his throne in heaven, and his kingdom rules over all."

One of the interesting stories concerning God's sovereignty is Nebuchadnezzar's own experience with God. When his sanity was restored, he stated,

> Then I praised the Most High; I honored and glorified him who lives forever. His dominion is an eternal dominion; his kingdom endures from generation to generation. All the peoples of the earth are regarded as nothing. He does as he pleases with the powers of heaven and the peoples of the earth. No one can hold back his hand or say to him: "What have you done?" (Dan. 4:34–35)

A major aspect of the doctrine of the kingdom is what is considered a spiritual kingdom, that is, the rule of God over those who believe in Him as God, including all who are saved and the holy angels. In contrast to the universal kingdom, this kingdom involves submission and recognition of God on the behalf of those who exercise their faith. This concept is more clearly revealed in the New Testament than it is in the Old Testament.

The Old Testament also deals at length with the political kingdom of David, often described as a theocratic kingdom; that is, God selected David to be king over the house of Israel. This selection was revealed to David in what is called the Davidic covenant. As recorded in 2 Samuel 7, David had raised the question as to whether he should build a permanent temple for God to replace the tent in which the ark of God remained. Nathan had replied that he should go ahead with it (v. 13). However, the word of the Lord came to Nathan that night with other instructions, as recorded in 2 Samuel 7:5–16:

> Go and tell my servant David, "This is what the LORD says: Are you the one to build me a house to dwell in? I have not dwelt in a house from the day I brought the Israelites up out of Egypt to this day. I have been moving from place to place with a tent as my dwelling. Wherever I have moved with all the Israelites, did I ever say to any of their rulers whom I commanded to shepherd my people Israel, 'Why have you not built me a house of cedar?'"
>
> Now then, tell my servant David, "This is what the LORD Almighty says: I took you from the pasture and from following the flock to be ruler over my people Israel. I have been with you wherever you have gone, and I have cut off all your enemies from before you.

> Now I will make your name great, like the names of the greatest men of the earth. And I will provide a place for my people Israel and will plant them so that they can have a home of their own and no longer be disturbed. Wicked people will not oppress them anymore, as they did at the beginning and have done ever since the time I appointed leaders over my people Israel. I will also give you rest from all your enemies.
>
> "The LORD declares to you that the LORD himself will establish a house for you: When your days are over and you rest with your fathers, I will raise up your offspring to succeed you, who will come from your own body, and I will establish his kingdom. He is the one who will build a house for my Name, and I will establish the throne of his kingdom forever. I will be his father, and he will be my son. When he does wrong, I will punish him with the rod of men, with floggings inflicted by men. But my love will never be taken away from him, as I took it away from Saul, whom I removed from before you. Your house and your kingdom will endure forever before me; your throne will be established forever."

As the Scriptures make plain, David is given a comprehensive statement that his theocratic kingdom will continue forever and that the descendants of David will reign. This statement is commonly interpreted as referring to Jesus Christ as the ultimate person to sit on the throne. Amillenarians try to find this prophecy fulfilled in the present age with Christ sitting on the throne in heaven, but premillenarians regard it as something that will be subject to the second coming of Christ and, in keeping with the prophecy connected with this, pictures Christ ruling over the whole earth.

The Davidic covenant also provided that Solomon would build the temple. There is a fine line drawn in 2 Samuel 7:13, which states, "He is the one who will build a house for my Name, and I will establish the throne of his kingdom forever." Clear here is the fact that Solomon's lineage, which leads us to Joseph in the New Testament, does not sit on the throne forever, and although the promise is that the throne will continue forever, the lineage of Solomon is not included. It is true, of course, that as the promise is given, Solomon lived a long life and was blessed of God. David, by contrast, is promised that not only his throne and kingdom but also his house, which is his lineage, will endure.

In connection with the reestablishment of the Davidic kingdom, David will be resurrected and will be coregent under Christ in His rule over Israel throughout the millennial kingdom. This point is stated in Ezekiel 34:23–24: "I will place over them one shepherd, my servant David, and he will tend them; he will tend them and be their shepherd. I the LORD will be their God, and my servant David will be prince among them. I the LORD have spoken."

A similar thought is contained in Ezekiel 37:24–25:

> My servant David will be king over them, and they will all have one shepherd. They will follow my laws and be careful to keep my decrees. They will live in the land I gave to my servant Jacob, the land where your fathers lived. They and their children and their children's children will live there forever, and David my servant will be their prince forever.

The Davidic kingdom, therefore, will have its ultimate fulfillment in the promise that David and his posterity, including Christ, would reign over the house of Israel forever.

The Old Testament contains many references to both the first and second comings of Christ that, in the Jewish understanding in the gospel period, were understood to be the same coming. But from our modern view, it is clear that the passages referring to the suffering of Christ refer to the first coming, and the passages to His glorious reign to the Second Coming. The triumph of God over Satan and the wicked is introduced in Genesis 3:15, which predicts that the seed of the woman "will crush your head," referring to Satan.

In the many passages dealing with the restoration of Israel, this prophecy is a climax, and the regathering of Israel is related to the Second Coming to restore Israel both politically and spiritually. Many passages in the Psalms speak of Christ as ruling after His Second Coming. The major statement in Psalm 2:9 predicts, "You will rule them with an iron scepter; you will dash them in pieces like pottery" in reference to the nations of the world. On this basis, Psalm 2:12 exhorts, "Kiss the Son" and trust in Him. Other major psalms dealing with the rule of God include Psalms 24, 50, 72, 96, and 110.

Old Testament prophetic books contain many references to Christ's rule at His Second Coming, including Isaiah 11, 12, 65, and 66. The Minor Prophets add their own words, as in Zechariah 2:10–12. Understandably, in light of all of these verses, Israel believed that this prophecy would be fulfilled when Christ came. He would deliver them from their enemies and assert His righteous rule over the earth. But they did not understand the difference between the first and second comings of Christ.

In addition to the universal kingdom of God over the whole world and the kingdom of David, the New Testament reveals a spiritual kingdom that stands in sharp distinction to the other kingdoms. Whereas both the kingdom of David and the kingdom over the whole world include unsaved people, the kingdom of God in the New Testament includes only those who are born again. Although this point was true in the Old Testament to some extent, the full revelation does not come until the New Testament.

In Christ's conversation with Nicodemus, He pointed out that it is necessary to be born again to enter this spiritual kingdom. Christ declared, "I tell you the truth, no one can see the kingdom of God unless he is born again" (John 3:3). This statement was a puzzle to Nicodemus, as he could not understand how a person could be born twice. However, as the Scriptures make clear, Nicodemus was born again and was one of those who ministered to Christ in His burial (19:38–40). All forms of the kingdom—God's rule over the whole earth, God's rule over the House of Israel, and God's rule over His spiritual kingdom—are combined in the millennial kingdom following the Second Coming.

THE SECOND COMING OF CHRIST IN THE NEW TESTAMENT

Throughout the New Testament are many references to both the Rapture and the second coming of Christ. From the Gospels, the references are entirely to the Second Coming, except in John 14. A major statement is found in Matthew 24:3–25:46, with the other Gospels citing similar prophecies (e.g., Mark 13:24–27; Luke 12:35–48; 17:22–37; 18:8; 21:25–28).

As was indicated earlier, the disciples, having ignored the promises concerning His sufferings and death, were laboring under the false belief that Christ would fulfill His Second Coming promises at His first coming, After being with Christ for more than three years, however, and seeing no progress in His reigning over the whole world, they began to have questions.

The disciples had been greatly disturbed by His discourse

on the unbelief of the religious leaders of Israel in Matthew 23 and were bothered by His predictions of coming desolation. So four of the disciples—namely, Peter, Andrew, James, and John, according to Mark 13:3–4—asked Christ about this, as recorded in Matthew 24:3: "'Tell us,' they said, 'when will this happen, and what will be the sign of your coming and of the end of the age?'" In response, Christ delivered a major discourse on the events preceding the Second Coming, as well as on the Second Coming itself, and climaxed the dissertation by making a number of practical applications.

Few passages in Scripture have been more manipulated by interpreters than have Matthew 24 and 25. Each interpreter has attempted to harmonize these chapters with his preconceived ideas, whether premillennial, amillennial, or postmillennial. First, one should observe that in His discourse Christ is not talking about the Rapture, concerning which He had given no previous revelation, but rather about the Second Coming.

In answer to the disciples' question, Christ predicted first that certain general signs would precede the Second Coming. These signs are itemized in Matthew 24:4–14:

> Jesus answered: "Watch out that no one deceives you. For many will come in my name, claiming, 'I am the Christ,' and will deceive many. You will hear of wars and rumors of wars, but see to it that you are not alarmed. Such things must happen, but the end is still to come. Nation will rise against nation, and kingdom against kingdom. There will be famines and earthquakes in various places. All these are the beginning of birth pains.
>
> "Then you will be handed over to be persecuted and put to death, and you will be hated by all nations because of me. At that time many will turn away from

> the faith and will betray and hate each other, and many false prophets will appear and deceive many people. Because of the increase of wickedness, the love of most will grow cold, but he who stands firm to the end will be saved. And this gospel of the kingdom will be preached in the whole world as a testimony to all nations, and then the end will come."

Observe that all of these indications are general signs, things that will occur in the whole present age, and Christ's statement anticipated the course of the last two thousand years.

Beginning in Matthew 24:15, however, He begins to deal with specific things, events that will mark the beginning of the end. As was mentioned earlier, He urged Israel at that time to flee to the mountains of Judea (v. 16). He told them that the signal will be "the abomination that causes desolation" spoken through the prophet Daniel (v. 15). Daniel 9:27 predicted that in the middle of the last seven years leading up to the Second Coming the temple would be desecrated and the sacrifices stopped. Because this event would occur on a specific day, it also becomes a definite sign that the Great Tribulation is beginning and that the world ruler is taking over the entire world. This will precipitate the breaking of his covenant of protection for Israel.

This persecution, which Christ made plain, would be such a time of trouble as had never before occurred and would result in the destruction of the world population unless it were stopped. This fact is stated in Matthew 24:21–22: "For then there will be great distress, unequaled from the beginning of the world until now—and never to be equaled again. If those days had not been cut short, no one would survive, but for the sake of the elect those days will be shortened."

The Second Coming itself will follow these signs. Christ

warns them that they are not to believe that He comes secretly as described in Matthew 24:26. Actually, the Second Coming would be a very visible event, like lightning in the sky. He said, "For as lightning that comes from the east is visible even in the west, so will be the coming of the Son of Man" (v. 27). Christ also described the disturbances in the heavens and the Second Coming itself: "At that time the sign of the Son of Man will appear in the sky, and all the nations of the earth will mourn; they will see the Son of Man coming on the clouds of the sky, with power and great glory" (v. 30). In anticipation of His millennial kingdom, the elect—referring to those who are the chosen of God, whether Jews or Gentiles—will be gathered from both earth and heaven to enter into the millennial kingdom.

In Acts, at the time of the ascension, the angels predicted that He would come back (1:11). Acts 15:16–18 emphasizes the difference between the present age and the future millennial kingdom. James stated the conclusion of Amos 9:11–12 that at the present time the Gentiles are prominent, but in the future David's kingdom will be restored.

Added light is given in the Epistles, such as in Romans 11, which explains gentile prominence in the present age and unfolds Israel's future at the time of the coming of Christ.

The question considered in Romans 9–11 is that of how the gospel and God's purposes relate to Israel. In chapter 11, particularly, the question is raised as to whether Israel has a future. Paul writes,

> I ask then: Did God reject his people? By no means! I am an Israelite myself, a descendant of Abraham, from the tribe of Benjamin. God did not reject his people, whom he foreknew. Don't you not know what the Scripture says in the passage about Elijah—how he appealed to God against Israel: "Lord, they have killed your

> prophets and torn down your altars; I am the only one left, and they are trying to kill me"? And what was God's answer to him? "I have reserved for myself seven thousand who have not bowed the knee to Baal." So, too, at the present time there is a remnant chosen by grace. And if by grace, then it is no longer by works; if it were, grace would no longer be grace. (vv. 1–6)

As chapter 11 unfolds, Paul points out how in the present time Israel is temporarily set aside because of their unbelief. Using the figure of the olive tree, he explains that their branches are broken off temporarily and the Gentiles are grafted in for the blessings of the special age, which is primarily Gentile. Just as the branches of Israel are broken off and the Gentiles are grafted in, however, the time will come when Israel will be grafted in again. This illustration is found in Romans 11:13–24. The chapter concludes with the prediction "and all Israel will be saved," meaning that a remnant of Israel will be delivered from end-time judgment in fulfillment of the Old Testament Scriptures: "The Deliverer will come from Zion; he will turn godlessness away from Jacob. And this is my covenant with them when I take away their sins" (vv. 26–27). All of these references should clarify that the second coming of Christ is one of the most important future events in prophecy.

The New Testament reveals repeatedly that the Second Coming will be a time of judgment on the wicked, as 2 Thessalonians 1:7–10, 2 Peter 3:3–4, and the book of Revelation state. At best, the Second Coming will be a climax to all of the judgments of God that fall on the earth during the Great Tribulation. As revealed in Revelation 19:19–21, the armies gathered against Christ are instantly annihilated, and the Beast, who is the Antichrist, and the False Prophet associated with him are cast into the lake of fire. It is a terrible judgment that will serve God's justice on the wicked but that will result in His deliverance of the righteous.

As portrayed in Scripture, the Second Coming is a literal event in which Christ comes bodily to the earth, accompanied by the saints of heaven and with the heavens ablaze with the glory of God. A long procession from heaven to earth takes place, as is described in Revelation 19:14–16, just as Revelation 1:7 had predicted. As Revelation 19:11–16 describes, the second coming of Christ will be an event that manifests His glory and will be visible to the entire earth:

> I saw heaven standing open and there before me was a white horse, whose rider is called Faithful and True. With justice he judges and makes war. His eyes are like blazing fire, and on his head are many crowns. He has a name written on him that no one knows but he himself. He is dressed in a robe dipped in blood, and his name is the Word of God. The armies of heaven were following him, riding on white horses and dressed in fine linen, white and clean. Out of his mouth comes a sharp sword with which to strike down the nations. "He will rule them with an iron scepter." He treads the winepress of the fury of the wrath of God Almighty. On his robe and on his thigh he has this name written: King of Kings and Lord of Lords.

In contrast to the Rapture, when no one accompanies Christ from heaven, at the Second Coming the saints come from heaven to earth, including all of the multiplied millions of angels and saints who will share in Christ's millennial kingdom. This fact is mentioned frequently in Scripture, as in Matthew 25:31 and Jude 14–15.

As is indicated in Zechariah 14:4, the destination of Christ's

Second Coming will be the Mount of Olives, from which He ascended. When His feet stand there again on the Mount of Olives, geographical changes will occur, including the splitting in half of the Mount of Olives. Then, where the Mount of Olives is today, a great valley will run from Jerusalem to Jericho. Many other physical changes will take place at the Second Coming, including the raising up of Jerusalem (v. 10).

The second coming of Christ will be the occasion of the judgment of God on the wicked world. When the glory of the Second Coming appears in the heavens, the armies of earth that have been fighting among themselves for power, will forget their differences and will unite to fight the armies of heaven. Satan encourages all of the armies of the world to come there for this very reason; he is marshaling all of the military might of the world to contend against the might of God. But it will all be futile. As the Scriptures make clear, Christ just speaks the word, and all of the armies are destroyed: "Out of his mouth comes a sharp sword with which to strike down the nations" (Rev. 19:15). The result is a great slaughter, and the vultures are invited to feed upon the dead bodies.

In connection with the Second Coming, the world ruler (described as the Beast) and the False Prophet are captured alive and cast into the lake of fire: "But the beast was captured, and with him the false prophet who had performed miraculous signs on his behalf. With these signs he had deluded those who had received the mark of the beast and worshiped his image. The two of them were thrown alive into the fiery lake of burning sulfur" (Rev. 19:20). The doom of the rest is summarized in Revelation 19:21: "The rest of them were killed with the sword that came out of the mouth of the rider on the horse, and all the birds gorged themselves on their flesh."

Just as the Old Testament is designed to present Jesus Christ as the Messiah of Israel and its Savior, so the Second Coming emphasizes that He is the King of David, and King of Kings and Lord of Lords over the entire earth, as Revelation 19:16 states.

A period of 1,335 days follows the Second Coming before the millennial kingdom begins. In this period, the judgments on the Gentiles and Israel are completed, as will be discussed later, and the regathering of Israel is undertaken. Few events in prophecy are more spectacular or more important; they result in major changes in the world situation.

At the beginning of the new millennium, the world stands poised to fulfill the dramatic sequence of events, beginning with the Rapture, the time of trouble that follows, the second coming of Christ, and the beginning of the millennial kingdom. Because the world situation today is situated precisely where one would expect it to be in such a sequence, those who are awaiting the Lord's return may eagerly anticipate it to occur any day. The tremendous prophetic series of events that follow will engulf our present world.

CHAPTER 9

THE RESURRECTIONS

The doctrine that all human beings will be raised from the dead is a central feature of Christian theology and is supported throughout Scripture. Two types of resurrections are obvious: (1) the resurrection unto life and salvation and (2) the resurrection unto eternal punishment.

Some theologians flagrantly disregard the details and attempt to make both of these types of resurrections into one major event in which all of the dead are raised and eternity begins. To do this, they must disregard the literal interpretation of prophecy and merge many conflicting events. The careful reading of Scripture concerning the doctrine of resurrection, however, reveals that instead of one general resurrection, actually seven resurrections are mentioned in the Bible.

Scripture records in both the Old and New Testaments many instances of those who died and were restored to life. All of these instances, as illustrated in the resurrection of Lazarus, were mere restorations and those individuals again went through the process of death. There were no permanent resurrections until the resurrection of Christ.

THE FIRST RESURRECTION: JESUS CHRIST

Accordingly, the resurrection of Christ is the first major resurrection recorded in the Bible, and it is a historical fact that is not only recorded by all four of the Gospels (Matt. 28:1–7; Mark 16:1–11; Luke 24:1–12; John 20:1–18) but also attested to in other portions of the New Testament. The resurrection of Christ is the historical basis for our Christian faith; apart from it, there would be no Christian theology or truth in Scripture.

As the Scriptures make plain, Christ's physical body, which died, was received back again in a restored form. As such, He was recognized many times subsequent to His resurrection. The Christian gospel was founded on the belief that He had actually been raised from the dead in His physical resurrection, followed later by His ascension into heaven.

THE SECOND RESURRECTION: THE TOKEN RESURRECTION IN JERUSALEM

On the occasion of Christ's own resurrection, a token resurrection occurred, as Matthew 27:50–53 records. This event was preceded by an earthquake that opened the tombs of some people in Jerusalem. After the resurrection of Christ, some of these people were raised from the dead and appeared on the streets of Jerusalem. Tremendous events also occurred when Christ died, including an earthquake that opened the tombs and the tearing of the curtain of the temple from top to bottom. This token resurrection was the climax of these events. The Scriptures do not record what happened to these bodies, but we must assume that they were raptured and taken to heaven. If they had died again, it would not have been a proper token of the resurrection of Christ.

The question is then raised about the significance of this special resurrection. The Scriptures do not state the connection, but it probably relates to the order of the feasts of the Lord in Leviticus 23, the first of which is the Passover, which is a type of Christ's death. This feast is followed by the Feast of

Unleavened Bread (v. 6). The third feast of the Lord, however, is a ceremony before the harvest, when a sheath of grain is waved before the Lord as a token of the expectation of the future harvest (vv. 9–14). Fifty days later, the fourth Feast of Pentecost is observed, recognizing the new grain that is reaped in the harvest. In keeping with this feast, the token resurrection at the resurrection of Christ corresponds to the sheaf of grain that was presented to the priest before the harvest. As there was more than one stalk of grain offered then, so there was more than one resurrected body in this token resurrection. It anticipates, of course, the ultimate resurrection of all believers that occurs later in God's prophetic program, which will fulfill the fourth feast, that of Pentecost in Leviticus 23.

THE THIRD RESURRECTION: THE RAPTURE

As was noted in earlier discussions, the Rapture of the church will be both a resurrection of the dead in Christ and a transformation of living Christians. Those believers who are raptured, according to Scripture, are described as "in Christ," referring to the baptism of the Spirit that began at Pentecost. Accordingly, although discussion on this point continues, the Rapture seems to include only those people who have been saved since Pentecost.

At the Rapture, all Christians who have died will be raised instantly and given resurrection bodies that are patterned after the resurrection body of Christ. Living Christians will be changed instantly (1 Cor. 15:50–53), receiving bodies that are suited for heaven. Both the resurrected dead and all living Christians will rise from the earth to meet the Lord in the air and be taken to heaven as Christ promised in John 14. The first two resurrections are now history; the third resurrection is still subject to fulfillment.

THE FOURTH RESURRECTION: THE TWO WITNESSES

In Revelation 11, a prophecy is given of two witnesses who will testify to the power of God for three and a half years, or 1,260 days (vv. 1–3). They are protected supernaturally, and no one is able to kill them. They have power to destroy anybody who attacks them (vv. 4–5). They also have power over rain and are able to inflict plagues on the earth (v. 6). After three and a half years, however, the Lord allows them to be killed, and the Scriptures record that their bodies are left to lie in the streets of Jerusalem for three and a half days. Then a miraculous event takes place: they are raised from the dead and ascend into heaven. Simultaneously, an earthquake will occur in Jerusalem and a tenth of the city is destroyed and seven thousand people will be killed (v. 13).

Much speculation has arisen regarding the two witnesses. Many people have tried to link them to Enoch and Elijah, who in the Old Testament were taken to heaven without death. The basis for this view is that all have to die and be raised. This view, however, is contradicted by the Rapture, at which time a whole generation of Christians will go to heaven without dying. Other people believe that the witnesses are Elijah and Moses, as on the Mount of Transfiguration.

A more sensible approach is to limit interpretation to what the Scriptures actually say. Nothing indicates that these two witnesses are people out of the past who have been resurrected and then die a second time. A more probable explanation is that these two witnesses, who are not named, are people of that generation. Accordingly, although they die, they are also resurrected and caught up to heaven in much the same way as is the church at the Rapture. We have no hint here of either a general resurrection of all of the dead or a reference to the Rapture of the church as some people try to find. As supernatural as the event is, it is described very plainly and literally in Scripture.

THE FIFTH RESURRECTION: THE MARTYRED DEAD

Contrary to the teaching of posttribulationists, no general resurrection occurs before the second coming of Christ or on the day itself. But in Revelation 20:4–6, the martyred dead of the Tribulation are raised several days after the Second Coming. As was discussed earlier, these people are martyrs in the Great Tribulation who refused to worship the world ruler and so were executed just before the Second Coming. The Scriptures declare, “They came to life and reigned with Christ a thousand years” (v. 4).

Because this view is a refutation of both amillennialism and posttribulationism, all kinds of attempts have been made to deny the literal fulfillment of this prophecy. Some amillenarians have gone so far as to make this the salvation of a lost soul, which is entirely contradicted by the passage. The people who are to be resurrected have been beheaded because of their faith in Christ and now are restored to life for the purpose of reigning with Christ a thousand years. The passage not only affirms a resurrection but also states that it will be followed by the thousand-year reign of Christ known as the millennial kingdom, indicating that the Second Coming is premillennial.

The passage, taken in its plain literal meaning, supports the second coming of Christ, with the resurrection of these martyred dead occurring a few days later. They will reign with Christ for a thousand years before the final state of the new heaven and the new earth.

The term “the first resurrection” raises an exegetical problem. Attempts have been made to make this the Rapture of the church on the grounds that it is declared to be first.

Although posttribulationists never recognize them, two resurrections are in this passage: (1) the resurrection of the martyred dead before the Millennium and (2) the seventh and last resurrection, which is the resurrection of the wicked dead that follows. Of these two resurrections, the resurrection of the martyred dead is first, not in the sense that no resurrection is before it but in the sense of its being a resurrection that is before the second resurrection at this time. We have already noted Scriptures that explain the fact of previous resurrections. In the chronological order of all of the resurrections, this one is the fifth.

THE SIXTH RESURRECTION: THE OLD TESTAMENT SAINTS

In connection with the events after the Second Coming is a record of Old Testament saints' resurrection from the dead, but they are not included in the Revelation passage. Obviously, they are to be resurrected and participate in the millennial kingdom, which requires them to be resurrected in the period between the Second Coming and the establishment of the kingdom. The relationship of this event to the resurrection of the martyred dead is not mentioned in Scripture, and the order is not stated.

Following the account of the Great Tribulation in Daniel 11, Daniel 12:2–3 states, "Multitudes who sleep in the dust of the earth will awake: some to everlasting life, others to shame and everlasting contempt. Those who are wise will shine like the brightness of the heavens, and those who lead many to righteousness, like the stars for ever and ever."

The fact of the resurrection of all men is stated in verse 2, but as the New Testament makes plain, both resurrections are not at the same time and, as Revelation 20 makes clear, at least a thousand years will elapse between the resurrection of the righteous and the resurrection of the wicked. The fact is that all human life, whether righteous or otherwise, is subject to resurrection.

The Old Testament provides few Scriptures that deal with the subject of the resurrection of the Old Testament saints. In addition to the Daniel 12 passage, another prediction is found in Isaiah 26:19: "But your dead will live; their bodies will rise. You who dwell in the dust, wake up and shout for joy. Your dew is like the dew of the morning; the earth will give birth to her dead." A third reference is found in Ezekiel 37, which predicts the resurrection of the nation Israel and describes her as a valley of dry bones that are given life and restoration:

> Therefore prophesy and say to them: "This is what the Sovereign LORD says: O my people, I am going to open your graves and bring you up from them; I will bring you back to the land of Israel. Then you, my people, will know that I am the LORD, when I open your graves and bring you up from them. I will put my Spirit in you and you will live, and I will settle you in your own land. Then you will know that I the LORD have spoken, and I have done it, declares the LORD." (vv. 12–14)

Although the context of this passage is the resurrection of Israel and the restoration of the land of Israel, it also seems clearly to indicate the resurrection of those who died in faith in the Old Testament, a view that is supported by references in Daniel and Isaiah.

THE SEVENTH RESURRECTION: THE WICKED DEAD

In connection with the Great White Throne Judgment (Rev. 20:11–15) is a resurrection of the unsaved dead who are now in hades as a temporary place for their souls. They will be raised from the dead and apparently given resurrection bodies that are suited for punishment. Then they will be cast into the lake of fire as the place of their punishment forever (vv. 14–15). This judgment will be followed immediately by the destruction of the current earth and heaven and then the creation of a new heaven, a new earth, and the city of New Jerusalem as the residence of the saints of all ages. Obviously, from the facts of history and prophecy, no general resurrection will occur but rather a series of seven resurrections. Also, there is only one Rapture of the living before the Tribulation, and this is the prophetic future of the church. No Rapture is mentioned to occur at the second coming of Christ.

In the nature of the case, other future resurrections may occur, such as that of the righteous who die in the millennial kingdom and the saints who are living at the end of the Millennium and who will need to be raptured and given bodies suited for eternity. The Scriptures do not mention these important events because they do not concern any of us who are living today. These Scriptures emphasize the fact that life does not end at death; it continues into eternity, and the destiny of human souls is determined by what they do in this life.

CHAPTER 10

THE RAPTURE QUESTION

The major problem with the doctrine of the Rapture is the question of when it will occur on God's prophetic calendar. The details of the Rapture are quite clearly stated in 1 Thessalonians 4:13–18 and 1 Corinthians 15:51–53. Although these passages are often neglected, ignored, or misinterpreted, they communicate effectively to the one who reads them that the Rapture is the movement of the saints from earth to heaven and as such is quite in contrast to the doctrine of the Second Coming.

In the history of the church, the Rapture has been largely neglected. It was assumed to be a posttribulational part of the second coming of Christ, or at least it was believed to occur in the general period of the consummation.

Those who interpret the prophecies of Scripture literally point out that the Bible is quite clear that the Rapture occurs before the end-time catastrophes that the Bible pictures for the Tribulation. It is impossible to interpret the tribulation period literally, take the church through it, and at the end still have the prospect of the Rapture as a blessed hope. Posttribulationism is impossible if prophecy of the Tribulation is interpreted literally. A literal interpretation makes clear that a host of martyrs will exist, as described in Revelation 7:9–17, rather than the preservation of the saints intact through this terrible period. Evidence also exists that the Rapture occurs years before the end-time catastrophes and judgments of God.

The only view that interprets prophecy literally and consistently is that of the pretribulational, premillennial position. But other views have emerged from those who do not take all prophecies literally. The most prominent and common in the church is that of the posttribulational view, which interprets the Rapture as occurring as a phase of the second coming of Christ. The traditional post-tribulational explanation is that as Christ descends from heaven to earth at the Second Coming, the church rises to meet Him and then makes a U-turn and comes back with Him to earth. The problem, of course, is that absolutely no Scripture supports this view, and it involves a nonliteral interpretation of the tribulation period.

Amillenarians universally regard the Rapture as part of the Second Coming. Premillenarians who are also posttribulationists tend to interpret the Millennium period literally but do not take the tribulation period literally. For them, the Tribulation is equated simply with the struggles of the church in history without any exegesis of the tribulation predictions.

The midtribulational view considers the Rapture as occurring about three and a half years before the Second Coming and before the Great Tribulation, which precedes the Second Coming. A modification of this view is the recent prewrath position, which pictures the Rapture as occurring somewhere in the middle of the last three and a half years but before the catastrophes of the bowl judgments in Revelation 16. All of these views cite no specific Scripture as predicting the Rapture. The major division that separates the pretribulation view from all other views is the question of literal interpretation. Every view other than the pretribulation view requires a nonliteral interpretation of at least some prophecy.

The fact that the question of the Rapture has been answered

with major differing views based on the difference in the method of interpretation necessitates a study of why the nonliteral views are not satisfactory. The author's book *The Rapture Question* attempts to study the issue completely in three hundred pages. He will attempt a much briefer statement here.

DEFINITION OF THE CHURCH

Because the issue is whether the church is raptured, we must define what is meant by *the church*. A very common interpretation applies the term *church* to the saints of all ages. All saints who are saved in the Old Testament are born again. In the New Testament, the church is defined as the union of Jews and Gentiles on an equal basis. The New Testament word *church* comes from the Greek word *ekklesia*, which is a general word for "assembly." It was used in the Greek states where the citizens were gathered to vote on various motions and the gathering would be called an ekklesia. Accordingly, this word is found in the Greek translation of the Old Testament Septuagint to translate several Hebrew terms, including *moed*, *edah*, and *kahal*. In all cases in the Septuagint, it means "an assembly," not necessarily with any religious connotation. In the New Testament, the same word is used with reference to any assembly of people, such as Israel in the wilderness (Acts 7:4–38) or a legal assembly (19:39).

In the New Testament, the word is often used for the assembly of professing Christians in a local church (Acts 8:1–3; 11:22, 26) or, in its plural form, for a group of such churches (1 Cor. 16:19; Gal. 1:2). Revelation 2–3 notes the fact that not everyone in the assembly of the church is necessarily a true believer. The word is also used of all professing Christians (Acts 12:1; Rom. 16:16; 1 Cor. 16:19; Gal. 1:13; Rev. 2:1–3:22).

In the New Testament, the word has a religious connotation when it refers to the body of Christ as composed of all true believers baptized into one body (1 Cor. 12:13). In the Old Testament, *ekklesia* is never used in a religious sense, although it was used of an assembly of Israelites. Clearly, in Matthew 16:18, where Christ predicts the church, it was still a future undertaking of God and therefore not in the Old Testament. The church as the body of Christ was formed at Pentecost, and as new believers are added to the fold, they are baptized into the one body by a work of the Holy Spirit.

The teaching of the doctrine of the church as the Body of Christ introduces something that the Old Testament never anticipated—that Jews and Gentiles would be united into one religious body. Therefore, this teaching supports the idea that the present age, which is often passed over in the Old Testament, is a new dispensation that was not anticipated in the Old Testament revelations. From this view is derived the fact that when the Rapture occurs, it concerns only those who are baptized into the body of Christ that began at Pentecost; accordingly, the expression "the dead in Christ" (1 Thess. 4:16) refers to only the saints of the present age. This position supports the doctrine that the Rapture concerns only the saints of the present age and that the resurrection and judgments of other people occur later. Therefore, the Rapture should be dissociated from the resurrection of the Old Testament saints or the tribulation saints who are martyred. Therefore, the doctrine of the church, correctly defined, supports the pretribulational view.

THE RAPTURE: AN IMMINENT EVENT

In the survey of future events as predicted in the Bible, that the Rapture is never mentioned in any of the passages that relate to the Great Tribulation is most significant. Every reference to the Rapture in the New Testament is presented as an imminent event, and no preceding events are ever revealed.

When some of the Thessalonians died, it raised the question of what would happen to them when the living were raptured. They apparently had the idea that the resurrection of the dead in Christ would not occur at the Rapture but would be some time later. How much they understood about the coming Tribulation and the second coming of Christ is not clear in Thessalonians. When they asked Timothy to clear up this difficulty, he was unable to do so and brought this question, along with other theological questions, to Paul, and Paul answers them in 1 Thessalonians.

The experience of the Thessalonian Christians makes quite clear that they were expecting Christ to come at any time but did not anticipate going through the Tribulation because no mention is made of it. In 1 Thessalonians 4:13–18, Paul gives them details as to what will happen at the Rapture, as was discussed earlier. In this revelation, Paul makes clear that the resurrection of the dead in Christ will not be delayed because they will be raised from the dead a moment before the living are instantly changed to meet the Lord in the air. They will go up together to the Father's house in fulfillment of the promise of Christ to His disciples in John 14 that He would take them to the Father's house.

A more important, often-overlooked fact is that not a single passage about the Rapture ever mentions the preceding events. The exhortation is always to be looking for Christ. No exhortation exists for Christians to be looking for the Tribulation or for the Antichrist. The fact that the Rapture is offered as a comfort and reassurance in both John 14:1–3 and 1 Thessalonians 4:18 demonstrates that they were not looking for a Tribulation that would kill most of them.

All posttribulationists have to take the Tribulation nonliterally. In fact, before World War II, they affirmed that it was already fulfilled. The most recent view is that there is some tribulation ahead but that it is greatly reduced and that the church is carried through it without much loss. This view simply is not supported by the book of Revelation, which pictures the martyred dead in Revelation 7, as well as the destruction of a fourth of the world population in Revelation 6:7–8, and a third of the remainder in Revelation 9:18.

In addition, we have the terribly destructive judgments of Revelation 16, which climax with an earthquake that destroys practically the whole earth, except Israel. How could the passage of the church through this time of trouble, in view of the clear indication of the great loss of life and the martyrdom of believers, be regarded as a blessed hope?

A rapture that will occur at the end of the Tribulation can hardly be a comfort to believers if the church has to go through the Tribulation. The Christians, as described in 1 Thessalonians 1:4–10, are those who "wait for his Son from heaven." In every chapter of 1 Thessalonians that speaks of the Rapture, its imminence is used as the basis for exhortation, as in 2:15 and 5:6 and especially in 1 John 3:2–3: "Dear friends, now we are children of God, and what we will be has not yet been made known. But we know that when he appears, we shall be like him, for we shall see him as he is. Everyone who has this hope in him purifies himself, just as he is pure." Similar factors exist in regard to the Second Coming. With the Rapture already fulfilled, those living after the Rapture will face the future Second Coming and will be subject to admonitions to prepare for this event.

THE DETAILS OF THE RAPTURE

A comparison of the Rapture to the Second Coming immediately brings out distinctions that separate the two major events by a considerable time. At the Rapture, saints will meet the Lord in the air; at the Second Coming, Christ returns to the Mount of Olives. At the Rapture, living saints are translated; at the Second Coming, no translation occurs and even the resurrection is later. At the Rapture, Christ transports the saints to heaven; at the Second Coming, He remains on earth and reigns for a thousand years. The Rapture is said to be before the wrath (1 Thess. 5:9); the Second Coming clearly follows the Great Tribulation, which is the time of wrath and predicts the great coming judgment. The Rapture is presented as an imminent event; the Second Coming has many prophesied signs that precede it and must be fulfilled before it will occur.

The Rapture and the doctrine of the Second Coming are the subject of prophecy in the New Testament, and whereas the Rapture occurs in relation to the saved, the Second Coming relates to both the saved and the unsaved. Obviously, the comings that are described are not the same. This fact tends to support the pretribulation Rapture view. There is only one Rapture but a series of resurrections, beginning with the resurrection of Christ and the token resurrection of the saints at the time of the resurrection of Christ.

THE RAPTURE AND THE RESURRECTION OF THE TWO WITNESSES OF REVELATION 11

Some people have interpreted the resurrection of the two witnesses in Revelation 11 as referring to the Rapture. As earlier discussion indicated, no justification exists for interpreting the two witnesses as representing the entire church. They are literally two people who experience what the Scriptures declare, and their resurrection is an event that occurs after the Rapture rather than at the time of the Rapture. It is probably a revelation of events just before the Second Coming.

RESURRECTIONS THAT FOLLOW THE SECOND COMING

The resurrections that follow the Second Coming include the resurrection of the Old Testament saints (Dan. 12:1–2), and the resurrection of the martyred dead of the Tribulation (Rev. 20:4–6). Both events occur some time after the Second Coming, and no Rapture of the living is involved. The saints who survive the Tribulation enter the Millennium in their natural bodies. The final resurrection is that of the wicked dead at the end of the Millennium before the creation of the new heaven and the new earth.

In conclusion, in putting all of these facts together, the Scriptures clearly express prophecy in literal terms and are to be interpreted in that way. The passages dealing with the Second Coming and the Rapture in the New Testament—such as the Gospels, 1 and 2 Corinthians, 1 Thessalonians, and Revelation—unite to describe the Rapture as a totally different event than the Second Coming, with the Rapture occurring more than seven years before the Second Coming.

WILL THE RAPTURE OCCUR SOON?

One of the problems in the doctrine of the Rapture is that it was declared to be imminent in the first century when it was first revealed. It has not occurred for almost two thousand years, and the question is how much longer we will have to wait.

As was pointed out earlier, the Rapture has no signs, and the associated exhortation always is to be looking for the coming of the Lord, not for events that will follow. Although the Bible clearly teaches that the Rapture is imminent, it is a different problem to prove that the Rapture could be soon. The answer involves a comprehensive view of all of the prophecies of the end time. Although no signs predict the Rapture, the Bible does describe in great detail some of the things that will be in existence at the time of the Rapture, either just before or just after the event occurs.

As was also pointed out earlier, the Bible contains three major areas of prophecy:

1. prophecy concerning Israel,
2. prophecy concerning the church, and
3. prophecy concerning the nations.

An amazing movement has occurred in all three areas of prophecy during the period since World War II, seemingly in fulfillment of prophecy and setting the stage for the Rapture.

All prophecies of the end time picture Israel in the land (e.g., Matt. 24). This, of course, was not true until 1948, when Israel was formed as a nation.

A major feature of the end time is the prediction of a world government under the Antichrist. Until the twentieth century, such a world government was impossible because the components for such a government—including rapid transportation, rapid communication, and financial and military control of the world—did not exist. These factors were impossible before World War II.

In the twentieth century, the early efforts to form a world government after World War I failed with the failure of the League of Nations. In World War II, however, the broad program of what is called the United Nations emerged. Although the formation of the United Nations is not a direct fulfillment of Scripture, its purpose is to teach that a world government is the way out of world chaos, especially in an atomic age. Such a philosophy is the foundation for the acceptance of the world dictator (Antichrist) when he comes at the beginning of the Great Tribulation.

Since World War II, rapid transportation has been developed, as giant planes carry men and supplies around the world in a relatively short period of time. This capability made all of the difference in the world during the Gulf War when the rapid air deployment of men and war materials to Saudi Arabia made possible the defeat of Saddam Hussein.

Also developed in the twentieth century are giant computers that have the capacity to control the financial transactions of the entire world, thereby enabling the Antichrist to control buying and selling (Rev. 13:16–17). The development of the atomic bomb and missiles capable of sending a bomb anywhere in the world places tremendous power in the hands of a potential world dictator. In addition to these factors, we have a world church movement that is anticipated in the book of Revelation that will have its ultimate display in the first half of the last seven years, leading up to the Second Coming.

In Revelation 17, the harlot is described as sitting on a scarlet-colored beast (v. 3). She clearly represents a religious aspect, and the beast is the political aspect of the ten nations. The apostate church and the ten nations' governments work together for world domination. At the middle of the last seven years, however, when the world dictator takes over, the ten nations rise up and destroy the apostate church because the dictator wants to be worshiped himself without any intervening church support (v. 16).

When all of these factors are combined, it is obvious that we now have a window where the background for the Rapture is already present in our world. Also clear is the fact that in our rapidly moving world these conditions will change. Accordingly, a prophetic window exists immediately at the opening of the new millennium in which it is reasonable to assume that the Rapture will occur and that the other prophetic events will follow in their predicted order. Never in the history of the church has there been a time during which more evidence existed that the Rapture is near.

The fact that the Rapture is imminent and could occur any day presents a challenge to practical Christian living. We must examine our hearts to ensure that we are born again and qualify for the Rapture. We should live for Christ and for the things that have eternal value. After all, the Rapture is not a theological argument but a practical exhortation to be ready for the Lord when He comes.

CHAPTER 11

THE INTERPRETATION OF THE MILLENNIUM

Although the doctrine of the Millennium does not immediately determine the character of one's life in the present age, it is a major factor in biblical interpretation. Once again, the interpreter faces the problem of whether to interpret prophecy literally. If prophecy is interpreted literally, it clearly points to what is known as premillennialism, that the second coming of Christ is followed by Christ's reign on earth for a thousand years. The idea of such a kingdom is mentioned many times in the Old Testament. Added to the Old Testament is the statement six times in Revelation that the kingdom will last a thousand years or a millennium (20:2–7).

The premillennial view is based on the system of interpretation that finds Revelation 19–22 in chronological order. In other words, the destruction of the enemy follows the second coming of Christ in chapter 19. Satan is bound in Revelation 20:2, and the martyred dead of the Tribulation are resurrected in verses 4–6. As was pointed out earlier, the Scriptures here are very explicit:

> And I saw the souls of those who have been beheaded because of their testimony for Jesus and because of the word of God. They had not worshiped the beast or his

> image and had not received his mark on their foreheads or their hands. They came to life and reigned with Christ a thousand years. (20:4)

The people involved in this resurrection are those who lived in the Great Tribulation, the three-and-a-half-year period preceding the second coming of Christ. The context is that they refused to worship the Antichrist and therefore were beheaded. A few years later, after the Second Coming has taken place, their resurrection is revealed and they are resurrected with the purpose of reigning with Christ for a thousand years. If this language is taken in its ordinary meaning, it can lead only to the conclusion that the Second Coming occurs first, then the martyred dead are raised several days later, and the Millennium then follows these events.

Not only is Revelation 20 clear that these events precede the Millennium, but also that chapter reveals what will happen at the end of the thousand years. In Revelation 20:7–9, Satan stirs up the rebellion against God and attempts to take the capital city of Jerusalem by force, only to be destroyed by fire that comes down from heaven. Following this, Satan who had been bound for a thousand years and then loosed for a season, is captured and cast into the lake of fire, along with the False Prophet, as recorded in Revelation 20:10. This passage specifically supports the premillennial view and confirms many other passages that speak of a rule of Christ on earth, which will be discussed later.

By contrast, the amillennial view is the view that the Millennium is not a literal period. People who hold this position generally follow the Augustinian explanation that it is fulfilled in the present age when Christ rules in the hearts of those who believe in Him. Proponents of this view make no attempt to provide an exegesis of the passages involved, but they assume without evidence that the prophecies cannot be taken literally. For instance, they do not interpret Revelation 20:4, which speaks of the martyred dead who are beheaded and resurrected, literally.

The amillennial position is that this verse refers to the salvation of believers, something that is totally foreign to this passage. To confess that it is literal would be to give up their amillennial view. Amazingly, men of stature and scholarship, whose opinions are weighed carefully, will nevertheless adopt such a strange interpretation of this passage just because their system of theology dictates it. Although most amillenarians follow the Augustinian explanation that the millennial passages are being fulfilled nonliterally in the present age, some of them more recently have taken the position that it applies to the souls that have died and who are in the intermediate estate awaiting resurrection. Somehow they are viewed as fulfilling the reign of Christ by letting Christ rule them spiritually.

One of their scholars has adopted still another view that the Millennium is fulfilled in the eternal state in the New Jerusalem. Supporters of this position carefully pick their way through various Scriptures, avoiding the passages that contradict their view. Such passages speak of sin and death in the millennial kingdom, something that, of course, never happens in heaven. As is always true in nonliteral interpretation, once a person denies that the passage means what it says, it is an open door to all sorts of speculation because no one develops a solid interpretation.

A third view, known as postmillennialism, has become prominent in recent centuries. It is the idea that the gospel will be triumphant, that the whole world will become Christianized, and, after a thousand years of glorious success, Christ will come at the climax to that thousand-year period.

In a sense, amillennialism is also postmillennial because Christ is viewed as coming after the Millennium, but the postmillennial view is more optimistic. In history, the postmillennial view has stood largely on the theory of evolution, the belief that things are getting better and better. The fact that this view is absolutely contrary to the Scriptures is often ignored. Even worthy expositors and outstanding contributors to the Christian faith, such as Charles Hodge, nevertheless went along with this postmillennial idea, although he did not develop it in his systematic theology.

To a large extent, in the last part of the nineteenth century, evangelicals were contending against secular evolution. Postmillennialism was advanced as the biblical answer to this idea of progress. Many prophecy conferences were held in the last twenty-five years of the nineteenth century, initially including people of diverse eschatological positions. Gradually, however, the amillenarians dropped out (as did the postmillenarians later), leaving fundamentalism to be largely supported by the premillennial view as the twentieth century began.

Nevertheless, in the latter nineteenth century, evangelicalism was largely postmillennial, and that view formed the basis of many of our popular hymns that speak of the Promised Land as if it were heaven, instead of viewing it as the future millennium. Postmillennialism was, however, almost entirely futuristic; that is, no one claimed that the world was in the Millennium now, but that there would be still a future period of a thousand years when the gospel would be triumphant.

With the advent of World War I, Germany was the major contributor to the Protestant movement. At the same time, however, it was also guilty of committing horrible atrocities; as a result, postmillennialism suffered a mortal wound from which it has never fully recovered. The world was not getting better. Most postmillenarians moved from their position of optimism to the more realistic amillennial view.

In contemporary theology, undoubtedly, the amillennial

view, along with the view that prophecy cannot be interpreted literally, is the majority view of the organized church, whether Roman Catholic, Greek Orthodox, or Protestant. Coupled with this view of eschatology, however, is often the concept that the Bible is not inerrant and that each interpreter must determine for himself what is true or false in the Bible, which, of course, completely destroys its authority. Among those who insist on the inerrancy of Scripture and the supernatural character of the Bible, many are premillennial, though not exclusively.

PREMILLENNIALISM IN THE OLD TESTAMENT

Numerous passages of Scripture in the Old Testament anticipate a rule of Christ on earth. If the Old Testament is interpreted literally in its prophetic anticipation, it leads directly to the concept that when Christ returns, He will bring in His kingdom on earth. Even scholars of other persuasions often admit that such is the case. Not only do they concede that the Old Testament interpreted literally yields such a doctrine but clearly recognize that the people of Israel anticipated such a Messiah and such a kingdom.

Opponents of premillennialism follow two lines of argument, disputing the concept of a kingdom on earth and that prophecy should be interpreted literally. This argument is often stated very dogmatically without any proof from the text. As was explained earlier, about five hundred prophetic passages have already been literally fulfilled. One would expect that the five hundred passages that remain unfulfilled naturally would be fulfilled in the same way. Amillenarians ignore any such factual basis for a literal interpretation.

A second view is followed by the amillenarians on the premillennial issue in that they make the promises literal but conditional; that is, God would have done something if the Jews had met the conditions for the kingdom. Amillenarians do not seem to realize that they are contradicting themselves. If only a spiritual fulfillment is expected, then no conditions exist. If the predictions are literal, then one must prove that they are conditional. Although it is true that some prophecies of the Bible are offered conditionally, the fact of the kingdom on earth is stated so dogmatically and so clearly without reference to conditions that the explanation of a conditional basis is not supported in Scriptures.

The subject of the kingdom on earth is a frequent revelation of the Psalms. In Psalm 2, for instance, Jesus Christ is revealed to be the coming King who will rule over the nations with an iron hand (v. 9). In the messianic psalms, such as Psalm 8, Christ is put in charge of the earth, and its beasts, birds, and every other part of creation are put under His feet (v. 6). In Psalm 22, Scripture speaks of the death of Christ and the climax is revealed: "All the ends of the earth will remember and turn to the LORD, and all the families of nations will bow down before him, for dominion belongs to the LORD and he rules over the nations" (vv. 27–28).

The coming of Christ as the King of Glory in the Second Coming is mentioned in Psalm 24:7–10, which speaks of His rule over the earth. Psalm 72 is an outstanding picture of the glorious kingdom that goes far beyond anything achieved by Solomon: "He will rule from sea to sea from the River to the ends of the earth. The desert tribes will bow before him and his enemies will lick the dust" (vv. 8–9). It is stated again in Psalms 72:11: "All kings will bow down to him and all nations will serve him." The next-to-last verse of the psalm states, "Praise be to his glorious name forever; may the whole earth be filled with his glory. Amen and Amen" (v. 19).

Psalm 89, which repeats the promises of the Davidic covenant, is an extensive statement of how David will rule over the earth with Christ. The statement in Psalm 89:19–36 is a specific prediction of how David will inherit the throne and, with the Messiah, will reign over the whole earth after His resurrection. The summary line states, ". . . his line will continue forever and his throne endure before me like the sun" (v. 36). In Psalm 110, Christ is pictured as waiting for the time of His rule on earth: "The Lord is at your right hand; he will crush kings on the day of his wrath. He will judge the nations, heaping up the dead and crushing the rulers of the whole earth. He will drink from a brook beside the way; therefore he will lift up his head" (vv. 5–7).

In addition to the Psalms, Isaiah 11 describes His righteous judgment on the earth. The whole chapter deals with Christ's reign on earth in His millennial kingdom. The theme of the kingdom on earth winds its way through all of the Major Prophets and is the major theme of the Minor Prophets. For this reason, the Jews expected that when Messiah came, He would deliver them from their enemies, not realizing that the prophecy of His death had to be fulfilled first before the promises of His victory in the Second Coming would be fulfilled.

The New Testament, of course, offers solid confirmation of the premillennial view. In Luke 1:32–33, Mary is told that she will be the mother of the Messiah and that He would reign over the house of Jacob forever. In view of the common expectation of the Jews, how could Mary interpret this prophecy other than that her son would reign over the earth and that the promises given to David, of whom she was a descendant, would be fulfilled literally? Others in the Gospels quite clearly looked to a literal fulfillment of the kingdom on earth, such as the mother of James and John, who sought special privileges for her sons (Matt. 20:20–23).

In Acts 1, when the disciples asked about confirmation of the kingdom that they were seeking, Christ did not tell them that they were wrong in their expectations but that it was not for them to know the time (Acts 1:7). The apostle Paul also raises the question of the kingdom and the future of Israel in Romans 9–11. A survey of these chapters indicates that for the time being Israel has been set aside and the Gentiles are being blessed, but the time will come when once again Israel will be under God's blessings and their deliverance will come out of Zion.

The history of the early church reveals a total lack of controversy regarding a literal millennium, although some of the early church fathers do not speak on the subject, and amillenarians tend to claim them because they are silent. Those who did speak out held that the coming of Christ and a thousand-year kingdom to follow was the prevailing opinion of the apostolic fathers. On the contrary, no evidence whatever exists for the first-century amillennial view. The second century of the Christian church continued this form of interpretation of prophecy.

Of the many adherents to premillennialism, Justin Martyr, in his classic work, *Dialogue with Trypho the Jew* (chap. 81), is often quoted:

> But I and whatsoever Christians are orthodox in all things do know that there will be a resurrection of flesh and in a thousand years, the city of Jerusalem built, adorned and enlarged, according as Ezekiel, Isaiah and other prophets have promised. For Isaiah saith of this thousand years (ch. 65:1–17): "Behold, I create new heavens and a new earth: and the former shall not be remembered, nor come to mind; be glad and rejoice in those which I create: for, behold, I create Jerusalem to triumph, and my people to rejoice."

Because the quote from Justin is subject to some question and is such a vital proof of premillennialism, it has been attacked very vigorously by those who do not accept the premillennial view. However, any overall view of the early church fathers does not reveal any amillennialism in the first two centuries, and if such existed, it would be almost impossible to have this total silence.

In the third century of the Christian church, opposition arose for the first time, originating in a school of theology at Alexandria, Egypt. Scholars in this school—which included such men as Gaius, Clement, Origen, and Dionysus—taught that the Bible should be harmonized with the pure idealism of Plato, a popular philosopher at the time. To do this, they held that the entire Bible should not be taken literally but is a huge allegory in which the truth behind the text should be sought.

The early church recognized this position at once as a total attack upon Christian theology and refuted it successfully, and the interpretation of the Bible in most areas was returned to the grammatical-historical-literal interpretation that characterized the previous period. In the area of prophecy, however, it was more difficult to prove this view as right or wrong because the prophecies had not yet been fulfilled. The result was that it destroyed the premillennial view, first in North Africa and then in the rest of the church.

For several centuries, unrest and uncertainty about the Millennium existed. But then Augustine, a famous African bishop, attempted to solve the problem by stating that the Bible as a whole should be interpreted literally and grammatically but that prophecy was a special case. Augustine, however, was quite inconsistent in this position because he believed that heaven and hell were literal, that purgatory was literal, and that resurrection was literal, but the one thing that he opposed as being literal was the millennial kingdom.

Never has any reasonable explanation of this position been offered because Augustine's support for his view is so minimal. It might be that this view was a form of anti-Semitism because the Millennium largely exalted the Jews and the church. Perhaps Augustine, who was a Gentile, resented this exaltation of Israel. In any case, the church became largely amillennial and departed from the premillennial interpretation, and in the centuries that followed, the Alexandrian school of prophecy was adopted. Although some premillenarians have existed throughout the history of the church, they did not possess the dominant position that they had held in the early centuries.

Since the Protestant Reformation, an intensive study of the Scriptures as the authority of Christian theology has arisen in contrast to the claims of the Roman Catholic Church. Through the Protestant Reformation, many of the great doctrines of the church, such as the priesthood of the believer, were advanced. Only in the twentieth century, however, has a large resurgence of the study of prophecy occurred in an attempt to find one's way through the conflicting viewpoints.

PREMILLENNIALISM IN CONTEMPORARY THEOLOGY

In the twentieth century, a general deterioration has occurred in the biblical character of theology in the widespread attack on the inerrancy of the Bible and its complete inspiration. The majority of theological seminaries today do not systematically support the concept that every verse of Scripture is inerrant. The opinion that each interpreter has to determine for himself what is true and what is not true in the Bible is widespread. This view, of course, destroys completely the authority of the Bible as the revelation of God and reduces the truth to the judgment of the interpreter. The inadequacy of this position is manifested in the fact that no central agreement exists as to what the Bible teaches once you depart from the fact that Scripture is inerrant.

Even those who hold to biblical inerrancy destroy their arguments for the authority of Scripture if they hold that prophecy is not literal. This weakness has been coupled with a failure to clarify the gospel message of salvation and many other truths that are central to Christian faith. The battle for premillennialism is much broader than the controversy concerning eschatology, and the lack of premillennial interpretation has its effect upon almost every area of prophetic interpretation.

In the current theological context, premillennialism is clearly more than a system of eschatology; it is actually a system that affects theology as a whole, building as it does upon literal interpretation and the inerrancy and inspiration of the Bible. Those who attack premillennialism have claimed that it is a new and untried doctrine and ignore the history of the doctrine and the clear premillennial character of the early church.

PREMILLENNIALISM AND THE BIBLICAL COVENANT

As was discussed earlier, the biblical covenants with Abraham and David and the new covenant have important contributions to make in the determination of the millennial future. The promises to Abraham that he would be the father of many nations and that his seed would inherit the Holy Land provide a solid view for the premillennial doctrine. The promises to David, brought out in the Davidic covenant and confirmed by Psalm 89, reveal that God has a purpose in restoring the kingdom of Israel in which David will be resurrected and be a coregent with Christ.

Much disagreement has arisen concerning the interpretation of the new covenant, even among scholars who agree on other doctrinal issues. The point of view that clarifies this issue is to understand that the new covenant is the theological covenant of grace, which proceeds from the fact that Christ died for the sins of the whole world. As such, it is the basis for the salvation of all people from Adam onward. It is also the basis of God's blessing upon Israel, as indicated in Jeremiah 31, where the restoration of Israel in the millennial kingdom is an act of grace, not something that they deserve but that is made possible by the death of Christ.

The new covenant is also revealed in the grace that is bestowed upon the church, of which the Lord's Supper is the commemoration. The salvation of those in the future who will come to Christ also is based upon this new covenant. The new covenant is in contrast to the covenant with Moses and the promises given to Adam. The fulfillment of the new covenant is integral to the whole premillennial interpretation. The large subject of Israel in prophecy, which we have already discussed, also supports the concept that a future fulfillment for Israel is made possible by grace, and a regathering, restoration, and spiritual renewal will occur in the millennial kingdom when Christ will reign not only in Jerusalem on the throne of David but also over the entire world.

PREMILLENNIALISM IN RELATION TO THE CHURCH

An important part of premillennialism is to distinguish between God's program for Israel, which will have its fulfillment in the millennial kingdom, and His program for the church, which will have its fulfillment in the Rapture. The church will reign with Christ on earth in the millennial kingdom and will be in the New Jerusalem in eternity.

As was discussed earlier, the Old Testament saints, although saved and born again, were not baptized into the body of Christ and do not qualify for what the Scriptures describe of the church on the Day of Pentecost and at the time of the Rapture. The Rapture itself is declared to be limited to those who are "in Christ," and that position of being in Christ is the result of the baptism of Spirit that was fulfilled for the first time on the Day of Pentecost (1 Thess. 4:16).

The church, having been raptured, will have no part in the Tribulation that follows, and the Rapture, preceding the second coming of Christ, is not mentioned in any tribulation passage that deals with the end-time period.

THE GOVERNMENT OF THE MILLENNIAL KINGDOM

If the approach is accepted of interpreting prophecy literally, the Bible presents evidence of the literal government that will be administered by Christ in the millennial kingdom. In earlier discussion of the kingdom concept, we pointed out that a number of kingdoms are in the Bible, including the universal kingdom of God as Creator, the kingdom of David (a political kingdom), the kingdom of God (a spiritual kingdom), and the messianic kingdom that will be fulfilled in the millennial kingdom. Although amillenarians attempt to make this future form of the millennial kingdom the same as the current spiritual form of the kingdom, major differences obviously exist in Isaiah 11. For instance, the reign of Christ on earth is described as a righteous reign, and it is the period when the prophecy of peace in the animal world is described. In this period, Christ reigns on the throne in Jerusalem (Isa. 9:7; 11:1–16). As was noted earlier concerning Psalm 2:6, God's purpose is to set Christ upon the holy hill of Zion to reign over the earth.

A number of Scriptures support the concept of Christ as the supreme King of the millennial kingdom when He will sit on the throne of David (2 Sam. 7:16; Ps. 89:20–27; Isa. 11:1–16; Jer. 33:19–21). When He came, He was also rejected as King (Mark 15:12–13; Luke 1:32–33; 19:14). In His death, He was said to die as a King (Matt. 27:37). And His return will be that of King of Kings and Lord of Lords, as is stated in Revelation 19:16. So many references to Christ's reigning in the millennial kingdom exist that the realization that scholars have attempted to refute it is amazing (see Isa. 2:1–4; 9:6–7; 11:1–10; 16:5; 24:23; 32:2; 40:1–11; 42:3–4; 52:7–15; 55:4; Dan. 2:44; 7:27; Mic. 4:1–8; 5:2–5; Zech. 9:9; 14:16–17).

As we noted earlier, David will be resurrected and serve with Christ as a regent under Him and will share the throne (Ezek. 34:24; 37:24). The millennial government of Christ will for the first time cover the entire earth and will fulfill what the Devil tried to imitate by bringing in his universal kingdom before the Second Coming, as is stated in Daniel 7:14: "He was given authority, glory and sovereign power; all peoples, nations and men of every language worshiped him. His dominion is an everlasting dominion that will not pass away, and his kingdom is one that will never be destroyed."

This government will be absolute in both its authority and its manifestation (Pss. 2:9; 72:9–11; Isa. 11:4). Those who are saved and survive the Tribulation will enter the kingdom in their natural bodies. They will bear children, and these children, in turn, will need to come to faith in Christ or be judged. A certain amount of Christian profession without reality will be permitted, and this condition is judged at the end of the millennial kingdom when those who are not saved join Satan in his revolt against Christ. Obviously, many Scriptures support the position that Israel will have an important place in the millennial reign of Christ.

THE SPIRITUAL LIFE OF THE MILLENNIAL KINGDOM

The facts that Christ will be on the throne in Jerusalem, assert-ing His authority and judging sin, and that Satan is bound leads to the conclusion that the spiritual life of the kingdom will be very unusual. In the previous experience of human history, the appeal is sometimes made that Satan is the cause of the sin of human beings. But in the Millennium, Satan will be bound for a thousand years, and the only evil that can then come will be from the evil heart of man. Most significant is the fact that even under ideal circumstances—in which Christ is visibly present, when every school is a Bible school, and where no restrictions hinder the distribution of scriptural truth—unbelief and rebellion will still exist and come to a head at the end of the millennial kingdom.

The millennial kingdom will be characterized as a time of universal knowledge of Christ. As Isaiah 11:9 states, ". . . the earth will be full of the knowledge of the LORD as the waters cover the sea." The Holy Spirit will be active in teaching people the truth of God. As Jeremiah states, God will do a magnificent work in the hearts of His people:

> "This is the covenant I will make with the house of Israel after that time," declares the LORD. "I will put my law in their minds and write it on their hearts. I will be their God, and they will be my people. No longer will a man teach his neighbor, or a man his brother, saying, 'Know the LORD,' because they will all know me, from the least of them to the greatest," declares the LORD. (Jer. 31:33–34)

Included in the righteousness that will characterize human conduct, as described in Isaiah 11:3–5 will also be peace and a lack of war. This is stated in Isaiah 2:4: "He will judge between the nations and will settle disputes for many peoples. They will beat their swords into plowshares and their spears into pruning hooks. Nation will not take up sword against nation, nor will they train for war anymore."

Psalm 72:7 also speaks of peace, but in addition to peace, there will be joy, as described in Isaiah 11:3–4, and the Holy Spirit will be active in the millennial situation, as is stated in frequent Scriptures (e.g., Isa. 32:15; 44:3; Ezek. 39:29; Joel 2:28–29). The millennial kingdom, therefore, is not a materialistic, carnal situation that Augustine described for the Millennium, which he rejected. It has basic spiritual characteristics that were not found in earlier periods.

THE PLACE OF THE MILLENNIAL TEMPLE AND WORSHIP

A major problem in the millennial kingdom is the description of the millennial temple in Ezekiel 40:1–46:24. The details of the temple include provision for animal sacrifices and the rituals connected with it. This issue has become a major stumbling block for those who want to follow the premillennial interpretation.

A number of different explanations have been given for this problem. Some people have tried to connect it with the temple of Solomon or a later temple built after the Babylonian captivity. The details of Ezekiel, however, do not correspond to either of these temples (see 2 Chron. 3:3–4:22; Ezra 6:3–4). Some people also consider Ezekiel's temple as an ideal, but there is nothing to substantiate this view. Still another idea is that the temple is a typical presentation of the church in the present age, but no exegesis supports this view and it presents many problems.

The only explanation that follows the text of Ezekiel is to interpret it literally as a sacrificial system fitted to the millennial kingdom. This explanation raises the question, of course, of why sacrifices are necessary in the millennial kingdom when the sacrifice of Christ was supposed to have ended the Old Testament sacrifices. Many expositors ignore the problem, but still Ezekiel and other prophets refer to the sacrificial system of the millennial kingdom (Isa. 56:7; Jer. 33:18; Zech. 14:16–21).

A close examination of the sacrificial system of the millennial kingdom, however, reveals that it has a different purpose. All conservative Bible scholars agree that the sacrifice of Christ is the only efficacious sacrifice. The Old Testament sacrifices looked forward to this in type, but they, in themselves, could not take away sin. Similarly, the millennial sacrifices have no efficacious value and do not replace the sacrifice of Christ. Although debate on this subject will continue, one can fairly say that if the Old Testament sacrifices were ordained by God to look forward to and anticipate the death of Christ, the millennial sacrifices could also be used as a *reminder* of the sacrifice of Christ, just as now the Lord's Supper for the church is a reminder of the death of Christ on the cross.

Worthy scholars can be quoted on either side of this question, but if one interprets the Scriptures literally, the sacrifices of the Millennium are no criticism of premillennialism. After all that Ezekiel wrote about it, our problem is simply that it seems to reflect on the one sacrifice of Christ. The best explanation, therefore, is that whereas the sacrifices have no value as far as redemption is concerned, they are a reminder of the necessary sacrifice of Christ and the major fact that without the shedding of blood there is no remission of sin.

The question has been raised as to why this sacrifice is necessary. In the ideal situation of the millennial kingdom, sin will not take on the ugly character that it has now, and it is possible that some people would question whether it was necessary for Christ to die. The sacrifices are a reminder of the necessity of sacrifice for forgiveness, and those who avoid considering them as literal do so by criticizing the Scriptures themselves.

In general, the spiritual life of the kingdom is one of joy, peace, righteousness, and worship. In contrast to previous ages, it is probably more advanced than anything achieved before the second coming of Christ.

Because the rule of Christ is perfect, it also affects other aspects of life on earth. Clearly, the curse that was brought upon the earth by Adam and Eve's transgression now is lifted, as revealed in Isaiah 35:1–2, which speaks of the abundance and fertility of the soil:

> The desert and the parched land will be glad; the wilderness will rejoice and blossom. Like the crocus, it will burst into bloom; it will rejoice greatly and shout for joy. The glory of Lebanon will be given to it, the splendor of Carmel and Sharon; they will see the glory of the LORD, the splendor of our God.

Other passages speak of abundant rainfall (Isa. 30:23; 35:7), and food seems to be abundant (30:23–24). With the reign of Christ on earth, of course, comes universal justice, as is pointed out in Isaiah 11 and Psalm 22. Although no Scripture passage speaks directly to the subject, the majority of people living in the millennial kingdom probably will be saved. At the beginning of the Millennium, all of the adults will be saved because the unsaved will have been put to death. As children are born and grow up, however, they, too, will have to make spiritual decisions. It is possible for them to go through the motions without reality; thus, some of them will rebel against God at the end of the Millennium. It is probably safe to conclude that more people will be saved in the millennial kingdom proportionally to the population than in any other world situation.

All of the ideal circumstances continue to support the idea that there will be a worldwide abundance of food and material prosperity (Jer. 31:12; Ezek. 34:25–27; Joel 2:21–27; Amos 9:13–14). Apparently, there will also be much less sickness, and health and healing will characterize the period. Reference to this fact is found in Isaiah 29:18 and 33:24, and the health of the human race is also mentioned (35:5–6; 65:20).

Certain changes will also take place in the physical characteristics of the Holy Land. A cleavage will form a valley through the middle of what is now the Mount of Olives. This will be achieved when Christ's feet touch the Mount of Olives at the Second Coming (Zech. 14:3–4). Jerusalem also seems to be elevated (v. 10). Other changes will also occur, such as living waters that will go out of Jerusalem toward the western sea (v. 8). Also, during the millennial kingdom, the land of Israel will be divided among the twelve tribes, as indicated in Ezekiel 47:13–48:29, thus fulfilling the Abrahamic promise (Gen. 12:7).

If the Rapture of the church is imminent, then the millennial kingdom will be fulfilled soon. In relatively few years, the earth may see the fulfillment of all of these predictions of marvelous change in the world.

CHAPTER 12

THE NEW HEAVEN AND THE NEW EARTH

The climax of history in prophecy is recorded in the final two chapters of the book of Revelation. It is remarkable that in the Bible—where thirty-eight chapters of Genesis are devoted to the life of Abraham, Isaac, and Jacob—only two chapters are devoted to the eternal state where the saints will live forever. The reason is that it is not necessary for us to know all of the details of the future, as long as our destination and its general character is clearly indicated in the Bible. By any standard of judgment, the final two chapters of Revelation are tremendous in their scope and revelation.

The New Jerusalem and the new heaven present the tremendous future that awaits the saints of God. These end-time prophecies are introduced with the following statement: "Then I saw a new heaven and a new earth, for the first heaven and the first earth had passed away, and there was no longer any sea" (Rev. 21:1). Biblical scholars have debated whether the scene here is a renovated earth and heaven or an entirely new creation. The evidence seems to weigh heavily in favor of an entirely new creation. Revelation 20:11 states, "Earth and sky fled from his presence, and there was no place for them." This verse implies from chapter 21 a destruction of the current earth and heavens and their replacement with a completely new order.

Additional revelation is given in 2 Peter, which declares that our current earth will be destroyed with a roar: "But the day of the Lord will come like a thief. The heavens will disappear with a roar; the elements will be destroyed by fire, and the earth and everything in it will be laid bare" (3:10).

This day of the destruction of the earth is clearly amplified in 2 Peter 3:12, which states, "That day will bring about the destruction of the heavens by fire, and the elements will melt in the heat."

As science has shown that our material world is composed of atoms that contain incredible power when released (as indicated in atomic explosions), it is obvious that the same God who created the universe and locked in this power in the atomic structure can also unlock it. A possible reference is found in Colossians 1:17, which states of Christ, "He is before all things, and in him all things hold together." Just as the power of the atom is locked in by Christ, so it can be unlocked at the time when God is finished with our present earth. From the description that follows, it is quite clear that there is an entirely new physical order in the world in the eternal state. The monument of our current earth apparently will be destroyed and with it all of the oceans and bodies of water are eliminated, which would be a dramatic change from our current situation. This situation is comprehended in a very brief statement in Revelation 21:1: "There was no longer any sea."

The description that follows focuses not on the new earth or the new heaven, but on the New Jerusalem. Revelation 21:2 states, "I saw the Holy City, the new Jerusalem, coming down out of heaven from God, prepared as a bride beautifully dressed for her husband." Because the book of Revelation contains much symbolism, debate has resulted as to whether the New Jerusalem is a literal city or merely a nonliteral description of the eternal state. From the details given in Revelation 21:22, however, it appears to have all of the elements of a literal city.

The question, then, is why it is described as a bride, which raises the issue of whether it is related to the church as the bride of Christ. This matter is complicated by a later statement in Revelation 21:9: "I will show you the bride, the wife of the Lamb." In the verses that follow, John is given a revelation of the city.

One can reasonably assume that the New Jerusalem cannot be both a nonliteral and a literal city. The evidence is heavily in favor of considering it a literal place of residence for the saints of all ages, as described in these two chapters. The New Jerusalem is compared to a lovely bride prepared for her husband, just as the city is prepared to be the temple of God and the home of the saints.

Before examining the city itself, however, some of the major features of the situation are described in Revelation 21:3–4:

> And I heard a loud voice from the throne saying, "Now the dwelling of God is with men, and he will live with them. They will be his people, and God himself will be with them and be their God. He will wipe every tear from their eyes. There will be no more death or mourning or crying or pain, for the old order of things has passed away."

The sorrows of earth will be abolished, and God is described as wiping away every tear, and the saints then experience no more death, mourning, or pain.

Some expositors have said that we will be so sorry for our sins that we will spend considerable time in heaven shedding tears for our past sins. This view seems to be contrary to what the Scriptures say because there certainly will not be any sickness, death, or pain. Also, it seems more reasonable to assume that the passage is referring to the sorrows of this life, and the tears are wiped away by the fact that we are in heaven, where there are no tears.

In the verses that follow, Christ is introduced as the Alpha and the Omega (Rev. 21:6), which, in speaking of His eternality, is defined as the Beginning and the End. Salvation is depicted as a spring of water of life from which those who hear are invited to drink. Clearly, however, the ungodly and the unsaved will not enter into the New Jerusalem (v. 8). This verse says that those who are characterized by their sin will not be allowed to enter: "But the cowardly, the unbelieving, the vile, the murderers, the sexually immoral, those who practice magic arts, the idolaters and all liars—their place will be in the fiery lake of burning sulfur. This is the second death" (v. 8).

THE NEW JERUSALEM DESCENDING FROM HEAVEN

In Revelation 21:2, the new Jerusalem comes down from heaven. This thought is repeated in verse 10, which states that John sees the city coming from God: "And he carried me away in the Spirit to a mountain great and high, and showed me the Holy City, Jerusalem, coming down out of heaven from God."

The description of Jerusalem coming down from heaven has created a good deal of discussion. From Scripture we learn that heaven and earth clearly are created new. But the New Jerusalem is not said to be created at this time; instead, it is described as coming down from heaven, as having a prior existence. The Bible does not enlarge on this fact, but it leaves open the question as to whether the New Jerusalem is in existence during the millennial kingdom.

Clearly, the New Jerusalem could not rest on the earth

because it is described as such a huge city that it would blot out the whole Promised Land, making impossible the fulfillment of other elements of the millennial kingdom. If it is in existence during the millennial kingdom, it would have to be a satellite city, situated in space. Here we are faced with a lack of revelation, and all one can do is try to fit this description into the situation. Some people have suggested, however, that it may be that those who have been resurrected or translated will live in this satellite city over the earth and be able from that position to come to the earth to carry out functions that they are described as fulfilling, such as administrative government. This explanation seems to have some support from Isaiah 65:21–23, which describes life in the kingdom of those living in the Millennium:

> They will build houses and dwell in them; they will plant vineyards and eat their fruit. No longer will they build houses and others live in them, or plant and others eat. For as the days of a tree, so will be the days of my people; my chosen ones will long enjoy the work of their hands. They will not toil in vain or bear children doomed to misfortune; for they will be a people blessed by the LORD, they and their descendants with them.

The passage goes on to speak of tranquillity among otherwise hostile beasts, as there will be no harm in this situation. In view of the fact that millions of people will be resurrected and translated, there is no indication that they will live alongside those who are still in their natural bodies. It would solve one problem, at least, if they lived in a satellite city in a separate situation, but still connected to the earth, so that they would share in the millennial reign of Christ. These possible conclusions, however, are conjectures and do not have the status of doctrine, but they still introduce many interesting possibilities that further revelation will make clear, once we get into the Millennium and the eternal state.

THE NEW JERUSALEM AND OTHER SCRIPTURES

In connection with the hope of Abraham, Scripture states that Abraham "was looking forward to the city with foundations, whose architect and builder is God" (Heb. 11:10). Abraham, of course, anticipated the millennial kingdom when Israel would inherit the land. But in addition to this, he was looking forward to the eternal city, as described in Hebrews 11. Later, Hebrews 12:22–25 describes those who will live in the New Jerusalem:

> But you have come to Mount Zion, to the heavenly Jerusalem, the city of the living God. You have come to thousands upon thousands of angels in joyful assembly, to the church of the firstborn, whose names are written in heaven. You have come to God, the judge of all men, to the spirits of righteous men made perfect, to Jesus the mediator of a new covenant, and to the sprinkled blood that speaks a better word than the blood of Abel.

Although the church and Israel are specifically mentioned, this passage and others make clear that the New Jerusalem includes the saints of all ages. Nevertheless, these saints will retain their individual and appropriate identity but will be dwelling together in the heavenly city in eternity future. Accordingly, all of the saints from Adam on—including the church, the tribulation saints and the millennial saints—will live forever in this holy city.

Scripture frequently mentions the New Jerusalem (see Isa. 65:17; 66:12; 2 Peter 3:13; Rev. 3:12). Sometimes the New Jerusalem is mentioned in the context of the millennial kingdom, as in Isaiah 65. It is not unusual for Scripture to put together things that are actually separated by a long time, as in Daniel 12:2, which mentions the resurrection of the righteous and the wicked in the same verse, even though these two events are separated by a thousand years.

Accordingly, the New Jerusalem, in the context of the millennial kingdom, is not speaking of the Millennium itself. This problem must be resolved because it is not correct to merge the New Jerusalem and the Millennium or the Millennium and the eternal state, as some amillenarians do. Obviously, the New Jerusalem is an entirely different geographic context than the Jerusalem in the millennial kingdom, which Scripture describes in considerable detail as being different than the New Jerusalem. Obviously, of course, those who are saved in the millennial kingdom will also later be in the New Jerusalem.

THE NEW JERUSALEM DESCRIBED IN DETAIL

The New Jerusalem is described as a glorious jewel in Revelation 21:11: "It shone with the glory of God, and its brilliance was like that of a very precious jewel, like a jasper, clear as crystal." The New Jerusalem is described as having the glory and beauty of a jasper stone that is defined as "clear as crystal." The jasper stone, as we know it, is opaque, not clear. Possibly, the reference is to a jewel that is like a diamond.

The physical features of the city are described as being surrounded by a high wall:

> It had a great, high wall with twelve gates, and with twelve angels at the gates. On the gates were written the names of the twelve tribes of Israel. There were three gates on the east, three on the north, three on the south and three on the west. The wall of the city had

> twelve foundations, and on them were the names of the twelve apostles of the Lamb. (Rev. 21:12–14)

As described in this passage, the city is square and surrounded by a high wall, with three gates on each of the four sides. The gates have the names of the twelve tribes of Israel, implying that Israel is in this city. The foundations have the names of the apostles, implying that the church is also involved in this city.

The tremendous size of this city is mentioned. It is 12,000 stadia in both length and width. The wall is declared to be 144 cubits high by man's measurement, and the usual interpretation is that it is approximately 200 feet high. Obviously, access to the city is possible only through the gates.

The materials of the city are fabulous. The wall is said to be made of jasper, and the city itself is basically pure gold that is described as "pure as glass" (v. 18). Apparently, the gold is not the same gold that we have today but rather a translucent gold through which light passes.

Revelation 21:18–20 describes the foundations of the city in great detail:

> The wall was made of jasper, and the city of pure gold, as pure as glass. The foundations of the city walls were decorated with every kind of precious stone. The first foundation was jasper, the second sapphire, the third chalcedony, the fourth emerald, the fifth sardonyx, the sixth carnelian, the seventh chrysolite, the eighth beryl, the ninth topaz, the tenth chrysoprase, the eleventh jacinth, and the twelfth amethyst.

The foundation of the city is composed of twelve magnificent jewels, as described in verses 19–20. The first jewel mentioned is that of the jasper, previously used to describe the city as a whole, which is a clear stone, possibly like a diamond or is the diamond itself. The second stone, the sapphire, is another jewel that is similar to a diamond but blue. The third stone, the chalcedony, is an agate with stripes of various colors, probably mostly blue. The fourth stone is a green stone similar to the emerald that we know today. The sardonyx is a red and white stone. The carnelian is a more common stone, usually reddish or honey colored and is distinguished as being used for the glory of God in Revelation 4:3. The seventh stone, the chrysolite, is believed to have been golden and somewhat different than the modern stone. The beryl is a deep green stone. The topaz is a trans-parent, yellow-green stone. The chrysoprase is also green. The jacinth is violet, and the amethyst is a shade of purple. All these colors together form a glorious multicolored picture of the wall of these precious stones.

Revelation 21:21 comments further on the gates, saying that they are composed of a large stone called a pearl. The gold of the city is described as transparent glass, indicating that it is apparently translucent. In fact, all of the stones and materials of the New Jerusalem seem to transmit light and give the impression that the city is going to be a brilliantly lit city and a demonstration of a glorious God.

THE TEMPLE IN THE CITY

In both history and in the millennial kingdom, the Lord is worshiped in various temples. Here, by contrast, the city itself is declared to be the temple: "I did not see a temple in the city, because the Lord God Almighty and the Lamb are its temple" (Rev. 21:22).

The city has no need for the sun or the moon; in fact, they do not exist in the eternal state, as the glory of God gives light, as Revelation 21:23 states. It mentions also how the saved of various kingdoms and their kings will enter into the city. The gates are declared never to be shut, and no darkness will ever exist in the city: "there will be no night there" (v. 25). Verse 27 mentions the purity of the city; only those who have their names in the Book of Life are allowed into the city.

THE RIVER OF LIFE

The opening five verses of Revelation 22 describe the river of the water of life that flows from the throne of God. If the throne is at the top of the city and the city is in the form of a pyramid, then the water will flow down from the throne to the various levels of the city until it reaches the bottom, where it can flow through the middle of the street of the city. Apparently, the street is divided by the river, but it is still considered as one street. The fountain of water symbolically represents eternal life and is significant because the water borders the Tree of Life in verse 2. In the Millennium, a similar stream flows from the sanctuary (Ezek. 47:1, 12; Zech. 14:8). This river, of course, flows from the throne of God after the earth has been destroyed.

THE TREE OF LIFE

Revelation 22:2 describes the Tree of Life: "On each side of the river stood the tree of life, bearing twelve crops of fruit, yielding its fruit every month. And the leaves of the tree are for the healing of the nations." Some people have held that a row of trees is called the Tree of Life. However, the Tree of Life probably is so large that its branches reach over the entire street and bear its fruit on both sides of the river.

The first mention of the Tree of Life in Scripture is in the

Garden of Eden (Gen. 3:22, 24). Adam was driven out of the garden so that he could not eat of the Tree of Life, or he would not have died. Under the circumstances of a sinful human race, it is better that saints die and be resurrected in a sinless body than that they continue in their present sinful body forever. Everyone in the city, of course, is already assured of eternal life, and the Tree of Life is most likely a reference to the quality of life.

Expositors have puzzled over the validity of the production of fruit each month and also of the statement that the leaves of the tree have something to do with the healing of the nations. If there is no sickness in heaven or the New Jerusalem, why would there be need of healing? The Greek word that translates "healing" is *therapeian*, which is translated in English as "therapeutic." The thought seems to be that it relates to their general health and well-being. Obviously, there is no need of healing in the eternal state. Some people have tried to relate this to the millennial kingdom, but the context does not deal with the millennial kingdom.

The fact that the fruit is produced monthly also raises questions because there is no moon or other way of marking a month. Despite this, the language doubtless is used in reference to a time period similar to what a month would be on earth.

THE LIFTING OF THE CURSE ON EARTH

According to Revelation 22:3, there will be no curse on earth during this period: "No longer will there be any curse." When Adam and Eve sinned, a curse was pronounced upon the earth, making it more difficult to raise food. Apparently in the millennial kingdom, this curse will be partially lifted, but here in the eternal state, there is no curse at all.

THE THRONE OF GOD

The most important reference to the throne of God in the Bible states, "The throne of God and of the Lamb will be in the city, and his servants will serve him" (Rev. 22:3). Unlike earlier temples, the city itself is the temple of God, as Revelation 21:22 states. God's throne is in the city because God's presence is there. The question has often been raised as to what we will do in heaven. The simple answer is, "His servants will serve Him" (22:3). Apparently, God's plan is to create a human race from which will come many saints who will manifest their allegiance and love for Him in various forms of service. As we pointed out in the discussion on the judgment seat of Christ, it is entirely possible that the privileged service that we will have in heaven will in some ways be determined by how well we serve Him here.

THE INTIMACY OF THE SAINTS WITH GOD

The question is often considered to what extent we will be able to see God. Revelation 22:4 states, "They will see his face, and his name will be on their foreheads." In other words, it will be possible for saints in their sinless bodies to be in the presence of the holy God and worship Him and be able to see God as He really is, as revealed in various Scriptures that picture heaven.

OTHER ASPECTS OF BLESSINGS IN THE NEW JERUSALEM

As was indicated earlier, the New Jerusalem will be ablaze with the glory of God and will not need the light of the sun or the moon. As a result, Scripture states in Revelation 22:5, "There will be no more night." Darkness is limited to this life; thus, in the life to come is no darkness, and the city, with all of its beautiful colors, will be ablaze with light.

The final statement reaffirms once again the important role of the saints in the government of God: "And they will reign for ever and ever" (v. 5).

THE CERTAINTY OF FULFILLMENT OF PROPHECY

Recognizing man's tendency not to take prophecy literally and not be subject to literal fulfillment, the angel reasserts that the words are trustworthy. The message of prophecy is, "The Lord, the God of the spirits of the prophets, sent his angel to show his servants the things that must soon take place" (Rev. 22:6). The message of prophecy is summarized in the statement "Behold, I am coming soon!" (v. 7). The use of the word *soon* should make obvious the fact that the prophecy does not mean that it would be immediate, but rather that in the eternal timetable of God, it will come suddenly and, from God's point of view, soon.

Once again, because prophecy is certain and trustworthy, a blessing is pronounced upon those who observe prophecy: "Blessed is he who keeps the words of the prophecy in this book" (v. 7). Remarkable also in the Bible, especially in the book of Revelation, is the special commendation and special attention given to the message of prophecy.

JOHN AND THE ANGELS

Several verses of Scripture record the conversation of John with the angel who has been revealing these things. When John falls down to worship the angel, as recorded in Revelation 22:8, John is told not to do so, but rather to manifest his reverence to the Word of God by keeping the words of prophecy and worshiping God.

The angel specifically tells John, "Do not seal up the words of the prophecy of this book, because the time is near"(v. 10). God anticipates in prophecy that wickedness will continue, but the time will come when God will reward the righteous and judge the wicked.

THE FINAL INSTRUCTION OF CHRIST

In Revelation 22:12–16, John receives a comprehensive instruction with a reaffirmation, a reward for the wicked and judgment for unbelievers:

> Behold, I am coming soon! My reward is with me, and I will give to everyone according to what he has done. I am the Alpha and the Omega, the First and the Last, the Beginning and the End. Blessed are those who wash their robes, that they may have the right to the tree of life and may go through the gates into the city. Outside are the dogs, those who practice magic arts, the sexually immoral, the murderers, the idolaters and everyone who loves and practices falsehood.
>
> I, Jesus, have sent my angel to give you this testimony for the churches. I am the Root and the Offspring of David, and the bright Morning Star.

On the basis of the word of Christ, the righteous are assured that they will be rewarded and the wicked will bear the consequences of their sin and unbelief. This assurance is related to Jesus, who describes Himself in verse 16.

THE LAST INVITATION OF THE BIBLE

Once again, the Scriptures invite those who are willing to trust in Christ and receive His salvation. This invitation is embodied in Revelation 22:17: "The Spirit and the bride say, 'Come!' And let him who hears say, 'Come!' Whoever is thirsty, let him come; and whoever wishes, let him take the free gift of the water of life."

The final and most significant warning in the book of Revelation is then given, but it is soon neglected by the church at large and misinterpreted. There should be a special warning about the sanctity of the actual words of this prophecy. John states,

> I warn everyone who hears the words of the prophecy of this book: If anyone adds anything to them, God will add to him the plagues described in this book. And if anyone takes words away from this book of prophecy, God will take away from him his share in the tree of life and in the holy city, which are described in this book. (vv. 18–19)

What is meant is that intrinsic in trusting to Christ as Savior is trusting His Word and the Bible. Those who do not trust the Word are not trusting Christ and are in danger of not being saved.

As the book closes with a final word of exhortation, Christ repeats the statement: "Yes, I am coming soon" (v. 20). This statement is followed by the final prayer of the Bible: "Amen. Come, Lord Jesus" (vv. 20–21). It then reminds one of the grace of God: "The grace of the Lord Jesus be with God's people. Amen" (v. 21).

Just as the Gospels portrayed Christ's life on earth with

His glory hidden, so the book of Revelation pictures Christ in glory as our coming Judge and Savior, with whom we will deal in eternity. The solemn words of the Bible are a constant reminder of how important it is to trust in Christ and to commit our lives to Him in obedience, worship, and love if we expect commendation at the judgment seat of Christ.

SCRIPTURE INDEX

SUBJECT INDEX